Niall Cherry was born in London in 1959 and recalls becoming interested in military history as a schoolboy from watching films such as *The Battle of Britain* and *A Bridge too Far*. He later found out that one of his grandfathers had fought in the Great War, serving as a Chemical Corporal at Loos. His father served in the Royal Electrical and Mechanical Engineers during the early 1950s. He continued in the family tradition by serving in the Royal Army Medical Corps, qualifying as a Combat Medical Technician Class 1, an instructor in First Aid and Nuclear, Biological and Chemical Warfare. He finished his service as a senior NCO.

Deeply interested in the Great War, he has visited numerous battlegrounds on both the Western Front and at Gallipoli. He is a long-standing member of the Western Front Association, the Gallipoli Association and the Military Heraldry Society. He also has the honour of being the first non-Arnhem veteran to hold the post of UK representative for the Society of Friends of the Airborne Museum in Oosterbeek, Holland.

In 2000, Niall's first book was published, *Red Berets and Red Crosses: The Story of the Medical Services in the 1st Airborne Division in World War 2*. The following year, answering an appeal from the Manchester Regiment Museum, he wrote *I Shall Not Find His Equal*, a biography of Brigadier Noel Lee. In the last few years he has also contributed articles to *Battlefields Review* and *After The Battle*, together with helping with around 20 other books on the Airborne Forces and Gallipoli.

Niall currently lives in Lancashire with his wife and two daughters, working for BAE Systems helping build fast military jets.

MOST UNFAVOURABLE GROUND

The Battle of Loos 1915

Niall Cherry

Helion & Company Ltd

Helion & Company Limited
26 Willow Road
Solihull
West Midlands
B91 1UE
England
Tel. 0121 705 3393
Fax 0121 711 4075
Email: publishing@helion.co.uk
Website: http://www.helion.co.uk

Published by Helion & Company Limited 2005
This paperback reprint 2008

Designed and typeset by Helion & Company Ltd, Solihull, West Midlands
Cover designed by Bookcraft Limited, Stroud, Gloucestershire
Printed by cPod, Trowbridge, Wiltshire

ISBN 978 1 906033 21 7

British Library Cataloguing-in-Publication Data.
A catalogue record for this book is available from the British Library.

Front cover: Sergeant Harry Wells, 2nd Battalion The Royal Sussex Regiment, winning the Victoria Cross at the Battle of Loos, 1915. Oil painting by Ernest Ibbetson. Reproduced courtesy of The Royal Sussex Regiment Museum Trust.

For details of other military history titles published by Helion & Company Limited contact the above address, or visit our website: http://www.helion.co.uk.

We always welcome receiving book proposals from prospective authors.

Contents

List of Maps

Maps 1-9, 12-13 drawn by the author and Eugène Wijnhoud
Maps 10-11 drawn by Major McNaught-Davis, 8th Lincolns

List of Tables

Foreword

I first met Niall in Albert at the Hotel Basilique, when he was on a battlefield tour organised by Martin Middlebrook, whom I wished to contact in order to further a research project of mine on the Battle of Arnhem. Over dinner we found out that we had mutual interests both in the Great War and the Battle of Arnhem and since that initial meeting we have corresponded regularly, and have met at Oosterbeek in Holland on several occasions. After Niall's successful debut as an author in his book *Red Berets and Red Crosses*, which covered the work of the Royal Army Medical Corps Units during the Arnhem battle, he obviously developed a taste for military history. In this, his third book I know he has again carried out extensive and detailed research to get the story right and his work fills a vacuum, as the Battle of Loos has not received the detailed attention of historians, as have the later conflicts of 1916 and 1917.

This battle was an important landmark in the development of the British Expeditionary Force in France and Flanders. After the defensive battles of 1914 the expanding British Army was encouraged by the French to go on the offensive. There followed in 1915 a series of battles at Neuve Chapelle in March, Aubers Ridge and Festubert in May, with little success due mainly to the lack of artillery and a shortage of ammunition. Direction of these battles proved a severe challenge to the High Command, with almost no imagination or skill being demonstrated. The Battle of Loos was fought with orders that showed that little had been learned from the earlier encounters; the Germans on the other hand were quick to use these experiences to improve their defence tactics.

The Loos battle, which started on 25th September and finished on 13th October involved units from all sections of the British Army: Regular, Territorial and the first major use of Kitchener's Volunteer Army. The action was on a larger scale than the previous 1915 battles but suffered from using the same strategy and tactics with the ongoing deficiencies of artillery. The inept use of 150 tons of gas by the British, released despite unfavourable conditions, proved to be counter-productive and did not compensate for these shortcomings.

The author has dealt with the battle unit by unit rather than attempt to cover the whole period on a day to day basis, and this enables the reader to follow their performance during the battle, identifying their movements and casualties. The inclusion of the organisation and performance of the medical services before and during the battle forms an important part of this book.

Although the battle did not finish as a victory due to the misjudgement of the generals, the gallantry of the troops did produce a breakthrough at Hill 70, only to be nullified by a slow reaction by the High Command. The final failure of the attack led to a falling out between the two major commanders. The general disquiet at the performance of the Commander-in–Chief, Field Marshal French, since the outbreak of the war, and in particular regarding the use of the reserves during the Battle, culminated in General Haig leading a concerted and eventually successful campaign to discredit and replace French.

I feel this book should be widely read, for in understanding this account it would be difficult for us not to remember and acknowledge the men whose sacrifice and endeavours made up that distant history, including, as I recently found out, the author's grandfather. I hope it receives the credit it deserves.

Paul Hanson
Chairman of The Western Front Association
Coventry 2003

Preface

When surveying the proposed battlefield of Loos in the middle of 1915, the then commander of IV Corps, from the 1st Army of the British Expeditionary Force, Lieutenant General Sir Henry Rawlinson, said: "It is most unfavourable ground and we shall be heavily taken upon".

He was not wrong in his comment and the battle was not far short of a total failure. Perhaps for this reason, and that it was a relatively small attack (with only six divisions on the first day) compared to battles in the following three years, Loos seems to be a forgotten battle of the Great War. I hope with this book to fill a gap in the history of the Great War, as books on Loos are few and far between. I have not intended this to be a battlefield touring book but a detailed look at the fighting and its aftermath. Although perhaps more eminent authors than myself consider Loos a 'forgotten battle' it is not to me. My grandfather was present at Loos: he joined the Honourable Artillery Company on or about (as his service record puts it) 28th August 1914 and proceeded to France with the HAC on 18th September 1914. In July 1915 he was transferred to the Royal Engineers Special Companies and as his AF W3723 says 'promoted to Cpl.' - one of the original Chemical corporals - he had been an engineer in civvie street. In March 1916 he was granted a commission and posted to No 1 Special Company RE where he remained till the end of the war, ending up as a Captain and second in command of this unit dispensing poison gas using Stokes mortars. Through earlier research I found out he was present at Loos, the Somme in 1916, Arras in 1917 and involved in the fighting during the March Retreat of 1918.

Since I was a schoolboy in the 1960s and 70s I seem to recall having an interest in the two major conflicts of the 20th Century. I have followed up this interest up visiting many of the battlefields of Northern France and beyond. However in the early 1990s I recall reading Philip Warner's book on Loos and found I still had unanswered questions. I first went to Loos in 1998, which only fuelled my interest, especially after seeing the billiard table-like layout of Loos, and I wanted to know what happened there. My journey of five years or so has seen a few highs and equally some lows but I hope that I have educated, entertained and informed here about what happened in the autumn of 1915.

Many people have helped me on my journey and I feel it would be appropriate to mention some of them here. Perhaps I should start with my very good Dutch friend Robert Sigmond who, without his offer to publish my first book, this story probably wouldn't have even seen the light of day. I was also grateful to him for pointing out the story of the 7th Battalion Kings Own Scottish Borderer pipers at Loos and Renkum Heath in 1915 and 1944.

Numerous members of the Western Front Association and the Great War Discussion Forum have helped, including Chris Baker (the most helpful webmaster of www.1914-1918.org, of which I am a PBI), Peter Boalch, Neil Bright, Rob Elliott, Richard Howells (and his web site: www.weforenglanddied.co.uk), Bob Jervis, Ken Lees for information on the 9th Kings, Les McKerricher, Geoff Parker and Chris Preston. A special word of thanks to my

The author's grandfather, Captain H. Polan RE, pictured after being awarded a
commission. In September 1915 he was one of the chemical corporals at Loos.
(Niall Cherry)

battlefield touring companion and totally unpaid research assistant Keith Harris
who helped with various photographs taken during the 1998 trip when we faced
some of the worst weather ever experienced (by us anyway) on the Western Front. I
am also grateful to Paul Hanson, Chairman of the Western Front Association, for
writing the Foreword. We were introduced to each other by Martin Middlebrook
in the bar of the Basilique in Albert some years ago and met again in Holland in
2001 when I helped with a battlefield tour of the Arnhem area. On that tour he
kindly or otherwise told me I must finish my research, so if you have any com-
plaints you know where to go! Since then we have become good friends and I hope
Paul will forgive my choice of words. Also, to Duncan Rogers at Helion for taking
a leap of faith with my manuscript. I only hope, Duncan, I have repaid your trust
in my ability.

The staff of the Liddle Collection and the Imperial War Museum were most helpful during various research trips, especially John Stopford-Pickering. Also, much information was obtained from the National Archive Kew, and I would like to say a big 'thank you' to the numerous staff that work there. Crown Copyright material in the National Archive is reproduced by permission of the Controller of Her Majesty's Stationery Office.

My one regret is that I never managed to meet a veteran of Loos, but I still dream. With the benefit of hindsight is it likely that errors crept into some of the veteran's accounts but I must accept full responsibility for the text. However this is not to say that the story is complete, and any new information would be gratefully received. A final word of thanks must go to my long suffering wife Deborah, and children Claire and Sarah for putting up with 'yet another research project'.

1

The Road to Loos September 1915

The year of 1915 was a difficult one for the British Expeditionary Force (BEF) - the war that had broken out in August 1914 was not over by the expected time of Christmas. Additionally, many of the original BEF had either been killed or wounded in the opening year of the Great War. By the beginning of 1915 the BEF was still a relatively small player on the Western Front with two armies, comprising Regular and Indian divisions (these armies consisting of 11 infantry divisions and 5 cavalry divisions). Even though many thousands of volunteers had answered Kitchener's call to arms it was going to be September till they were ready to take part in active operations. Meanwhile, in the early part of 1915, the BEF were involved in fighting in the Ypres Salient (2nd Army) and further south around Neuve Chapelle, Aubers and Festubert (1st Army).

At a conference in late 1914 Sir John French, commander of the BEF, met with his French opposite number, General Joffre. Joffre, like French, firmly believed that the war could only be won on the Western Front, and more importantly, his Government and people wanted the invaders removed from French soil. Discussions about offensives and rumours of impending attacks elsewhere meant nothing to him. Sir John French was of the same opinion, but the Government in London thought that perhaps it might be better looking elsewhere. I am sure they were thinking of Kitchener's 'New Armies' in training, whom they did not want to be wasted away in fruitless attacks.

Kitchener himself had made it very clear that he could not see the German lines being broken on the Western Front. Various options were discussed back in London, probably the most strategic one being a campaign in the Mediterranean - namely Gallipoli. However in early 1915 Sir John was advised that for the moment the main emphasis of the British Army would remain the Western Front, for as long as the French required it. The stage was now set for the first major British offensive of the War. Sir John informed London that he was optimistic for success during the coming year. Nevertheless he did not guarantee success, but emphasised that he must have the men and materials to achieve it. However, as usual in warfare, the other side will always have their say. At the beginning of 1915 the Germans were moving men to the Eastern Front. Around 14 divisions were sent but this still left a formidable 98 divisions behind! The rationale behind the German thinking was that they could only fight one main enemy at a time and had decided for the moment to concentrate on the Russians. This meant the adoption of a defensive policy in the West. The Allies had a much better plan (or so they thought) - attack everywhere without enough of anything and hopefully achieve a decisive victory. Things turned out somewhat different. On 8 February Sir John French issued a memorandum to his two army commanders, to be prepared to take the offensive in conjunction with the French. Following closely on behind this was Sir John French's instruction to the General Officer Commanding (GOC) 1st Army General Sir Douglas Haig, to prepare a plan for an offensive with a line from La

General Joffre. (Private collection)

Bassée to the Aubers Ridge as its final objective, these all being in the vicinity of the village of Neuve Chapelle.

Haig's plan of attack called for two divisions to break through the German lines at Neuve Chapelle between Port Arthur and the Moated Grange. These two attacking divisions were the Meerut Division from the Indian Corps and the 8th Division from IV Corps. Once through the German lines they were to swing to their left and right; the Lahore Division and the 7th Division would then follow on either side of the breach. Finally the Cavalry Corps would push on through to the Aubers Ridge and wheel behind the enemy lines, while their supporting infantry would consolidate the gains on the ridge line. The attack was planned to go in on 10th March 1915.

48 infantry battalions were to attack, faced by what Intelligence thought were only 9 German battalions. They were correct and the British had overwhelming superiority in numbers. The attack was preceded by a barrage fired by nearly 300 howitzers and field guns, concentrating on destroying the German wire and trenches. What heavy artillery there was, was to concentrate on counter-battery work. Initially things went very well. The gunners did their work well, destroying much barbed wire and other defences, leaving significant gaps in the German lines. Shortly after H Hour a gap nearly a mile wide had been made in the German line. However problems arose on the flanks, with troops moving in the wrong direction and fire coming in from German defensive positions left unscathed by the barrage.

Sir John French. (R. Haines)

In the centre the infantry had been told to advance only 200 yards beyond the front line and then wait while the village of Neuve Chapelle was shelled. During this pause the Germans took the opportunity to reorganise and man a second line of defences about 1000 yards behind the front line. When the advance resumed in the centre, the infantry did manage to clear the village but again halted on the outskirts. Here they were again ordered to wait until both flanks advanced. Communication was poor, both Corps commanders were about 5 miles away from Neuve Chapelle with their HQs yet apparently not in touch with each other. In the early afternoon the commander of IV Corps (Lieutenant-General Sir H. Rawlinson) found out about the stalled attack and ordered a new assault in conjunction with the Indian Corps. The orders for the new attack took over three hours to reach the battalions earmarked for the assault. The troops did not start their attack until it was nearly dark; needless to say it yielded no success. In spite of this a further attack was called for the next morning. Due to a mist over the battlefield and a shortage of Forward Observation Officers (FOO) the artillery support was negligible. Additionally, the Germans had brought up reinforcements during the night. This attack was also unsuccessful.

On 12th March a further British attack was called for, but was pre-empted by a German counter-attack. This was also unsuccessful and heavy losses were inflicted on the Germans. Again communication was poor, 1st Army HQ received very little accurate information about the German attack for many hours. At 3pm

General Sir Douglas Haig.
(Private collection)

Haig issued an order, which I suppose with the benefit of hindsight gives an interesting insight into his mentality for most of the war: "The Germans are much demoralised and both corps are to push through the barrage regardless of loss." The two-pronged corps attack would be supported by the 5th Cavalry Brigade. The orders took several hours to reach the front line. The attack went in piecemeal: some battalions never left the trenches. Those battalions that did suffered heavy casualties, and no ground was gained.

British casualties for this three-day action were over 11,000, and nearly all the ground gained had been taken in the three hours after H Hour on 10th March. In spite of this French and Haig were convinced they had found a recipe for success and were determined to learn the lessons and get it right next time. Perhaps the major failure of Neuve Chapelle was the inability of some commanders to push forward when the opportunity of a breakthrough occurred. Some commanders were deemed not to be tough enough as a 'thruster' and were given suitable advice in an 'interview without coffee'.

The next time the BEF was sent into the attack was again in the area of Neuve Chapelle, although the fighting is normally known as the Battle of Aubers Ridge. Haig's plan called for an attack both north and south of Neuve Chapelle preceded by a 40 minute artillery barrage. The northern part of the attack was to be carried out by the 8th Infantry Division. They were to attack in a south-easterly direction towards the village of Rouges Bancs. After this they were to secure a line from Rouge Bancs to Fromelles, then to advance along the Aubers Ridge where it would join up with the Meerut Division. The southern part of the assault was to be carried out by the 1st Division and the Meerut Division. Attacking between Chocolat Menier Corner and Port Arthur, once the initial objective had been taken and secured the Meerut Division was to swing north-east. Their next objective was to take a German strong point at La Cliqueterie Farm and then join up with the northern attack. This attack was originally intended to be on 8th May but was put back 24 hours, so it coincided with a large French effort further north near Vimy Ridge. However the Germans were one step ahead of the game, in that they had absorbed the lessons of Neuve Chapelle far better than the BEF. The German front line defences had been greatly increased. The breastworks in nearly all places was widened to a width of 20 feet, the trenches were made deeper and the barbed wire defences were strengthened and increased in depth up to 15 yards. More concrete dugouts were built to shelter troops. The Germans also dug many communication trenches to prevent troop movements being observed. The frontage of each regiment was reduced from 3,000 yards to 2,000 yards and their ammunition reserves were increased. All in all the German defenders were now waiting in strengthened positions supported by artillery and machine guns (these at one every 20 yards).

The British artillery bombardment started at 5am, with an increase in the rate of fire after 30 minutes for 10 minutes. At 5.40am it would lift to 600 yards beyond the German front line aiming at prearranged targets. The infantry in both the north and south attacks were to go in at 5.40am. The northern attack saw around 7,000 men from IV Corps attacking around 1,600 German defenders. A similar ratio in favour of the attackers was present in the southern area. The attack was a disaster, probably the worst of the war so far. The German defences were too strong. The fire support provided was just not good enough. The Germans did not rate the bombardment very highly. Indeed they probably had an idea the attack was coming, as on the previous day a large chimney near the front line was demolished to give the artillery a better field of fire. However the attacking battalions advanced with great gallantry and determination. The artillery bombardment of the German front line had looked very impressive – "a long sheet of flame and bursting shells" – but most of the machine guns had not been touched. Casualties started even before the attack started. The Derha Dun Brigade suffering heavily, the four battalions sustaining over 1,000 casualties, one in particular, the 1st Seaforth Highlanders, losing over 500.

When the artillery fire lifted from the front line, the German machine gunners stopped the advance completely, the fire being so intense that troops who tried to advance were either killed or wounded close to their own starting point. Within 40 minutes both attacks had stalled completely and no ground was gained. British casualties amounted to over 11,500. On 10th May Haig issued a special order of the day which stated that the attack had "proved of great assistance to our Allies". This suggested that the attack had prevented the Germans from moving reserves to counter the French attack. German accounts do not support this claim.

It was not long before the situation forced the BEF into another attack. The French 10th Army had so far been unable to take the heights at Vimy Ridge, which would greatly help the British 1st Army, as it hopefully crossed the open terrain to

Lens. Sir John French was under increasing pressure from the French to launch another attack, especially after the disaster at Aubers Ridge. Back in England, if that attack did nothing else, it caused the Government to realise that if they were to have any chance of winning the war, the country had to be on a better war footing. At last it was realised that the output of war material was grossly insufficient to meet the demands of the BEF. Added to this was the need to feed the troops on Gallipoli. Indeed 22,000 rounds of artillery ammunition were sent to the Dardanelles on the instructions of Lord Kitchener. Reserves of rifle ammunition in France was down to less than 100 rounds per rifle. Some of the new divisions forming in England could not be sent to the BEF, the reason being that there was a threat of a German invasion. In spite of this the French insisted on action. Joffre, the French Commander-in-Chief (C-in-C), believed that the Allies would lose the war if they did not strike while the Germans were involved on two fronts. He pressed Sir John to take action and have another go. French agreed and Haig was again instructed to use his 1st Army in the attack.

Haig's plan was to launch an attack north of the village of Festubert. This plan was proposed by Haig on 12th May. It was very similar to the previous attack at Aubers Ridge, but this time the artillery barrage was scheduled to last for 36 hours and this time the heavies would be targeted against the German breastworks. The attack was again to be a two-pronged assault but this time the gap between the two prongs was 600 yards rather than 6,000 yards. There were also limited objectives, these being envisaged to be a 1,000 yard advance to a road called La Quinque Rue towards the village of La Tourelle. The first attack was to be a night one, and was to be carried out by troops from the 2nd Division and the Meerut Division. A night attack was chosen as the ground had previously been attacked over. Following this night attack would be a daylight one carried out by the 7th Division. The artillery barrage started on the morning of 13th May and because of a shortage of shells, the fire was in a very deliberate orderly fashion, with the fall of shot being observed and recorded. However, as was usual, numerous shells failed to explode and it was raining heavily, making observation difficult. It was therefore considered necessary to extend the barrage to 60 hours.

The attack began at 11.30pm on 15th May and there was good initial success. The leading battalions of the 6th Brigade from the 2nd Division captured the German support trench. But on their left the 5th Brigade (again from 2nd Division) and the Garhwal Brigade from the Meerut Division were caught in the open by German machine gun fire and few men reached the German front line. At dawn the following morning, two brigades (20th and 22nd) from 7th Division left the British front line. The 22nd Brigade managed to advance about 600 yards, but the 20th Brigade was halted by heavy enfilade fire from their left. In spite of this the right hand units of the Brigade did manage to get past the German front line. The situation as usual was confused and communication and accurate information poor, and the Germans fought tenaciously. The troops that had taken part in the night attack had to support the attack from 7th Division. The casualty figures for the battalions taking part in both these attacks speak for themselves (see Table 1.1)

During the night of 16th/17th May the Germans began a withdr awal of about ¾ mile to a new defensive line, however the British were unaware of this for a few days. A join-up between the 7th and 2nd Divisions occurred on 17th May.

Table 1.1
Casualties suffered during attacks on 15/16 May 1915

2nd Royal Inniskilling Fusiliers 5th Brigade 2nd Division	649
2nd Ox and Bucks Light Infantry 5th Brigade 2nd Division	395
2nd Worcestershires 5th Brigade 2nd Division	311
2nd Leicestershires Garhwal Brigade Meerut Division	308
39th Garhwal Rifles Garhwal Brigade Meerut Division	154

Over the next few days various attacks were made which resulted in some small gains. Additionally some 'new' divisions - the Canadian and the 47th (2nd London) Division - were later 'blooded' on 25th May and took some ground east of Festubert. When the battle was called off the casualty total was over 16,600. The gains had equated to about 600 yards on a 4,000 yard front. The breakdown of casualties by divisions for Festubert was as below.

Table 1.2
Casualties suffered at Festubert May 1915

	Officers			Other Ranks			
	Killed	Wounded	Missing	Killed	Wounded	Missing	Total
2nd Div	46	120	12	536	3725	1006	5445
7th Div	57	98	12	674	2628	654	4123
47th Div	26	138	2	207	1387	595	2355
Canadian	25	70	2	356	1536	215	2204
Meerut	31	68	3	194	1969	257	2522
Total	185	494	31	1967	11245	2727	16649

I have included this table as most of the divisions used at Festubert were used again at Loos later in the year, and it ought to be noted that for two of these losses were in the region of 40%. These losses would, of course, have led to a dilution of the experience of these units. However it must be said that valuable lessons were learned from these three attacks:

1   The longer bombardment seemed to work
2   There were limited objectives (certainly only at Festubert - no talk of the cavalry exploiting the gains)
3   Better co-ordination between the divisions
4   The gap between the attacking forces was closer and gave the benefit of mutual support.

All in all Festubert was a useful lesson for the BEF. The night attack by the 6th Brigade proved successful by the plan being kept simple, prior planning and preparation and good reconnaissance. Surprise enabled the attackers to reach the German lines without a shot being fired by the defenders. However in the adjoining

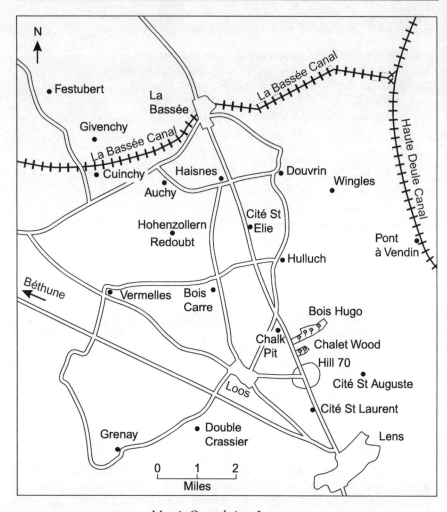

Map 1: General view, Loos area

sector the 5th Brigade suffered heavily - only about half of one battalion was able to reach the German lines. By the time the battle was called off, it had in some respects achieved its aim, that of assisting the French. It also had given the Germans something to think about. The question was who would absorb the lessons better?

Whilst these joint Anglo-French attacks were taking place, the French General Staff were finishing their plans for the culminating offensive for the latter part of 1915. Several large French assaults were planned in various areas and the BEF were expected to play their part in it. On 4th June, Joffre sent a draft of the plan to Sir John French, with the hope that the arrangements for this combined offensive be ready to take place in early July. The French hoped that the BEF would assist in two ways. Firstly by taking over 20 miles of trench currently held by the French

2nd Army. These were in the area from Chaulnes (30 miles south of Arras) across the Somme to Hebuterne (15 miles south west of Arras).

This would free up this Army for an offensive in Champagne. Secondly, to assist another French attack in Artois, either by attacking on the left of the French 10th Army, north of Lens, or alternatively to attack on its right across the Somme area south of Arras. Sir John French agreed in principle to these proposals - the strength of the BEF was increasing with Territorial and New Army divisions trickling into France. On 19th June during a meeting with Foch (the French commander of Army Group North) Sir John said that he hoped the BEF's preparations for the proposed attack would be completed by 10th July. It was envisaged that the BEF would attack on the left of the French 10th Army on a frontage of 4½ miles from the village of Grenay northwards to the La Bassée Canal. The divisions nominated to take part were the 1st and 2nd, supported by the 15th and 47th. The French High Command were happy with this and on the following day, Sir John asked Haig (1st Army Commander) to submit a detailed plan for this operation.

It would be interesting to know what the veterans of the 1st and 2nd Divisions would have said in June if they knew they were going to be thrown into battle once again. I hope the reader will bear in mind that at Festubert, only a few weeks before, the 2nd Division had suffered 5,445 casualties - nearly 50% of the establishment of a division. Perhaps the troops would have been encouraged if they had learned the contents of Haig's reply. On 23rd June Haig wrote to Sir John saying that after a personal reconnaissance of the ground south of the Canal, he was forced to the conclusion that the area was not a favourable one for an attack. Haig

Aerial view towards Givenchy showing German trenches. (IWM HU92184)

continued in his report that the German defences were so strong that until a greatly increased establishment of heavy artillery was provided, they could only be taken by siege methods. The ground, for the most part bare and open, would be so swept by machine gun and rifle fire both from the German front line trenches and the numerous fortified villages immediately behind them, that a rapid advance would be impossible. The Germans had the superiority of artillery position and observation nearly everywhere south of the Canal, and could concentrate the fire of their heavy batteries both to prevent the assembly of any considerable force for the proposed attack, and, if an assault were made, to enfilade it from both flanks. Moreover, the preliminary step of assembling a mass of troops south of the Canal was rendered hazardous by the open nature of the country, and by the fact that newly dug forming-up trenches in the chalky soil would be most difficult to conceal.

Haig further stated that if an attack on the left flank of the French 10th Army was imperative, he recommended that only subsidiary, diversionary attacks should be made south of the Canal. He suggested that the main attack should be directed astride and north of the Canal, with the intention of capturing the village of Auchy and the spur that ran easterly from Givenchy, threatening the village of Violaines and the town of La Bassée. He completed his report by saying that in his opinion, having visited the area, there was a most strong case for not attacking here, pointing out the shortage of artillery pieces and ammunition to fire from them.

This report may have had a profound effect at the BEF's GHQ at St Omer. On 11th July, at a meeting between Sir John French and Joffre, the plans for the forthcoming operations were discussed. This followed closely behind a conference at Boulogne on 19th/20th June at which far ranging comments were presented. At

View taken north of Loos, looking south-easterly towards Lens. (IWM Q41809)

this conference the BEF had suggested they would not be in a position to launch a large successful offensive till 1916. It was hoped by March 1916 that there would be 50 divisions in the BEF, more than double the strength in June 1915. The idea from the British was that an offensive with a reasonable chance of success would have to be delivered on a continuous front of 25 miles undertaken by more than 36 infantry divisions, supported by an artillery force of at least 1,100 heavy guns and howitzers and the normal complement per division of field guns. All of these constraints pointed to an attack by the BEF in the summer of 1916!

The BEF's proposals did not go down well with General Joffre. He dismissed out of hand the idea of not joining in till 1916. He further argued about the manner in which they proposed to participate if they accepted his plans. Joffre urged Sir John to initiate "A powerful offensive on the north of the French 10th Army. Whilst avoiding the buildings and towns of Lens and Lievin, your attack will find particularly favourable ground between Loos and La Bassée." The interesting comment behind this statement must be why Joffre found the ground in this area so favourable? I have been unable to find any reason for this except it was close to the French 10th Army!

Sir John French fully agreed with Haig's assessment of 'altogether unfavourable'. He sided with Haig's plan that the main thrust of the BEF's attack should be on the north side of the Canal, some 10 miles from the left flank of the French 10th Army. One suspects that there was serious 'political' manoeuvring behind the scenes before Sir John French finally agreed to Joffre's plan, and consented to the BEF supporting the French. However he added that the support would only be given provided that the French attack south of Loos was in sufficient strength to ensure that the German artillery around Lens would be neutralised. In such a case the two planned attacks by the BEF south of the Canal would be strongly and quickly reinforced and if circumstances warranted be turned into the main attack.

Hand in hand with the joint Anglo-French attack was the relief of the French trenches south of Arras. Sir John French insisted that his Government did not wish for their forces to be separated and they desired that the new divisions relieve French troops in the north, near the Channel ports. Joffre, however, would not agree to this. As is now becoming clear to the reader, Sir John opted out of a serious confrontation and suggested that his forming 3rd Army should gradually relieve the two French corps astride the Somme, as Joffre wanted. This would leave the French 10th Army sandwiched between the BEF. Sir John did get a concession from Joffre - that if the Germans attacked on the Somme front, then the French would give support to the British 3rd Army. It was agreed that the 3rd Army would start relieving the French on 18th July 1915 with the hand over to be complete by 8th August. In view of this and to give time to properly plan the Loos attack and to allow time for supplies to be built up, it was decided to delay the proposed offensive until the end of August.

It would be good to pause here and to briefly look at the German reaction to Festubert. They quickly absorbed the lesson that the prolonged bombardment (i.e. 60 hours) had had a great effect on their defences. They set to with their usual efficiency at strengthening their defences. Their peacetime manuals had suggested that only one line of defence was necessary. This was now changed to the idea of having a second line of defence some miles behind the front line. This gave the

Germans the benefit of choosing the best available positions for defence, often using the advantage of reverse slope positions. This meant the positions were concealed from effective observation (and fire) by the FOO's and consequently fire from the guns they controlled. Also, they usually had a much better barbed wire belt in front of it; this was hardly difficult as they could be constructed in daylight and at virtual leisure. These belts of barbed wire were often 15 yards or more thick and of a type of wire difficult to cut with the cutters used by the British Infantry. It was thought at this time that field artillery could not cut barbed wire at ranges in excess of 2½ miles. The Germans recognised this weakness, and therefore sited second line defences in excess of this distance behind the first line. This meant that should the first line be taken, a fresh attack and bombardment would have to be prepared and fired before a successful attack could be attempted. This, quite rightly the Germans realised, would give them time to move reinforcements to the area and probably still have the time to construct defensive positions behind the 'new' front line. During July 1915 the Germans worked at a rapid rate improving defences. Allied aerial photographs revealed the new construction but little was done to hinder its progress. By the end of that month, it became clear that whilst it would take some time to complete all the work, a strong point or redoubt had been built about every mile.

The knowledge that the Germans had built new defences in the Loos sector did at least cause a rethink in the High Command of the BEF. Sir John French looked at the area and this increased his doubts as to the possibility of any success in this sector. He wrote to Haig at the end of July asking if he wished to make any changes to his original plan. His letter said:

> If you are still of the opinion that the area between the French left and the La Bassée Canal is not favourable for an attack, it will be for consideration whether we should co-operate with our Ally by drawing off the enemy's reserves by an attack delivered further to the north.

Haig replied that he now had more knowledge of the area and it was his opinion that this sector was not favourable for an attack. It had become clear that the defences had been greatly strengthened and he recommended the abandoning of any offensive south of the Canal. He further suggested that the offensive should be "limited to the Aubers Ridge (north of the Canal), connecting it with our present line further north and extending it southwards towards the Canal by attacking at the same time towards Violaines."

He also suggested another strategic move by holding the front in less strength, freeing up about six divisions. These troops would then be sent to the right of the French 10th Army near Arras, where it was thought the German defences were not so strong and the ground was easier for an attack. But Sir John French disagreed with this as his main aim was to protect the Channel ports and so the idea was dropped. Again we now have an impasse, the French wanting the BEF to attack around Lens with the BEF not happy with this suggestion. The answer was of course to call another conference and this took place on 27th July at General Foch's HQ at Frevént.

At this meeting Sir John, although making it clear the BEF had every desire to assist the French 10th Army, said he wanted the BEF to attack somewhere where they had a sporting chance of success. In fact he wanted anywhere but south of the La Bassée Canal. He suggested Haig's alternative plan - that of the attack on Aubers Ridge and also an attack in the Ypres sector. The attack there would be against the Wytschate-Messines Ridge. This was a tactical attack as it would remove the Germans from the heights at Messines, which allowed them good observation over the Salient. We now find total French intransigence: Foch maintained it was of vital importance, and regardless of the ground and strength of the German defences, that the British 1st Army should make its main attack south of the Canal. For perhaps the first time he gave a reason for this, that it was so that the German artillery could be actively subjected to counter-battery fire along the whole front of the joint attack. With the benefit of hindsight this seems one of the poorest reasons ever given for an attack. Foch also admitted that a frontal attack against Lens and Lievin had virtually no chance of success. But perhaps the main reason for his insistence then came out into the open: Foch did not believe that an attack either in the Ypres Salient or north of the Canal, would produce the same effect, or give the same assistance to the French 10th Army as an attack going in alongside it. Perhaps Foch had some valid case for this view, as it had been proved earlier in 1915 that subsidiary attacks launched some distance away from the main thrust were generally found wanting in the purpose of drawing away reserves. It was thought that to be of any use these subsidiary attacks had to be sufficiently powerful to force a breakthrough on their own. Perhaps the overriding thought in Foch's mind was that if the BEF gained some ground in the Loos area, coupled with the French gaining Vimy Ridge, this would make the Douai Plain uninhabitable to the Germans, thus forcing them back a considerable distance.

To his credit Sir John French remained unconvinced by these arguments, given the nature of the ground and his constraints in troops and artillery. He held little faith in the French scheme. He thought that the best the attack could achieve was another salient in the German lines and a total breakthrough was out of the question, until the conditions were more in favour of the Allies. Therefore on 29th July he sent his summary of the Frevént conference. Whilst he admitted that he had before agreed to attack on the immediate left flank of the French 10th Army, he now said that at that particular time he had been unaware of the tremendous problems that an offensive at Loos would face. He also added that should an offensive take place south of the Canal, it had very little chance of success. He again tried to convince the French that places north of the Canal offered far better chances of success. He wrote:

> The expulsion of the enemy from the Aubers Ridge and from the Wytschate-Messines Ridge will not only permit the troops to occupy a much more favourable line for entrenchment under winter conditions, but the possession of these important ridges will be of the greatest advantage in the offensive operations in the early spring, which we will hope will result in driving the enemy out of France and Belgium.

He wrapped up his summary with three further points. The first was that success to the north of the Canal would be better support for the French 10th Army than attacking on its immediate flank. Secondly, he hoped that any offensive in the west would force the Germans to bring reserves across from the east and relieve pressure on the Russians. Lastly, he again reiterated his opinion that the offensive was too ambitious given the limited resources then available. He ended his report with what must be one of the best examples of a mixed message, which was seized upon by the French. In spite of all his reservations Sir John assured Joffre: "That, whatever might be decided, the BEF would assist the general operations in whatever manner and direction the French High Command thought best."

Joffre, after consulting with Foch, responded to Sir John on 5th August in a manner which ignored everything that had been said before:

> It seems to me that no more favourable ground than that which extends from the north of Angre to the La Bassée Canal can be found on which to carry out the general offensive of the British Army. Such an offensive delivered in the direction of the Loos-Hulluch Ridge is in close touch with the attack of the French 10th Army, and turns from the north that mass of miners' houses and cottages, Lens-Lieven, which we shall outflank from the south. Our double attack will therefore result in our bringing a destructive fire from both sides against Lens-Lieven, and in silencing the enemy's artillery located there, which might, if we attacked alone, imperil our success. The experience of this war constantly shows the importance of attacking on wide fronts as the only means of preventing the enemy from concentrating his artillery fire from both flanks. The attack I have described fulfils this most important obligation, as we mutually cover our interior flanks. I am very strongly of the opinion that any British action in any other part of the line would merely be a separate and divergent effort, and therefore not so helpful to an attack in the Arras region. I agree therefore entirely on these several points with General Foch, and I cannot suggest a better direction of attack than the line Loos-Hulluch and the ground extending to the La Bassée Canal, with final objective Hill 70 and Pont à Vendin.

Sir John French replied on 10th August to Joffre that his letter had not caused him to change his opinion in any shape or form, but he would not continue to press his views. He added: "Since I promised that on receipt of your reply I would direct the movements of the British Army in accordance with the wishes which you as Generalissimo expressed, I have no more to say as to the general plan." The first seeds had thus been sown for an attack in totally unfavourable conditions. However, Sir John was convinced that his 1st Army should not become involved in large scale offensive operations except in the very best circumstances for them. To fulfil his promise to the French he intended at the outset to co-operate by providing artillery support only. He tried to play the French at their own game, given the previous compromise, and await the neutralisation of the German artillery in the Loos area, this stemming from the French advance south of Lens before Sir John sent his infantry into the attack. He tried to make this clear to the French GHQ in his reply by saying:

> I am therefore making all the necessary arrangements to afford you the support you request in the direction of Loos and Hulluch. With that object, I am reinforcing my 1st Army, and I have directed it to assist the attack of your 10th Army by neutralising the enemy's artillery, and by holding the infantry on its front.

This confirmed instructions given three days earlier on 7th August to General Haig in which Sir John tried to limit the scale of any potential disaster. These instructions stated:

> The attack of the 1st Army is to be made chiefly with artillery, and a large force of infantry is not to be launched to the attack of objectives which are so strongly held as to be liable to result in the sacrifice of many lives.

This letter from Sir John stirred up a hornet's nest. Joffre took great exception to his reply and fired off a furious response on 12th August. This baldly stated that the support of the BEF could only be effective if it took the form of a large and powerful offensive using all available forces and pressed home regardless of local conditions. He summed up by stressing the large effort the French Armies were planning. Joffre had to some extent forced Sir John into a difficult position as he had suggested to the French Minister of War, Millerand, on 30th July, a proposal which would give him some control over the BEF. Joffre proposed an accord that would give him some power, but also take into account any British intransigence by subordinating them into a temporary but precise objective, this being the liberation of all occupied French territory. This accord proposed:

> During the period in which the operations of the British Army take place principally in French territory, and contribute to the liberation of this territory, the initiative in combined action of the French and British Forces devolves on the French Commander-in-Chief, notably as concerning the effectives to be engaged, the objectives to be attained, and the dates fixed for the commencement of each operation. The Commander-in-Chief of the British Forces will of course fully retain the choice of means of execution.

Political manoeuvring continued behind the scenes as Joffre invited Kitchener to visit in mid August 1915. Soon after his arrival at the French HQ at Compiègne he met with Millerand and Joffre. At this meeting he apparently agreed to this accord. This is backed up by the minutes of a meeting of the Dardanelles Committee for 20th August in which they refer in coded language to a new and secret agreement with the French. It appears with the benefit of hindsight that Kitchener looked upon this agreement as a temporary one. He felt that nothing decisive would be achieved on the Western Front in 1915, and it was best to go with the French plan. It would therefore be possible with larger forces in the field in 1916 for the BEF to assert itself. In any case on 26th August Millerand informed Joffre that Kitchener had accepted the accord. There was no doubt that the BEF would have to co-operate with the French.

Also going on in the background was the deteriorating situation in nearly every part of the world where the Allies were fighting. The landings at Suvla Bay at Gallipoli had failed to realise any material gains, the Italians had failed at Isonzo against the Austrians and news of defeat after defeat was coming from Russia. Against this background in a private conversation Kitchener told Sir John French he was unsure how long the Russians could hold on. Kitchener also said that up till then he had been in favour of a policy of active defence until the BEF was in a position of sufficient strength to strike hard. However because of deteriorating circumstances he now felt it was necessary to act vigorously and launch a large offensive on the Western Front. It was thought this would take some of the pressure off the

Russians. Kitchener said to Sir John: "We must act with all energy and do our utmost to help France in their offensive, even though by so doing we may suffer very heavy losses." When Kitchener arrived back in London on 20th August he was greeted with the news of another defeat on the Eastern Front, and so on the following day he telegraphed Sir John confirming the conversation and telling him to take the offensive and to act vigorously.

Sir John was under great pressure from all sides - at home Kitchener was urging him to act under instructions from the French, whilst Joffre and Foch were pointing the way for him to go. He was now in the unenviable position of being forced to order an attack when he considered he did not have enough troops, over ground he considered unfavourable and against the advice of one of his senior commanders. The loneliness of command is not a bad description of his position at this time. Therefore, on 23rd August, at a meeting with Joffre, Sir John informed him that the British 1st Army would attack with all the resources at its disposal south of the La Bassée Canal. Joffre expressed his satisfaction with this support and owing to the seriousness on the Eastern Front, asked that the joint attack begin on 8th September, just over two weeks away. Sir John meekly agreed to this date. As things turned out, due to various problems in other areas of the French-held front, the attack was put back on 31st August to 15th September. Then on 4th September Joffre advised Sir John that a further ten day delay was necessary and the date was set for the 25th September.

2

The Plan for the Attack at Loos

As with any offensive the commander of the attacking forces must assess the likely strengths of his enemy, and in September 1915 this was the case. It was thought by Allied Intelligence that between Arras and the Channel coast, a distance of around 65 miles, that the defenders were from the German 4th and 6th Armies. These two armies contained 30 divisions, so each one held just over 2 miles of line. In fact, according to the British Official History these two armies contained more divisions than any other German Army and also held less ground than the other five armies in the west. It is not difficult to wonder why an attack was considered in the Loos sector, as it was the area of greatest enemy strength. The Chief of the German General Staff, General von Falkenhayn, had expected the Allied offensives to continue after Aubers Ridge, but the lack of attacks led him in August to doubt whether any more would be undertaken. However by early September he had changed his mind as he wrote:

> From the beginning of September onwards, more and more frequent reports went to show that we had to expect an early attack by the British, supported by the French, in the neighbourhood of Lille, with a simultaneous offensive by the French in Champagne.

Indeed as a result of these reports, two corps (the Guards and X) were taken out of the line in the east and moved to the west around 15th September. These moves were unknown to the Allies and at yet another conference on 14th September held at Chantilly Joffre gave a final briefing to Sir John French and the three French Army Group Commanders - Foch, Dubail and de Castelnau. It was believed the French armies were approaching the peak of their strength and coupled with the increase of British troops, arriving in France, Joffre considered the time was right for a vigorous offensive. It was even thought it might even lead to final victory. The Germans were believed to have about 33% of their troops on the Eastern Front, leaving about 800,000 fighting troops to face over 1,000,000 Allied fighting troops. How these figures were arrived at even today remains a mystery. Even so, it was expected to have an attackers to defenders ratio of six to one. This was achieved by thinning out the defences on other sectors and concentrating the attackers in specific areas. An additional reason for optimism was the increase in heavy artillery from earlier in the year. Joffre therefore believed that the preliminary bombardment, the likes of which had not been seen on the Western Front before, would enable the numerical superiority of the Allies to strike a decisive blow. Joffre announced that the forthcoming attack was to consist of two simultaneous assaults- one from Artois and the other from Champagne - both aimed in the direction of Namur. The main thrust was to come from Champagne. This was basically because the Germans still held the heights of Vimy Ridge and therefore would be easily able to see the build-up of troops and artillery for a large assault. Joffre therefore felt compelled to reduce the strength of the assault from Lens and Arras and to increase it at Champagne. It was a change which probably suited the French more than the British Exeditionary Force (BEF). In the Artois area, as well as being under observation, there were many fortified villages which had given the French great trouble in previous attacks (now to be the responsibility of the BEF), whilst in Champagne there were few local 'hot spots'. In fact the French Official History reports "The tactical advantage of not having to storm villages against which our heavy artillery is still impotent, tipped the scales in favour of Champagne."

The Artois attack was still an Anglo-French affair across the plain of Douai, while the Champagne effort was a wholly French effort. Here they were to attack northwards across the Ardennes, west of the River Meuse. When both offensives succeeded the Germans holding the Noyon Salient would be cut off and isolated. Joffre's intention was then to prevent the Germans re-establishing their line and then concentrate on destroying the divided Germans piece by piece.

The attack in Artois was to be delivered by the French 10th Army and the BEF's 1st Army under the supervision of General Foch. It had been finally decided to attack along a frontage of 20 miles between Arras and the La Bassée Canal. The 1st Army was allocated a front of about 6 miles from Grenay to the La Bassée Canal itself. The attack was to be carried out by 6 divisions, with a further 3 divisions in General Reserve and (as usual) the Cavalry Corps and the Indian Cavalry Corps to be ready to exploit the gap when the assault was successful. Sir John French issued his orders for the BEF's part in this attack on 18th September in the shape of a document called 'General Instructions for the Commanders of Armies and GHQ Reserve.' These were as follows:

1   The Allies are about to assume the offensive with the object of:
     (i) Breaking the enemy's front

     (ii) Preventing him from re-establishing his line

     (iii) Defeating decisively his divided forces.

2   The offensive is to be carried out by:
     (i) The 4th, 2nd, 3rd and 5th French armies east and west of Reims, in the direction of Sedan-Le Nouvion

     (ii) Our 1st Army and the French 10th Army north and south of Arras, in the direction of Le Quesnoy-Frasnes lez Buissenal.

3   The main attack of the 1st Army will be made on the general front Lens-La Bassée (both inclusive) in accordance with instructions already issued to the 1st Army Commander. The right of the attack of the French 10th Army is to pass through Ficheux, and the left immediately south of Lens.

4   Subsidiary attacks will be made by the 1st Army north of the La Bassée Canal and by the 2nd Army east of Ypres in accordance with instructions already issued to the 1st and 2nd Army Commanders respectively.

5   The Cavalry, Indian Cavalry and XI Corps will form the General Reserve at the disposal of the Field-Marshal Commanding-in-Chief. Separate instructions will be issued for the concentration of these troops. The 2nd

Army will keep one Division in Army Reserve west of Bailleul to reinforce either the 1st or 2nd Army as the Commander-in-Chief may decide.

6   As soon as the enemy's front line is broken:

(i) The 1st Army will secure the crossings over the Hauté Deule Canal from Courrières to Bauvin both inclusive.

The next objective of the 1st Army will be the general line Henin-Liètard-Carvin. The dividing line between the 1st Army and the French 10th Army is the Lens-Henin-Liètard-Flers-Waziers-Lallaing road inclusive to the 1st Army.

(ii) The general mission of the Cavalry Corps will be to pursue the enemy and to prevent him from re-establishing connection between his forces north of the break and those to the south.

With these objects in view it will move through the 1st Army front and will secure the crossings over the Hauté Deule Canal between Douai and Courrière, both inclusive, and then moving by the north side of Douai, seize the crossings over the Scheldt between Condé and Tournai (both inclusive) as quickly as possible, cutting the railways Valenciennes-Lille and Ath-Lille.

In carrying out its mission the Cavalry Corps will act, as far as possible, in close combination with General Conneau's Cavalry Corps of the French 10th Army. The left of General Conneau's Cavalry is to move in the direction of Condé-Le Quesnoy by Douai and to the south of that town.

Circumstances may require the Cavalry Corps and General Conneau's Cavalry to move through the front of the 1st Army, or both may be required to move through the front of the French 10th Army. In the former case General Conneau's Cavalry will pass through the 1st Army by arrangement with the Commander of that Army, and in the latter case the Cavalry Corps Commander will make the necessary arrangements with the Commander of the French 10th Army.

(iii) The Indian Cavalry Corps will be held in readiness to support the Cavalry Corps or the French Cavalry as the Commander-in-Chief may decide.

The Bus Companies of each Army will be placed under GHQ control so as to be available to convey Infantry forward to assist the Cavalry if required.

7   The role of the 2nd Army will at first be to hold the enemy in its front, and to deceive him as to the direction of the main attack. It will be prepared, however, rapidly to take the offensive when the enemy retires, or to detach troops to follow up a success gained elsewhere.

8   The 3rd Army will assist with its artillery the right of the French Army attack in accordance with instructions already issued, and will be prepared to

advance at once in co-operation with the French troops on its flanks in the event of the enemy retiring.

9   Once the enemy's defences have been pierced a situation must be created in which manoeuvre will become possible, and to do this the offensive must be continued with the utmost determination directly to the front in the first instance. It must be impressed on Commanders that to delay the advance in order to work outwards to the flanks will give the enemy time to re-establish his front. The advance must be made in depth so that rapid manoeuvre may be possible.

10   General Headquarters will be at St. Omer.

W.R.Robertson, Lieut.-General, Chief of the General Staff.

The main assault was to be carried out by the 1st Army under the command of Haig, the six attacking divisions coming three each from I and IV Corps. The other two corps of this Army - the III and Indian, were to carry out diversionary and subsidiary attacks north of the La Bassée Canal. The other armies in the BEF also had to play their part. The 2nd Army in the Ypres Salient was to carry out diversionary attacks. Two of this Army's divisions (3rd and 14th) were to carry out an attack around Bellewaarde Lake, together with an attack towards Messines. The Army's commander, Plumer, was also warned to be ready to carry out a general offensive should the Germans have a general withdrawal or to send troops to other areas should a success be gained. The 3rd Army on the Somme, south of the French 10th Army, had to support their attack with artillery fire and also to be ready to send troops forward to co-operate with them in the event of a general withdrawal.

Sir John French, meanwhile, decided that as there were numerous potential situations that could develop, he would need a strong force to act as the General Reserve. Indeed he also decided this would remain under the control of GHQ. The Reserve consisted of the Cavalry Corps, the Indian Cavalry Corps and XI Corps. The two cavalry corps were, of course, relatively experienced in warfare, but for the major part of the Reserve it was only a hastily thrown together formation. It is worth noting that the cavalry units were not really the numerical strength of an 'infantry corps' but more like an infantry division in manpower. XI Corps consisted of the Guards Division, the 21st and 24th divisions. It might be useful to pause here and briefly look at the raising and experience of these divisions and corps before continuing with the actual plan for Loos.

The Guards Division was formed at St Omer in August 1915. Up till then the required 13 battalion to form a division had been split up amongst nearly all the 'Regular Army' divisions. There had been 9 Guards battalions in pre-war Britain, and 6 of these had gone to France with the original BEF (2 with the 1st Division and 4 with the 2nd Division). Two more battalion went with the 7th Division in October 1914. The Grenadier, Coldstream and Irish Guards each formed a new wartime battalion and in early 1915 the Welsh Guards were formed. This makes 12 battalions, and if we add in the last pre-war battalion still in England - the 3rd Grenadier Guards - we have the necessary number of units. This total of course includes one of the units acting as the Division's pioneers and this was the 4th

Coldstream Guards. The first commander of the Division was Major-General The Earl of Cavan.

The 21st Division was in essence one of Kitchener's 'New Army' divisions, formed after the flood of volunteers in 1914 after his famous appeal 'Your Country Needs You'. The 21st were one of the third wave of divisions that were formed and so can be called a K3 Division. It was formed around Tring in Hertfordshire from regiments from the north of England together with a battalion of Somerset Light Infantry and one from the Lincolnshire Regiment. They crossed to France between 7th and 15th September 1915. The GOC was Major-General G.T. Forestier-Walker.

The 24th Division was again a K3 Division and was formed around Shoreham in Sussex, mainly from battalions recruited from the eastern part of England - Norfolk, Suffolk, Essex, Bedfordshire and Northamptonshire. The numbers were made up by men from London and the South-East, such as the Middlesex Regiment, the Buffs, East Surrey and the Royal West Kents. They travelled to France in late August and early September 1915. The GOC was Major-General Sir J.G. Ramsay. The 3 divisions were formed into XI Corps under the command of Lieutenant-General R.C.B. Haking on 30th August 1915. Separate orders on 18th September were given to the units comprising the Reserve, different from the GHQ instructions. In these the majority were ordered to take up positions behind the 1st Army. They were to concentrate in an area north and south of Lillers (about 7 miles north of Béthune). The 1st and 2nd cavalry divisions were near Therouanne (about 10 miles north west of Lillers), the 3rd Cavalry Division was allotted to the 1st Army as their 'Army Cavalry', while the Indian Cavalry Corps was sent south to leaguer at Doullens supporting the 3rd Army.

General Haig as GOC 1st Army had been planning to some extent for a further attack somewhere, and he had with Sir John French's approval in early August assembled the six attacking divisions. These divisions came from two corps, the I and IV. These were commanded respectively by Lieutenant-General H. Gough and Lieutenant-General Sir H. Rawlinson. By early September the two corps were in position. In the northern sector was I Corps, holding the line from the Hulluch/Vermelles road across the Canal to join up with the Indian Corps at Givenchy. On the extreme left and therefore in contact with the Indians was the 2nd Division. Next to them was the first of the 'New Army' divisions to arrive in France - the 9th (Scottish) Division. They held the centre ground for this Corps and were opposite the much-feared German defensive position, the Hohenzollern Redoubt. Finally, the most southerly division was the 7th Division. The IV Corps held the line from the junction with I Corps at the Hulluch/Vermelles road southwards to the Grenay/Lens railway where they were in contact with the French 10th Army. The divisions holding the line from north to south were: the 1st Division from I Corps to a track between Vermelles/Loos; in the centre was a second New Army division - the 15th (Scottish) Division; on the extreme right, holding the line from just north of Grenay to the junction with the French, was the 47th (2nd London) Division.

So, of these 6 divisions we have 2 divisions from the original BEF (1st and 2nd) and a further Regular Division (7th), who had been in France since the end of September 1914. There was a Territorial Force Division - the 47th - who had been in France since March 1915 and had seen active service at Festubert. Finally there were two New Army divisions- one K1 (9th) and one K2 (15th). These New Army divisions had been formed rapidly from the mass of volunteers in the first few weeks of the war. Indeed 12 divisions (144 battalions) were formed in the first two months. The first K1 Division was the 9th (Scottish), formed from battalions raised at the regimental depots, the Division forming up at Bordon in Hampshire during September 1914. They sailed for France in May 1915. There is a similar story to relate for the 15th (Scottish) Division, except they can be looked on as a K2 Division. They were formed at Aldershot in September 1914, but did not arrive in France till July 1915. The total number of bayonets in these 6 divisions was around 70,000 and it was believed that there were only 10,000 to 11,000 Germans opposing them. This is well over the normal rule of thumb - for an attacking force to have a 3:1 advantage. Indeed it was also thought that the Germans had about a quarter of the field guns and howitzers and less than half of the heavy guns on the British front. However to some extent this inferiority must be balanced by the superior quality and quantity of the shells fired by the Germans compared to those by the BEF.

The situation facing the 1st Army was not helped by the many changes of plan. To recap: originally in August the 1st Army's role was to principally provide artillery support for a French attack from Vimy Ridge. The strength of the British attack was to depend on the success of the French attack there, since it was decided that until the French had gained control of the heights at Vimy there could be no major effort. Unless Vimy Ridge had been gained and the German artillery neutralised north of Lens it would be a killing ground. Despite this reservation, to fall in with French plans it was decided to launch a limited two division attack. Haig planned this attack with one division aimed at Loos village including Hill 70, and the other to assault the Hohenzollern Redoubt and Fosse 8 behind it. It is interesting to see which divisions Haig suggested for these roles - they were the 9th and 15th divisions. I feel that even for a Regular Division it would have been a hard assignment, never mind untried New Army troops. Perhaps Haig was mindful of the ground and the expected heavy casualties and wanted to save his Regular divisions from a needless slaughter.

Previous experience at Neuve Chapelle and Festubert had shown that troops attacking in a narrow frontage suffered heavily from concentrated artillery fire. It was therefore thought that to give the attacking troops from the 9th and 15th divisions a greater chance of success that the attack should be covered by smoke. However whilst this planning was being undertaken, a new weapon came on the scene that was thought might increase not only the chances of success but broaden the scope of the attack. This weapon was chlorine gas. It was thought that a gas cloud would be very effective weapon in neutralising the German defences, make up for the shortage of artillery and would allow for a broader attack making a six division frontage. It was therefore thought that even though there was still the chance of the attack being broken up by German artillery fire, the use of smoke together with gas might lead to a breakthrough in one or more places. This would allow the Reserve to come through and capture the German artillery. This was the theory. I shall now look at the plan for the artillery and the background for the decision to use gas and the plan for the gas cloud.

The Artillery at Loos

During the run up to the proposed offensive in September 1915 occurred the previously mentioned conference at Boulogne in June. One of the topics discussed was the critical artillery situation. This conference at least recognised that artillery was becoming the key to a successful attack by destroying German defences. In particular, it was decided that the supply of heavy artillery was now vital. It was revealed, based on intelligence estimates, that the proportion of field guns to heavy guns in the German Army was 2:1, the French acknowledged their ratio as 4:1, while the British was 20:1. This conference concluded that for offensive operations to have a chance of success the ratio ought to be 2:1. It was discovered and discussed at this conference that at Aubers Ridge in May 1915 an attack by 3 British brigades had been defeated by 15 German infantry companies supported by 22 machine guns and artillery fire. It is worth adding here that in theory, in 3 brigades there were at least 48 companies.

The next immediate problem was ammunition, or the lack of it. Again it was estimated that the Germans were producing around 250,000 rounds of artillery ammunition per day, the French 100,000 and the British 22,000, with no prospect of this last figure increasing until early 1916. The conference decided that at least 1,000 rounds of heavy and 2,000 rounds of field gun ammunition must always be available to any sector on offensive operations and 200 rounds per heavy and 500 rounds per field gun on the remainder of the front. A final decision (or advice) was that all future attacks should be conducted on a broad front policy to avoid dangerous enfilade fire from the flanks. This piece of news obviously went down well with

The northern part of the Loos Battlefield around Auchy les Mines. (IWM Q37770)

the 1st Army Commander General Haig, as he thought that a major offensive would need around 36 divisions. At the time there were three armies in the BEF encompassing (in June 1915) 21 divisions. The BEF would not reach a fighting strength of 36 divisions till 1916. Added to this was the idea that the artillery support for such an offensive would need 400 batteries of field guns (2,400 guns) and 200 batteries of heavy guns and howitzers (1,200 guns). The entire artillery strength for the BEF at this time was 1,406 field guns and 71 heavy guns.

The artillery plan at Loos called for 19 heavy guns per mile of front, but of course there was nowhere near enough heavies for the entire front, never mind the chronic lack of ammunition. To make up for this deficiency it was decided to use a new weapon - chlorine gas. The actual process of deployment is covered in another chapter, but it is necessary to say here that because of the uncertainty regarding wind direction two artillery plans were prepared: one with gas on a six division front, and one without on a two division front. Even then, with the six division plan there was not enough gas to cover the whole front. It was hoped that if used in conjunction with artillery it might suffice. The other hope was that it was known that the German gas masks were effective for around 30 minutes, so if a prolonged gas cloud of around 40 minutes could be manufactured, it ought to render the Germans incapable and ensure a breakthrough.

The artillery plan also introduced for the first time a new appointment, that of Commander Corps Royal Artillery (CCRA). The idea was that this Commander would control the artillery in his Corps. The two people appointed were (in I Corps) Brigadier-General J.F.N. Birch and in IV Corps, Brigadier-General C.E.D. Budworth. However a mistake was made in not placing the heavy artillery supporting the two corps under the CCRA but leaving them under the control of HQ 1st Army. This meant that vital counter-battery fire was not controlled by the HQs actually fighting the battle.

Artillery Order of Battle:

I Corps
2nd Division Artillery
34th Brigade RFA - 50th and 70th Field Batteries
36th Brigade RFA - 15th, 48th and 71st Field Batteries
41st Brigade RFA - 9th, 16th and 17th Field Batteries
44th Brigade RFA - 47th and 56th Howitzer Batteries

7th Division Artillery
14th Brigade RHA - F and T Batteries
22nd Brigade RFA - 104th, 105th and 106th Batteries
35th Brigade RFA - 12th, 25th and 58th Batteries
37th Brigade RFA - 31st and 35th Howitzer Batteries

9th Division Artillery
50th Brigade RFA - 160th, 161st and 162nd Batteries
51st Brigade RFA - 163rd, 164th and 165th Batteries
52nd Brigade RFA - 166th, 167th and 168th Batteries
53rd Brigade RFA - 169th, 170th and 171st Howitzer Batteries

Supporting (but under the command of 1st Army) were two batteries of heavies known as the 'Siege Group'.
5th Group Heavy Artillery - 7th and 14th Brigades RGA

Notes:
RFA - Royal Field Artillery
RGA - Royal Garrison Artillery
RHA - Royal Horse Artillery
The field batteries of the RFA and RHA used 18 pounder guns, the howitzer batteries had 4.5 inch howitzers and the heavy group whatever was allocated of calibre 6 inch and upwards. Thus the artillery support for I Corps was simple, direct and clearly defined. The opposite was true for the artillery support in IV Corps. Here the CCRA organised his troops in mixed packages.

IV Corps
1st Division Artillery
    Northern Group
        26th Brigade RFA - 116th and 117th Batteries
        C Battery 71st Brigade RFA
        A Battery 119th Brigade RFA
    Southern Group
        108th Brigade RFA- C and D Batteries
        30th Howitzer Battery RFA
        2nd Siege Battery 6th Brigade RGA

15th Division Artillery
    70th Brigade RFA - A, B, C and D Batteries
    71st Brigade RFA - A, B, and D Batteries
    73rd Brigade RGA - B, C and D Howitzer Batteries
    One section from 19th (London) Field Battery RFA
    5th Siege Battery 6th Brigade RGA

47th Division Artillery
    MacNaghten Group
        25th Brigade RFA- 113th, 114th and 115th Batteries
        39th Brigade RFA- 46th, 51st and 54th Batteries
        40th Brigade RFA- 21st (London) Battery
        109th Brigade RFA- C Battery
        24th Siege Battery RGA
    Massey Group
        5th (London) Brigade RFA- 12th, 13th and 14th Batteries
        G Battery RHA
        23rd Siege Battery RGA
    Divisional Reserve Group
        7th (London) Brigade RFA less two Batteries
        7th Brigade RHA- H, I and Warwick Batteries

This order of battle was further compounded by the different types of ordnance used. As well as 18 pounders and 4.5 and 6 inch howitzers, 15 pounders and 13 pounders were also in use. This unwieldy structure of support had in some degree been caused by the removal of the HQRA 1st Division to act as HQRA IV Corps. It was also envisaged that they should go back to the 1st Division HQ at some stage during the offensive.

Fire Plans

I Corps

Brigadier-General Birch decided on a simple fire plan on the following lines:

H Hour: Corps Artillery engage front trenches

H + 10: Guns lift by stages

H + 20: Guns to have moved their fire 1,200 yards east

H + 21: Guns lift back to front line trenches by stages

H + 30: Guns on front line trenches

H + 40: Guns lift from front line trenches to line 600 yards beyond

H + 50: Guns lift to a line a further 600 yards beyond

IV Corps

On the other hand, Brigadier-General Budworth gave a notional order to his Group Commanders to discuss their tasks with their relevant Divisional Commanders. His order stated: "Group Commanders will allow subgroup the greatest latitude in carrying out their tasks." There were five nominal tasks and these were:

Wire cutting

Bombardment

Searching and sweeping trench systems

Special tasks

Concentrations in response to Army HQ tasks

The relatively open nature of the ground coupled with the fact that the Germans had the better observation positions forced the heavy guns to deploy around 4,000 yards behind the front line. They were placed on a line roughly corresponding to Les Brebis, Mazingarbe, Noyelles and Annequin. The smaller field guns were placed about 500 yards in front of the heavies often in full view from the German lines. The British were very lucky here in that German counter-battery fire was poor and relatively small numbers of casualties were caused. If they had been on target it is likely the attack would have been postponed or cancelled. It was envisaged in the plan though that all gun batteries would advance in line with the successful attack and bridges over the trenches were constructed and marked.

The shell supply was not good. The British munitions industry back in Blighty was still struggling to increase production with a shortage of skilled workers (many had joined the Army in 1914) and unheard of levels of demand. As well as the BEF, the gunners and commanders in the Gallipoli campaign were also asking for shells. Indeed, the famous shell shortage at the previous battles in 1915 had led

Table 2.1
Allocation of ammunition by various types of gun during the offensives at
Festubert, Loos and Messines

	Festubert	*Loos*	*Messines*
Heavy Artillery			
60 Pounder	1107	4937	175479
6 inch Howitzer	2848	11241	540541
6 inch Gun	191	340	13647
8 inch Howitzer	0	3218	120934
9.2 inch Howitzer	443	2239	83664
12 inch Howitzer	0	0	6717
15 inch Howitzer	16	216	803
Totals	4605	22191	941785
Field Artillery			
18 Pounder	22602	203124	1977499
4.5 inch Howitzer	4014	30568	642246
Totals	26616	233692	2619745

Table 2.2
Table comparing rounds held by each gun against those allocated, 1 June 1915

	Normal Allocation	*Actually Held*
13 Pounder	1000	413
18 Pounder	1000	573
15 Pounder	1000	444
4.5 inch Howitzer	800	240
60 Pounder	500	649
14.7 inch	500	298
6 inch Howitzer	495	73

to numerous headlines in the newspapers at home. However the supply of ammunition had improved, as can be seen from the above tables. Just for a small comparison I have added the shells allocated for an attack at Messines two years later. Nevertheless, it should be stated that the situation by no means should be judged as satisfactory.

As bad as this seems, perhaps one ought to spare a thought for the gunners on the Gallipoli peninsula in the summer of 1915. In that theatre at certain times the gunners were limited to firing two rounds a day and then these only in an emergency.

The actual artillery operation was divided into three distinct phases:

• Phase One was a preliminary bombardment lasting for 96 hours

An artillery observation post at Philosophe, September 1915. (IWM Q49237)

- Phase Two to consist of artillery support during the actual fighting lasting for 48 hours
- Phase Three to consist of artillery support during subsequent operations lasting for 96 hours

Of the allocated ammunition two thirds of it was meant to be fired during the first phase, and this together with the gas cloud was one of the most vital parts of the battle. The artillery support was however complicated by the need to produce two fire plans.

In the first plan it was seen that some of the attacking divisions, notably the 9th Division against the Hohenzollern Redoubt, and the 15th Division opposite Loos, were (in theory) attacking without the support of gas. Therefore all possible artillery would support this limited attack. The attached divisional artillery would support the infantry, while all the other guns would cover the flanks with the heavy artillery engaged in counter-battery work.

In the second plan, in which it was envisaged to use gas, the artillery would have to support the entire attacking front of six miles and six divisional assaults. The fire would in this case be concentrated on enemy strong points, barbed wire, observation posts and counter-battery work. The need to produce two plans, which in itself caused confusion, was that no one was going to be able to decide which one was going to be used. It all depended on the weather or wind direction on the morning of 25th September. Coupled with this was the difficulty of siting the guns in the billiard table like countryside around Loos. However as in most cases the gunners just had to get on with it. As the selected date for the attack was 25th September, the preliminary bombardment was due to start on 21st September.

That day was a fine warm dry day. In order to conserve ammunition to sustain the prolonged bombardment it was necessary to restrict the number of shells fired. In the first 24 hour period, the field guns were allocated 150 rounds per gun and the heavies 90. After a while clouds of smoke and dust were billowing all over the front, making observation almost impossible. Over the next few days the weather changed into rain, with the wind changing direction and strength almost at will. During the preliminary bombardment, occasional feint attacks were made, which caused the Germans to man their parapets and left them open to shrapnel attacks. However, according to German records, they thought the barrage was a delusory one and did not think it was the precursor to the largest British attack of the war to date!

It is now time to leave the gunners and turn attention to the other element of support in the Battle of Loos - gas and the role of the Royal Engineers Special Companies.

The RE Special Companies had only been formed in that year as a result of one of the 'new' weapons developed during the Great War. It was on the afternoon of 22nd April, near a place called Bikscote in the Ypres Salient, when the Germans released around 150 tons of chlorine gas from 6,000 cylinders along a four mile front. The Germans had been waiting for 11 days for the wind to be blowing in the right direction. Within seconds of being released from the cylinders a dense yellow-greenish cloud was drifting towards the Allied lines. This area was held by mainly French troops from Algeria, with men from the 2nd and 3rd Canadian brigades on their right. The Germans probably came closer to achieving a total breakthrough on this day than any other in the Great War. Within minutes the French North African troops were seen in some cases running back to Ypres. Others staggered along roads coughing and vomiting up blood and liquid. The main effects of chlorine gas are to strip the lining of the lungs and windpipe- causing large amounts of blood and liquid to be produced. Chlorine is known as a choking agent - victims literally drown in their own fluids.

Some soldiers frantically attempted to bury their faces in the earth to avoid the cloud, while others ran away. The Germans had succeeded in opening a five mile gap in the Allied front line, but failed to capitalise on it for various reasons, one of which was the reluctance of the German soldiers to advance into the gas cloud. The situation was virtually saved by the actions of the Canadians and is today commemorated by the brooding Canadian Memorial at St. Julien.

Smarting from this attack Sir John French the very next day demanded of London that he be supplied with chemical weapons to unleash on the Germans. Kitchener, the Minister of War, replied: "Before we submit to the level of the degraded Germans, the request would have to be put before the War Cabinet because the use of poison gas in war is outlawed by international agreement." In trying to remain aloof from this controversy he ended up saying: "These methods show to what depths of infamy our enemies will go in order to supplement their want of courage in facing our troops."

In spite of this the War Cabinet agreed to French's request, with the proviso that "The British would only use chemicals which were no more harmful than those used against them by the enemy, although preparation and experiments might proceed for the employment of more deadly things." The man selected to investigate this new type of warfare was Major C.H. Foulkes of the Royal Engineers, who was appointed as 'Commander Gas Reprisals'. The plan was for Foulkes to find chemicals suitable to be used as weapons and then produce them in bulk, transport them to France, work out how to deploy them, and train soldiers in how to do this.

After looking at several alternatives, and after receiving help from scientists from various universities, it was decided as a stopgap measure to blow back the original German weapon - chlorine gas. The chosen and indeed only method at that time was release from cylinders. In 1915 there was only one factory in Britain, the Castner Kellner chemical plant at Runcorn in Cheshire, which could produce chlorine gas. Even then they could in theory only produce enough gas to fill 50 cylinders a day. Foulkes thought he would need at least 1500 cylinders to produce a suitably large enough cloud of gas. Enough gas had been produced and moved to France by 22nd August for a demonstration of a 'chlorine wave' at a small village called Helfaut not far from the coast near Calais. Indeed in July 1915 the RE Special Companies Depot had been established at this village. The first two Special Companies, 186th and 187th, were formed in July 1915 from men transferred from the infantry in France, and the so-called 'Chemical Corporals' from people specially selected in England who had the necessary qualifications. In August 1915 two more companies were formed - 188th and 189th. Early in September 1915 it was possible to send two companies (totalling 34 sections each on average 28 strong) to the 1st Army to assist in the forthcoming operation.

The demonstration in August had left a very definite impression on the observers, including Haig and nearly all his corps and divisional commanders. On the following day, 23rd August, Haig received Sir John French's new orders, based on Kitchener's instructions: "The Commander-in-Chief wishes you to support the French attack to the full extent of your available resources and not to limit your attack in the manner indicated in his letter of 7th August." It was therefore decided that with the news that gas would be available in quantity, to attack simultaneously with all six divisions instead of just two. This news was relayed to the senior commanders at a conference held at Army HQ at Hinges on 6th September. Haig had originally doubted whether an attack south of the Canal would succeed but the idea that the use of gas on a wide scale persuaded him otherwise. He was now of the opinion that there was the prospect of the German defences being completely overrun and that a local success at Loos could be turned into a strategic victory. He added:

> Provided that we and the French take reasonable precautions as to secrecy, and advance with the necessary vigour and strength on the general line Douai-Valenciennes, decisive results are likely to be obtained. The gas is to be lavishly employed on the whole front of attack. It will be carried by the wind in front of

the attacking divisions and create a panic in the German ranks, or, at least inca-
pacitate them for a prolonged resistance.

The final operational orders of the 1st Army were issued on 19th September
and these read as follows:

1st Army Operation Order No. 95

1

a) In conformity with the general plan of operations as notified to Corps
Commanders, the 1st Army will assume the offensive on the 25th September, and advance between Lens and the La Bassée Canal towards the
line Henin-Liètard-Carvin.

b) The French 10th Army will also take the offensive on the 25th September and advance towards Douai. The left of its attack will pass immediately south of Lens.

c) The dividing line between the 1st Army and the French 10th Army will
be the road Lens-Henin-Liètard-Flers, inclusive to the 1st Army.

d) The 2nd Army will break the enemy's front near Hooge and will hold
troops in readiness to support the 1st Army as opportunity offers.

e) The XI Corps and the Cavalry Corps (less one Division) will be in General Reserve. The Cavalry Corps will move through the 1st Army front
and secure the crossings over the Haute Deule Canal between Douai and
Courrières (both exclusive) as soon as the enemy's line has been broken.

2   Corps of the 1st Army south of the La Bassée Canal will attack with the
object of securing the line Loos-Hulluch and the ground extending to the
La Bassée Canal. As soon as possible after piercing this line units will be
pushed forward to gain possession of the crossings of the Haute Deule
Canal between Harnes and Bauvin. Corps of the 1st Army north of the La
Bassée Canal will vigorously engage the enemy in order to prevent him
from withdrawing troops for a counter-attack. Wherever the enemy gives
ground he must be followed up with the greatest energy.

3

a) The artillery bombardment will commence on the 21st September, and
will continue day and night under instructions already issued.

b) The IV Corps will assault the enemy's trenches between the Double
Crassier (inclusive) and the Vermelles-Hulluch road (exclusive). It will
advance with its left on the Hulluch-Vendin-le-Vieil road, and operate so
as to secure the passages of the Haute Deule Canal at Pont-à-Vendin and
the Lens-Carvin road south of Annay.

c) The I Corps will assault the enemy's trenches between the Vermelles-
Hulluch road (inclusive) and the La Bassée Canal. It will advance with its
right on the Hulluch-Vendin-le-Vieil road, and operate so as to secure the

passages of the Haute Deule Canal from Pont-à-Vendin to Bauvin. It will also assault the enemy's trenches at Givenchy and attack Canteleux.

d) The Indian Corps will assault the enemy's trenches in the vicinity of the Moulin du Piètre. It will take advantage of any weakening of the enemy on its front to operate so as to secure the high ground about Haut Pommereau and La Cliqueterie Fme.

e) The III Corps will assault the enemy's trenches in the vicinity of Le Bridoux. It will take advantage of any weakening of the enemy on its front to operate with a view to effecting a junction with the Indian Corps on the Aubers Ridge.

4   The attacks by the IV and I Corps south of the La Bassée Canal will be preceded by 40 minutes gas and smoke, in accordance with the directions already issued, and the assault will take place at 0.40. The attacks by the I Corps at Givenchy and by the Indian Corps will be preceded by 10 minutes gas and smoke, and the assault will take place at 0.10. The attack by III Corps will take place at daylight. It will not be preceded by smoke unless the hour of zero is suitable. The hour of zero will be notified later.

GOC's Corps will arrange for smoke to be discharged along the whole of the remainder of their line, commencing at 0.6, and will be prepared to take advantage of any retirement of the enemy in their front and to advance with their whole force in conformity with the general plan of operations.

5   The 3rd Cavalry Division (less one Brigade) will be in Army Reserve in the Bois des Dames, in readiness to advance on Carvin as soon as possible.

6   Advanced 1st Army Headquarters will remain at Hinges.

R.Butler, Major-General, General Staff, 1st Army.

Issued at 11 p.m.

This, then, was the top-level plan, and looking slightly below this it meant that the gas cylinders were to be turned on at a time predetermined the evening before the attack on 24th September. The gas and smoke were meant to be discharged for 40 minutes, accompanied by an intense artillery barrage. After this the six divisions would leave their trenches. The immediate aim was to punch a hole in the German first and second lines in the central sectors. The two flanking divisions were only given limited objectives so that they could form a solid base. In the north, the 2nd Division was expected to reach and hold the line of the Haisnes-Cuinchy railway with two brigades and then turn and face north-west. The other brigade of this Division operating north of the Canal was to capture the villages of Chapelle St Roch and Canteleux and then join up with the Indian Corps. On the southern flank the 47th Division was to swing on the Double Crassier and hold a line facing south-east including the Loos Crassier.

The four divisions in the central sector were ordered to "push on eastwards in the direction of Pont à Vendin and the Haute Deule Canal to the extreme limit of their power. Adequate reserves are behind us, and all attacks will be pressed forward with energy until the enemy's resistance is crushed." It was therefore deemed that the area of Lens could be overrun from the north whilst the French 10th Army enveloped it from the south. Not for the first time and indeed not for the last time in the Great War three divisions of cavalry were to move through the infantry and secure crossings over the Haute Deule Canal, then out into open country and rout the Germans.

It is worth pointing out that Haig did at least think tactically at times, as he remained convinced that without a lot more artillery pieces and shells, that the forthcoming attack would yield heavy casualties if the gas cloud failed. He thought that if the wind was not blowing in a favourable direction or of sufficient strength the attack should be postponed. Indeed as late as 16th September he wrote to the Chief of the Imperial General Staff (CIGS) Sir William Robertson:

> Without gas the front of our attacks must be reduced to what our guns can satisfactorily prepare, with the results normally attendant on small fronts; namely, concentration of hostile guns on point of attack, large losses and small progress. In my opinion under no circumstances, should our forthcoming attack be launched without the aid of gas.

However, as usual politics came into force and Haig's concerns were brushed aside and he was told that his attack was "not to be dependent on the use of gas, which in the nature of things, must be certain and the attack should take place on the 25th September, irrespective of weather conditions." Haig, not for the first time, tried an alternative track and submitted new proposals in which he suggested firstly that if weather conditions on the 25th were right, the attack on the entire front supported by gas would take place. Secondly, if the wind was not right, but otherwise conditions were good, and an attack must take place that day, then I and IV corps would attack with only one division each. In tandem with this would be demonstrations north of the Canal by III and Indian corps with the object of diverting attention. The main attack by I and IV corps, supported by the gas cloud, would be postponed till the following day, assuming the wind was then favourable. Finally, if weather conditions were also unfavourable on the 26th, then the main attack would take place on the 27th or else be completely cancelled. Sir John French approved these suggestions although he did add the condition that the date of the attack could not be altered without express permission from GHQ.

Thus at the late stage of the 19th, when the attacking troops should have been thinking about the actual assault, doing reconnaissance and generally preparing, there were two sets of orders to consider. One for a general attack using gas and the other a limited attack using just two divisions. The 'new' set of orders stated that the 9th Division was to assault the Hohenzollern Redoubt at daybreak on the 25th, and when taken join up the flanks of the Redoubt to the original British front line. Following on after this success they would then take Fosse 8 later on that morning. Meanwhile further south the 15th Division were to attack at 10am, the same time as French offensive south of Lens. The first objective of the Jocks was to seize a section of the German front line between the Lens-Béthune road and the Loos-Vermelles track. After this to roll-up all the defences in front of the village of Loos. The other four divisions of the I and IV corps were to be ready to extend these initial gains with all available men, later that day, or at night or even on the following

A

SECRET.—(Not to be carried forward in the Assault).

TIME TABLE OF GAS.

	Attacks South of the LA BASSEE CANAL.
(Minutes).	
0	Start the gas and run 6 cylinders one after the other at full blast until all are exhausted.
0-12‡—0-20	Start the smoke. The smoke is to run concurrently with the gas if the gas is not exhausted by 0-12.
0-20	Start the gas again and run 6 cylinders one after the other at full blast until all are exhausted.
0-32—0-40	Start the smoke again. The smoke is to run concurrently with the gas, if the gas is not exhausted by 0-32.
0-38	Turn all gas off punctually. Thicken up smoke with triple candles. Prepare for assault.
0-40	ASSAULT.

‡ On the 3-cylinder and no-cylinder fronts the smoke will be started at 0-6.

Note:—From 0 to 0-40, front system of hostile trenches will be kept under continuous shrapnel fire. Defences further in rear under bombardment of H.E. shell of all calibres.

At 0-40 artillery fire will lift as required.

1st Army Printing Section, R.E. 465

Timetable of gas for 25th September 1915. (PRO WO 95/1733)

morning supported by the gas cloud, if the wind was correct. Which of these options would be chosen would depend on the gains made by the French south of Loos.

Meanwhile the main supporting weapon was slowly being built up in the rear areas. Supplies of chlorine gas started to arrive in France in early September and by 19th September over 5,000 cylinders of gas had arrived. To give the reader some idea of the difficulties involved in this attack were that around 8,000 men had to be engaged on moving the cylinders. The actual cylinders themselves were around 6 feet in height and weighed about 150 lbs. A great deal of thought and preparation by the RE Special Companies went into this attack. Special recesses in the front line trenches were dug to house the cylinders when they were brought into them, and once there were surrounded by sandbags, as the result of a cylinder being hit by shrapnel is obvious. There were 259 recesses dug in I Corps area and 205 in IV Corps. It has been calculated that 2,568 cylinders were allocated to I Corps and 2,460 to IV Corps. As a cylinder could discharge its contents in 2 minutes and the gas attack was to be of 40 minutes duration, each gas position would have needed 20 cylinders. This would have meant over 9,000 cylinders but only 5,000 were available. To cover this gap it was decided to alternate the gas with smoke. Each gas post was allocated around 12 cylinders and used smoke candles to make up the rest

Unexploded rare 4" Stokes Mortar bomb found near the site of the
Pope's Nose Redoubt. (Peter Boalch)

of the cloud. It had been discovered that the German gas mask was only effective for around 25 to 30 minutes, so it was necessary to have a prolonged assault of gas. In the last few minutes before H Hour special triple smoke candles would be lit to form a dense smoke screen, behind which (and through) the infantry would advance. The Special Companies specially selected and trained small parties in detecting the direction of the wind together with the wind speed and allocated them to the six attacking divisions. Other parties numbering nearly 200 were given the responsibility of turning on the cylinders. One man at each gas post was issued with a wristwatch and these were carefully synchronised shortly before the attack. The actual timetable for the attack was as follows:

- 0 (Zero Hour): Start the gas and run six cylinders one after the other at full blast until all are exhausted
- 0.12 to 0.20: Start the smoke. The smoke is to run concurrently with the gas if the gas is not exhausted at 0.12.
- 0.20: Start the gas again and run six cylinders one after the other at full blast until all are exhausted
- 0.32 to 0.40: Start the smoke again. The smoke is to run concurrently with the gas if the gas is not exhausted at 0.32.
- 0.38: Turn off all gas punctually. Thicken up smoke with triple candles. Prepare for assault
- 0.40: Assault.

In other areas a limited number (27) of a new 4 inch Stokes mortar were used to fire special smoke bombs. The Stokes mortar was an ordinary steel tube and fired either normal mortar bombs or smoke. It was decided in certain areas, such as on the flanks and against exceptionally strong positions such as the Hohenzollern Redoubt, that it would be easier to fire the 'smoke screen' rather than relying on it drifting to where it was wanted. So 27 mortars and over 10,000 bombs were provided. Later on in the war Stokes mortars would be the main weapons of Numbers 1 to 4 (Trench Mortar) Special Companies Royal Engineers, in one of which my grandfather served. All of these tasks were carried out on the three nights preceding the start of the preliminary bombardment, which of course was due to start about 60 hours before H Hour.

The Last Few Hours Before H Hour

In the last few days before the attack as well as the previously mentioned movement of the gas cylinders, all manner of preparations had to be carried out. In various areas it was deemed that No Man's Land was too wide to be safely crossed, sapping was therefore carried out to shorten the distance. This happened most notably in the 1st Division area. Stores of all descriptions were established near the front line, trench bridges for both infantry and cavalry prepared, medical aid posts established and so on. Underground mining operations were also being carried out by the tunnelling companies. The Germans must have heard the sounds of the diggers in the chalk but for unknown reasons chose to ignore them. In fact most of the preparations were carried out without much German interference. Then at last the hour for the start of the preliminary bombardment arrived.

As many guns as could be spared from the rest of the BEF had been allocated to the 1st Army. There were now nearly 1,000 guns on the 1st Army sector - over 100 super-heavy, heavy guns and howitzers with 850 lighter guns and howitzers. The first phase of the bombardment was to last for four days and nights, and it was envisaged in the plan that the first rounds would be fired as soon as observation was possible on the morning of 21st September. This day turned out to be a fine, warm dry one and fired opened soon after dawn. The heavies were limited to 90 rounds per gun and the field guns to 150 for the first 24 hours. The bombardment after this initial four days and nights was intended to develop into a second phase of two days firing for a two day battle. The third phase was deemed to be in support of 'subsequent operations', during which the guns would move to new positions. Of the 10 days scheduled firing in the artillery plan, the preliminary bombardment was deemed to be the most important phase, and about 66% of the total ammunition available was allocated to this phase.

As previously stated, the number of guns and ammunition were by themselves considered to be insufficient to support an attack of more than two divisions. But it was thought that with the use of the gas cloud, there would be enough guns and rounds to support six divisions. In this case, the heavy guns were to be scattered over the entire front and used mainly on counter-battery work and the destruction of villages, strong points and observation posts. The field batteries were left with the job of cutting the barbed-wire defences that were sited in front of the German lines. Each field battery was 'given' a sector about 600 yards long as their own allotted target. So far so good, but there was an unfortunate gap in the plan. The

Germans had also constructed barbed wire defences in front of their second line. These were generally out of the range of the field batteries, and so, where possible the task of wire-cutting was given to the heavies. But due to their already large workload and the difficulty of actually observing the results, it was not seriously attempted. These were the daylight objectives. At night the field batteries were to concentrate on the German lines of communication.

In the event of the conditions being unsuitable for the gas cloud, alternative orders were prepared for the limited two division attack. This was to be supported by all available heavies and by the field batteries of the divisions concerned. The flanking division's artillery would support by firing to the north and south of both attacks. This limited assault would be given the support of an hour's intense bombardment of the German front line. Intense in so far as the heavy ammunition lasted, the field guns being allowed to fire 100 rounds, the various howitzers (4.5, 5 and 6 inch) being allocated 60 rounds. The fire plan was arranged so it reached a peak at the moment of the assault. After the assault, the bombardment was to extend its range so that positions beyond and on both sides of the initial objectives were covered. Anyway this was the plan for the limited two division attack but all resources went into the wider attack. It is easy to see now that it would have been very difficult to lift and shift the guns to support at very short notice the two division attack. Hour after hour shells fell onto the German positions, and soon clouds of smoke and dust hung over the front line. This made observation almost impossible, but the barrage continued anyway. After two days of reasonable weather, the 23rd dawned wet with a variable wind. On the night of 23rd/24th there was a violent thunderstorm with torrential rain, which made movement, especially in the chalk bottomed trenches, nearly impossible. Conditions improved on the morning of the 24th and the bombardment continued all day. However the wind on the 24th varied considerably. Obviously for the gas cloud to prove effective the wind would need to be blowing from anywhere between north-west and south-west and at about a speed of 8 mph. On the eve of the assault at midday the wind was coming from the south but later on veered to south-east and east-south-east. That night it went from south to south-west and in certain areas to due west. Rarely can a senior commander have had to put so much thought into 'General Weather'. Perhaps the decision facing Haig was almost mirrored nearly 30 years later on the night of 5th June 1944 when Eisenhower said 'Let's Go' to Normandy and the invasion of France.

Meanwhile what was the effect of the barrage? Coupled with the barrage were several ploys intended to provoke and deceive the Germans. In certain areas units were told to open fire with small arms for a couple of minutes, show bayonets and dummies above the parapets and generally give the indication of an attack. In several cases it worked and the Germans manned their firing step and were caught in the 'open' by shrapnel shells. In certain parts of the plan though it appeared there were shortfalls. During the preliminary phase there was little fire in return from the German artillery, perhaps leading to the notion that the batteries had been put out of action. Also due to the shortage of guns and ammunition (and that that was available was of dubious quality) it was unlikely to effectively destroy all the targets envisaged. Reports from the FOOs showed that in places suitable gaps had been cut in the German wire, but at others it was virtually intact. It did not help that in places the wire had been sited on a reverse slope and therefore difficult or impossible to see from observation posts. Also some of the FOO parties and the actual batteries themselves were relatively new to the front and not experienced in this work.

But at the end of the day, regardless of the effectiveness of the artillery barrage, much faith had been invested in the new weapon - the gas cloud. Due to the technology (or lack of it at that time) the gas cloud needed a wind of about 8 mph from any point from the north-west to the south-west to have any chance of drifting into the German positions. Up till that point in the war never had the 'weather men' played any significant role. The arrangements for weather reporting at 1st Army HQ in September 1915 was the responsibility of Captain E. Gold, who was a member of the Royal Flying Corps. He received four weather reports a day from the Meteorological Office in London giving weather conditions from various places in Britain and Europe. Additionally 40 officers from the Special Companies sent reports to Lieutenant-Colonel Foulkes on the wind speed and direction. It was from all these reports that Captain Gold had to make a guess as to future conditions. In the evening of 24th September at 6pm Haig had a meeting with his two corps commanders, Rawlinson and Gough, at which Gold was also present. Gold reported on his observations from 7am and he also said that in his opinion that there was a small chance of a 'correct' wind on the following morning. There were further charts from 1pm, the opinion this time being that the wind would be either favourable or unfavourable! However he did qualify this expert opinion by saying there was a slight bias towards the wind being favourable. It was on these opinions that the biggest attack by the BEF in the war so far rested. Haig saw Gold again at 9pm during which he said that the wind which at 6pm had been blowing from between south-east to east-south-east would probably change during the night through south to south-west or west.

Gold's forecast for the 25th September was: "Wind southerly, changing to south-west or west, probably increasing to 20 mph." A wind blowing directly from the west was ideal for the deployment of a gas cloud and based on this forecast Haig issued the following instructions. Firstly he ordered the actual attacking troops to go into the forward trenches, he also issued the following message: "The weather forecast, at this hour, 9.45pm, indicated that a west or south-west wind may be anticipated tomorrow, 25th September. All orders issued for the attack with gas will therefore hold good. The hour of Zero will be notified later during the night." Soon after 10pm the wind started to blow from the west, although it was gentler than expected, it also brought a light drizzle that lasted most of the night. Meanwhile up at the front, the attacking brigades were making their way into their jumping-off trenches. By 2.30am on the morning of 25th September nearly all had reported in to 1st Army HQ that they were in position and ready to attack. Further back in the rear areas the Reserve from XI Corps spent the night on the march moving towards the front line. Their pre-allocated positions were all about seven miles behind the front line and as we shall see later was a very trying experience for all these three divisions.

Reports of the wind speed and direction came from the Special Company Officers continued to come in through the remainder of the 24th and during the early hours of the 25th. It must have been a tense time at HQ, at 9pm on the 24th the wind had changed from south-east to south. An hour later it appeared to be

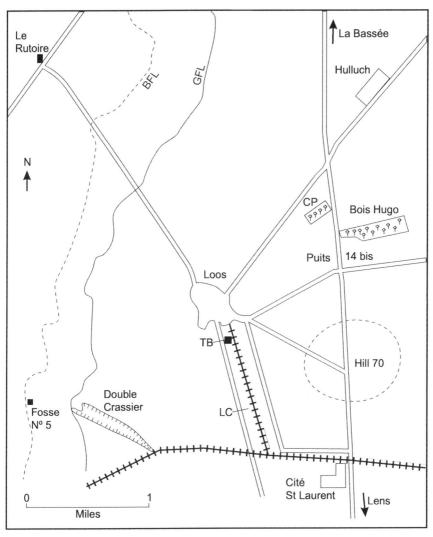

TB	Tower Bridge	GFL	German Front Line
LC	Loos Crassier	CP	Chalk Pit and Chalk Pit Wood
BFL	British Front Line	+++	Railway Line

Some roads and the rear trenches omitted for clarity.

Map 2: The Loos area

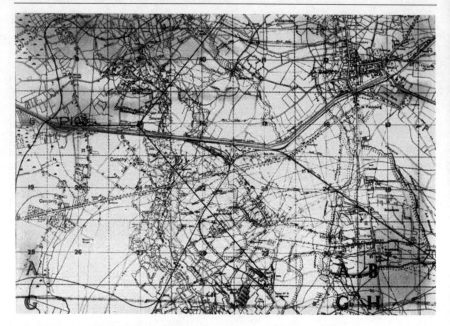

The Loos Battlefield north of Cuinchy. (IWM Q 41774)

blowing from the south-south-west, midnight and it was between south-west and west but was only being recorded at a speed of about 4 mph. Through the early hours the wind seemed to continue blowing from the south-west, but at times the wind speed was so slow it was almost unreadable - certainly not ideal conditions. During this anxious time Haig had a meeting with Gold at 3am the morning of the 25th, and the opinion was expressed that conditions were still favourable for a wind from the south-west later on that morning. Gold did add a rider that there were indications that conditions could become less favourable and the wind could veer to become one from the south. Gold further stated that it was likely that the wind would increase in speed after dawn and just before noon. When asked what time would be best for the release of the gas cloud, he replied that it would probably be as soon as possible. Haig therefore decided, probably at great personal anguish, to issue orders that Z Hour was to be 5.50am and the infantry attack was to go in 40 minutes later at 6.30am.

At 5am Haig and his senior ADC Major A. Fletcher went outside to gauge for themselves the wind speed and direction. The drizzle had stopped and there appeared to be a very slight wind. To gauge the wind Fletcher lit a cigarette and the smoke drifted away to the north-east. As stated before Haig now had probably the hardest decision to make in his life so far: should he go with the gas or not? The previous evening he had ordered the attack, but he had always reserved the right to limit the attack and had staff officers standing by to relay fresh orders. To attack without gas would probably lead to heavy losses, and the Germans might spot the massed infantry in the front line from the divisions that did not attack and bring down murderous artillery fire. Then, just after 5am the wind began to increase, and at 5.15am Haig gave the order to carry on. A few minutes later the wind seemed to die down and one of his staff officers telephoned I Corps to ask whether it was possible to stop the arrangements for the gas attack. General Gough responded that he considered it impossible to get word in time to the trenches and the attack would have to go in as planned.

In spite of this Foulkes had made alternative arrangements by arranging with Gassing Officers to have 20 slips of paper saying 'Attack postponed, taps not to be turned on until further notice.' Foulkes had also told officers at certain places that if the wind was unfavourable the gas was not to be turned on. Just before the attack started Haig was at the top of his wooden lookout tower, the wind speed seemed to be increasing and conditions seemed more satisfactory. The front line troops had been given special instructions as to the wearing of the new 'smoke hoods'. They were warned not to consume any food or drink found in the German lines as it would be gas contaminated, and that the gas would linger in the German trenches and dugouts, so they would need to wear their hoods. The infantry were, as usual, weighed down with kit. As well as the usual set of webbing each rifleman had 200 rounds of small arms ammunition, three empty sandbags, an iron ration and an extra cheese ration. Each platoon had been allocated a set of wire cutters and a pole with a coloured disc on the top to indicate their position to artillery spotters. Additionally 25 picks and shovels were distributed among each 100 men. In theory all was now set and the minutes ticked by towards H Hour 5.50am.

I think it would be appropriate now to take a brief look at the topography of the Loos battlefield. For the major part of the forthcoming battleground the area around Loos was basically a featureless plain, with the exception of a few small ridges, hills and villages. In 1915 the most dominant features were the numerous towers which supported the winding gear for mine shafts and the dumps of coal refuse (slag heaps). There was very little coal mining taking place for obvious reasons in 1915 and the surface of the fields was a barren plain intersected by trenches whose white chalk parapets gave away their positions.

In the south of the attacking area there were several villages, such as Cité St Auguste and Cité St Laurent, which were in effect the northern suburbs of Lens. In the north towards the La Bassée Canal was the village of Auchy. There were several areas of high ground and the Germans had sited their defences on these, such as Hill 70 and Lone Tree Ridge. In total there were six principal pit-heads or 'Fosses', each of these usually rose to about 100 feet and were very useful for observation purposes - until that is one side or the other destroyed them. Also close to each Fosse was their slag heap or 'Crassier'. Again these were useful for both observation and after adequate shelters had been constructed, to site machine guns. The Germans held Fosse 8 and the Crassier which were close to their front line, and from which they were given a complete view of the British lines. This included seeing all the roads leading back to Béthune. Indeed it was stated that the Germans could see every artillery piece brought up to within 3,500 yards of the German front line. This feature dominated the northern part of the battlefield. In the south the Germans were also well served by a Fosse in Loos village. This had a double wheel house and was consequently known to the Tommies as Tower Bridge. The British artillery had tried without success to destroy them. The British did have a Crassier for observation at Fosse 9 in the northern part, but as it was about two miles from the front line it only gave limited views. In the southern part at Grenay was the

Crassier of Fosse 5, this was only just behind the front line but again it had limited views due to a spur opposite it and the 'heights' of Hill 70. As can be guessed the Germans had the opportunity of siting their defences in the best places whilst the Allies normally had no option but to go in those with a tactical disadvantage.

Normally close by the Fosses was a village made up of miners' cottages known as corons. Although normally not of a very high standard of construction and easily demolished by artillery fire, they had the advantage of having a cellar. The Germans often sited defensive positions in these and they could hold about 15 men each.

To sum up then, it appeared that at both ends of the six mile front there was about a mile that would be a difficult nut to crack. The central four miles - a comparatively open stretch of undulating plain appeared to offer the best chance for a breakthrough. It was also the most open ground the BEF had ever attacked across. Whilst this meant there were no obstacles to progress, it equally provided no cover from enemy observation or fire, and was flanked by heavily defended German positions. Again it is worth saying that it hardly seemed like 'particularly favourable ground' as described by General Joffre. In fact the post-war British Official History described the area as follows; "A more unpromising scene for a great offensive battle can hardly be imagined."

3

Over the Top: 25th September 1915, I Corps

Soon after 5.50am the gunners unleashed an intense artillery bombardment on the German front line defences and at the same time the new weapon was used for the first time. However perhaps before looking at some experiences from the Special Companies, it might be worth diverting for a moment to relate the diversionary attacks that occurred.

There were three efforts all to the north of the actual offensive area, with some starting up to three hours before the attack at Loos. The earliest feint was carried out by the 8th Division situated at a place called Bois Grenier near Armentieres. It had been preceded by an artillery bombardment on 24th September and then on the 25th September by a 5 minute barrage immediately before the attack. The intention was for three battalions from the 25th Brigade to attack a 1,200 yard section of the German front line, push through towards Fournes and join up with the Indian Corps at Aubers Ridge. It was also supported by a small discharge of gas and smoke. Further south at 6am around Neuve Chapelle opposite Aubers Ridge elements of the Indian Corps were to attack a 1,500 yard German salient west of the Moulin du Piètre. If successful they were to push on through Piètre and gain a foothold on the Aubers Ridge. Again a small amount of gas and smoke was released, but the wind did not move the cloud as fast as expected and gas casualties resulted. The third diversion was carried out by the wholly British 19th Division from the Indian Corps in front of Festubert. This Division was to co-operate with 2nd Division from I Corps and they were to attack the Rue d'Ouvert as soon as the attack from 5th Brigade (2nd Division) had developed.

The experiences of these three attacks were all broadly similar in that the shortage of ammunition prevented suitable softening-up and there were no Reserves to exploit any gains. The following report from 7th Battalion East Lancashire Regiment, who were in the 56th Brigade, 19th (Western) Division, is typical:

> Zero Hour for the commencement of the Operation was 5.50am at which hour the artillery opened a very heavy bombardment which lasted for 40 minutes. At 6.35am a sheaf of rockets announced that 58th Brigade had gone over the top. The sheaf of rockets sent up from the HQ of 58th Brigade denoted that the left flank of the 2nd Division had advanced sufficiently far to enable the 58th Brigade to carry out its task. On the Battalion front hundreds of smoke bombs were thrown over the parapet and heavy rifle and machine gun fire was opened on the enemy trenches with the result that the enemy commenced to shell our trenches heavily with shrapnel and trench mortar bombs.
>
> This continued in varying degrees of intensity until nearly midday, when there was a slight slackening. For some time there was no news from other parts of the line, but it was quite obvious that the enemy was still in force in front of the Battalion. Later on, definite information of the failure of the 58th Brigade

Two soldiers demonstrating the use of the Vermorel Sprayer, a converted agricultural sprayer which contained a solution that neutralised puddles of gas remaining in trenches.
(IWM Q 51647)

was received, also some optimistic and pessimistic reports of the progress of the Battle south of the Canal, but it was quite clear that the attack north of the Canal had been a failure.

The 58th Brigade suffered 654 casualties, the 8th Division had 1,335 casualties and the Indian Corps around 2,000.

Meanwhile further south the Special Companies had been preparing their equipment. The gas cylinders weighed about 160 lbs, in addition there was a system of pipes. One pipe was bent at right angles about 5 feet long with a further bend about 1 foot from the end. There was also a shorter pipe also bent at right angles; one end was attached to the cylinder and the other to the pipe so that the length of the pipe was sufficient to reach from the top of the cylinder to the top of the parapet. One Special Company man commented that it was obvious to them that they would lose time in transferring the pipe from one cylinder to another and that it would not be an easy task. As well as containing the cylinders each gas post had double the number of pipe connections, assorted nuts and bolts and two

A group of soldiers pictured in December 1915 showing the various types of respirators used in 1915. The soldier on the extreme right is wearing the P helmet the version used at Loos. (IWM Q 17399)

wrenches, one of which was adjustable. The top of each cylinder was surrounded by a dome cap which protected both the turning-on tap and the outlet valve. The cylinders were turned on by two methods, one type had a spindle with a small rect-angular projecting rod, while others had a convex wheel handle. Each method re-quired the use of a different type of spanner and the outlet valve was capped off with a blind nut which needed removal before the connection of the jet-pipe. Ad-ditionally each post had two special Vermorel sprayers to neutralise the inevitable gas leaks in the trenches. The Vermorel sprayers were similar to insect sprayers and contained a solution of 'thio' which could absorb chlorine. Finally all the Specials had been given an armband of red, green and white to stop them being mistaken for deserters if found in a seemingly empty trench.

Finally, at 5.50am, as denoted by their newly issued and carefully synchro-nised watches, the long wait was finally over. Even though the wind appeared to be less than acceptable in many areas, the pipes went over the parapet and the valves were turned on. In spite of training behind the lines at Helfaut, it was a different proposition in the front line trenches, and the rain and trench mud had got into places where it wasn't wanted, such as on the joints of pipes, valves on the cylinders and spanners. Charles Ashley noted:

> To attach a pipe to twelve cylinders in succession and turn the tap on and off in a period of 38 minutes does not sound a difficult task, for the gas took less than two minutes to flow out of each cylinder and we had two pipes. However work-ing as hard as we could, and without intermission while smoke was being sent

The Battlefield of Loos looking towards Tower Bridge. (IWM Q49236)

over, we managed to empty only ten cylinders, which we later discovered was more than the average. The difficulty was caused by the release of pressure making the nuts so cold that they would not fit easily onto the new cylinder. One man, we were told, was so frustrated that he carried his cylinders forward and then tried to burst them by firing at them; another followed his example but turned the taps on without attaching any pipes.

This frustrated soldier was Company Sergeant Major Morrison from 186th Company. Regretfully, he was struck by a jet of liquid chlorine from a burst cylinder which killed him. If this account is correct, Morrison was only 23 years old, and had already been awarded a DCM. His date of death is given as 26th September 1915 and he now lies at Chocques CWGC Cemetery. Another account is given by John Thomas:

> Streams of gas were escaping from every joint in the pipes, and Skinner was busily spraying both Davies and myself with 'Hypo' solution from his Vermorel sprayer in an effort to neutralise the chlorine. I fastened onto the leaks and tightened the joints with my spanner, and when the first cylinder became empty proceeded to deal with the second. The escaping gas had so chilled the pipes by now, that it was almost impossible to unfasten the joints. There was a slight drizzle of rain also, and this turned to snow on the pipes and the outside of the pipes became covered with a slippery surface of ice. We had got the second cylinder on when the word came along to turn off.

Both of these accounts are from Special Company men who were with the 2nd Division in the extreme north of the attack area near the La Bassée Canal. The results along the entire six Division front were patchy. In many places where the wind was non-existent or indeed blowing in the wrong direction the results were disastrous. It seems that at about 6.20am that the wind changed direction once again. The following is taken from the War Diary of the 9th Glasgow Highlanders from the 5th Brigade:

> The gas when set free, travelled away from our trenches - though its direction was NE rather than E. No trouble occurred until about 6.25am when our trenches were suddenly enveloped in dense volumes of gas which rolled up from the Canal on our right, where it has apparently collected, and possibly blown back. Within five minutes our two leading platoons had only seven and nine men left respectively who were fit to carry on. Things were not made any better by the wearing of the smoke hoods.

These hoods were made of flannel impregnated with chemicals to neutralise the chlorine. They had a small insert of clear material - mica to enable the wearer to see out, but if worn correctly made the wearer uncomfortably hot and greatly restricted vision. Worse still, command and control wearing the smoke hoods was difficult and even today it is difficult to have effective communication in full NBC suits. Perhaps even worse, the troops had been told to wear their hoods with the fronts rolled up until the last minute, and the rain caused the chemicals in the cloth to run and irritated the eyes. In addition to these difficulties the onset of the gas attack caused a violent German reaction in the form of a heavy bombardment of the British front line. This also caused as well as the 'normal' casualties by blast and shrapnel, further gas casualties. German shells hits the pipes, connectors and sometimes the cylinders themselves with imaginable results. Still, the minutes passed by till it was nearing 6.30am when the infantry would go over the top. Before I look at the actions of the attacking divisions it might be best to see what effect the chlorine gas and smoke cloud had had on the Germans.

It must be said that the technology used for getting the gas across to the German lines, although the best (and only) method at that time, really was dependent on luck rather than judgement. This is easy to say with hindsight but additionally other factors have to be considered as well as relying on a favourable wind. The varying distance between the British and the German lines and the frequent dog-legs in the German trenches all have to be considered. All of these factors taken into account produce a varying picture of the effects of the gas cloud along the entire front. The one advantage the British did have was surprise; according to German records there was no idea that gas was to be used, an attack yes, but a gas attack no. On the extreme southern flank prisoners from the 22nd Reserve Regiment captured by Londoners from the 47th Division revealed that they had watched the cloud approaching them but did not realise what it was until it reached them. Very few had respirators handy and some men quickly fell unconscious, while others became temporarily incapacitated. A German officer remarked that as soon as the gas entered his trench, he lost all control over his men, a panic ensued and many of them broke and fled. In the middle sector where the 15th, 1st and 7th divisions were, perhaps gave the most varied results. Prisoners from the 157th Regiment were of the opinion that no gas was used. But in the Hohenzollern Redoubt, held by men from the 11th Reserve Regiment, opposite the 9th Division, the gas had the greatest effect. Perhaps this was due to its salient position and the gas drifted across the Redoubt from south to north. Generally speaking though the following account from the official history of the German 6th Army is worth recounting:

After the British had bombarded the line with very heavy shelling from 5.20am to 6.30am, and from 8.00am to 8.15am, they began a gas attack on a grand scale against the whole sector of the 117th Division. At intervals of ten to fifteen minutes, three to four smoke clouds, and immediately after each except the last, a gas cloud moving with one to two metres per second velocity rolled towards the occupied trenches. A light even west wind impelled it forward. The smoke was dirty white, the gas yellowish red. The clouds soon reached a height of 50 metres. Simultaneously the British artillery fired shells that emitted heavy gas and 'stinking' gas [this was not the case as no such shells existed at this time]. Gas and smoke hung about until 11.00am and stretched eastwards, always losing density, as far as the Divisional Headquarters in Wingles 2¾ miles behind the line. As the wind was slight, the clouds dispersed very slowly. In depressions the gas lay thick and obstinately; at other places smoke had the upper hand, and made the air far too dark to see through. Near the enemy one could not see more than three paces, in Wingles barely thirty. In general, the physical effect on the men was trifling.

Further examples are given in captured German documents dated 27th September 1915, which state that at 1500 metres from the British trenches, the artillery suffered greatly, at least machinery wise. Guns and rifles quickly rusted up and it became impossible to open breech blocks. It was difficult to give orders and it became clear that the 40 minute gas barrage was the right length of time, in that the German gas masks became less effective as time wore on.

The 56th Regiment opposite the 2nd Division in the northern area of the attack reported the following:

At 6.45am a thick white gas cloud was discharged from the British trenches against our position. Isolated observers stated that it had a bluish colour. The cloud came over our trenches, and after about five to ten minutes, a second and later a third. A strong chlorine smell was noticed. Between each cloud the air was clear and pure. The bulk of the gas disappeared over our trenches, but the lower layer sank down into them. Fires built on the parapet appeared to cause the gas to dissipate. The gas masks were satisfactory, but there were 72 gas casualties in hospital, a large proportion being cases of unconsciousness, some of bronchitis, and some discharge from the mouth. No deaths so far recorded.

At the southern end around Lens the German defenders were provided by the 26th Regiment and this is again from a captured German document:

A yellow white smoke welled up from the British trenches at intervals of fifteen metres. I ordered 'Gas masks on and man the trench!' In two minutes all was ready - no one to fire before the word is given. There was no doubt that the attack had come. The British trenches could no longer be seen. The gas cloud came near. In ten minutes it reached the first wire entanglement and was fifteen metres high. Now the British artillery took a hand. Howling and slaying, the shrapnel raged over our trenches. I gave the order 'Fire!' and everyone shot into the cloud. The machine guns clattered. All around us was now white mist. Breathing was difficult. The gas masks helped a little, however. In front of the first platoon the British clambered out of their trenches. Our fire compelled them to return. At 7.10am the cloud lifted and went northwards.

I suppose the most interesting detail from these reports is the lack of signifi-cance given to the 60 hour British bombardment, which was the heaviest fired by the BEF in the war thus far. Indeed it has been said that the Germans considered the barrage to be a relatively slight one. It was now the turn of the infantry to do their bit.

The Attack by I Corps in the North

The I Corps plan under Lieutenant-General H. Gough with its three attacking di-visions was to break through the German defences between the Vermelles/Hulluch road and the La Bassée Canal. After breaking through they were to press on eastwards to the German second line about a mile behind the front line. After tak-ing this line they were to move forward in the general direction of the Haute Deule Canal. The 7th and 9th divisions were to move towards the villages of Wingles and Douvrin respectively. The right flank of the 7th Division was to remain in touch with IV Corps. The 2nd Division on the left flank after capturing the village of Auchy, was to go firm on the railway line that ran from Haisnes to the Canal. The aim here was to cover the further advance of the 7th and 9th divisions.

The area was virtually a flat plain, ideal for defence, but dominated by a few prominent strong points. Firstly, the low crest of the Grenay spur curved in a wide arc behind the German lines between the Hulluch road and Fosse 8. There was also the posing question of two important redoubts: the Quarries, a chalk excavation on the crest of the spur, over a hundred yards long and liberally sprinkled with dug-outs; and Fosse 8, with its collection of mine buildings, miners' cottages and slag heap known as 'the Dump', all turned into fortified positions. It was by no means an easier nut to crack away from these areas - between the Dump and the Canal was the large village of Auchy, which again had been turned into a strong point. Also, should the front line be breached there was little cover between that and the second German line, and just behind that second line was a series of fortified villages - Hulluch, Cité St Elie and Haisnes. All in all, a very formidable challenge for the men of I Corps.

This is the I Corps Operational Order for the attack, dated 20th September 1915:

1   The 1st Army will assume the offensive on 25th September and advance between Lens and the La Bassée Canal towards the line Henin-Lietard/ Carvin. The I and IV Corps south of the La Bassée Canal will attack with the objective of securing the line Loos-Hulluch and the ground extending to the La Bassée Canal. Immediately after piercing this line units will be pushed forward to gain possession of the crossings of the Haute Deule Canal between Haisnes and Bauvin.

North of the La Bassée Canal the enemy will be engaged vigorously in order to prevent him withdrawing troops for a counter-attack. Wherever the enemy gives ground he must be followed up with the greatest energy. The IV Corps will advance with its left on the Hulluch-Vendin le Vieil road, and operate so as to secure the passage of the Haute Deule Canal at Pont à Vendin and the Lens-Carvin road south of Annay.

The 3rd Cavalry Division (less one Brigade) will be in Army Reserve in the Bois des Dames in readiness to advance on Carvin as soon as possible.

2   The general intention of the GOC I Corps is to break the enemy's line south of the La Bassée Canal and to advance to the line of the canal Pont à Vendin-Bauvin with his right on the Hulluch-Vendin le Vieil road. A main attack will be made by the 7th, 9th and 2nd Divisions against the enemy's front from the Vermelles-Hulluch road (inclusive) to the La Bassée Canal with the view to an immediate advance on Hulluch-St Elie-Haisnes railway line from Haisnes to La Bassée Canal. A subsidiary attack will also be made by 2nd Division from Givenchy.

3   Main attack. 7th Division, with two Brigades in front line and one Brigade in reserve, will assault the enemy's front line trenches from the Vermelles-Hulluch road (inclusive) to Quarry Trench (G.5.c.87) and will advance with its right on G.12.c.60-G.12.d.60- H.13.b.17.28.66 (exclusive) and its left on G.5.c.87-cross-roads G.6.b.52 (inclusive).

9th Division, with two Brigades in front line and one Brigade in reserve, will assault from Hohenzollern Redoubt to Vermelles Railway Triangle (inclusive) and will advance with its right on south end of Slap Heap-Slag Alley, south of Fosse No 8- crossroads G.6.b.52 (exclusive), and its left on A.27.b.93-Train Alley-Lone Farm-Cemetery Alley-Pekin Alley-A.30.a.74, all inclusive.

2nd Division, with two Brigades in front line south of Canal will assault the enemy's front trenches from left of 9th Division to the La Bassée Canal, and will advance with its right in touch with the left of 9th Division, and its left along the La Bassée Canal to Canal Alley (railway line Haisnes to La Bassée Canal).

Subsidiary attack. The left Brigade of the 2nd Division holding the line north of the Canal will attack the enemy's trenches opposite Givenchy and will capture the line A.9.b.09-26-43-A.9.d.79-A.10.c.03 and will push on to the line Chapelle St. Roch-Canteleux.

It must be impressed upon all commanders that to obtain success it is essential to push on the advance with the utmost rapidity in order to take advantage of the first surprise and to prevent the enemy's reserves occupying his rearward defensive lines.

4   The following distinctive screens will be used by Divisions to denote positions gained by the Infantry:

   7th Division- red and blue diagonal on one side- khaki on reserve side.

   9th Division- red and yellow diagonal.

   2nd Division- yellow- reverse side khaki.

   Smoke candles giving yellow smoke, and men raising their caps on bayonets, will also be used as signals to denote positions gained by Infantry.

Panoramic view of virtually the centre point of I Corps front. Auchy is on the left, with Fosse 8 and The Dump in the centre and Cité St Elie to the right. (IWM Q 37765)

5   Orders for wire-cutting, preliminary bombardment and barrages will be issued by the BGRA I Corps. The first day of bombardment will be the 21st September.

6   The hour of Zero will be notified later. The left Brigade of 2nd Division will attack from Givenchy at 0.10 hours, and the 2nd Division south of La Bassée Canal, 7th and 9th Divisions will attack simultaneously at 0.40 hours. Action during period from Zero to 0.10 and 0.40 hours will be in accordance with instructions already issued.

7   At 1.20 the Divisional artillery (1.10 for the artillery covering the left of 7th Division) will come under the Divisional control, subject to the following:

The heavy artillery will remain at the disposal of the Corps Commander and will be allotted to Divisions as circumstances demand. Should the Infantry attack checked at any period prior to 1.20 a special bombardment may be demanded of, and ordered by, the Corps. The hour at which this special bombardment will commence will be notified. It will last for thirty minutes from first to last gun, the last five minutes of this period being marked by a rapid rate of fire. Expiration of this period of intense bombardment will be the signal for the Infantry to assault.

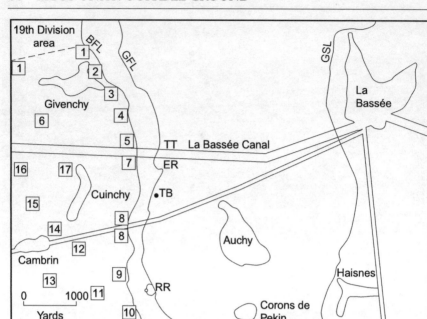

BFL   British Front Line

GFL   German Front Line

GSL   German Second Line

TB   The Brickstacks

TT   The Tortoise

ER   Embankment Redoubt

RR   Railway Redoubt

1   7th King's

2   2nd Ox & Bucks LI

3   1st Queen's

4   2nd Highland LI

5   9th Highland LI

6   2nd Worcestershire

7   2nd South Staffs

8   1st King's

9   2nd Argyll & Sutherland Highlanders

10   1st Middlesex

11   2nd Royal Welch Fusiliers

12   1st Scottish Rifles

13   5th Scottish Rifles

14   1st Hertfordshires

15   1st KRRC

16   5th King's

17   1st Royal Berkshires

Map 3: 2nd Division area of attack, 25th September 1915

8   The reserve Brigades of 7th and 9th Divisions will be assembled as far forward as possible in trenches of the Grenay line with a view to pushing forward the advance rapidly and avoiding delay.

9   No 7 Mountain Battery (less one section) is placed at disposal of 9th Division to support its advance. No 1 Motor Machine Gun battery is placed at the disposal of 2nd Division.

The 31st Army Troops Company RE and 1/1st Hants Fortress Company RE(T) will assemble at Sailly Labourse under the orders of CE I Corps. The 170th, 173rd and 176th Tunnelling Companies RE will retain such men in the different mining fronts as are considered necessary by 2nd Division, and the remainder will be assembled under orders of the 2nd Division. In the event of a general advance they will come under the orders of CE I Corps.

10   Advanced Corps Headquarters will be established at Prieure St. Pry at 6.00 p.m. on 24th September.

A.S. Cobbe, Br.-General,General Staff, I Corps.

This then was the operational order sent down from I Corps to the divisions, who in turn, sorted out their tasks and flowed them down to the brigades and battalions making up the division. As stated before, there were three divisions (2nd, 7th and 9th) in I Corps and they were positioned on the left of the attack astride the La Bassée Canal. The 2nd Division had been in France since August 1914 and had taken part in nearly every battle fought by the BEF so far. The main task of the 2nd Division at Loos was to form the flank guard to cover the major assault by the four central divisions. They had been allocated a section of front about 2 miles long, with two of their three brigades sited south of the La Bassée Canal. The 5th Brigade on the north side of the Canal were to advance towards Canteleux and Chapelle St Roch maintaining contact with other troops from the 2nd Division on their right as they advanced and the Indian Corps on their left.

In this area the front lines were less than 100 yards apart, and No Man's Land was pockmarked with many craters from previous mine detonations and general artillery fire. Two of the largest mine craters were known as Etna and Vesuvius, and each had lips about six feet high, preventing decent observation of each sides lines. To assist the 2nd Division three mines had been placed under the German lines and these were to be blown on 25th September.

In spite of the use of gas and mines, the Germans were in a strong position here, there were six defending battalions and a very strong point known as 'The Brickstacks'. This was a part of the La Bassée brickworks which had been turned into a viper's nest of concrete machine gun positions with shell-proof dugouts below them. There was also a strong second line defensive position about 100 yards behind the front line. The attack by the 2nd Division was due to go in after the gas and smoke cloud had done its work, coupled with the blowing of the three mines. The problems here started right at the outset in that the wind in the area was negligible. Here is a comment from a Special Company member:

> The wind was now practically nil and it was drizzling, so on receipt of Zero Hour only one hour before it was due I rang up 5th Brigade HQ and asked them if this meant I was to carry on. They said "Yes, why?" I explained that I had reported unfavourably on the wind all night and would not hold myself responsible for the effect of gas on our own men. An agitated voice said he would report to Corps, and I received the order to carry on.

A more senior officer in this sector also tried to stop the gas being discharged and the conversation is alleged to have gone all the way up to the Divisional GOC Horne. It went along the lines of: "The wind is unfavourable and I don't think I should release." Horne confirmed to the officer: "The order is to turn on the gas." The Gas Officer was reported as refusing to open the cylinders, upon which the reply from Horne was "Then shoot the bastard."

The 5th Brigade was to attack north of the Canal and at two places about half a mile apart. One attack was near to the Canal and the other near Givenchy. At the Canal attack the 9th Highland Light Infantry (Glasgow Highlanders) were to capture Tortoise Redoubt which dominated the ground on both sides of the Canal.

Looking towards the Brickstacks. The open nature of the ground is all too apparent from this view. (IWM Q 37769)

No Man's Land north of the La Bassée Canal. To the left, near the bank, was the Tortoise Redoubt. (IWM Q 41780)

Aerial view of the La Bassée Canal and the Brickstacks.
(IWM Q55714)

There was also another position called Embankment Redoubt which dominated the southern approaches. The elimination of both these redoubts was deemed as essential to allow the other two brigades (19th and 6th) to advance south of the Canal. The attack of the Glasgow Highlanders was to go in exactly at 6.30am, but due to an unexpected own-goal as previously stated the two leading platoons were unable to carry it out. The two follow-up platoons took their places and left the British front line at 6.40am, ten minutes late. They were at once came under heavy small arms fire from Tortoise Redoubt and suffered heavy casualties. Those survivors remained for the time being in No Man's Land and awaited further orders. Although the reserve battalions were sent forward, for once good sense prevailed and they were not thrown into the attack. The Glasgow Highlanders eventually returned to the safety of their own lines; they had suffered 119 casualties and the attack here was a total failure.

Slightly further north, the other attack by the 5th Brigade was meant to be a diversion to help the attacks south of the Canal. It was therefore due to go in at 6.00am and to be carried out by three battalions - 2nd Highland Light Infantry,

2nd Ox and Bucks Light Infantry and 1st Queens. Although a diversion, it still had tactical objectives, in that the troops were meant to capture a line between the villages of Canteleux and Chapelle St Roch, about 800 yards beyond the British lines. Gas and smoke was used here as well, but was only planned to be released for ten minutes. The gas and smoke did not have a great effect as the wind was not favourable and it hung around the British lines, but to assist a mine was exploded at 5.58am. Two minutes after this, at 6.00am, the three battalions advanced across No Man's Land. The assault came as a complete surprise and the leading men were able to reach the German barbed wire without too many casualties. The wire had been well cut and they entered the German front line to find it virtually deserted. Most of the defenders had gone back to their second line trench. They pressed on towards this trench and soon came under withering small arms fire. The advance was halted after less than 150 yards, the British literally pinned down unable to advance or retreat. Then the Germans launched their usual counter-attack and making much use of their superior hand grenades, bombed and gunned the British back to their original front line.

This disaster was summed up in the 2nd Highland LI War Diary:

> When about three quarters of the way across heavy machine gun fire was turned on them from their right. I think the Germans with machine guns and bombers were in deep dugouts somewhere along the communication trenches and came out when our leading lines were almost past them. The two leading lines closely supported by another company of the 1st Queen's meanwhile had almost reached the German second line and were in a similar manner intercepted by cross machine gun fire and forced back.

By 9.40am it was all over and it was decided not to throw the two reserve bat-

Table 3.1
5th Brigade casualties, 25th September

	Officers	Other Ranks	Total
2nd Highland LI	8	350	358
1st Queens	9	308	317
2nd Oxs & Bucks	8	270	278
9th HLI	1	118	119
7th Kings	0	17	17
2nd Worcs	1	6	7
Totals	27	1069	1096

talions into this mess. It should be said here that the 5th Brigade had six battalions under command rather than the normal four. The casualties of these six battalions for 25th September were as follows:
These figures include killed, wounded, missing and gassed

Further south, indeed just south of the La Bassée Canal on a front of about 800 yards, was the 6th Brigade. This Brigade also had six infantry battalions, four Regular and two Territorial Force. This attack was also fraught with problems.

The 2nd Division area. The canal area of Cuinchy looking towards La Bassée.
(IWM Q 41790)

2nd Division frontage south of the La Bassée Canal, with Auchy les Mines in the
distance. (IWM Q 37763)

The Brickstacks in September 1915 - the whole area was a mass of German strongpoints.
(IWM Q 41775)

About 15 minutes before the gas was due to be released the officer from the Special Company was so dubious about the direction and strength of the wind that he declined responsibility for turning on the taps. Others reported this to 2nd Division HQ as previously stated but the order came back that the gas must be discharged whatever the conditions were, but with the proviso that it could be turned off if it proved unsatisfactory. However it was about 6.00am before these instructions got through. The gas was therefore turned on and virtually failed to go anywhere except the British trenches. The battalion most severely affected was the 2nd South Staffords. Virtually the entire unit was affected, some obviously worse than others and the War Diary records that over 130 men were unable to take any part in the attack. In spite of this setback the attack was still pressed home. A and B companies were to attack the Brickstacks while C Company was left with Embankment Redoubt. A and B companies made little progress, as their War Diary related:

> As the signal for the assault was given, our men rushed gallantly forward, only to be met by cross fire from concealed machine guns and heavy rifle fire from the German front line trench, the enemy evidently being quite unaffected by the gas. A and B companies were held up on the craters nearest to their parapet and were unable to advance.

C Company's line of advance was along the Canal towpath and soon after 6.30am came under severe small arms fire from both sides of the Canal. The OC of the Company, Captain A. Kilby, led the attack with great gallantry, being wounded at least twice and having a foot blown off. Despite his wounds he continued to urge his men on but alas no one got into any of the German positions. At 8.00am orders were received to withdraw prior to an artillery bombardment on the

German front line. When it did come, this barrage had no effect and fortunately no follow up attack was ordered. After dark on 25th September volunteers looked for wounded in No Man's Land, but Kilby could not be found. He was later posted missing and recommended for a Victoria Cross, which was subsequently approved. He was originally commemorated on the Loos Memorial to the Missing but his body was found in 1929 and he now lies at Arras Road CWGC Cemetery, Roclincourt. The South Staffs lost 11 Officers and 280 Other Ranks this day. Another unit from the Brigade, the 1st Kings further south, had better fortune but still no success, attacking a German position known as Cabbage Patch Redoubt. For unknown reasons on their front the gas and smoke actually reached the German lines and caused local confusion. Two companies reached the German wire virtually unscathed, but to their horror found it virtually uncut. The Germans regrouped and started to cause casualties amongst the Kingsmen. One of the officers, Captain J. Ryan, made his way back across No Man's Land to report to his CO that there were at least two belts of uncut German wire which were stopping progress and it would be pointless sending the next two companies across. The advice was taken but Ryan returned to his men and was later killed. He is now buried at Cambrin CWGC Cemetery, which contains 57 officers and men from the 1st Kings who died on 25th September. Ryan had previously been awarded a Military Cross. The attackers here fell back as best they could but nevertheless, the Kings suffered 5 Officer and 222 Other Rank casualties this day.

This only leaves the final brigade attack from the 2nd Division - that of the 19th. The attacking troops were to be supported by the firing of two mines under the German front line dug by 173rd Tunnelling Company RE. For unknown reasons they were ordered by Division to be blown 10 minutes before Zero Hour. The War Diary of the 2nd Argylls detailed some of the preparations for the 19th Brigade attack:

> During the night the wire in front of our jumping off trenches was removed and trenches were bridged about 30 to 40 yards in rear of the fire trench. Forty short scaling ladders were in position in each trench. Two companies had two platoons formed up in these jumping off trenches, one standing at the ladders the other platoon standing beside the ladders, the other two platoons of these companies were formed up in the support trenches known as High Street. It was hoped that four waves of troops would emerge almost simultaneously, taking the Germans by surprise.

However the blowing of the mines gave the defenders both warning of the attack and time to prepare themselves for it. The gas had been discharged at the correct time, but due to an adverse wind direction the cloud was blown back into the faces of the attackers and then behind them. So when 6.30am was reached, not only had many of the attackers been affected by the chlorine gas but there was no smoke screen to cover the advance across No Man's Land. In spite of this the 1st Middlesex and 2nd Argyll and Sutherland Highlanders left the trenches. They were further hampered by their need to bunch to get through narrow gaps between the mine craters. The attackers managed to reach the German lines but again found the barbed wire uncut and both units halted in front of it. Further troops from both battalions were sent forward, including the machine gun platoons, but it had no effect apart from causing more casualties. Two companies of the 2nd Royal

Welch Fusiliers were also sent across No Man's Land. After consulting other senior officers At 9.00am the Brigade Commander - Brigadier P Robertson - ordered a halt to any further attacks, and asked those troops in No Man's Land and to get

Table 3.2
19th Brigade casualties, 25th September

	Officers	*Other Ranks*	*Total*
1st Middlesex	16	439	455
2nd Argyll & Sutherland	15	315	330
2nd R Welch Fusiliers	7	113	120
Totals	38	867	905

back as best they could. The men of the Middlesex Regiment had to wait until dark before coming back, the ground being flat and open with no cover. The casualty total for this three battalion attack was as follows:

Here is the post-action report by the CO 1st Middlesex Lt Colonel F. Rowley about the 25th September:

> The advance was slow on account of the gas which hung about, and at the same time fires were observed in front of the German trenches. A hot rifle and machine gun fire was opened onto the advancing lines from the front and flank particularly from Ryan's Keep and the line was brought to a standstill about 100 yards from our own trenches. Nearly all the officers being killed or wounded, and the casualties among the other ranks were very heavy. I at once ordered the three reserve Platoons to advance and assist the line forward, but owing to the heavy hostile fire, the line was brought to a standstill.

This is what the War Diary of the 2nd Argyll and Sutherland Highlanders records for the early part of the 25th September:

> At 5.45am the artillery opened fire and at 5.50 the gas was turned on for 40 minutes, the last five minutes combined with smoke. At 6.30am the assault started, the morning being very still, the gas hung about and was inclined to come back which hampered the leading platoons.

Not a very good morning for the men of the 2nd Division, but it could have been a lot worse. Around 9.00am ,when Major-General Horne, the GOC, heard of the failures he ordered a 30 minute barrage on his Division's front south of the Canal. The intention was for the reserve battalions to deliver a fresh assault, but at 9.10am a message was received from Brigadier Daly from the 6th Brigade. This starkly related: "The gas was a complete failure against the enemy, our men suffered very heavy casualties and are not in a position to attack again." Twenty minutes later at the end of the barrage, the COs of the reserve battalions let it be known that the artillery fire had had very little effect and most of the German strong points were untouched. They said to their brigadiers that they felt any attack would have little chance of success and could turn out to be a mass slaughter. The two brigadiers, Robertson and Daly, agreed with this and told Divisional HQ so. Around 9.45am it was agreed that there would be no attack by either the 6th or 19th

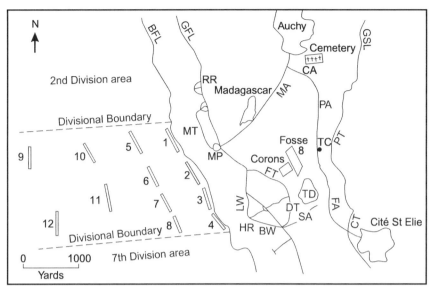

BFL	British Front Line	SA	Slag Alley
GFL	German Front Line	FA	Fosse Alley
GSL	German Second Line	CT	Cité Trench
RR	Railway Redoubt	TD	The Dump
MT	Madagascar Trench	1	10th Highland LI
MP	Mad Point	2	6th KOSB
MA	Mad Alley	3	5th Cameron Highlanders
CA	Cemetery Alley	4	7th Seaforth Highlanders
PA	Pekin Alley	5	9th Scottish Rifles
PT	Pekin Trench	6	11th Highland LI
TC	Three Cabarets	7	8th Black Watch
FT	Fosse Trench	8	8th Gordon Highlanders
DT	Dump Trench	9	6th Royal Scots Fusiliers
BW	Big Willie	10	11th Royal Scots
LW	Little Willie	11	12th Royal Scots
HR	Hohenzollern Redoubt	12	10th Argyll & Sutherland Highlanders

Map 4: 9th Division area of attack, 25th September 1915

Brigade until further orders. The 2nd Division official history states the total casualties for this day as 2,538, but the whole attack by them had failed and would have had knock-on effects in other sectors.

The next division in the line of attack heading southwards was the 9th Division commanded by Major-General G. Thesiger. This Division was the first New Army Division to reach France at the beginning of May 1915. It was entirely Scottish in flavour and had spent some time holding the line, but Loos was to be the first time they would be used in an attacking role. They were allocated an attacking front of about a mile, between the 2nd and 7th divisions. They were given several very difficult tasks and these including taking the mine buildings and Dump of Fosse No 8 and the Hohenzollern Redoubt. The Dump was a huge flat-topped slag heap, which although only 20 feet high offered commanding views of the

Aerial shot looking towards Haisnes, also showing the Hohenzollern Redoubt and the Dump. (IWM HU 73604)

surrounding area. It was being used as one of the main German observation posts and it was felt that it could fulfil the same job for the British in their planned advance. It had been turned into a warren of tunnels and strong points for both artillery observers and machine gunners. To protect this vital position the Germans had turned a small rise about 400 yards in front of the Dump into a feared redoubt known as the Hohenzollern Redoubt. The two trenches either side of the Dump were known as Dump and Fosse Trenches and these were connected to the Hohenzollern Redoubt by two communication trenches known as Big Willie and Little Willie. The Germans manning these defences came from the 11th Reserve Regiment. It was considered by many that the Hohenzollern Redoubt was the most strongly fortified position on the entire attacking front of the six division line.

At a conference in mid-August 1915 the then GOC of the 9th Division - Major-General H Landon - decided a plan of attack in conjunction with his brigade commanders. The agreed plan was an almost standard one with two brigades up and one in reserve. The 28th Brigade was to be positioned on the left with the 26th on the right, the 27th Brigade being in reserve. Following on the standard plan each attacking brigade was to have two battalions in the front line with two in reserve. These two brigades were firstly to capture the German front and support lines between the Vermelles-La Bassée railway (the junction with the 2nd Division) and southwards for about 1,500 yards to their junction with the 7th Division. To achieve this would mean taking the fearsome defences of the Hohenzollern Redoubt, the Dump and Fosse 8. Following this they were to press on to the Lens-La Bassée road. Pausing briefly to reorganise with reserve battalions and brigades pushing through as necessary, with the left flank centred around the village of Haisnes and the right on Cité St

Elie, they were to advance towards Douvrin and then to the banks of the Haute Deule Canal. These final operations were to be carried out in conjunction with the 7th Division. The senior officers were also told that once here the reserves from XI Corps would definitely take up the advance. Just to complicate things even further, an alternative plan was mentioned, in that if the 2nd Division failed to make a breakthrough, the 9th would then act as the flank division. They would have the role of taking and securing the German front line and occupying the northern end of Fosse 8. They were also to capture the communication trench known as Pekin Alley heading towards Haisnes, while the 7th Division attacked. As it turned out this plan was not used. A final point to note here, is that, there was a late change of command in September, on the 9th of that month when Major-General G. Thesiger took over from Landon, whose health had broken down.

In detail therefore, the tasks of the 28th Brigade were, firstly, that they had to secure the railway line from the Corons de Marons to the junction of Les Briques and Train Alley, their second objective being to take Pekin Trench. The 26th Brigade was first to take the Hohenzollern Redoubt, Fosse Trench and Dump Trench. Secondly, to take a line from the east side of Fosse 8 through Three Cabarets to the Corons de Pekin. Should this be achieved, the Brigade was to push on to Pekin Trench. If at this stage the line had been joined up with the 28th Brigade and 2nd Division, the two brigades were to advance eastwards on Douvrin. The reserve brigade - the 27th - was left about 3,000 yards behind the British front line. As is usual with a reserve, its role was unclear - it would be used initially to support the attack on Fosse 8 or to advance on Haisnes and Douvrin.

I feel it is worth commenting that the tasks given to the 9th Division were not easy ones, especially as it was their first time in battle. Perhaps the High Command had the impression that it was better to give this tough nut to an untried Division on the basis it would not show the caution usually displayed by more experienced troops. An added complication was the need to swing the axis of advance from one that was basically north-easterly to an easterly one and to converge on a narrower front. However, the difficulties of such a manoeuvre were diminished to some extent by the open plains and conspicuous landmarks, such as the villages of Haisnes, Cité St Elie and Douvrin.

The preparations for the assault in this sector certainly seemed to work better than in other areas. When the 9th took over the line at the beginning of September, the lines were deemed to be too far from the German lines to be suitable as the forward assembly trenches. The previous occupants, the 1st Division, had already dug a number of blind saps into No Man's Land. In one night's work these were opened up to form a new trench line, each battalion digging about 350 yards of trench. This brought some trenches to within 150 yards of the Hohenzollern Redoubt. In addition, a support line was dug in the rear, with numerous communication trenches running back to the old front line. This meant that it was now possible to accommodate the whole Division in the trench system. It was calculated that the Jocks dug over 12,000 yards of new trenches before the battle. It is also probable that the preliminary bombardment and ruses were effective here. The first feint was on 21st September at noon, when men from the 26th Brigade behaved as if an attack was imminent, in an attempt to get the Germans to man their positions on the Hohenzollern Redoubt. This appeared to have the desired effect and led to an intense barrage of shrapnel on the Redoubt. A similar effort was made on the 24th by the 28th Brigade opposite Madagascar Trench.

It will be best to look at the actions of the two brigades for the early part of the attack in isolation before bringing the story together. Firstly, in the northern sector was the 28th Brigade. This was composed of four battalions; the two attacking battalions being the 6th King's Own Scottish Borderers (KOSB) and the 10th Highland Light Infantry (HLI), supported respectively by the 11th HLI and the 9th Scottish Rifles. In support were 63rd Field Company RE and D Company from the 9th Seaforth Highlanders - the Divisional Pioneers. These troops were attached for the consolidation of captured positions and digging of new communication trenches. But the 28th Brigade did not get off to a good start. Again in this area the wind speed and direction was not favourable, indeed it was moving more from the south-east. This meant that the gas and smoke were in fact carried back into the faces of the troops waiting in the front line trenches. It again had negative effects on the attacking troops but by 6.30am most of it had drifted behind the British trenches. This meant the Germans were hardly affected by the gas, and the smoke gave no cover whatsoever. Additionally, some lucky German artillery shells hit gas cylinders with fatal results to those nearby. There were three impressive German strongpoints that would need to be neutralised. On the left, commanding the open ground on either side of the railway, was Railway Redoubt. In the middle was Mad Point, which blocked the Vermelles-Auchy road, near the small village of Madagascar. On the right was Strong Point, which was a sap projecting forward from the trench known as Little Willie. Two of these suffered very little in the bombardment, but it was reported that Mad Point had been damaged badly but was still occupied. All in all these three strong points were still able to bring fire upon most of the attacking frontage of the 28th Brigade.

Still, again at the appointed hour the Jocks left their trenches, the 6th KOSB being led by their second-in-command as the CO had already been wounded moving up to the front. The 6th KOSB attacked either side of the Vermelles-Auchy road, and were able to reach the German wire with very few casualties. However the wire was uncut. There was a ditch in front of the wire about eight feet across, filled with stakes and barbed wire which had been covered with turf to act as a booby-trap. Some of the attackers fell into this ditch but many managed to reach the German wire and tried to make passages through it. Most of the Battalion was now densely huddled close to the wire when the Germans woke up and machine guns from Strong Point opened fire on the 6th KOSB. It was a slaughter; fortunately, the last wave of attackers had only just left the British trenches and was able to get back to relative safety. Only a few of the stranded KOSB's were able to drift back. The casualties included Major Horsley (the acting CO), who had been wounded on leaving the British front line but insisted on going forward. In fact, of the 19 officers who went into action, 12 were killed and 7 wounded. The Other Rank casualties amounted to 630.

On the left of the KOSB's were the leading three companies of the 10th HLI, and they fared little better. The wind was too weak to carry the gas forward from the front line trenches, many men suffering from the effects of the chlorine. When the leading waves left the trenches they were subjected to heavy machine gun fire from Railway Redoubt. The first line was virtually annihilated before it had gone twenty yards. The second and third lines also suffered heavily on leaving the support trenches. The reserve vompany was thrown in about 15 minutes later but suffered the same and had to return to the original British front line.

The War Diary of the 10th HLI reported the sorry tale:

> The attack was launched; all the lines rose out of the trenches simultaneously, and advanced under a very heavy machine gun, rifle and shell fire. The first line were practically wiped out before they had gone 20 yards, the second and third lines lost very heavily before they reached our own first line. By the time all the first three companies were over we had lost 70% of the men who went over and about 85% of the officers. C Company advanced about 15 minutes afterwards and also lost very heavily.

At a roll call later that morning the casualties were found to be 15 Officers and 631 Other Ranks. Worse still, a shell had killed most of the signalling staff at Battalion HQ, so no definite news reached the Brigade commander.

At Brigade HQ, it must have been a very difficult time, with very few hard facts coming back from the front line. It is believed only one message was received by Brigadier S. Scrase-Dickens, received from the 9th Scottish Rifles at 8.15 am. This enigmatically said that the 10th HLI were asking for reinforcements. As it was known at 7.50am from Divisional HQ that the 2nd Division attack had failed, it probably sowed more seeds of doubt in his mind. In spite of this Scrase-Dickens ordered his two remaining battalions forward. The 11th HLI was ordered to advance at 9.30am and to send two companies to support the 6th KOSB. This they did and came under heavy fire from Strong and Mad Points. Again heavy casualties resulted and the situation remained unchanged. The 9th Scottish Rifles were ordered to send two companies to Madagascar to support the 10th HLI and form a defensive flank. When they did get to the front line trenches, it was obvious there were only dead and wounded in front of them and the order was sensibly cancelled, although only for the time being.

Around 11.15am the Corps Commander General Gough ordered the 28th Brigade to make another attack on Madagascar Trench in an hour's time, at 12.15 p.m.. It would be supported, they were told, by a barrage on the German defences between Auchy and Fosse 8 by as many guns from the 2nd and 9th divisions as possible. However the barrage, when it did come, had very little effect and was quite inadequate for the task in hand. At the last minute the CO of the 11th HLI suggested an alternative attack from the south, but it was not considered feasible and in keeping with orders from other commanders: "The attack will go in as planned." There were the usual predictable results and a high number of casualties (over 66%), but on the extreme right flank a small success. With great gallantry about 100 men reached the centre of Little Willie and established themselves there. At 1.30 p.m. Scrase-Dickens reported back to Divisional HQ that the second assault had failed with heavy losses and his Brigade was unfit for further offensive action. The rest of the afternoon was spent organising the shattered remains of these four battalions into positions to defend the original front line. Additionally a communication trench known as New Trench was dug forward to connect with the centre of Little Willie held by the 11th HLI. It will now be best to leave the 28th Brigade and look at the actions of the 26th Brigade and their experiences against the Hohenzollern Redoubt and Fosse 8.

This Brigade, under the command of Brigadier A. Ritchie, had been given arguably the most difficult task on the entire Loos Battlefield. The plan was for them to overrun in one rush the Hohenzollern Redoubt and Fosse 8 with the two leading attacking battalions. If they were able to reach the eastern side of a prominent landmark known as The Dump without reinforcements, they were to stop here and reorganise. The two reserve battalions would then pass through south of Fosse 8 and to advance to Haisnes. After the organisation these two battalions would follow in support, leaving the Fosse to be consolidated by the 28th Brigade. Again this seems a very tall order for virtually untested troops but the Highlanders rose to the occasion magnificently. But they were aided by some excellent support.

Firstly, two heavy guns - 9.2 inch howitzers - had been brought forward and hidden in a wood near Beuvry. Although hampered by shortages of ammunition these two guns had used most effectively what was available. Many defensive positions in the Hohenzollern Redoubt were destroyed by fire from them. A successful sapping operation was carried out so that the attackers had less than 150 yards to the face of the Redoubt. Finally, the gas cloud worked. Stationed here in support of the 26th Brigade was a young officer by the name of Richard Gale. He related:

At 5.30 we again stood by for 5.50, by now it was lighter and the breeze a little more marked. One minute more, the intensity of our artillery rising in a roaring crescendo every moment, what an intensity of time that last minute seemed, at last Zero Hour arrived, the gas was turned on, and to the accompaniment of an inferno

Ninth Avenue Cemetery. This is an original 1915 cemetery, which contains many Cameron Highlanders. They were buried in a mass grave alongside a trench known as Ninth Avenue, which had been dug across No Man's Land to connect the original front lines after the initial attack. (Geoff Parker)

of fire from all caliber's, the greenish wall of gas grew slowly from our own parapets, rolling across No Man's Land to the Redoubt. In addition, smoke candles were used to render the gas cloud more opaque and form a screen of invisibility for our Infantry. While the gas attack was in progress, the Camerons prepared for their share of the proceedings with the greatest unconcern, and gave us their caps and scraps of tartan for souvenirs. Tea has just been handed round, with a stiff dose of rum added to it. Meanwhile the time passes and the gas will soon be turned off - 6.28. The gas and smoke cloud rolls on, now a great wall of greenish yellow fog. Then silence. A shouted order and the Jocks are up and over the top.

The left hand battalion of the Brigade was the 5th Cameron Highlanders, with the 7th Seaforth Highlanders on their right. These were supported respectively by the 8th Black Watch and 8th Gordons; also present were 90th Field Company RE and B Company of the 9th Seaforths acting as a working party to strengthen defences. At 6.29am the assaulting battalions left the trenches and formed up in front of the British wire, hidden by the smoke screen. This had the effect of steadying the lines and allowed the advance to be made at the outset without confusion or disorder.

Between Fosse 8 and the Hohenzollern Redoubt was a small ridge. The attackers used this as a landmark, with the Camerons advancing to the north of it and the Seaforths to the south. In spite of these advantages confusion reigned for a few minutes, the Seaforths going in a bit before the Camerons, who were slightly delayed by the gas cloud. The Seaforths dashed straight for the Hohenzollern Redoubt, suffering considerable casualties from small arms fire from the right flank. In spite of this, after a brisk fight, they captured the southern part of the Redoubt. Then they bombed and bayoneted their way up the communication trenches to the main German line, and without waiting for the Camerons, pushed on past Fosse 8, clearing the miners' cottages and seizing the position known as Three Cabarets. At this point, they had a quick reorganisation and took up defensive positions in the Corons Trench, immediately east of Fosse 8; the time was still only about 7.30 am. All in all, a very fine achievement for a novice Battalion. Unfortunately, their success was not repeated by the Camerons, as we shall now see.

The Camerons decided to wait for a few minutes at 6.50am to see if the wind might carry the gas and smoke cloud towards their objective - Little Willie. Alas it did not, and their attack went in through the smoke screen. As the waves appeared out of the smoke they were hit by heavy fire from their left front at Mad Point. Many casualties were caused but in spite of this they successfully entered Little Willie Trench as the wire had been well cut by the artillery bombardment.

Again the unit's War Diary relates the start of a disaster:

It was found that the whole line of advance was enfiladed by heavy machine gun and rifle fire from Mad Point and Madagascar. This fire had caused us very heavy losses, practically having wiped out the first two lines. With HQ the remains of D and the other lines pushed forward and reached the south west corner of the Corons.

Now the 5th Camerons were located in Little Willie they came under enfilade fire from the defensive positions at Madagascar. However the fire soon slackened as the German defenders shifted their fire to the men from the 28th Brigade who were directly attacking the small village. This gave the Camerons the chance to enter Fosse Trench relatively unscathed, which they had done by about 7.10 am. Just beyond this trench were some miners' cottages. These had been cleared by the left flank of the Seaforths, and at about 7.45am both battalions joined up between Three Cabarets and the Corons de Pekin, north of the Dump. Both battalions briefly paused here. A more graphic description can be found in the 7th Seaforths War Diary:

> At 6.29am the troops got out of the trench and formed up behind the smoke barrier. They advanced at 6.30am at a steady walk and, after having got a little distance, machine gun and rifle fire was spewed on us. This was not very accurate as the smoke, behind which we advanced, rendered it difficult for the Germans to see us clearly. A few men went down under this fire, which seemed to come from the machine guns to our right. The Germans were holding the Redoubt and we lost a good many officers in the Redoubt's first trench.

For the advance towards Dump Trench and Fosse 8:

> We continued to advance and bombed up the communication trenches from Hohenzollern to the main German trench. On our left we made good the miners' cottages, but the Camerons, whose business it was to keep touch with us, for some reason lost touch and we had to make good all these cottages, the orders which we had previously received being to press on and not to wait.

Soon afterwards the 8th Black Watch arrived and reinforced the Cameron Highlanders, with the orders that the Seaforths and Camerons were to hold fast and convert Corons Trench into a fire trench to cover Fosse 8. The Camerons had achieved their objective but at a horrific cost; around 800 officers and men left the trenches, but only 2 officers and 70 men were left standing.

It now became clear that the 2nd Division further north had failed to capture Auchy and their follow-on objectives, so the alternative plan for the 9th Division was now the only option. They were to form a defensive flank facing north-east between Fosse 8 and the village of Haisnes. It was also clear that the 28th Brigade on the left of the 26th Brigade had failed to capture Madagascar Trench. For these reasons it was impossible to advance towards Haisnes so they started preparing defensive positions. Meanwhile a word or two about the two reserve battalions of the 26th Brigade is necessary.

The 8th Black Watch and the 8th Gordon Highlanders left their reserve trenches at 6.30am and by 7.00am were in the old No Man's Land. They did however suffer casualties due to a German barrage on the British front line and small arms fire from the flanks. The CO of the Black Watch, Lieutenant-Colonel Lord Sempill, amongst many others, was seriously wounded. On reaching the Hohenzollern Redoubt the Gordons took a number of Germans prisoner who had hidden when the Seaforths advanced. The Black Watch also fought a small action at Dump Trench, again with hidden Germans. The Gordons bombed their way down to a feature known as the Window in the German main line to try and clear the way for the 7th Division attacking on their right. Instead of changing direction to the south-east, after passing through the main German trenches most of the Black Watch pushed on through the Corons and ended up between the Seaforths and Camerons beyond the miners' cottages. The rest of the Battalion - about a company strong - went with the Gordons down Fosse Trench and then moved off in an easterly direction towards Cité St Elie and Haisnes. They pushed on through Fosse Alley and headed towards Pekin Trench soon after 8.00am but due to a large number of casualties felt they did not have the numbers to go on. Here they halted and started to put the newly gained trenches into a state ready for defence. By around 10.30am it was estimated the defenders - numbering about 400 Seaforths, 100 Camerons and 250 Black Watch - had turned the areas around Fosse 8, the Dump and the Corons de Pekin into a reasonable position for defence. Meanwhile it was decided to continue the advance, with a limited number of men coming from the 8th Gordons and a company of the Black Watch. Moving forward they headed towards Pekin Trench, a position that had virtually been untouched by the bombardment and thankfully not manned by the Germans. In fact it was only partially dug, but did have a thick belt of barbed wire in front of it. The distance they had to cover to reach Pekin Trench was about 1,000 yards and it was completely open ground. By sheer good luck annihilation was avoided and they reached the barbed wire virtually unscathed. Their biggest difficulty was cutting the barbed wire. But they managed to cut their way through and get into Pekin Trench - the last German line of defence, on a front between the Loos-Haisnes road and the Auchy-Haisnes road. There appeared to be no Germans in the immediate area and Haisnes village was there for the taking. However the local commander Lieutenant-Colonel H .Wright decided to await the arrival of the 5th Camerons and the 7th Seaforths which he believed were following close behind in support. With the benefit of hindsight we know they were not coming but Wright did not know this.

I will leave the men of the Gordons at this point and go up the chain of command and look at the role of the Reserve Brigade commander, Brigadier C. Bruce. It was this Brigade that the GOC of the 9th Division had up his sleeve to try and exploit the advantages gained by the 8th Gordon Highlanders. His four battalions very handily placed, in that they had been in reserve trenches during the night of 24th/25th September and had moved into the 'empty' British front line at 7.30am. But Bruce had been given two sets of orders. On one hand, if the attack of the two leading battalions of the 26th Brigade on Fosse 8 was unsuccessful, he was to reinforce that attack. On the other hand, if that attack went well, he was to support the other half of the 26th Brigade in its advance on Haisnes. The situation however seemed to have resolved itself as at about 8.00am news came back that Fosse 8 had been taken by the Camerons and Seaforths. This meant that the Brigade should now head towards Haisnes. However it appears that there was a misunderstanding as to the time they should actually move. The GOC Thesiger thought they would wait till he gave the word, while Bruce was intending to move immediately he heard of the fate of the attack on Fosse 8. Upon hearing of the success there, he ordered three of his battalions - the 11th and 12th Royal Scots and 10th Argyll and Sutherland Highlanders - in the general direction of the church tower at Douvrin village, which could be seen against the horizon. The village of Douvrin was to the east of Haisnes, so proved to be a useful aid to navigation. Bruce kept the 6th Royal Scots Fusiliers behind as his reserve.

Meanwhile the fog of war was now to come into play. Unaware of these moves by the 27th Brigade, at 9.30am Thesiger ordered Bruce to send forward two of his battalions to support the 8th Gordons in their attack on Haisnes. About ten minutes later the Corps Commander Gough told Thesiger that the division on their right -

the 7th - had captured some strategically important villages and ordered him to use the whole of his Brigade to take Haisnes. However, around 20 minutes later, at 10.00 am, reports seemed to indicate there was a gap of around half a mile between the men of the 26th Brigade at Corons de Pekin and the troops of the right flank of the 28th Brigade at Strong Point, in front of Little Willie. There was the obvious need to plug this gap and of retaining a reserve to ensure that Fosse 8 could be held against the almost inevitable counter-attack. General Thesiger sent a message by telephone to Bruce telling him to carry on with the attack on Haisnes, but with only three battalions and to leave one in the area around Little Willie. He also promised that he would arrange for all the artillery support he could muster for the attack on Haisnes. Perhaps it was too late to change plans but for whatever reasons the original orders stood and the three battalions were all independently moving south of the Dump towards Pekin Trench to support the 8th Gordons. Bruce was able to keep his reserve the 6th Royal Scots Fusiliers in the original British front line.

The first battalion from the Reserve Brigade - the 12th Royal Scots - left their trenches soon after 8.00 am, and advanced in extended line across the old No Man's Land in relatively good order and without suffering too many casualties. By about 8.45am two companies had taken up positions in Pekin Trench, with the other two companies behind the trench line. The left flank of the 12th Royal Scots was in contact with the Gordons in the trench opposite Haisnes, and their right flank was in position at the junction of Pekin Trench with Cité Trench. The second unit to leave, the 11th Royal Scots, was slightly delayed by traffic jams in the communication trenches and it was about 9.00am before they set off towards the German lines. After passing Fosse Alley the two leading companies unfortunately lost their bearings and wheeled too far left, so that they were heading towards the Haisnes-Auchy road. On reaching this they were fired on from Auchy Cemetery and took casualties. However this enabled them to realise their error and shifted direction to the right astride the road to Haisnes. After an advance of a few hundred yards they came up against a thick belt of barbed wire in front of Haisnes Trench. This trench was a continuation of Pekin Trench heading north to the west of the village of Haisnes. The Royal Scots tried to cut a path through this belt of barbed wire, but they came under fire from the village of Haisnes. It is believed that the Germans were from the Reserve Battalion of the 16th Regiment which had literally only just arrived in the village after being rushed up from their rear area position. It is believed only a few men managed to reach Haisnes Trench, the rest either becoming casualties or withdrawing back to Fosse 8. The other two companies of the 11th Royal Scots which had not made the navigation error headed towards the church tower at Douvrin and around noon reached the area of Cité Trench, going into the line south of the Gordons and Royal Scots. They managed to do this without suffering many casualties, but from this moment it appears that any opportunity of making further progress slipped away.

The third battalion in this brigade was the 10th Argyll and Sutherland Highlanders. They moved off about 30 minutes after the 11th Royal Scots. They skirted the southern end of the Hohenzollern Redoubt, crossed the captured trench Big Willie and also headed in the direction of Douvrin church tower. However after passing south of the Dump they came under a heavy barrage from German artillery. Some of these guns were positioned between Haisnes and Auchy, but it is believed that a field battery positioned less than a thousand yards away was firing over open sights. In spite of this heavy fire they continued with their advance and managed to reach Fosse Alley around noon. On hearing that there were already a large number of troops in Pekin Trench, the CO of the 10th Argylls, Lieutenant-Colonel A. MacKenzie, decided to temporarily halt in his current location until re-inforcements were called for. Around 1.30 p.m. they were asked to supply assistance to the troops in Pekin Trench, so a company was sent forward, but they received very heavy attention from German artillery and infantry as they tried to cross nearly 1,000 yards of open ground. The CO declined to send any more troops across, as it appeared to be totally useless.

Now even more problems of command and control were to come into play. It seemed to be clear that a promising situation (in front of Haisnes) was in fact becoming potentially a very dangerous one. The Germans reserves were arriving in the area and strengthening their defences, and although there were no signs of an imminent counter-attack it was to be assumed that one would soon come. It appeared to the High Command that the men from the 26th and 27th brigades in Pekin Trench were in danger of being cut off. To support them and also to ensure some sort of security for them, it was essential that the area around Fosse 8 be held. I Corps therefore sent some messages - firstly to 24th Division, that at 1.00 p.m. their 73rd Brigade was to advance immediately to Fosse 8. It is worth adding here that Haig had advised Gough in the morning of 25th September that the 24th Division had been passed from GHQ Reserve to I Corps. Also, some more guns were sent into the area. The 7th Mountain Battery RGA with four 2¾ inch guns were already in support just behind the original British trenches, south-west of the Hohenzollern Redoubt, and they were joined by B Battery from L Brigade RFA and A Battery from LII Brigade RFA. A little later that afternoon D Battery LIII (Howitzer) Brigade RFA also came up into the area. But it was clear that the German artillery had better observation and locations than the British.

The plight of the troops in Pekin Trench to the south-west of Haisnes was becoming more and more dangerous. To use a military term 'both flanks were up in the air' and German artillery fire began to fall on the position. Under cover of this the inevitable counter-attack followed. German infantry, using their superior hand grenades, began to bomb their way southwards along Pekin Trench from the direction of the Auchy-Haisnes road, while another group moved northwards from Cité Trench. The fighting went on for most of the afternoon and their toehold on around 1,500 yards of enemy trench gradually weakened.

Brigadier Bruce had by now gone forward to the area of the Dump and hearing of the situation in Pekin Trench had in the early afternoon called up his last remaining reserve - the 6th Royal Scots Fusiliers. They eventually reached Fosse Alley, where it was decided to send forward two companies to support the men in Pekin Trench. Despite these reinforcements there was no chance of maintaining the gains here and by about 5.00 p.m. less than 50% of the original trench remained in British hands. The senior officers in Pekin Trench decided the position was untenable and ordered a withdrawal, although the War Diary of the 6th Royal Scots Fusiliers put a slightly different spin on things:

> Darkness was setting in and the situation was critical. Our bombs, being soaked with rain, were useless, and the men's rifles were clogged with mud. The flanks,

particularly the left, became very unsteady, and it was necessary to rally the men three times and to reoccupy Pekin Trench, which the men had been leaving in large numbers.

It is believed that around 800 men struggled back under heavy German artillery fire. Remember that these men came from four battalions - 8th Gordons, 11th and 12th Royal Scots and 6th Royal Scots Fusiliers. The 10th Argylls were faced with this large group or groups of men coming towards them and recorded:

> A great mass of troops appeared on our front about 1,000 yards away. At first we thought they were the enemy, but they turned out to be our own troops retiring. The confusion was great and the mixture of units also. Every attempt was made by the officers of the battalion to rally the fugitives, unfortunately with but little success, and they passed right through us leaving the battalion with its

Table 3.3
9th Division casualties, 25th September

8th Black Watch	511
5th Cameron Highlanders	406
7th Seaforth Highlanders	378
11th Royal Scots	267
8th Gordon Highlanders	249
12th Royal Scots	197
Total	1708

flanks exposed.

Perhaps now is a good point to briefly break off from the account to list casualty figures for some of the battalions of the 9th Division for the 25th September:

As has happened on other occasions, the discipline of these men had almost broken down. The men from the 6th Royal Scots Fusiliers rejoined their comrades in Fosse Alley, but the others, despite some officers trying to stop them, went back to the original German front line trenches, Dump Trench and Big Willie. This meant that Fosse Alley now became the front line in this area. The Germans, for the moment at least, seemed satisfied with retaking Pekin Trench and made no attempt this day to attack Fosse Alley. I consider the untested men of the 9th Division had been given a very difficult job and had nearly achieved a major breakthrough. It would have been a tough nut to crack for a Regular Division and they had achieved virtually the only success of the day so far.

To review the situation therefore at nightfall, the 27th Brigade and part of the 26th Brigade held Fosse Alley from north of the Quarries to the junction of Fosse Alley with Slag Alley, west of the Dump. The majority of the 26th Brigade carried on from here north-westerly around the Corons de Pekin, with their left flank facing Madagascar. The 28th Brigade were back in their original trenches save for a small party from the 11th HLI that was established in Little Willie. The Divisional artillery support, which had only proved of limited use during the assault, was withdrawn to a firing position around Cambrin and west of the La Basseé-Vermelles railway. However a useful lesson was learnt in that the chief drawback

The 7th Division front, Cité St Elie on the left horizon. (IWM Q 37766)

for close artillery co-operation was the lack of information about the infantry's position. Whilst it was a lesson learnt, it was one that was to dog the British Army for most of the Great War, the days of walkie-talkies being a long way off. This account from an Officer back at I Corps HQ recounts some of the difficulties with communications:

> The actual front line was completely blurred. The middle distance between the front line and our slag heap was now in constant convulsion, rising in columns of black earth and smoke. The gas which we had released was drifting heavily down across the left of our front, obviously in the wrong direction. We peered and peered through our glasses, trying to catch sight of anything where the smoke had drifted away. Through a gap the horizon showed up like a sinister purple streak. Suddenly someone shouted, "What's that near Fosse 8?" We all focused our glasses on the slap heap and for a second figures appeared, as one might see bathers surge up in the troughs of rough seas.
>
> Our telephones buzzed feverishly; messages were coming in on the wires, all more or less confused. Someone caught a visual message and spelt the words out to another who took it down, repeating every syllable with that slow cadence that gives special significance to tidings, and leaves an indelible impression on the mind: "We-have-no-Officers-left-..." Then something happened. The shutter flashing the message had closed. Contact was lost.

It will now be best to look at the actions of the final division under Gough's command in I Corps, that of the most southerly one - the 7th Division.

The 7th Division was in some respects an interesting division; it was formed around September 1914 from three Regular battalions based in Britain and nine battalions recently returned from overseas stations. These places ranged from

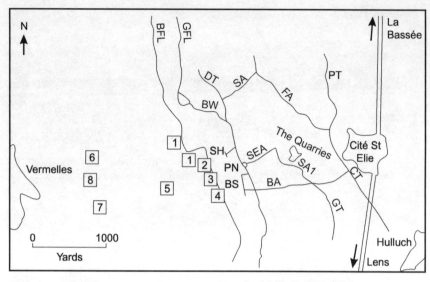

BFL	British Front Line	BA	Breslau Alley
GFL	German Front Line	GT	Gun Trench
DT	Dump Trench	SAI	Stone Alley
BW	Big Willie	1	2nd Royal Warwickshires
SA	Slag Alley	2	1st South Staffords
FA	Fosse Alley	3	8th Devons
PT	Pekin Trench	4	2nd Gordon Highlanders
CT	Cité Trench	5	2nd Border Regiment
SEA	St Elie Alley	6	1st Royal Welch Fusiliers
SH	Spurn Head	7	6th Gordon Highlanders
PN	Pope's Nose Redoubt	8	2nd Queen's & 9th Devons
BS	Breslau Sap		

Map 5: 7th Division area of attack, 25th September 1915

Guernsey, Cairo, Gibraltar (two units), Malta (two units), Natal and Transvaal (two units), this being possible by the arrival of Territorial Force units in certain stations such as Gibraltar and Malta. It did originally include two Guards battalions, and the Division had landed at Zeebrugge and Ostend in October 1914 in an attempt to prevent the Germans capturing Antwerp, although they were unsuccessful in this. They later moved south to join the BEF, becoming the first British unit to take part in the defence of Ypres. In 1915, its two Guards battalions, the 1st Grenadier Guards and the 2nd Scots Guards, had been taken by the forming Guards Division. Their places were taken by two New Army battalions - the 8th and 9th Devonshires. Indeed by the time of Loos it was a Division that had 14 infantry battalions in it. In addition to its two Regular units and the 8th and 9th Devonshires, the 20th Brigade had been given a TF Battalion, the 6th Gordon Highlanders. The 21st Brigade contained four Regular battalions and also a TF unit, the 4th Cameron Highlanders. One of the attached units was also TF - the 1st/2nd Highland Field Company RE.

This Division had been allocated an attacking frontage of about 1,400 yards between the Hohenzollern Redoubt and the Vermelles-Hulluch road. Their left flank was to be in contact with the 9th Division, whilst their right was the Corps boundary and the attacking flanking division was the 1st Division. The usual preparations for the attack had been carried out, including the digging of around five lines of parallel lines of trenches behind the British front line, so that the attacking waves of infantry could form up quickly. It was said that the three RE Field Companies in the period prior to the 25th September made 2,500 trench bridges and 3,500 ladders. Again, with the benefit of hindsight, the area appeared not to be ideal to launch an offensive. The ground was pretty much open and there were several strong German defensive positions, the most important perhaps being the Pope's Nose Redoubt. This was virtually in the centre of the attacking sector and the Redoubt formed a salient from which machine guns could enfilade fire over a large area on both flanks. Behind the German front line at a distance of about 600 yards was a second line of defences located on and around the crest of the Grenay Spur. A particular trench on the reverse slope of this crest was known as Gun Trench. There were also some German field guns located here. North of this were other positions known as Stone Alley and The Quarries. There were also the usual communication trenches to the front line, named Breslau Trench and St Elie Alley 1 and St Elie Alley 2. It was believed the defences were only weakly held by a couple of companies from the 11th Reserve Regiment with a couple more in reserve at the Quarries and Cité St Elie.

The plan was that once the front line defences had been breached the troops would push on almost directly east over the crest of the Grenay Spur, capture Gun

The area of the 22nd Brigade's attack, with the Quarries on the horizon. (IWM Q42185)

Trench and The Quarries. From here the left hand side was to push on to Cité St Elie, while the right was to head for the northern part of the village of Hulluch. As well as the defences already mentioned, there were two large defensive positions known as Stützpunkt II and Puits Trench, which were both in the open ground between these two already mentioned villages. As was usual, it was the classic two-up attack, the 20th and 22nd brigades in the leading wave with the 21st Brigade in reserve. Going in with the 20th Brigade were the 55th Field Company RE and No 1 Mortar Battery, while the 22nd had the 54th Field Company and No 10 Mortar Battery. The Divisional artillery was also organised into two mobile groups to follow each brigade together with a small reserve force.

The preliminary bombardment and gas support in this area appeared to have very little effect. Most of the German barbed wire appeared to be uncut, and on the morning of 25th September the wind in some places was acceptable, in others it was not, being more like a gentle breeze. In certain sectors therefore the gas and smoke was used, but in others it was not turned on, as it would have blown across the British lines. The most northerly brigade, the 22nd, was responsible for a front of about 600 yards. Here is an account from a Special Company man, G. Mitchell:

> The day broke dull and a slight drizzle was blowing from the left of us about 5 mph. The 1st South Staffordshire Regiment was occupying our part of the line. We received our order and Zero time fairly early on. Zero was 5.50am. We started our performance on the minute. I got a big mouthful with the first cylinder and then, of course, pulled my helmet down. We had only two pipes for twelve cylinders and had to change over when one was empty. God, what a game! The rotten apparatus they had given us was leaking all over the place and we were working in a cloud of gas. We sweated ourselves to death and only got eight off. All gas had to be turned off at 6.28 am. At 6.30 the infantry had to go over the parapet. We finished on time.

Again, the Brigade Commander, Steele, had opted for two up, with two in reserve. The two leading battalions were the 1st South Staffords and the 2nd Royal Warwickshires. The gas and smoke cloud had seemed to work and the first part of the advance was through this screen, but it appears due to some quirk of fortune the last 50 yards or so to the German wire was free of gas and smoke. Even then, the wire was a very thick belt and virtually uncut. The leading waves of both battalions attempted to cut gaps in it, but suffered very heavy casualties. One man from the 2nd Royal Warwicks, Private A. Vickers, was instrumental in this. On his own initiative, he went forward and in the open under heavy fire managed to cut two gaps in the barbed wire. He was recommended for a Victoria Cross which was gazetted on 18th November 1915. His citation read:

> On 25th September 1915 at Hulluch, France, during an attack by his Battalion on the first line German trenches, Private Vickers on his own initiative, went forward in front of his Company under heavy shell, rifle and machine gun fire and cut the wires which were holding up a great part of his Battalion. Although it was broad daylight at the time, he carried out this work standing up and his gallant action contributed largely to the success of the assault. Vickers survived the war ending up as a Sergeant and finally dying in 1944 aged 62.

In spite of heavy losses the two battalions forced their way through the barbed wire belt and entered the German front line trenches. In view of the heavy losses one of the reserve units, the 1st Royal Welch Fusiliers, was immediately sent across to assist. By around 7.30am the leading troops had captured the German support trench with the exception of Slit Redoubt, but this soon fell with help from a party from 20th Brigade approaching from the south. A number of prisoners were taken.

The communications in this Brigade must have been working well, as the reserve battalion, the 2nd Queens, arrived about 8.30 am, and carried on to the area known as The Quarries. By about 9.30 am, the 2nd Queens had taken The Quarries and the trench immediately to the north of it, again taking a number of prisoners. Not resting on their laurels they pushed on again and reached the area of Cité Trench, which covered the western outskirts of the village of Cité St Elie. Meanwhile the South Staffords were trying to push along a communication trench towards Cité Trench, but they came under a heavy attack by bombing parties. In spite of this they fought through to the junction of the communication trench and Cité Trench, literally on the outskirts of the village. Lots of Germans could be seen moving around the village. But they came under a renewed attack and found the position untenable and they withdrew back a few hundred yards. However as the morning drew on, the casualty figure continued to mount and German fire seemed to be increasing and around noon all the troops were pulled back to an area around The Quarries - to the north and east of it, which was being prepared for a state of defence. However an attempt around 2.00 p.m. was made to enter Cité St Elie by a company from the 2nd Queens. They entered the village but came under heavy shell fire, it is believed from British guns, and came back. There were no further attempts that day to enter the village, and the men from the 22nd Brigade remained

Table 3.4
22nd Brigade casualties, 25th September

2nd Royal Warwicks	527
1st South Staffs	448
1st Royal Welch Fusiliers	442
2nd Queens	272
Total	1689

around The Quarries for the rest of the day. Much effort was spent in building defences and on the night of 25th/26th September the Divisional engineers put up barbed wire in front of them. It is not surprising to see a lack of drive after these initial gains when you look at the casualty figures for the 22nd Brigade:

Here is a post-action report from Captain C Swinhoe of the 2nd Warwicks:

On the morning of 25th September the Battalion assaulted in the following formation:
    A Company First Line
    B Company Second Line
    C Company Third Line
    D Company Fourth Line
    Battalion HQ in the middle of D Company.

The Battalion went into the attack with 17 Officers and about 650 Other Ranks.

At first the smoke screen completely hid everything. It was impossible to see more than 10 yards in it. Direction was difficult to keep.

I came through the smoke and on to the German wire at the same moment. I can well remember my amazement. Hardly a shot had passed me so far and now the ground was strewn with bodies. The fire must have been entirely enfilade and to make it easier for the Germans the smoke had stopped about 30 yards from their trenches. The wire was as far as I could see absolutely untouched by our bombardment.

I personally got through a gap which had been left when the Germans had dug a sap-head through the wire. I was shot just as I got clear, in three places: below the knee a rifle bullet, through the thigh a machine gun and in the shoulder a shrapnel fragment. I then fell into the sap-head. I later crawled into the German front line to get away from our own gas, but I found it worse there and so crawled back again.

The right hand brigade in the southern sector was the 20th, and their first objective was a trench known as Breslau Trench. The two battalions in the leading wave were Regulars from the 2nd Gordon Highlanders and a New Army unit, the 8th Devons. The gas and smoke cloud can again be said to have been relatively ineffective, lingering in and around the British front line. Many men felt compelled to remove their smoke hoods, due to their own apparent suffocation and suffered the consequences of chlorine gas poisoning. The Germans did not help by firing artillery shells into the cloud which caused many casualties.

But for once on the front of the 20th Brigade, the artillery had done a good job, and within about ten minutes the leading waves of the 2nd Gordons were in the front line, although at a heavy cost. The CO of the Battalion. Lieutenant-Colonel J. Stansfield, was seriously wounded and died on 28th September at Chocques. The 1st Casualty Clearing Station RAMC was here, and there was some post-battle controversy over the medical arrangements at Loos which will be discussed later. Further north, in the area of the 8th Devons, the artillery fire had been less successful and only a few gaps had been made in the German wire. This unfortunately led to bunching around the gaps, a problem that would be repeated on the Somme the following year. This gave the defenders in Breslau Trench an ideal target and in a few short minutes they wreaked havoc amongst the men of the 8th Devons. Suffice to say that over 600 men from this unit became casualties on this day. It is believed only 3 of the 19 officers who left the British trenches at H Hour entered the German lines. In spite of the high casualties the Gordons and Devons managed to capture most of the objectives, including Breslau Trench and its support trench, and take a number of prisoners. Undaunted by the losses the battered survivors of both battalions regrouped and moved forward to the crest of the ridge line. The few defenders here were overwhelmed and the advance continued down the reverse slope towards Hulluch. A German field battery of four guns was also captured. Two of these captured guns were presented by the War Office to the County of Devonshire, who gave them on loan to the Mayor and Corporation of Exeter.

Captured German artillery at Béthune, possibly some of those captured by
the 8th Devons. (IWM Q 28963)

The Gordons meanwhile, in spite of their heavy losses, carried on forward to
the Lens road, which they reached about 8.45 am. They deployed on the eastern
side of this road for about 200 yards south of the junction of the Vermelles-
Hulluch/Lens roads. An additional opportunity soon appeared in that a party of
several hundred German reserves could be seen marching into Cité St Elie without
apparently a care in the world. Rapid fire was quickly poured into the ranks causing
some casualties and the men quickly took cover in ruined cottages around the main
street of the village. These Germans from the Reserve Battalion of the 11th Reserve
Regiment quickly recovered from this early shock and proceeded to fight stubbornly for the rest of the day. Meanwhile on their left the 8th Devons struggled on.
By now they only numbered around a hundred all ranks, and ended up astride the
Lens road, north of the crossroads previously mentioned.

It is now best to bring into play the story of the other three battalions in the
20th Brigade. Two of them can be usefully called the second wave (6th Gordons
and 2nd Border), while the last (9th Devons) had been nominated as brigade reserve. It is worth quoting this comment from a soldier who was in one of the units
in the second wave, the 6th Gordon Highlanders, about the gas cloud: "Half of us
were gassed, you see; those helmets wouldn't take the gas, and we were choking
there and spitting and choking and I got terribly sick, and I was sick and vomiting
and I couldn't cut it there any longer, and there were others a lot like me just the
same." Even so, both battalions followed quickly behind the leading wave. Two

companies from the 6th Gordons took up positions to the right of their sister battalion the 2nd Gordons on the Lens-La Bassée road, with the rest of the unit taking up defensive positions behind them.

Reinforced by these new arrivals, the acting CO Major Ross, decided to send a party of around 50 men forward to assess the strength of the German defences in and around Hulluch. After only going around 200 yards they came under cross fire from both the village of Hulluch and the position known as Stützpunkt II. There was also some very thick undamaged barbed wire defences and it was decided by Ross that no advance could be attempted till Cité St Elie and Puits Trench were in British hands. Just further north but not so far forward as the Gordons, the 2nd Borders had captured the parts of Gun Trench and Stone Alley north of the Vermelles-Hulluch road and settled down into defensive positions facing Cité St Elie and waited for the 22nd Brigade to appear on their left flank.

Due to these relative successes the Brigade commander ordered his reserve battalion the 9th Devons forward, in the direction of Gun Trench. Their passage across the open ground was a nightmare, being under fire most of the way from a variety of weapons, but it seems that artillery fire claimed most victims. From this unit - the 9th Devons the CO, the second-in-command, three out of four company commanders and seven other officers all became casualties in a matter of minutes. Indeed, only about 300 men reached Gun Trench, with only five officers present, and one of these was killed immediately after arrival. It seemed unlikely that a successful attack could be launched on the formidable Puits Trench with their limited numbers so they attempted to strengthen the defences against the inevitable counter-attack. Before looking at the actions of the 21st Brigade and tidying up the days actions, the following comment from *The Devonshire Regiment in the Great War* is worth quoting:

Hard hit both battalions had certainly been. The 8th had 19 officers and 620 men in their casualty list, and it was even more in the quality than in the quantity of their losses that they had suffered so much. To lose so many of the officers and NCOs who had borne the brunt of the work of raising and training the new battalion, was a shattering blow. Colonel Grant, Major Carden and Captain Kekewich had all done great work for the 8th and their loss was severely felt. The Colonel, himself a great worker, had expected the 8th to work hard and to learn rapidly. With the keen raw material with which he had to deal his exacting demands and his high standards had been a great incentive. The 8th had been keen to satisfy one who showed himself in every respect a competent soldier, and for the high level they reached and maintained their first CO deserves not a little credit.

The 9th losses, though less by a quarter than those of their sister battalion, came to 15 officers and 461 men, but, fortunately, they faired better in that far fewer officers had been killed. In the 8th, besides the officers already mentioned, the wounded included Captains James, Pryor and Broadbridge, Lieutenants Hulm and MacMichael, Second Lieutenants Nixon, Balderson, Bridson and Cracroft, and the Chaplain, the Reverend Hewitt, had been killed. No less than 148 men were killed, 129 missing and 343 wounded or gassed. The 9th with Lieutenants Tracey, Martin, Upcott, Glosson and Worrall and Second Lieutenants Allan, Davies, Hinshelwood and Pocock and Lieutenant

O'Reilly RAMC and 59 men killed, 76 men missing and 326 wounded, were almost as much in need of reconstruction.

Still the 8th and 9th could look with pride on their first battle. At that period in the war but few other battalions could boast of having captured German guns. It was a notable achievement for a new Battalion, it spoke well for the Battalion's training and for the spirit by which it was inspired, that, when nearly all their officers had fallen with so many of the men, the survivors should have carried on the attack with such vigour and resolution.

Among the officers of the 9th Devons was Lieutenant William Noel Hodgson, who won a Military Cross in October 1915, was killed the next year at Mansell Copse on the Somme, and is one of the well known war poets. After his death a volume of his work was published titled *Verse and Prose in peace and War*. His most famous poem is probably 'Before Action', which he wrote on the Somme in 1916, but perhaps sums up the feelings of many men waiting to go into battle:

I, that on my familiar hill
Saw with uncomprehending eyes
A hundred of thy sunsets spill
Their fresh and sanguine sacrifice
Ere the sun swings his noonday sword

Table 3.5
20th Brigade casualties, 25th September

8th Devons	619
2nd Gordons	457
2nd Border	234
6th Gordons	297
9th Devons	256

Must say good-bye to all of this;-
By all delights that I shall miss
Help me to die, O Lord.

The casualty figures for the 20th Brigade can be summarised as follows:
The role of the reserve brigade, the 21st, was as usual in the plan to continue the advance after the two forward brigades had punched the necessary holes in the German defences. Soon after Zero Hour they had moved forward from their reserve positions around Vermelles into the recently vacated front line trenches. The original plan called from them to pass through the two attacking brigades and advance to the Haute Deule Canal. However, as most commanders know, their plan rarely lasts after the first initial contact with the enemy. The plan of the GOC of the 7th Division, Major-General Capper, was no exception to this rule and he was forced into a rethink. He decided to order them to support the 20th Brigade on the right of his Divisional area, with the intention of taking the village of Hulluch. This manoeuvre, he hoped, would free up the 22nd Brigade held up by Slit

Redoubt. However at 9.30 am, he heard that this bottleneck had been overcome, so he changed his orders once again. As there were five battalions in this Brigade, it was decided to split it into three parts, which for ease can be called the left and right hand forces and as usual a reserve force. The left hand force consisted of the 2nd Green Howards and the 4th Cameron Highlanders, and was to pass through the 22nd Brigade and take Cité St Elie. The right hand force comprising the 2nd Bedfordshires and the 2nd Wiltshires were to pass through the 20th Brigade and seize and hold Hulluch, in fact their original task with less numbers.

The left hand force managed to reach the area of The Quarries without too many casualties, but when they arrived here they started coming under fire from both small arms fire from Cité Trench and artillery fire from Haisnes. Both battalions therefore dug in around The Quarries - south of its southern edge and in the northern part of Stone Alley.

Meanwhile the right hand force comprising the 2nd Bedfords and the 2nd Wiltshires went forward in the manner required and suffered very few casualties until around 11am when they reached the area of the Loos-Haisnes road, east of the original German front line. Cresting a small rise heading towards Gun Trench (where the Devons and Borders were) they came under intense small arms fire from the village of Cité St Elie. The casualty roll included the CO of the Bedfords, his Adjutant and all four company commanders; the Wilts lost over 200 men. The survivors rushed forward and settled down into the relative safety of Gun Trench. It was obvious it would be difficult to move forward so they set about turning the trench into a defensive position. These troops were lucky in that they had the support of some guns about 1,000 yards behind them - these being from T Battery RHA, 35th (Howitzer) Battery 37th Brigade RFA and 59th Siege Battery RGA.

Meanwhile it was decided to send two officers forward from Gun Trench to discover the defences around the village of Cité St Elie, their report stated: "The enemy's second line strongly held on northern and western edges of the village with rifles and machine guns; houses loop-holed and a strong wire obstacle in front of Cité Trench undamaged by our bombardment." This news was relayed to the 21st Brigade's commander, Watts, along with the decision that further attacks would be a disaster unless properly organised and supported by an adequate (at least) artillery bombardment. Major-General Capper therefore issued orders that the artillery was to bombard the village of Cité St Elie and other German positions in the environs until 4.00 p.m. when the 21st Brigade would renew the attack. It would probably be better to say what elements of the 21st Brigade that could be mustered would renew the attack. In any case by 4.00 p.m. it was obvious to those in Gun Trench that the bombardment had been totally unsuccessful. The wire, Cité Trench nor the fortified cottages in Cité St Elie had been damaged. Fortunately the CO of the Wiltshires, Lieutenant-Colonel Leatham, was brave enough to report that an attack against the undamaged defences with tired troops and insufficient numbers was only likely to lead to a disaster. Both Watts and Capper agreed with this stance and the attack was cancelled. In the meantime two lines of support trenches behind Gun Trench were started and

Table 3.6
1st Brigade casualties, 25th September

2nd Bedfords	255
2nd Wiltshires	207

additional defensive measures taken to safeguard Stone Alley on the left flank. There was no more movement in the Divisional area on this day and according to a Corps Order issued at 6.05pm which was received at Divisional HQ at 7.30pm the ground was to be consolidated. Before reviewing the position of the Division at the end of the day, a few casualty figures:

This is the entry in the 2nd Wiltshires War Diary for the 25th September:

Following the advance of the 20th Brigade, the Battalion occupied the front and support German lines. Lieutenant-Colonel Leatham then gave orders for the Battalion to advance in open order in direction of Cité St Elie. Keeping to the north of Hulluch road, our right flank connecting with the 2nd Bedfordshires left. Extremely heavy rifle and machine gun fire was experienced from the front. Eventually the Battalion came to a line held very weakly by a mixture of 8th Devons and 2nd Borders. The trench contained 4 German Field Guns and ammunition. Our losses were heavy.

At dusk the Battalion was relieved by 9th Devonshire Regiment and took up a new front at Breslau Avenue our right resting on the latter Regiment.

Astride the Vermelles-Hulluch road close to the junction of the Lens-La Bassée road holding a front of around 500 yards were the survivors of four units, 2nd and 6th Gordons and 8th and 9th Devons. Their right flank was in contact with IV Corps but had an exposed left flank facing Cité St Elie. They had been ordered to dig in here, with engineering stores being sent forward together with two 1½ inch mortars to provide some local fire support. The remainder of the 20th Brigade, together with two battalions from the 21st (Bedfords and Wiltshires) held Gun Trench from the Vermelles-Hulluch road to Stone Alley. The other battalions from the 21st Brigade (2nd Green Howards and 4th Cameron Highlanders) held Stone Alley up to and including the southern edge of The Quarries. The 2nd Royal Scots Fusiliers were back in the area of the original British and German front lines acting as Divisional Reserve. The 22nd Brigade meanwhile in much depleted numbers was holding the northern and eastern edges of The Quarries. All in all a reasonable day for the 7th Division, its mixture of youth and experience had worked well. The question was now, could they hang on to their gains although bought at a heavy price and perhaps exploit them with the reserves on the following day? Or would the Germans launch their inevitable counter-attack and would it be able to be repulsed? We will come back to the actions of I Corps later, but now it is right to look at the position on the southern sector of the battlefield - those of IV Corps.

Before I do, here is an interesting comment from an officer with the 1st Leicesters in the Meerut Division, part of the diversionary attacks for the I Corps.

For Loos, September 25th 1915, we rehearsed the attack, well behind our lines for a week or two beforehand. The relative positions of our front line and 'theirs' was clearly pegged and indicated. But it was all to no purpose, for when we went over the top we could hardly see anything, due to our smoke screens blowing down on us between the lines instead of, as they were intended to do, staying on our flanks to hide us from enfilade fire. Also our own gas hung around us instead of going where it had been meant to go - over to the enemy lines, and because we were all (at first) wearing flannel helmets with mica eyepieces.

We were suffocating in the helmets, so took a chance and threw them off. We all seemed to suffer no ill-effects, leaving a doubt about what effect it would have had on the enemy, if it had reached him!

This comment came from Lieutenant G. Grossmith, who was wounded in the attack by the Meerut Division on the 25th and got a 'Blighty One.'

4

IV Corps

The southern part of the Loos Battlefield was the responsibility of IV Corps under the command of Lieutenant-General Sir Henry Rawlinson. The first objective of his Corps, which comprised a mixture of Regular, Territorial and New Army divisions was the capture of the German front line defences along the heights of the Grenay spur between a feature known as the Double Crassier and the Vermelles-Hulluch road.

The IV Corps Operational Order was as follows:

20th September 1915

1   a) Under orders received from 1st Army, the IV Corps will attack the enemy's position between the Double Crassier (inclusive) and the Vermelles-Hulluch road (exclusive)

b) Simultaneously with this, strong attacks will be made south of the IV Corps front by the French, and to the north by the I Corps, while the III Corps and Indian Corps will make minor attacks. The 2nd Army will make an attack on Hooge

c) The objectives of the IV Corps are Loos, Hill 70, Cité St Auguste, southern part of Hulluch, and the enemy's defences between the two latter villages, with the ultimate objective of securing the passage of the Haute Deule Canal at Pont à Vendin, and the Lens-Carvin road south of Annay, advancing with its left on the Hulluch-Vendin le Vieil road

d) The objectives of the I Corps will be Fosse 8, St Elie, Puits 13 and the northern part of Hulluch, with the ultimate objective of securing the passage of the Haute Deule Canal from Pont à Vendin to Baudin, advancing with its right on the Hulluch-Vendin le Vieil road.

2   The offensive of the I and IV Corps will commence with a steady bombardment by all available guns night and day during the first four days and up to the time of the Infantry assault on the fifth day.

In order to conceal as far as possible, the points of attack, the bombardment will be distributed over the whole front of the 1st Army, whilst counter-battery guns deal with any of the enemy's batteries that may disclose their positions.

3   At 0.00 on the morning of the fifth day, gas and smoke will be discharged for 40 minutes along the whole of the IV Corps front, and this discharge will be immediately followed by the Infantry assault at 0.40.

4   Instructions regarding the use of gas and smoke have been issued separately.

5   During and after the 40 minute discharge of gas and smoke the artillery will add to the effect of the gas by firing on the hostile front line system of trenches with shrapnel only, and on their objectives beyond, with HE and shrapnel, in accordance with the artillery timetable already arranged.

6   With a view to forming a defensive flank southwards to cover the advance of the 1st and 15th Divisions, the objectives of the 47th Division will be:-

a) The Double Crassier as far as M.4.d.8.8.

b) Hostile front line system of trenches from M.4.a.1.3. to G.34.a.6.5.

c) The second line trenches from M.4.8.8. to the cemetery in G.35.a. (inclusive)

d) New School G.35.d.7.8. Building G.35.b.2.2. and G.35.d.1.8.

e) Enclosure in G.35.d.

f) Copse in M.6.a.

g) Fosse in G.36.a.

Demonstrations will be made by 47th Division between the Double Crassier and Puits 16.

7   The objectives of the 15th Division will be:-

a) The hostile front line system of trenches from G.34.a.6.5. to the hostile sap G.22.d.6.3-3.8

b) The second line trenches between the cemetery in G.35.a. (exclusive) and G.29.b.3.9

c) Loos village (less buildings G.35.b.2.2 and d.1.8. and New School G.35.d.7.8.)

d) Hill 70

e) Cité St Auguste

f) The high ground north of Loison.

8   The objectives of the 1st Division will be:-

a) The hostile front line system of trenches from sap G.23.a.4.3-G.22.b.9.7. to Vermelles-Hulluch road (exclusive)

b) The second line trenches from G.29.b.3.9. to G.12.d.6.0.

c) Line of the Lens-Cité St Elie road from Puits 14 bis (inclusive) to house H.13.a.2.8. (inclusive)

d) Bois Hugo

e) Hulluch between H.13.d.2.5 and trench H.13.b.1.7.-b.6.6. (inclusive)

f) Puits 13 bis- Redoubt H.20.d.

g) The passages of the Canal at Pont à Vendin.

9   Divisions, on reaching the enemy's front line system of trenches, will send out bombing parties to join up with neighbouring formations and secure their flanks.

10   The 7th Division will be on the left of the 1st Division, and their objectives will be:-

Puits 13 bis and northern part of Hulluch.

The right of this Division will be directed on-: G.12.c.2.1-G.12.c.6.0-G.12.d.6.0-H.13.b.2.8.-H.13.b.7.8. and along the Hulluch-Vendin le Vieil road.

11   The assaulting troops will advance as fast as possible from one objective to another. Divisions will push up fresh troops from the rear to hold the successive lines captured by the assaulting troops.

12

a) The following guns of the 1st Group H.A.R. Will carry out the bombardment and support of the attack of the 1st, 15th and 47th Divisions:-

1 15 inch howitzer
4 9.2 inch howitzers
8 8 inch howitzers
4 6 inch Mark VIII guns
7 batteries 60 pdrs (28 guns)
3 batteries 4.7 inch (12 guns)
2 9.2 inch guns on railway trucks
4 batteries 18 pdrs (24th Division)

b) The artillery of the 1st, 15th and 47th Divisions, four batteries of 6 inch howitzers, two batteries (4.5 inch) 109th Brigade, and two batteries (18 pdr) 107th Brigade, divided into three Divisional groups, will be under the command of Brigadier-General C.E.D. Budworth, MVO, and will support the 1st, 15th and 47th Divisions in their respective attacks, under instructions already issued

c) A map showing the 'lifts' of the artillery of the 1st Group H.A.R. and IV Corps Artillery, during the various phases of the Infantry assault has been issued to all concerned

d) A proportion of the Divisional Artillery will be detailed beforehand by the Corps Artillery Commander to follow up the Infantry advance and furnish closer support as the attack moves forward

e) As soon as possible after the hostile advanced trenches have been captured, the Divisional Artillery of the 1st, 15th and 47th Divisions will be placed under direct control of the Divisional Commanders, and Brigadier-General Budworth will resume command of the 1st Divisional Artillery. Two batteries of 6 inch howitzers will be allotted to the 1st Division and two to the 15th Division, at the same time. Two batteries 107th Brigade RFA (24th Division) and two batteries 109th (Howitzer) Brigade (24th Division), will then receive orders from Corps Headquarters.

13   The bombardment will commence on the 21st September. The hour of Zero in reference to the gas attack on the 25th will be notified later.

14   The attack of the IV Corps will be pressed home to the utmost extent of its power, and all commanders must exert their maximum of effort in driving the enemy from his positions.

15   The 3rd Cavalry Division and XI Corps will be held in Army Reserve in rear of the I and IV Corps and will be brought forward in support as occasion demands.

16   The IV Corps Advanced Headquarters will open at Vaudricourt from 10.00 a.m. to 7.00 p.m. on the 21st, 22nd and 23rd, and at 10.00 a.m. till further orders on the 24th September.

A.A.Montgomery, Brigadier-General,
General Staff IV Corps.

As we have just seen once the initial gains had been made, the southern-most division, the 47th, was to halt astride the Loos valley in the area between the Double Crassier and the Loos Crassier and form a defensive line facing Lens. They were also expected to seize and hold a German position known as The Chalk Pit.

Meanwhile the other two divisions, the 1st and 15th, were to advance past Hill 70 and the Lens road, pushing on through the German second line between Cité St Auguste and Hulluch, and then on to the banks of the Haute Deule Canal. The right flank of the 15th Division was also expected to join up with the French 10th Army in the area of the Lens-Carvin road, east of Cité St Auguste. It was expected by nearly everyone from the Corps commander downwards that a huge breakthrough would be achieved and the nominated reserves would be close up to exploit it. It is perhaps significant that there were no reserves detailed by Rawlinson and he intended for his commanders to attack with nearly every available man. Perhaps the thinking behind this strategy came from intelligence that suggested that there were only small numbers of German troops opposite them - two regiments or six battalions. In theory this gave IV Corps an overwhelming superiority 40 infantry battalions against 6. Although I looked at the actions of I Corps from north to south, I will look at IV Corps from south to north, so we can look at the actions of the flank guard first, the 47th Division, or to give them their correct title the 47th (2nd London) Division.

This Division was one of the pre-war Territorial Force formations, and because London was able to attract so many recruits it was able to field two complete divisions. These were obviously the 1st and 2nd London divisions, and when the Territorial Force (TF) divisions were numbered in 1915, the 2nd Division was given the number 47. The other London division was allocated the number 56. Now I realise this may seem a bit strange but the 1st London's Infantry had been

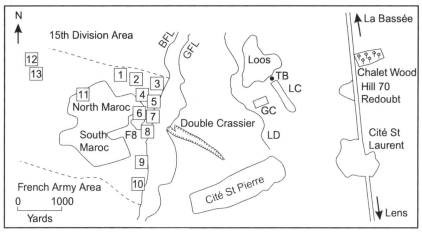

F8	Fosse 8	4	20th London Regiment
BFL	British Front Line	5	6th London Regiment
GFL	German Front Line	6	8th London Regiment
TB	Tower Bridge	7	7th London Regiment
LC	Loos Crassier	8	15th London Regiment
GC	Garden City	9	22nd London Regiment
LD	Loos Defences	10	21st London Regiment
1	17th London Regiment	11	4th Royal Welch Fusiliers
2	19th London Regiment	12	23rd London Regiment
3	18th London Regiment	13	24th London Regiment

Map 6: 47th Division area of attack, 25th September 1915

sent all over the place - to overseas garrisons such as Gibraltar, to act as reinforcements for the BEF and to make up other divisions shortages. The authorities were not able to pull together all the dispersed elements until early 1916, which is why it got a number higher than the 'junior' London Division. The 47th Division's units were mainly from South-East and South-West London, and were all from the London Regiment, a wholly TF unit. But amongst the exotic names such as the Post Office Rifles, London Irish Rifles and the Civil Service Rifles were the 22nd and 24th London Regiments which were linked with the Queen's (West Surrey) Regiment. Other units of the Division incorporated local place names in their titles, such as the 6th and 7th Londons known as the City of London Rifles and the 17th - Poplar and Stepney Rifles and the 20th - Blackheath and Woolwich. The Division left England for France in March 1915, being the second complete TF division to join the BEF and had prior to Loos taken part in the actions at Aubers Ridge and Festubert. The 47th Division took over at the end of August 1915 the sector extending from the Maroc-Puits No 16 road northwards to the Béthune-Lens road. As was common with other areas at the time, the front line positions were deemed not suitable for an attack, they lay in a concave curve north of the Double Crassier, and diverged, to a distance of some 700 yards from the German front line. A new line was therefore dug to cut down the distance between the lines. It was the usual form of joining up the heads of long saps dug out into No Man's Land.

Work on this new trench system envisaged to be nearly a mile in length was started on 27th August by men from the 141st Brigade under the direction of the Division's Royal Engineers. As usual most of the work was done at night with the men being brought up from their billets in and around Noeux les Mines by London Omnibus vehicles. An officer with the 19th London Regiment, Lieutenant A Waterlow, recalls digging this new trench system:

Our job was a somewhat ticklish one. The whole Battalion was to go up to the front line armed with picks and shovels, file out along the various saps which had been extended out into No Man's Land and spread out along a line about two hundred and fifty yards in front of our front line, where patrols usually only crawled about on their stomachs. We were then to dig a new front line, which would be previously marked out in white tape by the Royal Engineers. It was to run slightly in front of our present front line at the Béthune-Lens main road (where the British and Bosche trenches were closest together) in a straight line to meet our present front line in front of South Maroc, so straightening out two re-entrants, taking in a considerable area of No Man's Land and making a convenient jumping-off trench for the coming attack. We had instructions to carry on with the digging, no matter how heavy the casualties might be. They were expected to be fairly heavy because the London Irish had been digging the new line in front of the right hand sector on the previous night and, with the new trench running in a straight line and suddenly ending 'in the air', it should have been obvious to the Bosche during the day what our game was and to get the exact range of the new line and have us taped at night.

When the time came we filed out of the sap-heads like mice and spread out along the taped line. Every man had to take the utmost care not to jangle the picks and shovels against one another or against his equipment. Any slight noise might give us all away, and if the Bosches chose to turn a machine gun on to us they could have practically wiped us out. We were simply a line of men across No Man's Land with absolutely no cover. The men with the picks got to work at once, while the men with shovels lay at full length on the ground, with the shovel blade in front of them to protect their heads until their turn came. Never have I seen men dig at such a rate! They seemed to be two feet deep in no time.

The policy was for each pair of men to dig a hole to give them both as much shelter as possible and, when this was the required depth, to join up the various holes into one continuous line of bays and traverses. By a marvellous piece of good fortune we only had desultory rifle fire from the Bosches, in spite of the fact that they were sending up Very lights regularly which seemed to light us all up so plainly that we could not fail to be observed. In fact it gave one the impression of standing naked and unable to take cover in front of a vast throng of people. But it was two hours before they sent any shells over and by that time the men had dug some cover for themselves. We got a few salvoes at intervals but altogether only two men were wounded. The Bosche knew where we were right enough, for all the shells landed only a few feet behind the new line we were digging, so that it passes comprehension of the Bosche mentality why he did not turn on a machine gun or rifle fire, when he definitely knew that we were there! Our artillery had been given instructions to retaliate with compound interest on the Bosche trenches if we got shelled at all but their reply was somewhat feeble. I heard they got 'strafed' by the higher powers.

This new front line trench was deep and well traversed, and in alternative bays special recesses were made for the gas cylinders. As assembly trench was also dug about 50 yards behind the new front line. The assembly trench was fitted throughout with hurdles to assist the attacking troops in climbing out of the trenches, and many connecting saps were cut. It has been calculated that over two miles of new trenches were dug in three weeks. Fortunately, the Germans allowed this work to be carried out almost unmolested, and caused only a few casualties. As well as the digging other preparations were in progress. In the rear areas, ground resembling the objectives of the 47th Division was marked out by flags and tape so that every trench and noticeable feature was shown on the ground. The units detailed for the assault trained on this model, so that in theory come the day everybody knew what they had to do and the ground was well known to them.

I know I have said this before but it needs repeating - the 47th Division had also been given a tough nut to crack. The Division had a frontage of around 2,500 yards along the western head of the Loos valley. The Division's left flank was on the Béthune-Lens road and its right on the Grenay-Lens railway where the French 81st Territorial Division was positioned. Behind the British front line were the dump and buildings of Fosse 5 and the miners' cottages of North and South Maroc. Some of these cottages on the eastern side had been converted into observation posts. Additionally the cellars of most buildings were useful for either storing men and supplies or using as medical facilities.

Looking south from Dud Corner at the Double Crassier. (Geoff Parker)

The Double Crassier at its western end. (IWM Q 37911)

View from the top of the Double Crassier giving an idea of the advantage gained from its heights. (IWM Q 37914)

In front of the Division was an open valley about 1,500 yards across; it almost resembles the Valley of Death from the Crimean War. At its head about 6,000 yards away was the village of Cité St Auguste, the northern side bounded by Loos itself, the southern edge the villages of Cité St Pierre and Cité St Laurent. Virtually down the middle were the formidable Double Crassier, Chalk Pit and the Loos Crassier. The waste from Fosse 11 had been piled into two high embankments - the Double Crassier - about 1,200 yards in length and both about 100 foot high. The waste from Fosse 12 had only been piled into one bank - the Loos Crassier - about 800 yards long but over 150 foot high. However, this was dwarfed by the twin lattice-girder wheel houses of the mineshaft of Fosse 11, which became known as Tower Bridge. These positions had been turned into strongholds by the Germans, and also scattered around were other defences such as Stützpunkt 69 by the Chalk Pit. This is a good place to relate the Operational Order issued for Loos by the GOC, Major-General C. Barter, for the forthcoming attack:

Operational Order No 19
20th September 1915
1   The 1st Army has been ordered to assume the offensive in connection with the French to the south. The 2nd Army attacks Hooge. The 81st (French) Division immediately to our right is to demonstrate only.

The IV and I Corps are to attack the enemy's positions south of the La Bassée Canal, with Loos, Hill 70, Cité St Auguste, Benefontaine, Hulluch and St Elie as ultimate objectives.

The 3rd Cavalry Division and XI Corps are in Army Reserve.

The 47th Division forms the right of the attack of the 1st Army and is to cover the flank by forming a defensive flank southwards.

The 15th Division on our left has Loos, Hill 70 and Cité St Auguste as objectives, and the 1st Division on the left on the 15th Division, directs its right attack on Puits 14 bis.

2   The GOC intends to attack with the 140th and 141st Infantry Brigades. The 142nd Infantry Brigade (less two Battalions) will be in Divisional Reserve. Two Battalions of the 142nd Infantry Brigade will maintain the right of our present defence line.

3   The attack will be preceded by four days continuous bombardment by Heavy and Field Artillery, commencing on 21st September, with a view to:

(i) Removing obstacles and cutting wire.

(ii) Destroying artillery observation stations.

(iii) Bombarding defences and connections.

(iv) Damaging buildings in order to make them more susceptible to gas attack.

(v) Lowering the enemy's morale.

The artillery programme is issued separately.

4   The assault will be preceded by 40 minutes gas attack opposite the points to be assaulted combined with the formation of a smoke screen along the whole of the 1st Army front. The commencement of the gas attack on 25th September will be timed 'Zero' and movements will be regulated from this. The exact time of 'Zero' will be communicated later.

Staff officers will be sent to Advanced Divisional Headquarters at 7.00 p.m. on 24th September to set watches.

5   Separate instructions have been issued as regards:

Artillery objectives, co-operation and affiliation

Royal Engineer co-operation

Gas and smoke attacks

Concentration for assault

System of messages in case of postponement of gas attack

General Instructions, Tactical-Administrative

Detailed instructions - Road Controls, Prisoners of War and Veterinary arrangements.

6

(a) The right of our present defensive line, Sub-section W.1. and that part of W.2. south of the Quarries (exclusive) will be maintained by:-

2 Battalions of the 142nd Infantry Brigade
142nd Infantry Brigade Machine Gun Battery
142nd Infantry Brigade 95m/m Battery (4 guns)
2 Sections 1/3rd London Field Company RE
No 7 Trench Howitzer Battery (2 inch) (less 2 guns)
'G' and 'I' Trench Mortar Batteries

This portion of the line will demonstrate only

Commander:- Lieutenant-Colonel E J Previté 22nd Battalion London Regiment.

(b) The 140th Infantry Brigade will form the right attack and will also be responsible for the present defensive line- Sub-section W.2. (less that portion south of the Quarry).

Commander:- Brigadier-General G J Cuthbert, CB.

Troops:

140th Infantry Brigade
140th Infantry Brigade Machine Gun Battery
140th Infantry Brigade 95m/m Battery (4 guns)

2 Sections 1/3rd London Field Company RE
1 gun of No 7 Trench Howitzer Battery
No 8 Trench Howitzer Battery (1 ½ inch) (less 2 guns)
1 Platoon and 2 machine guns 4th Bn. R.Welch Fus.

Front of assault - M.3.b.7.2 to Sap 1 (exclusive).

Objectives-the hostile system of defences:-

(i) The Double Crassier- G.34.c.9.2. (inclusive). Artillery fire is lifted south and east of this before 0.40'.
(ii) M.4.d.8.8-G.35.c.6.2. Artillery fire is lifted south and east of this before 0.50'.

(c) The 141st Infantry Brigade will form the left attack and will also be responsible for our present defensive line, Sub-section W.3. and Sap 18 (inclusive).

Commander: Brigadier-General W Thwaites.

Troops:

141st Infantry Brigade
141st Infantry Brigade Machine Gun Battery
141st Infantry Brigade 95m/m Battery (4 guns)
2 Sections 4th London Field Company RE
2 guns of No 8 Trench Howitzer Battery (1 ½ inch)
1 Platoon and 2 machine guns 4th Bn. R.Welch Fus.

Front of assault- Sap 1 to Sap 18 (both inclusive).

Objectives - the hostile system of defences:-

(i) G.34.c.9.2. (exclusive)- G.34.a.6.5. (inclusive). Artillery fire will be lifted south and east of this before 0.40'.
(ii) G.35.c.8.2. (exclusive)-G.35.a.6.3. (inclusive) Artillery fire will be lifted south and east of this before 0.50'.
(iii) Enclosure in G.35.d. Houses at G.35.d.2.9. and G.35.b.2.2. School House. Artillery fire will be lifted south and east of this before 1.15'.
(iv) Copse and Chalk Pit. Artillery fire will be lifted south and east of this before 1.30'.
(v) Loos Crassier. Artillery fire will be lifted south and east of this before 1.15', as 15th Division are timed to be at Puits No 15 by 1.15'.

(d) Line of demarcation between 140th and 141st Infantry Brigades for all purposes is a line from G.35.c.6.2 through Maison des Mitrailleurs produced westwards to Brebis Keep south-east.

(e) The Divisional Reserve will be formed of:-

Divisional Mounted Troops (less special duties) - Square L.21. (1 mile west of Mazingarbe)

6th London Fd. Arty. Bde. (less 1 ½ Battys) - Haillicourt
7th London Fd. Arty. Bde. (less 2 Battys) - Haillicourt
1/3rd Lon.Fd.Coy. RE (less 4 sections) - Les Brebis
2/3rd Lon.Fd.Coy. RE - Les Brebis
4th Lon.Fd.Coy. RE (less 2 sections) - Les Brebis
4th Battn. R.Welch Fus. (less 2 Platoons and machine guns) - North Maroc
142nd Infantry Brigade (less 2 Battalions) Commander: Brigadier-General F G Lewis, CMG
Headquarters - At Headquarters W Section Les Brebis.
Two Battalions in the Grenay Line.

(f) The assault is to be made over the open as to be rapidly and vigorously pushed home. All positions gained are to be consolidated for defence and to be held at all costs.

(g)Lateral connection between our attacking Brigades and between the 141st Infantry Brigade and the 15th Division attack will be established as soon as possible and maintained.

(h) Communication trenches between our present defence line and the hostile front system will be constructed under instructions issued to the CRE.

7   All units will be 'mobile' in all respects and instructions on this point have been issued.

8   8 Artillery Brigade Ammunition Columns remain at Haillicourt and supply SAA to refill

Depots:-

7th London F.A. Bde to 140th Inf Bde.

6th London F.A. Bde to 141st Inf Bde.

5th London F.A. Bde to 142nd Inf Bde.

Divisional Ammunition Column remains at Labuissière as at present.

9   Divisional Train remains at Haillicourt as at present.

10   Reports to Advanced 47th Division at the Mines Office, Les Brebis after 11 a.m. 24th September.

B. Burnett Hitchcock Lt-Colonel.
General Staff 47th (London) Division

These then were the orders for the 47th Division. On the nights of the 23rd and 24th September, the 140th and 141st Brigades relieved the 142nd Brigade in the W3 and W2 sectors. W3 extended from the Grenay-Loos road to the northern limits of W Sector and W2 extended southwards from the Grenay-Loos road to the south-east corner of the village of South Maroc. In the area of IV Corps it was decided at a Corps conference as late as the 24th September that unless the wind was suitable for the gas and smoke cloud, the 47th Division would attack without its support. As it turned out the Gas Officer for the area decided shortly before Zero that the wind was blowing in a southerly direction at about one mile per hour, which was satisfactory.

To put a bit more flesh on these bare orders, the following were the specific brigade objectives: The 140th and 141st brigades were to form the defensive crust around the Loos Crassier and the Double Crassier. On the left was the 141st Brigade under the command of Brigadier W. Thwaites; their first objective after taking the German front line was the southern part of the Loos defences. These were about 1,200 yards behind the German front line between the Béthune-Loos road and Loos Cemetery, at the south-west corner of the village. Thwaites deployed his battalions for the attack as follows: 18th Battalion (London Irish Rifles) in the front line, with the 19th Battalion (St Pancras) and 20th Battalion (Blackheath and Woolwich) on their left and right respectively. On capturing the trenches of the Loos defences, the 18th Londons were to halt and let the other two battalions pass through them with new objectives in mind. The 19th Londons were to wheel right and to carry on to the line 'Mine Buildings and Loos Crassier-Puits 15', while the 20th Londons were also to veer to the right and to move forward to the line 'Chalk Pit-Chalk Pit Copse'. The fourth unit in the Brigade, the 17th Battalion (Poplar and Stepney Rifles) were to remain behind in the original British front line as brigade reserve.

On their right was the 140th Brigade, commanded by Brigadier G. Cuthbert, with an initial objective of the German front line, then to take about 800 yards of the German second line trench. This stretched from approximately the middle of the Double Crassier northwards to the Béthune-Lens road. All in all it was a 'relatively small excursion' into enemy-held territory of just over 1,000 yards. Two of the Brigade's battalions had been chosen for the assault, these being the 6th and 7th battalions (both City of London). The other two battalions were in reserve, but had been detailed to remain in the seized German front line. These units were the 8th Battalion (Post Office Rifles) and the 15th Battalion (Prince of Wales's Own Civil Service Rifles).

The third brigade of the Division- the 142nd commanded by Brigadier F. Lewis - had a mixed bag of duties. Two of the battalions - the 21st Battalion (1st Surrey Rifles) and the 22nd Battalion (The Queen's) were to give fire support only from their positions. They held a front of approximately 1,200 yards from a point virtually opposite the Double Crassier southwards to the junction with the French. The others - mainly the 23rd Battalion and the 24th Battalion (The Queen's) together with Brigade HQ, 2½ batteries, a field company RE, the Divisional mounted troops and the pioneers (4th Royal Welch Fusiliers) were to be positioned near Les Brebis, acting as divisional reserve.

Meanwhile the 47th Division's artillery resources were organised into two groups. The first group in the north was to fire in direct support of the two attacking brigades - the 140th and 141st. The southern group was tasked with firing a continuous barrage on the German front line trenches in that area and on the village of Cité St Pierre to provide some sort of diversion for the northern attack. The 47th Division had been in action before Festubert (with one of its men winning a

Victoria Cross), and as at that battle had been able to spend some time beforehand in rehearsing their role over similar ground identified in the British rear areas. The men were additionally carrying flags and coloured discs to indicate progress and a sketch map of the area to be attacked had been issued down as far as section commanders.

The gas was turned on promptly at 5.50am and at 6.30am the leading waves of the 140th and 141st brigades stepped out into No Man's Land. The troops from the 142nd Brigade used a variety of dummy figures to try and attract enemy fire. It was noted that the gas probably had some of the best results of the entire Loos sector here, possibly due to the slope of the ground into the Loos valley. The attack was also covered by an effective smoke screen fired by two batteries of Stokes mortars located in South Maroc. The smoke shells fired burst behind the German front line with the intention of forming a screen along the length of the Double Crassier hindering German observation. As well as achieving this, the wind blew the smoke towards the village of Loos, which it eventually enveloped. Behind this gas and smoke cloud came the men of the 47th Division. An eyewitness said every line went forward into the valley and was quickly lost in the smoke. It is a credit to this Division that in spite of the thick smoke and the possible confusion, direction keeping was spot on.

On the 140th Brigade front, the 7th Battalion advanced on the Double Crassier, the west end of which, with a German trench running just under it, was their first objective. Their second objective was some 400 yards of the German second line north of its junction with the Crassier. The 6th Battalion attacked on the immediate left of the 7th with objectives of the first and second German lines. The 8th Battalion was to follow close behind, with the 15th being in reserve. Both the 6th and 7th Londons reached the German front line without too many casualties; but it remained strongly held by defenders from the German 22nd Reserve Regiment, who appeared to be more frightened than incapacitated by the gas cloud. However it did weaken the German's resolve and the trench line was taken, and they pressed on to the German second line. The wire in front of this line was relatively uncut and presented for a short while a serious obstacle as casualties started to be inflicted. However the wire was cut and this line also was taken by 7.30am. Private W. Morley of B Company 7th Londons later recalled:

> We went over the top into a perfect hail of machine gun bullets - they let us have it properly; still we kept on and soon reached the German trenches. Most Germans turned tail and bolted, and we had some fine sport bringing them down. About four of us in five minutes turned about twenty out, eleven of them in one dugout.

Here are some comments from L/Cpl R Thorpe-Tracey, who was a member of D Company. about his experiences both before and during the battle:

> The trench digging we carried out prior to the battle was all done at night. The Battalion moved to the front line and a certain number were detailed as guards, others as diggers. We all went out in No Man's Land, the guards would be posted and when this had been carried out the diggers would dig frantically at first so as to get some sort of cover. I seem to recall some German activity, Very

lights and machine gun fire together with some artillery rounds, but it did not really disrupt the digging.

Then a few days before the 25th we were issued with extra stores, most men either got a picks or shovel and everyone got three empty sandbags, 2 Mills bombs, an extra iron ration together with ammunition and a gas helmet. Then on the 24th we were briefed by the Company Commander - Captain Meyer, we were told D Company would follow A, B and C and consolidate the German front line. One of the most important things we were told was that if we found a wounded man with a tool to take it off him and make sure it got to the German lines. Also any artillery signalling discs found on wounded men must be collected. Finally we were given a gas briefing.

Then on the morning of the 25th it was our turn to go over the top. I remember having difficulty in breathing and was stumbling along. After a few minutes of this I thought I would sniff the air, it didn't seem too bad to me so I took my helmet off. I thought I was completely alone in No Man's Land but then I started to stumble on wounded men - three of them. From them I collected as I recall a shovel, a pick and an artillery disc. So weighed down with all this extra kit I carried on towards the German lines, then when I got to within about 20 yards of their wire, I realised there may still be some Germans there and I wouldn't be able to fight with all this extra kit so I threw it aside.

I got to the German front line and it seemed much deeper than our trenches and I thought it was unoccupied, although very quickly other members of D Company appeared and we started work in consolidating the position. There was soon a shortage of sandbags so a working party was organised to scrounge these from men in the old No Man's Land. Then on another occasion one of my soldiers said to me "Corporal, there's some Germans in this dugout." So I said "Well, get them out!" The reply came back "Corporal, they won't come out." So I then said "Well, we'll see about that." It seemed that there were two entrances/exits to this particular dugout so I posted two men at one of them and I went down the other with one other man, I led with my bayonet fixed and he had a grenade ready. I shouted down "Anybody there?" A reply came in reasonable English - "Yes." I said "How many?" The response to this question was "Two." So I ordered them to come out one at a time and we retired to the dugout entrance, eventually nine Germans appeared, we took possession of their very fine helmets and any official documents and then sent them back under escort to the rear.

Later on that day the 8th Londons were sent forward to support them. The German defenders reacted quite quickly and a counter-attack was made on the right flank of the 7th Londons from south of the Crassier. The brunt of this attack fell upon A Company of the 7th Battalion commanded by Major W. Casson. Several attacks were repulsed helped by bombers from the 8th Battalion, and gradually a firm foothold was established on the Crassier but at a high cost. Out of 18 officers from the 7th Battalion who took part in the attack, 14 became casualties, including 10 killed, of whom Major Casson was one. He now lies in Loos CWGC Cemetery. Later that day the Battalion's Padre buried 87 men from the unit including Major Casson. He later wrote:

Bill Casson's only thought was for the Regiment and for the well being of his men. He was a perfect type of Regimental Officer, absolutely selfless, untiring,

Loos Memorial Cross to the 6th London Regt in St Sepulchre without Newgate Church in the City of London. The cross stood upon the battlefield for over three years before being replaced by a more permanent one in 1919. (Neil Bright)

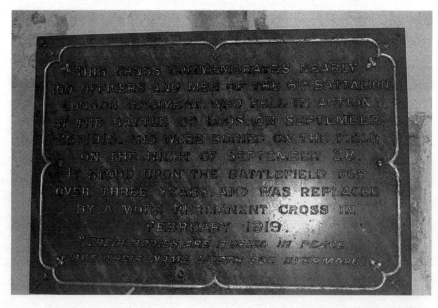

Headstone of Major W. Casson, 7th Londons,
in Loos Cemetery. (Richard Howells)

utterly loyal and completely fearless in battle, with an acute sense of humour and enjoyment of the simple things in life which made him the vast number of friends who felt that his death left a gap impossible to fill.

Major Casson also got a mention that day in the 140th Brigade's War Diary:

A determined effort was made by the enemy from the south of the Double Crassier to drive the 7th Battalion from the first line trenches captured, chiefly by means of grenadiers working round the point of the Double Crassier. The attempt was defeated by the promptitude with which Captain Casson commanding A Company of the 7th Battalion led his men against the Germans coming over and round the south western edge of the Double Crassier, and by the rapid reinforcement of this point with the grenadiers of two companies of the 8th Battalion.

Part of the 8th London Regiment's War Diary entry for 25th September is as follows:

Tower Bridge, with the Loos Crassier stretching out below it. (IWM Q43123)

Loos village, with the Loos Crassier overlooking it. (IWM Q 43114)

At 6.30am a slight wind being just sufficient to enable gas and smoke to have been used since 5.50am the 6th and 7th Battalions London Regiment left their trenches and successfully assaulted the Double Crassier and first and second line of German trenches to the north. The Battalion immediately occupied the trenches vacated by these Battalions and held themselves in readiness to support. A German bombing counter attack seriously threatened the right flank of the 7th Battalion and sections of 2 and 3 companies were ordered up in support.

Another present here was Corporal F. Moylan, who was a member of C Company of the 7th Londons, in the second wave. This is his account:

A and B companies took the front line. C and D were to go through them and take the second one. I was in C. We had the furthest to go. Now, war is peculiar. C Company had the fewest casualties and went the furthest distance. B Company lost every officer - the whole lot on the right, a hell of a lot, got killed. We were lucky. We'd found gaps in the wire. It was all a matter of luck.

We went up the night before this attack. We were pretty tight in the trench and we sat down on the floor of it. I'd got somebody in between his legs and somebody else behind me had got me in between his legs. There was a fellow named Brockhurst behind me and a man named Emersfield in front of me and Emersfield got cramp and it meant we both had to get up and we changed positions. I was in front then and Emersfield was in the middle. We had ladders in the trench to go up, and when it came to the time we went over and we hadn't got very far when this chap Emersfield flopped down. Must have been a machine gun bullet. Of course, he was where I would have been if we hadn't changed places! I remember thinking that as I saw him go down.

In an attack the whole thing seems a bit like a dream. It doesn't take as long as you think. Crossing No Man's Land, you imagine beforehand what a hell of a journey that's going to be - but it's not, and either the Germans are dead or there's no one there. There were a lot of our dead in No Man's Land as we crossed and more at the places where they'd arrived at the wire and it wasn't cut. Then they were just sitting ducks. We just went through gaps in the wire, but we weren't in the first wave luckily.

We got to the German front line and they were mopping it up - there were prisoners there being mustered, and there were dead lying about. Then we got to the second line and they'd gone from there. Where we were the gas blew over the Germans and that may have driven them out of that second line. There were some dugouts there and we went down one of them - deep, long, steep it was, very well made - and I got a terrific fright then. It was pitch black and we were just feeling our way. Somebody had a glimmer of light ahead but where I was it was really dark, and I suddenly felt this arm grabbing me and pulling me flat in the dark. I toppled right over. I nearly died of fright. I must have yelled out because someone struck a light, and there was a wounded German, lying there in the dark. He was alive but somebody must have thrown a bomb down there. He got peppered all over and he was a mass of dried blood. He was calling for his mother and for water. He was muttering, "Mutter, Mutter, Wasser." We got him out and it was a hell of a job up those stairs, and when we got him out it was raining. We laid him out in the trench there and he was taken away after a while.

When we got back in the trench I saw the most extraordinary thing happen. I got up to look over - it was quite safe, because the fighting was a good bit ahead - and there were civilians knocking about. Loos village was on our left, and suddenly out came these civilians. Of course they were shepherded away as quickly as possible but I remember seeing an old woman wounded, hobbling along and thinking that she must have been shot in the leg. There was a whole bunch of them, at least a dozen, maybe more.

By around 8.00am all of the 140th Brigade's objectives had been taken together with nearly 300 prisoners and three machine guns. On their left was the 141st Brigade, with further to go than their sister brigade. This Brigade's attack was led by the 18th Battalion, or the London Irish Rifles. Their objective was the German second line from the Loos-Béthune road (where they joined up with the 6th Battalion) to Loos Cemetery. Two battalions followed behind them, the 19th on the left and the 20th on the right, with the intention of passing through the London Irish at their objective. After this the 19th Battalion were to take the Cemetery, the southern edge of Loos village and Tower Bridge. The 20th were directed towards features south of Loos - a copse and Chalk Pit, a small enclosed 'garden city' and a Crassier running south-east towards Lens from Tower Bridge. In reserve was the 17th Battalion.

The London Irish Rifles started off by kicking a football in front of them, a feat which, of course, was repeated the following year on the Somme. No Man's Land was crossed without much difficulty but casualties started to be suffered at the German front line. But they pressed on to the second German line which, although it had a thick belt of barbed wire in front of it, had few defenders in it. On their right, the 20th Battalion successfully advanced up to the garden city which was quickly taken. A Company of the 20th successfully advanced to the Chalk Pit. The German barbed wire here was uncut, so the 20th Londons bombed the Germans out and in the process captured two field guns, which were displayed a few weeks later on Horse Guards Parade in London. So far so good, nearly everything had gone to plan, and the famous Army saying of 'Prior Planning and Preparation Prevents Poor Performance' was coming true. The northern end of Chalk Pit Copse was also entered, but then a snag arose. Men from the German 26th Regiment equipped with at least two machine guns were stubbornly holding a section of trench in the southern part of the Copse astride the Béthune-Lens road and resisted all efforts to dislodge them. Owing to a shortage of bombs, it was decided to leave this position alone for the time being and a line close up to it was consolidated. By 9.30am the 20th Battalion, which had been reinforced by a company and some machine guns from the 17th Battalion, was able to report back that they were firmly established in the Chalk Pit, had taken all their objectives except the southern edge of Chalk Pit Copse, and as previously planned had positioned a Platoon astride the Loos Crassier, and they had been in position since 7.45am.

The 19th Battalion had had a hard fight for the Loos Cemetery, but fought their way through and joined up with men from the 15th Division in clearing houses in the village of Loos. Two officers from the 19th Londons won gallantry awards in the village. Both were the DSO, and one of these was a rare award to a Lieutenant. He was Lieutenant F. Pusch who was awarded his for gallantry during bombing operations in the village; sadly he was killed later in the war. He died as a

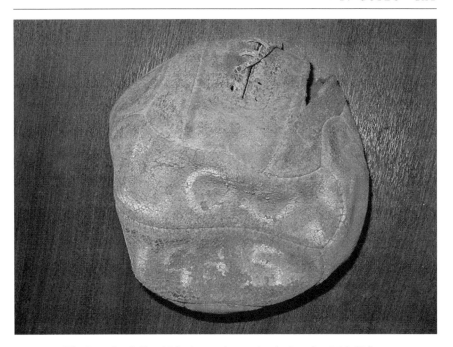

The Loos football as kicked over the top by the London Irish Rifles.
(London Irish Rifles Regimental Museum)

View across No Man's Land over which the London Irish Rifles kicked their football.
(Peter Boalch)

Lieutenant with the 1st Battalion Irish Guards in the Ypres sector on 27th June 1916 and was buried at Essex Farm CWGC Cemetery, perhaps one of the more famous and most visited cemeteries on the Western Front. The other was Major E Blogg of the 4th London Field Company RE, who defused several mines in the church.

Unfortunately, in the village, men became intermixed and communication started to break down. The CO of the 19th Battalion, Lieutenant-Colonel C. Collison-Morley, was killed shortly after leaving the British front line, and Lieutenant-Colonel A. Hubback of the 20th Battalion assumed control of both units - not always an easy operation. Soon after 9.00am all objectives except those in Chalk Pit Copse had been taken, but for various reasons the 47th Division, although not a spent force, was facing difficulties. The rest of the day was spent in consolidating the positions captured and beating off a few local counter-attacks, notably on the Double Crassier, Chalk Pit Copse and the south-east corner of Loos village. The defenders were helped by artillery support previously arranged in anticipation of the counter-attacks. The Division suffered over 1,400 casualties for 25th September, the majority of these being in the attacking battalions and again the majority occurring early in the attack:

Table 4.1
47th Division casualties (all London Regiment), 25th September

	Officers	*Other Ranks*	*Total*
6th Battalion	7	274	281
7th Battalion	14	250	264
18th Battalion	9	235	244
19th Battalion	14	372	386
20th Battalion	9	162	171
Overall Totals	53	1293	1346

The difficulties alluded to earlier which will be examined soon, stemmed from the pre-planned notion that a German counter-attack might develop west of the Loos Crassier. Additionally the depleted 19th Battalion on the left flank of the Division, and the failure to extend the defensive flank to cover the 15th Division were all to have serious repercussions. I would like to end this look at the actions of the 47th Division by quoting Major-General Barter, who later wrote about the gas and smoke cloud:

> The enemy opened heavy rifle and machine gun fire immediately the gas was launched, but the fire was very wild and high and gradually died down: our assault coming up behind the thick curtain of gas and smoke practically took the enemy by surprise. There is no doubt that the success of our assault was entirely due to the gas and smoke attack, which, if it affected nothing more, formed a screen to cover the attacking troops.

It is now the time to look at the actions of the division to the north of the 47th - the 15th Division.

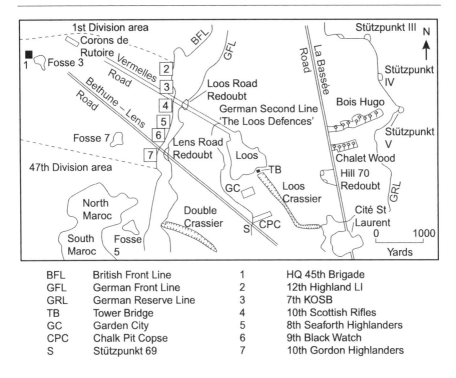

BFL	British Front Line	1	HQ 45th Brigade
GFL	German Front Line	2	12th Highland LI
GRL	German Reserve Line	3	7th KOSB
TB	Tower Bridge	4	10th Scottish Rifles
GC	Garden City	5	8th Seaforth Highlanders
CPC	Chalk Pit Copse	6	9th Black Watch
S	Stützpunkt 69	7	10th Gordon Highlanders

Map 7: 15th Division area of attack, 25th September 1915

This Division, the 15th (Scottish) Division, was a Kitchener New Army one, being a K2 Division, the first of the second block of six to be raised. It was composed entirely of Scottish battalions being formed at Aldershot in September 1914 and crossed to France in July 1915. It consisted of 12 battalions from some of the famous Scottish formations such as the Royal Scots, King's Own Scottish Borderers, Argyll and Sutherland Highlanders, Gordon Highlanders and Seaforth Highlanders. One small problem seems to have been the allocation of support weapons. The Brigade Major of the 45th Brigade, Major E. Beck, wrote post-war: "The supply of machine guns had run short before the 15th Division went overseas, we therefore had to be content with Lewis guns allocated 12 per Battalion."

On 25th September 1915 this Division, commanded by Major-General F. McCracken, was responsible for an attacking front of around 1,500 yards from a line either side of the Béthune-Lens road and the Vermelles-Loos road. In keeping with a lot of other plans it was a two-up attack, with the 44th and 46th brigades in the leading wave. The plan was for these two brigades to rush and capture the Lens Road and Loos Road Redoubts and then to push on eastwards towards the village of Loos. The Germans attached considerable importance to the village of Loos, which although it was in a depression, it still held the key to the commanding heights of Hill 70 to the east of the village. The Germans had dug extra defences on the western side of the village, which the British called the 'Loos Defences'. This was a continuous trench line interspersed with strong points and machine gun positions. A notorious strong point in this line was known as Fort Glatz, which dominated the area around the Vermelles road as it entered Loos. Even so it was thought by British Intelligence that there were only around two companies (400 men) from the 157th Regiment defending the area, so there was a high ratio in favour of the attackers. After the leading two brigades had cleared the village of Loos they were to head towards Hill 70. Local objectives were then to neutralise Hill 70 Redoubt - this being the right hand flank's task with the left being on the mine buildings of Puits 14 bis. The orders then became a little vague, with the plan being that the first brigade to reach the Lens road, which passes over the top of Hill 70, was to leave behind sufficient forces (probably a battalion) to consolidate the position for defence, whilst the remainder of the two brigades were to carry on almost due east to the village of Cité St Auguste. The portion of the 46th Brigade at Puits 14 was to advance eastwards along a track between Chalet Wood and Bois Hugo.

These then were the first set of objectives, the second was to take the German second line, which, to quote the Official History, skirted "the western edge of the northern suburbs of Lens, Cité St Laurent, then turned sharp to the eastwards for 1,200 yards across the Lens-La Bassée road to Cité St Auguste." The Germans had also taken advantage of some reverse slopes to site defences on Hill 70 and then northwards past the eastern ends of Chalet Wood and Bois Hugo. Near Hulluch the line formed another big flank by turning westward and then round the village. If the planners knew that the 15th Division, after crossing the crest of Hill 70, might be under enfilade fire from both left and right flanks during the advance towards Cité St Auguste, they kept it quiet. After passing through Cité St Auguste the attackers from the 15th Division were to take the village of Loison and Annay about another 1½ miles away. No notice or plans were made for the defences in the north of Lens, as it was believed the Germans would by now be either on the run or simply not have enough men to hold them in any strength.

The units selected to lead the attacks were from the 44th Brigade, the 9th Black Watch and the 8th Seaforth Highlanders, while the lead units for the 46th were the 10th Scottish Rifles and the 7th King's Own Scottish Borderers, supported by two companies of the 12th Highland Light Infantry. I will refer to them as the Scottish Rifles to avoid confusion with the Cameron Highlanders, as strictly speaking the Scottish Rifles should be called the Cameronians. It was also intended for some close artillery support to be available and at least one gun from A Battery of the 236th Brigade RFA were involved in this. Here is the story as told by Battery member Bombardier A Dunbar:

> After a busy time at Festubert and Givenchy my battery came into action from Vermelles, near the main road from Béthune to Loos. Preparations were obviously in hand for a big push. From our battery positions we could see the towers of the Hulluch mine workings, part of Hill 70 and the Double Crassier nearby. Beyond this and out of sight was the town of Loos. We suspected that it would be one of the objectives in the attack. My gun was detached from the battery and was to be used only on the day of the opening attack for cutting the wire of the enemy's trenches to provide spaces through which our Infantry could advance. For this to be effective the gun had to be taken as near to the target as possible so that the trajectory of the shrapnel shell and its bullets would be almost

parallel to the ground when the shell burst so as to do the maximum damage to the wire.

Alongside the main road and about a mile in front of the other guns of the battery was a row of houses (or partly demolished houses) and their backs looked across open ground to the front line trenches. Between the German and our front line the distance was about 60 yards. One of these houses had a ground floor room intact and from the corner of the house we could look straight across to the wire about 400 yards away. My gun was brought up at night and after cutting through the back wall of the room we positioned it facing the back corner. We then made a right-angled frame of wood and covered this with canvas which we painted to resemble bricks. We cut out the bricks in the corner and replaced them with our dummy - hoping that the Germans wouldn't see the deception. But I went up to our front line the next day and I couldn't distinguish our dummy wall from the real bricks even with binoculars. It was perfect match and this was on the 15th September.

We got about 200 rounds of shrapnel and a few HE shells and put plenty of sandbags around the gun and the inside walls of the room. After three or four days a bombardment started up and it seemed that all the guns for miles were taking part except us.

On the morning of the 25th just before dawn we pulled aside the false walls of the ruined cottage and ran the muzzle forward into the opening and started work. Through my telescopic sight I had an excellent view of the target and I could pick out the section of wire I wanted to cut. This was the first occasion I had used direct firing and I found it much more interesting than laying on an aiming post and never seeing the target.

After firing about 50 rounds, I noticed that my eyes were beginning to water and before long I could hardly see at all. I put this down to the fumes of the cordite which came from the breech every time it was opened.

We will return to Bombardier Dunbar shortly.

Here are some extracts from the Divisional Order for the attack:

Assaulting Columns
a) The assault will be delivered by four columns, two from each of the leading brigades. Each column will consist of one battalion (with machine guns), one Section RE, and one platoon 9th Gordon Highlanders (the Divisional pioneers), and will be formed up in depth on a front of two platoons.

b) The task of the assaulting columns will be to move straight forward to their ultimate objective. Parties for cutting wire, blocking side trenches and bombing down communication trenches, will be told off from the leading two companies. Assaulting columns will not be entrusted with the tasks of occupying and consolidating positions won, or of digging communications back to our own trenches; these tasks will be allotted to parties told off from the Brigade reserves (who were to work under the direction of the CRE-Lieutenant-Colonel G Cartwright). The assaulting columns must push on.

c) The fourth company in each column will carry a proportion of picks and shovels; the RE Section will carry explosives for hasty demolition; the platoon of the 9th Gordon Highlanders will carry six sandbags per man and tools.

These then were the brief instructions for the attack of the 15th Division, with the usual gas and smoke discharge preceding the assault. It must be said here with the benefit of hindsight that the wind in the 15th Division sector was in parachuting terms very marginal. Indeed the War Diary for the 15th Division itself says: "The troops were wondering if the wind conditions justified the gas discharge." An Officer with the Special Companies here, Lieutenant Charles, gave the orders to start the gas and smoke at Zero. He later recounted:

The Germans, who had not fired a shot all night, immediately plastered our parapet with shrapnel, machine gun and rifle fire. The shrapnel did a large amount of damage to our pipes, and, through this fact and the eagerness of the men to turn on the gas before tightening up the connections, our trench was very soon filled with gas. The infantry in the trenches, finding the heat inside their smoke helmets trying and experiencing some difficulty in breathing, were inclined to draw them up to get a couple of breaths of fresh air, with the result that quite a number of them were more or less seriously gassed. Directly these men found themselves coughing they wrenched their helmets off and staggered down the trench, making it very difficult for us to work or even to work at all. Also at this period the wind changed slightly and some of the smoke poured down the trench.

Back at the house Bombardier Dunbar recalled his first experiences with gas:

The others didn't seem affected so I thought that the extra strain of laying was responsible for the trouble with my eyes. I changed places with my number 2, but after a few rounds he was crying his eyes out. Just then we became aware of a beautiful smell of lilac filling the room. This was the last thing we expected. Perhaps there was a field of lilac nearby and a changing wind had brought the smell to us. We were puzzled.

We managed to continue firing by frequently swapping places. We hoped our infantry were keeping their heads well down when we were cutting their wire. With fuses correctly set and with such a flat trajectory there was not much risk of bullets going into our own trenches. At Zero plus 30 we ceased fire. We had fired about 150 rounds and blown some useful gaps in the wire on both sides.

It was against this sort of background that the leading waves from both attacking brigades climbed over the parapet at 6.30am. An account written at the time said: "The effects of the white clouds of smoke rolling slowly towards the enemy trenches was extraordinary. It looked as if a curtain, stabbed here and there with red bursts of shrapnel, had come down across the Division's front." Within seconds men had disappeared from sight, and it seemed as if the advance would falter as on the left hand side many men from the 46th Brigade had suffered from the effects of the gas and others bunched at places clear of gas bays in an effort to avoid the cloud. An officer, Lieutenant Lovell from the 10th Scottish Rifles, who went over the top in the fifth wave, claimed later that the wind was actually blowing towards the British lines. The situation seemingly was saved by the actions of just one man - Piper D. Laidlaw from the 7th KOSB. According to contemporary sources at 6.30am, when the order was given to attack, nobody moved. Piper Laidlaw who was standing close to his Company Officer Second Lieutenant M. Young heard him shout: 'For God's sake, Laidlaw, pipe 'em together!' Ignoring the gas and enemy shelling Laidlaw got over the parapet with Second Lieutenant Young and started to march up and down the 7th KOSB frontage playing the Regimental March *Blue Bonnets O'er The Border*. I am reminded here to say that almost exactly 29 years later on 17th September 1944 Piper Willie Ford played the same march to rally the 7th KOSB on Landing Zone S at Wolfheze in Holland at the start of Operation Market-Garden.

Galvanised by the sound of the pipes, and Young's urgings, the KOSB finally went over the top and advanced into No Man's Land. Other troops from the 46th

Piper Daniel Laidlaw VC 7th KOSB.
(KOSB Regimental Museum)

Brigade, the 10th Scottish Rifles and 12th Highland Light Infantry, followed close behind. Laidlaw continued to march up and down and incredibly was not hit whilst playing on his own in No Man's Land. He then headed towards the German lines, playing all the time. As he neared the German lines he was hit in the left leg and ankle. In spite of this he continued to limp along, changing the tune to *The Standard on the Braes O'Mar* before being hit for a second time again in the left leg. Laidlaw later said: "I kept on piping and piping, and hobbling after the laddies until I could go no further, and then, seeing that the boys had won the position, I began to get back as best I could to our own trenches." He also dragged his bagpipes back with him too. It is said Laidlaw had been wounded by shrapnel from a shell which also wounded Second Lieutenant Young, but he insisted on walking back to a dressing station rather than being carried by stretcher bearers. Sadly, Young died from his wounds the next day, he is now buried at Noeux-les-Mines CWGC Cemetery. Another account from someone who was there, although from the 6th Cameron Highlanders, who were in support of the 7th KOSB, said, "I heard quite clearly a piper piping them into action. It was an act of intense bravery under

Piper Laidlaw's present day headstone at Norham, Northumberland.
(Les McKerrichter)

intensive fire. As we passed through the KOSBs I saw a badly wounded piper sitting on the ground in a severe state."

Happily though, Laidlaw survived, and he was promoted to Corporal for distinguished service in the field. Perhaps more importantly he was recommended for and awarded a Victoria Cross. Part of his citation reads: "During the worst of the bombardment, Piper Laidlaw, seeing that his Company was shaken from the effects of gas, with absolute coolness and disregard of danger, mounted the parapet, marched up and down, and played his Company out of the trench."

Laidlaw survived the war and died in June 1950, and was buried in Norham Churchyard, Northumberland. The KOSB Regimental Association placed a plaque to his memory in the Church, but, until June 2001, he strangely laid in an unmarked grave. His grandson Daniel Laidlaw decided that something had to be done and on 2nd June 2001 a dedication service was held and a headstone placed over his grave. The Pipe-Major of the 1st Battalion KOSB, Pipe-Major E. Stuart, played *Blue Bonnets O'er The Border* and *The Standard on the Braes O'Mar* - the 'Piper of Loos' as Laidlaw had become known at last had a fitting memorial.

So, an unpromising position had been rescued by the actions of a few men and the troops steadily advanced across No Man's Land. Just before reaching the German wire they were spotted by machine gunners in the Loos Road and Lens Road Redoubts. For a few minutes (or so it seemed) withering fire was poured onto the Jocks causing many casualties. Fortunately the wire had been well cut and the attackers were able to get into the German trenches and neutralise the redoubts and the small number of German soldiers in the front line. In accordance with their orders they did not stop here but pressed on towards the Loos defences, albeit with less numbers and some of the troops being mixed up with other units - a good example of the Fog of War.

An officer present was later to record the following about the conduct of the men from the 15th Division as they advanced across No Man's Land:

It was magnificent. I could not have imagined that troops with a bare twelve month's training behind them could have accomplished it. As the men reached our wire they made their way through it with perfect coolness and deliberation, in spite of the enemy's increasingly heavy rifle fire. Once in No Man's Land they took up their dressing and walked - yes, coolly walked - across towards the enemy trenches. There was no running or shouting; here and there a man finding himself out of line would double for a pace or two, look to his right and left, take up his dressing and continue the advance at a steady walk. The effect of these seemingly unconcerned Highlanders advancing upon them must have a considerable effect on the Germans. I saw one man whose kilt had got caught in our wire as he passed through a gap; he did not attempt to tear it off, but, carefully disentangling it, doubled up to his correct position in the line and went on.

It was in this sort of scene that the Jocks pressed on over the open 1,000 yards towards the Loos defences on the outskirts of the village, using as a reference point the twin landmarks of Tower Bridge, slowly appearing through the mist. Around 7.00am, the area of the Loos defences was reached. Here they were lucky because the defences were unmanned, if not I suspect heavy casualties would have been sustained. The barbed wire in front of these defences had only been partially cut and a

Picture taken 30th September 1915. It is likely this road was on the route taken by the
9th Black Watch and the 18th Londons (London Irish Rifles) into Loos.
(IWM Q28987)

small delay occurred. This gave the opportunity for some German machine gun
positions to open fire from the flanks. One position was in a house east of the Cemetery and another in Fort Glatz. However they were soon overrun and the troops
entered the village of Loos. It is believed the units from the 46th Brigade - the 9th
Black Watch and the 8th Seaforth Highlanders followed by the 7th Cameron
Highlanders - were the first troops into the village and they found a scene of confusion. It seemed the Germans had not expected the front line defences to fall so
quickly and were completely unbalanced by the appearance of British troops in the
village. Many Germans remained hidden in the cellars of houses, some for several
days. Valuable time was spent searching and clearing houses, while other Germans
put up a spirited resistance, but weight of numbers, cold steel and bombs overcame
their efforts. However some Germans had already fled, some to the village of Cité
St Laurent, and others, probably in greater numbers, to the heights of Hill 70 and
the Redoubt near the top. Here is a comment from the War Diary of the 7th
Cameron Highlanders about the street fighting in Loos:

> In Loos itself there were still parties going about bombing and bayoneting Ger-
> mans running out of houses, and also taking prisoners. I sheltered behind a
> strongly built house close to Loos church, but was heavily shelled and went in
> search of cellars. I found one which was occupied by Germans, who were killed,
> and this was used as my HQ for a quarter of an hour. When one of my men
> came along with a Vermorel sprayer I sent him to the lower cellar of the house,

where a German officer was found still telephoning to the enemy. He was killed.

But nothing could stop the flow of the Jocks through the village, and in the southern part of the village men from the Black Watch and Cameron Highlanders steadily advanced. Some slight resistance was met in the village square near the church but this was also swept aside. Heading on past the pylons of Tower Bridge, meeting some men from the 19th Londons, they pushed on to the eastern side of the village. By around 8.00am all of Loos village was in British hands, the Seaforths having cleared the northern parts of the village.

Meanwhile, slightly north of Loos, the 46th Brigade was also performing relatively well. Their initial objective had been Loos Road Redoubt and then to head north of Loos towards Puits 14 bis and the small copses east of the La Bassée road. The most northern battalion, the 7th KOSB, after recovering from their initial setbacks, and supported by a company from the 12th HLI, made steady progress into German-held territory. Six abandoned field guns were discovered and slowly the ever-growing sight of Puits 14 bis guided them towards this objective and the Lens-La Bassée road and Bois Hugo. In the early part of the advance patrols were sent northwards in an attempt to get in touch with the right flank of the 1st Division, but no contact was made. Around 8.30am the 7th KOSB, wheeled to the right to conform with the operational plan and a message from Major T. Glenny, timed at 9.15am, recorded: "Have reached 300 yards south of Puits 14 bis. Going strongly. Have halted for another blow as our artillery are firing a bit short. Shall push on again immediately." This message was most likely sent from the area of the Lens road.

Meanwhile on their immediate right the 10th Scottish Rifles had gone past the trenches east of the Grenay-Hulluch road, when they came under small arms fire from the northern houses of Loos. Eventually men from the 44th Brigade overrunning the positions stopped this fire, but, quite naturally, a number of men deviated from their 'proper' line of attack and headed towards Loos village, around a company actually entering the village. They became mixed up with the 8th Seaforths and ended up taking part in the fighting there. This was only the start of the difficulties faced by the 15th Division. Just to go back in time a little, it is easy to see with hindsight how things went wrong. One of the lead units, the 8th Seaforth Highlanders, had to change their plan almost immediately after H Hour, as this comment from their War Diary shows:

Captain A. Ravenhill killed on the parapet smiling as he helped his men out to the attack; and the two leading platoons of A Company followed by the two remaining platoons swept down on the German trenches. It seems as if uncertainty arose among some of the men, owing to the unfavourable conditions that drew back the gas, if the attack was to proceed. The Officer Commanding decided to later his intentions regarding his own movements and to convey the assurance to all that the attack was on, he, himself, now proceeded over the parapet at the head of B Company instead of at the head of C as planned.

Company now followed after company without hitch, until - within, indeed, only a few minutes after starting - the whole Battalion was launched to the attack. The failure to have a definite policy in the event of any misfunction or abandonment of the gas programme being necessary or, appearing to be necessary was to be regretted. Known to all, this could have avoided all uncertainty, and left the attack free from the danger of being robbed of vigour and decision, when these features were most necessary. As it was, the gas programme was adhered to in circumstances which seemed unfavourable. It was a question, therefore, whether on balance it was an advantage or disadvantage to the attack. With reference to our own men, gas calculated to give confidence to the leading troops as giving them the assurance of everything preceding them in the run of the assault, but on the other hand, the doubtful success of the gas owing to unfavourable nature of wind must have robbed the moral effect of some of the force; and the casualties it caused in our ranks were a positive and palpable factor against it.

The four reserve battalions from the 44th and 46th brigades had been called forward, and the 10th Gordon Highlanders from the 44th Brigade were prominent in the rush forward. It is recorded that the Gordons somehow managed to meet up with the original attackers before they reached the eastern side of Loos. The reserve from the 46th Brigade had originally been tasked with keeping up close behind the 12th HLI and keeping the advance going. Now that the battle was underway, they were sent forward in independent company groups. One company losing their way ended up joining the 10th Scottish Rifles on the eastern side of Loos, but the others appeared to navigate correctly. They were sent to south of Puits 14 bis, to provide a flank guard for the left of the Division, as it was recognised that the Division had lost direction.

Meanwhile in the village of Loos, soon after 8.00am, there was a bunching of units from the 44th and 46th brigades with companies and platoons becoming intermingled. However, the men knew what they had to do, and streamed out of Loos and began to climb up Hill 70. I am reluctant to use the words "they advanced in a somewhat leisurely manner", but the War Diary of the 8th Seaforth Highlanders said: "The spirit of the attack relaxed, a kind of holiday mood came over the men." It is believed there were about 1,500 men in this group. This was in some respects good but in the confusion the whole thrust of the 15th Division was now drifting south-east instead of east. This body of men advanced straight up the slope. The confusion is well summed up in the War Diary of the 8th Seaforths:

> In advancing the village of Loos and Crassier behind the pylons seemed to exercise a bad fascination on the firing line. The line also was inclined to the right by the desire to get in touch with the London Division. The result was that the Seaforth Highlanders and Black Watch mixed up with the Gordons and Camerons left the German work at H31 Central on their left and advanced on the Cité St Laurent rather than the Cité St Auguste. The right of the line emerged directly on Puits 12, where its further advance was impossible owing to the fact that our heavy artillery was shelling the mine and apparently searching for a battery right up against which we had arrived and which continued to fire in our immediate neighbourhood until one gun was knocked out by one of our shells. As advance was obviously impossible here the line then inclined to the left and directed its attack against a position extending from Puits 12 to the Dynamitière at N.1.B.1.2.. The Dynamitière was strongly held by machine guns and our guns began wasting their ammunition at this point.

Meanwhile back at Divisional HQ, as things seemed to be going well based on reports received, the 74th Field Company RE and the 180th Tunnelling Company RE were ordered forward to start bridging trenches and prepare tracks so that the field artillery could advance.

Now another factor came into play: poor staff work. It should be added that many of the Division's staff were still finding their feet with regard to the actual fighting. It is clear with hindsight, that there was ambiguity in the orders of the sub-units of the 15th Division as to the movements of their sister division, the 47th, further south. It was not made sufficiently clear that the 47th Division was to halt after reaching the Loos and Double Crassiers. The 44th Brigade orders mentioned that the 47th Division was to form a defensive flank, and gave its objectives, but did not say that these were its final objectives. The 46th Brigade orders said that the 47th Division would be attacking on the right of the 15th Division with no further information. It is clear that many officers from the 15th Division believed that during their advance to Cité St Auguste and beyond, their right flank would be covered by a simultaneous advance by the Londoners through and beyond the northern part of Loos.

The leading company of the 9th Black Watch on the extreme right flank therefore right wheeled as it emerged from Loos towards the Loos Crassier, expecting to make contact with men from the 47th Division. It had expected to find them around the southern end of the Crassier and also north of it, but the battalion

German bunker still situated on Hill 70 looking towards the village of Loos.
(Peter Boalch)

detailed for this job, the 19th Londons, had been split apart. One company was at the north end of the Crassier rather than the southern, while the other three companies were in Loos village and a few men even approaching Hill 70. When some of the 9th Black Watch arrived at the southern end of the Crassier, they decided to occupy the crest about 200 yards from Fosse 12. About a platoon's worth of men were also sent forward to take up a defensive position facing south along the railway embankment that ran between the Fosse and what was known as Dynamitière - a building used to store explosives used in the mining operations, but turned into a German strong point in front of their second line defences. It is thought that this action, even though intended to be a temporary measure, pulled the attention of the Division in a southerly direction.

Back at the outskirts of Loos and Hill 70 the sight of Germans in apparent disarray running away and disappearing over the southern side of the hill was enough to raise the Jocks' blood and make them head in the same direction. Instead of advancing with the right flank on Hill 70 Redoubt, the 44th Brigade moved with its left flank there and its right along the Loos Crassier. Meanwhile the 46th Brigade, instead of leaving its left flank on the Loos-Cité St Auguste track, swung round astride the Lens-La Bassée road, while their right flank unit, the 10th Scottish Rifles, was heading towards Hill 70 Redoubt (the right half) and their left near the Bois Hugo. Meanwhile the actions of a few Germans almost certainly caused more confusion and deviation from the plan.

These few Germans occupying Hill 70 Redoubt, guessing that they were heavily outnumbered by the troops streaming out of Loos village, decided to withdraw to Cité St Laurent. It is reported that as they ran south towards this village, they could be seen by many of the men from the 44th Brigade as they neared the crest of Hill 70. These men cheered, which seemed to raise the blood even further of those not near Hill 70 and gave a further push towards the south. Then the fog of war descended again with word going around the 46th Brigade, as they were swinging round south of Bois Hugo, that the 44th Brigade had captured a village, meaning Loos. But unfortunately almost directly in their line of sight was Cité St Auguste and a number of soldiers could be seen entering the village. The British thought they were their own troops, but they were in fact Germans. Nevertheless the 46th Brigade headed straight for Cité St Auguste but soon came under small arms fire from there and the trenches in front of it.

Here is an account from a member of the 10th Gordon Highlanders in the 44th Brigade, Sergeant J. Cavers:

> On the morning of the 25th we attacked. Our objectives were enemy redoubt Béthune-Lens road, first and second line trenches, Loos village and Hill 70. The Battalion went forward as Brigade reserve, but we found ourselves in the front line at the village. The whole Brigade had suffered heavily from enemy barrage and machine gun posts. The street fighting was very hot, barricades were climbed, houses bombed and enemy detachments made prisoner. We carried our advance to Hill 70, where we encountered an enemy redoubt on the crest. When this obstacle had been disposed of we advanced over the hill towards Cité St Auguste. Here we found the enemy busily manning the houses. Our Lewis gunners accounted for a good many of them. The enemy opened machine gun fire on our open position and we were compelled to make head cover. During a

lull we tried advancing by short rushes with the intention of clearing the enemy from the houses, but we did not count on the volume of fire poured into us from the houses in front and from those on the right. We were consequently unable to execute more than two short rushes. When what was left of our line dropped to take cover we found ourselves right on the enemy position but separated from them by barbed wire.

After this I found myself with three or four casualties on either side of me: our Lewis gunners were knocked out and the enemy was enfilading us from the right. We could only hold our ground and wait for night to relieve us from our untenable position. Our rifle fire got weaker as the day wore on and I could not communicate with my right or left. Later in the day the enemy counter-attacked us from the right flank.

The situation now became even more confused: the advance was off track, the summit of Hill 70 had been crested and the men began to move down the slope with a few going in the correct direction to Cité St Auguste, the majority headed for Cité St Laurent, about 600 yards away. The men were heading into a pocket of German defences bounded by Cité St Laurent, Bois Hugo and Cité St Auguste. From these positions a murderous crossfire developed causing many casualties. Some of the surviving commanders realising the danger managed to regroup behind the crest line of Hill 70 with about 400 men.

Some of the messages sent back by the 44th Brigade to Divisional HQ showed that many were unaware of the change of direction. One surviving message said that they could see the village of Cité St Auguste (actually Cité St Laurent) and were still heading eastwards. Apparently apart from using a compass to orientate yourself the two villages were virtually the same distance from Hill 70 and appeared the same with a mine wheel-house, one large two-storeyed house and a mass of small houses. Perhaps it is no surprise that such a mistake was made. An additional problem was also the apparent rigidity of the orders, and although probably correct they are worth recapping here. The Divisional Order had stated that the first brigade to gain Hill 70 was to detail a sufficient force to consolidate and hold it until troops from the Divisional reserve could be pushed up to take it over, whilst the remainder pushed on to the German trenches in front of Cité St Auguste. The 44th Brigade Orders had covered the possibility of them being covered on Hill 70 first by saying that: "The sufficient force would be probably one battalion and it would be impossible to nominate any particular one, the senior Commanding Officer on the spot will issue the necessary order for consolidating that position against possible attack from direction of Lens." The 9th Black Watch's Commanding Officer Lieutenant-Colonel T. Lloyd, was the senior CO of the 44th Brigade, and one of the first onto Hill 70. But he had realised there was the yawning gap between his force and the 47th Division, so he had gone to the right flank to try and sort it out. This left the CO of the 7th Cameron Highlanders, Lieutenant-Colonel Sandilands, as senior and he, together with the CO of the 10th Gordon Highlanders, started to issue orders for the consolidation of the position with the few remaining men in the vicinity. There was no way of stopping the majority who had carried on in the direction of Cité St Laurent. Perhaps even more worrying, there was no sign of the 1st Division appearing on the left flank of the 15th

Division, although they were relatively safe for the moment, as the majority of the 8th KOSB continued to cover the flank towards Bois Hugo.

Meanwhile what of the large band of men from mixed units who were rushing headlong towards Cité St Laurent? At first things went well, they managed to get to within circa 300 yards of the German defences outside the village when rifle fire from there and machine gun fire from the area of the Dynamitière brought them to a shuddering halt. The words of Rawlinson made many weeks before now had a resounding meaning: "Very difficult for attack. It will cost us dearly and we shall not get very far." The ground the Jocks were sheltering in was almost devoid of cover, but in the best traditions of the British Army they attempted to get forward, and it is believed nearly 100 got to within 80 yards of the German trenches. Here they found hidden in some long grass an apparently uncut thick belt of barbed wire. The attack petered out here. The few remaining Jocks attempting to scrape out some cover with whatever they had to hand. The unintended shift of direction southwards now exposed the men on Hill 70 and made any advance eastwards, in the correct direction impossible. Fortunately the men on Hill 70 were now reinforced by the 7th Royal Scots Fusiliers from the reserve 45th Brigade. Their original role had been to dig communication trenches but had moved forward on the initiative of their CO, Lieutenant-Colonel C. Henning. They started to consolidate the hill for defence; a trench was dug along a bank that ran just below the crest. It roughly ran from the area of the southern end of the Loos Crassier, through Hill 70 Redoubt with its other end near Chalet Wood on the Lens-La Bassée road. Messages were sent back asking for artillery support against German positions in Dynamitière and Cité St Laurent, but as usual in these kind of situations in the Great War, it was not appreciated exactly what the position was.

From surviving accounts Divisional HQ believed that the two attacking brigades were stopped east of Hill 70 facing Cité St Auguste. Indeed at 10.50 am, General Rawlinson ordered McCracken to push on with the advance by sending the 45th Brigade through the other brigades at Cité St Auguste. He obviously cannot have appreciated that at least one of this Brigades units, the 7th Royal Scots Fusiliers, was already digging in on Hill 70. Rawlinson also ordered that all the available heavy artillery bring down its fire onto the area around Cité St Auguste for 30 minutes to act as a preliminary softening-up for an infantry attack. The only problem was there were no available troops to do this assault and the men hugging the ground in front of Cité St Laurent could have done with this artillery support. Also having a major effect now was the usual quick reaction by the Germans to the apparent threat to Lens. Early in the morning, around 9.00am, a message was sent back to the German 7th Divisional HQ in Lens that the British had advanced through Loos and were heading towards Cité St Laurent and Cité St Edouard. At 9.30am an entire battalion from the 178th Regiment in IV Corps reserve was ordered to move up to Cité St Laurent to reinforce the line - they arrived about two hours later, around 11.30am. Then a further report came back saying that the 'English' were continuing to advance, had occupied Hill 70 and were moving towards Lens. The local commander, General Lucius in Lens, considered the situation extremely critical. He appreciated that the rising ground on which the villages of St Laurent and St Edouard lay overlooked Lens and all its approaches, and that occupation of this by the British would threaten the lines of communication of most of the German IV Corps. He therefore decided that the 'Schwerpunkt' was here and must be stopped at all costs. Around 10.45am all available men in Lens were ordered forward to hold a line between the Lens-Béthune and Lens-La Bassée roads. It was a mixed bag of troops comprising about three battalions strong together with some pioneers and cavalry.

Meanwhile the first German counter-attack had already started, trying to force the few men lying on the open slope in front of Cité St Laurent back. The first effort coming from the railway embankment west of Dynamitière was beaten back by about 20 men from the 9th Black Watch from their position on the southern end of the Loos Crassier. When the German reinforcements arrived, more fire was brought down on the men in front of Cité St Laurent and around 1.00pm an effort was made by the Jocks to get back to Hill 70. This movement caused several parties of Germans to leave their lines, move through gaps in the barbed wire and charge forward. Their cheers and advance seemed to galvanise the other reinforcements on the Lens-La Bassée road, who also left their trenches and rushed forward in an extended line towards the summit of Hill 70. Of the men in front of Cité St Laurent some attempted to run back to Hill 70, but nearly all were killed or wounded. Of the 900 or so who rushed down Hill 70 towards Cité St Laurent it is probable only 20 or 30 got back to British held ground. The losses of the 15th Division will be tabulated later but of the men captured by the German 26th Regiment on this day only 50 were unwounded.

There now ensued a bitter struggle for control of Hill 70. The Germans managed to reach the summit of the hill but were held up by fire from the Redoubt and the reverse slope positions. The attack was also held up for a time by the 9th Black Watch from their positions either side of the Loos-Lens track near the Loos Crassier. Some of the hardest fighting was for the Hill 70 Redoubt and the 73rd Field Company RE were prominent in this. This company of engineers had been attached to the 44th Brigade with the intention of helping the infantry dig in and consolidate any positions gained. However, as most readers will be aware, the role of any soldier is to be an infantry soldier first and a specialist second, which is why the unit's War Diary states that: "The Company acted as infantry practically the whole time."

The company was divided into four sections, no's 1 and 2 sections had followed the Black Watch and Seaforth Highlanders respectively into the attack. No's 3 and 4 were behind the 10th Gordon Highlanders waiting to follow them when it was time for their advance. While they were waiting for the Gordons to move No 4 Section was ordered to bridge a trench over the Loos road, but while this was being done one officer and ten men were wounded. The officer wounded was the OC Lieutenant Nolan, and a Captain Cardew assumed command of 3 Section. He then ordered 4 Section under Second Lieutenant F. Johnson and the survivors of 3 Section to follow the Gordons into Loos village. Somewhere in or near Loos village the CO of the Gordons ordered the Sappers up to Hill 70. They reached the crest of the hill around 9.30am, from where they could see the hard-pressed men in the Redoubt. They joined in here in an attempt to consolidate the position but all of them were forced to withdraw due to the weight of German fire. They went back to a position on the reverse slope, but after Captain Cardew and 2nd Lieutenant Johnson 'borrowed' a machine gun, they decided to have another go at taking the

Redoubt. The attacking force was made up of RE only and about 10 men actually got into the Redoubt but unfortunately were forced back out, and the Redoubt was lost for good. Captain Cardew was seriously wounded and Johnson was hit in the leg. In spite of his wounds Johnson led several more attempts to retake the Redoubt but all failed. Nevertheless his conduct under heavy fire was noted and the Company War Diary records: "Second Lieutenant Johnson, who, although wounded, carried on till midnight, rallied his men and the parties of infantry without officers, and showed great coolness and gallantry." He was recommended for a Victoria Cross, which was gazetted in November 1915, and his citation read as follows:

> For most conspicuous bravery and devotion to duty in the attack on Hill 70 on 25th Sept. 1915. Second Lieutenant Johnson was with a section of his company of the Royal Engineers. Although wounded in the leg, he stuck to his duty throughout the attack, led several charges on the German Redoubt, and at a very critical time, under very heavy fire, repeatedly rallied the men who were near him. By his splendid example and cool courage he was mainly instrumental in saving the situation and in establishing firmly his part of the position which had been taken. He remained at his post until relieved in the evening.

Johnson was promoted up the ranks, reaching Major in late 1917. Sadly he was killed in action on 26th November 1917 and is now commemorated on the Cambrai Memorial to the Missing.

While this fighting was going on, at last there was some limited support for the BEF: the French attack was going in, albeit at 12.45pm, six hours after the initial effort. But it did have the effect of diverting German attention and for the moment no more German reserves could be moved into the Loos sector. In the area of Hill 70, apart from shelling, they were quite happy to hold onto Hill 70 Redoubt because it dominated such a large area.

Meanwhile it would now be appropriate to look at the actions of the reserve brigade, the 45th, commanded by Brigadier F. Wallerston. In spite of Rawlinson's plan that they be employed in one drive to take Cité St Auguste, they went into action piecemeal. As stated before, the 7th Royal Scots Fusiliers had, around 9.00am on the 25th, gone after the 7th Cameron Highlanders through Loos and onto Hill 70. Here they gave valuable assistance in holding the line against the German counter-attacks. Also, typically for a reserve unit, some of its strength was dissipated to units in trouble. At 9.00am Brigadier Matheson had asked for support for the left flank of his Brigade (the 46th). On this flank, you will recall, were the 7th and 8th KOSB near Puits 14 bis. He, quite rightly, had deduced that his flank here was exposed due to the no-show of the 1st Division and he also felt vulnerable to his front as he was overlooked by Hill 70. The first decision taken was to send a platoon of the 6th Cameron Highlanders to him together with about 100 bombers. Later the whole of the 6th Cameron Highlanders was sent forward. Here is a comment about the early part of the day from their War Diary:

> Hot tea was issued to the men at 3.00am. At 5.50 the Battalion moved slowly up towards the firing line. At 6.30am the attack started and the Battalion occupied the fire trenches. Parties began to dig communication trenches to the German first line. About 9.30am the Battalion moved forward.

The Cameron Highlanders were ordered to head towards Puits 14 bis and, when there, they came under the orders of Brigadier Matheson. They were ordered to form a defensive position from the north-west corner of Chalet Wood to Chalk Pit Wood, this being in existence by about 12.30pm. Meanwhile the remaining two battalions of the Brigade, the 13th Royal Scots and the 11th Argyll and Sutherland Highlanders, were tasked to carry out Rawlinson's orders. They set off to Loos village and did not reach the area until after 1.00pm, by this time it was too late for them to have any effect. The Germans had retaken Hill 70 Redoubt. From this position they had commanding views down the western slope into Loos, and it appeared impossible to make an attack against the summit of Hill 70 without a heavy artillery bombardment, which was virtually impossible to arrange due to the communication difficulties. They therefore remained in Loos in close support of the intermixed units of their sister brigades holding the improvised line from Chalk Pit Wood to the Loos Crassier. The rest of the afternoon was spent in a sort of stalemate/holding position with the exception of enemy artillery fire. This caused many casualties, especially on the Béthune-Lens road, which seriously delayed the evacuation of wounded and may have led to Rawlinson's famous comment in June 1916 when he took an interest in the medical arrangements for his 4th Army's attack on the Somme (see *Stand To!* Number 64 April 2002).

In the early evening of the 25th, around 7.45pm, McCracken sent a staff officer forward to investigate the situation his Division was in. Coincidentally when this officer, Major Wace, found 44th Brigade HQ in Loos, the CO of the 7th Cameron Highlanders (Lieutenant-Colonel Sandilands) had just left his position on Hill 70 to get some new instructions and the two met. It was decided that the two battalions from the 45th Brigade, currently in Loos village, should relieve those men left up on Hill 70, with the CO of the 13th Royal Scots (Lieutenant-Colonel W Maclear) taking over command of the area from Sandilands.

In keeping with many other units, it was understood that fresh troops from the Reserves would be readily available, and McCracken had expected them to be with him at 10am, but in fact the reserves from the 62nd Brigade of the 21st Division got to Loos around 7.30pm. The reasons for this will be explained later but McCracken was to say: "They were not in a condition to enter such a fight." They were ordered to relieve the remnants of the 46th Brigade holding a line between Loos-Hill 70 track and Puits 14 bis.

At the end of this day the 15th Division had done far more than I feel anyone had realistically expected them to achieve and certainly caused the Germans some dangerous moments but at a very high cost. They had broken through the first line of German defences and came close to causing a major breach in the second line and if reserves had been available may have got into open country. As it was they finished their first day of action somewhere between the original German first and second lines from the Loos Crassier to Chalk Pit Wood.

Here is a comment from Private L. Hedges, who was a member of C Company of the 7th Royal Scots Fusiliers, who were initially in reserve on the morning of 25th September:

On the Saturday morning 25th September 1915, we went into action as supports to the Black Watch. I believe it was the 8th Battalion. We suffered along

Looking towards Hill 70 across the northern outskirts of Loos village.
(IWM Q43111)

with the Black Watch. I think all our officers were casualties. I was fortunate to survive although I was wounded twice.

We had severe casualties in the charge for Hill 70 which we captured, but we were driven back, as the supporting Division was late in arriving, they did not arrive until Sunday afternoon (the 26th) and we tried to dig ourselves in with our entrenching tools. The weather was appalling, raining all the time and we had no greatcoats.

Another present was Private C. Tain, again from the 7th Royal Scots Fusiliers:

At dawn on 25th September, we went over the top. We went into action and advanced through the German front line trenches into, and through the village of Loos. Thereafter we attempted to capture Hill 70, but when going over the crest and half way down the slope the enemy opened fire, there was no shelter of any kind, the Scots Division was almost annihilated. I myself received severe wounds resulting in the loss of my left arm and also a severe gunshot wound in my right leg. The firing was so intense and prolonged, consequently it was two days before I was picked up by stretcher bearers.

Second Lieutenant Gilbert was a platoon commander in the 10th Gordon Highlanders from the 44th Brigade and this is taken from a letter written shortly after the attack:

Just a line to let you know that I am quite fit and well, I suppose you've seen in the papers all about the large advance we've made here. Well I came through the whole thing.

We attacked the Germans lines, captured them all; we then attacked and after a lot of street fighting captured Loos and then we pushed onto the Hill 70 and I was in command of the Company by then. Well I pushed forward, captured Hill 70 and went on about 500 yards past it and there I was hit in the arm. Well we hung on there under the most terrible fire, with no cover at all and with the Germans firing from behind loop holed walls for five hours until eventually we had to retire onto Hill 70 again.

During that retreat I was hit four times in the kilt, about six times in my haversack and all my shaving materials, towels, food etc, were all riddled and dropped out of the latter. Then they attacked us all night, but we were not had on by them and drove them off. About twelve hours later we were relieved by another brigade and we went back and I had my arm dressed. It was only a scratch through my left arm above the elbow.

Later Lieutenant-Colonel Sandilands wrote this about the relief of his men by the 62nd Brigade:

I never saw any of the 62nd Brigade until I was leading back the remnants of the Camerons about midnight. I looked into a neighbouring trench and to my astonishment it was crammed with English soldiers. I got hold of a senior officer and asked him what they were supposed to be doing. He said: "Relieving the 15th Division." I said, "Why the devil don't you get out of the trench and relieve overground?" At that time there was practically no shelling and I pointed out that he was in a German trench and neither I nor anyone else knew where it led. But they would not get out, so I left them, as it was my chief duty to look after my own men. I later found out that they evidently thought that a relief could only be carried out in trenches, as taught to them on Salisbury Plain.

The total casualty figure for this one day for the 15th Division is actually open to some speculation, the British Official History does not give any figures for the whole Division, just the 44th and 46th brigades. As is usual with a return given at the time there is always a number who had been counted as 'missing' but later turn up. The uncorrected figures for the 44th Brigade are as follows:

Table 4.2
44th Brigade casualties, 25th September. Corrected post-action figures are given in brackets.

	Officers	Other Ranks	Totals
9th Black Watch	20	672 (660)	692 (680)
8th Seaforths	19 (23)	700 (479)	719 (502)
10th Gordons	7	374	381
7th Camerons	14 (19)	534 (668)	548 (687)
Grand Total	60 (69)	2280 (2181)	2340 (2250)

Unfortunately the similar report for the 46th Brigade is for the 25th and 26th September but it is worth noting that the majority of the casualties were incurred on the 25th September:

Table 4.3
46th Brigade casualties, 25/26th September. Corrected post-action figures are given in brackets.

	Officers	Other Ranks	Totals
7th KOSB	19 (20)	645 (611)	664 (631)
8th KOSB	14	379	393
10th Scottish Rifles	21	638 (464)	659 (485)
12th Highland LI	18 (21)	558 (532)	576 (553)
Grand Total	72 (76)	2220 (1986)	2292 (2062)

Other figures for the 25th September I have seen mention 4,474 all rank casualties and another for the period 25th to 27th September calculates 6,606 all rank casualties. Whatever the number I think it is fair to say that the stuffing had been knocked out of the 15th Division. At the end of the 25th September it was just about able to field slightly more than 50% of its effective strength. Things could

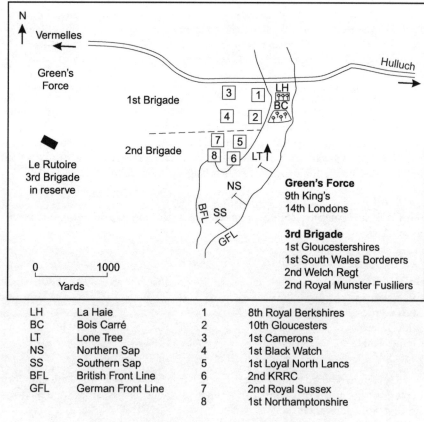

LH	La Haie	1	8th Royal Berkshires
BC	Bois Carré	2	10th Gloucesters
LT	Lone Tree	3	1st Camerons
NS	Northern Sap	4	1st Black Watch
SS	Southern Sap	5	1st Loyal North Lancs
BFL	British Front Line	6	2nd KRRC
GFL	German Front Line	7	2nd Royal Sussex
		8	1st Northamptonshire

Map 8: 1st Division area of attack, 25th September 1915

Lone Tree pictured before its destruction.
(London Scottish Regimental Museum)

have gone so much better, but like other opportunities before and later they were allowed to slip away.

The final part of IV Corps was the 1st Division, who were in the most northerly sector of the Corps area. The 1st Division was the senior division of the British Army and was one of the first to land in France after war had been declared in August 1914. Its first action was at Mons and had taken part in nearly every major action of the war up till then. By September 1915 it still comprised three brigades but instead of the usual grouping of four battalions per brigade, two of the brigades (1st and 2nd) had five battalions. It had been an all Regular division but two of its battalions had been Guards units, and these had been transferred to the newly-formed Guards Division. Their place had been taken by two Territorial Force units - the 14th London Regiment, better known as the London Scottish, and the 9th King's Regiment. Somewhat surprisingly the 1st Division was also sent two New Army battalions- the 10th Gloucestershires and the 8th Royal Berkshires. This now meant the Division had 14 battalions in it instead of the usual 12. For unknown reasons the TF and New Army units were not allocated to all the three brigades but just two, with three going to the 1st Brigade and one to the 2nd Brigade. Another interesting thought is how many pre-war Regulars were still serving with the 1st Division?

Anyway, as was common with other parts of the overall plan, the 1st Division had been given alternative roles. In the original mid-August plan when it had been believed that it was impossible for the 15th Division to capture both the German front line and the Loos Defences in one assault, the 1st Division was to have been kept in reserve to support them. The envisaged plan was that if the Loos defences held out, to use the 1st Division to attack Loos and the defences from the north, while the 15th went in from the west. However the decision to use gas changed all this and as the plan called for a six division attack, in early September the 1st Division took over a section of front line. This stretched for about 1,400 yards on the left of the 15th Division, from opposite Northern Sap to the Vermelles-Hulluch road, where its left flank was in touch with the 7th Division from I Corps, this being the inter-corps boundary. Upon taking over this sector it was decided that the German trenches were too far away from the British lines (approximately 600 yards), so jumping-off trenches about 300 yards nearer the German lines were dug close up to the crest of the Grenay Spur. It was still not an entirely satisfactory conclusion, as the German front line was still around 300 yards away on the other side of the ridge. To help the Germans maintain their positions, they had dug two trenches forward known as Northern Sap and Southern Sap, and these were relatively strongly defended.

To avoid bumping into these positions it was decided not to attack the area directly between them, but as soon as the attacking brigades from the 1st and 15th divisions had by-passed them on either end, it would be a task for the 15th Division to roll-up Southern Sap by bombing the defenders out. Two companies from the 12th Highland LI were detailed to carry out this role. However as a result of this plan there would be about a 600 yard gap between the 1st and 15th divisions.

For the attack the 1st Division was deployed in the regulation two-up, one back formation, the two attacking brigades being the 1st (in the northern part) and the 2nd (in the south) with the 3rd Brigade being in reserve. The 1st Brigade was responsible for an area from the Vermelles-Hulluch road and a landmark known as Lone Tree. This was a solitary cherry tree which was in No Man's Land that had somehow survived the shelling, albeit only about a 15 foot stump with broken branches. Their objective was to drive due east heading for the southern part of the village of Hulluch. The 2nd Brigade in the southern sector was to attack on an approximately 600 yard front between Lone Tree and Northern Sap. After taking the German first and second line trenches, they were to swing south-eastwards and make contact with the 15th Division in the area of Puits 14 bis and Bois Hugo. If everything went to plan an ever-widening gap would be opening up between these two attacking brigades, so an auxiliary force was cobbled together. The units making this force up were taken from the extra Brigade units. Those chosen were the 14th Londons (London Scottish) and the 9th King's from the 1st and 2nd brigades respectively. To stiffen it up a bit the Regular 2nd Royal Sussex were taken from the 3rd Brigade and the whole force was named after the CO of that unit, becoming Green's Force. The aim was for them to move behind the inner flanks of the 1st and 2nd brigades and on reaching the area of the Lens-La Bassée road to link both brigades up. From here after a brief consolidation they were to attack some German defences between Bois Hugo and Hulluch - those known as Stützpunkt III and IV. This would be supported by the remainder of the 3rd Brigade. The plan then came together saying that the attack would be carried out in co-operation with their sister divisions - the 15th on their right and the 7th on their left. Again the ultimate objective was the Haute Deule Canal.

Most of these points and orders were expanded upon in a Divisional Order on 18th September which (as many points are of interest) is given now:

1 Consolidation of captured positions

(a) The consolidation of the ground won will, in the first instance, take the form of constructing a series of strong points suitable for 50 rifles and a machine gun

(b) Locations for each Brigade/Force are outlined below

(c) As soon as the first objectives had been gained:

i) 2nd Infantry Brigade will put Puits No 14 bis in a state of defence and construct strong points at 98 (SW end of Chalk Pit Wood facing south) and at Chalk Pit (facing east)
ii) Green's Force will construct a strong point at H.19.a.66 (where road from Bois Carré joins Lens-La Bassée road)
iii) 1st Infantry Brigade will put the southern end of Hulluch village in a state of defence, and construct a strong point at H.13.a.2.8 to H.13.a.2.6 (buildings west of Lens-La Bassée road and 300 yards south of Tournebride Estaminet crossroads).

(d) The points in the line of the subsequent objectives to be consolidated are:

i) Farm des Mines de Lens and north-east corner of wood in H.27.c. (Bois de Dix-Huit)
ii) German second line trench from point H.27.a.2.6 to point H.26.b.9.8 (Stützpunkt IV)
ii) The Redoubt in H.20.d.3.7 (Stützpunkt IV)
iv) Point 93 (immediately north of (c))
v) Puits No 13 bis.

(e) It must depend upon the progress of the attack both on our own front and on the fronts of the 15th Division and of the 1st Corps as to whether it will be necessary to link up our own front line with that of the enemy. If the situation renders such a course necessary the following connections will be made:

i) By 2nd Infantry Brigade- to saps G.22.b.9.7 (Northern Sap) and G.17.c.8.1 (sap by Lone Tree)
ii) By 1st Infantry Brigade- to saps G.17.a.9.4 (sap at Bois Carré) and G.17.b.2.8 (sap at La Haie).

This work is, however, to be considered as of secondary importance to that indicated in sub-para (b) above.

(f) No consolidation work is to be carried out by troops of the assaulting columns. These must push straight on, and the work of consolidation entrusted to working parties pushed up from behind.

2 Working Parties

The following working parties will be organised by General Officers Commanding Brigades:

(a) First working parties

(i) By 2nd Infantry Brigade - 2 Sections 26th Field Company RE, 1 Company Infantry (not less than 200 strong), portion of Brigade wiring party

(ii) By 1st Infantry Brigade - 2 Sections 23rd Field Company RE, 1 Company Infantry (not less than 200 strong), portion of Brigade wiring party.

These parties will be stationed in the trenches of their Brigade areas in such a position as to follow up the assault behind the supporting Battalions. They will draw their tools and stores from the dumps on the line of the new fire trenches as they advance.

(b) Second working parties

(i) By 2nd Infantry Brigade- 26th Field Company RE (less 2 Sections), the Infantry mining detachment attached to the 26th Field Company, portion of Brigade wiring party

(ii) By 1st Infantry Brigade- 23rd Field Company RE (less 2 Sections), the Infantry mining detachment attached to the 23rd Field Company, portion of Brigade wiring party.

These working parties will be in reserve at the disposal of Brigadiers. The personnel of the Field Companies will be engaged on special duty in the front trench up to the moment of the assault. As soon as the assault is launched, these personnel will be collected at a place to be selected beforehand by the Brigadiers.

The mining detachments, which will be in Philosophe, will move up via French Alley as soon as the assault is launched under orders of the Officers Commanding Field Companies, to places selected by Brigadiers beforehand. They will draw their tools and materials as they advance from the dumps on the line of the new fire trench.

(c) Green's Force working party

(i) 1 Section Lowland Field Company RE, ½ Company Infantry (not less than 100 strong), portion of wiring parties from 1st and 2nd Infantry Brigades.

This party will be stationed in the trenches in Green's Force area and will accompany the advance of Green's Force. They will draw their tools from a dump that has been placed on the line of the Fosseway.

(d) Bridging Parties

(i) 1 Section Lowland Field Company RE, ½ Company Infantry (not less than 100 strong) to be detailed by GOC 3rd Infantry Brigade.

This party will be stationed at a point to be selected by GOC 3rd Infantry Brigade, and will follow up behind the supporting Battalions of the 2nd Infantry Brigade. Their task will be to repair the bridges and road between

Corons de Rutoire and the Lone Tree, and to make ways for guns and ve-hicles at all points where the enemy's trenches and wire cross the road from Lone Tree to the Loos-La Bassée road, thence to crossroads at C.18.c.1.6 (200 yards further east) and then to point G.24.b.1.8 (road junction 700 yards south-east of above crossroads). The ways are to be made by filling trenches with sandbags and earth, etc., and by bridging with specially prepared timber sent up from the rear in wagons. Material for repairing the bridges in our area will be stored at Le Rutoire Farm.

(e) A special party of 30 men, under an Officer, will be detailed by the GOC 2nd Infantry Brigade.

Their task is to proceed via Lone Tree, and having selected a suitable point in the German trenches between this and the Northern Sap, to make a route suitable for mounted troops across the German trenches by filling them with earth and sandbags, and by clearing away wire. The route to be marked by one or more red flags to be carried by the party.

[Author's note: I suppose the interesting point about all these working parties is the way in which the bayonet strength of the assaulting battalions was diluted by all these subsidiary tasks. It is little wonder that more and more thought and action was being given to the creation of a pioneer battalion in each division. Indeed soon after Loos, the 10th Battalion, Duke of Cornwall's Light Infantry was sent to act as the Divisional pioneers. A little known fact is that men in these units were paid an extra 2d per day as recognition of their special skills.]

3   Special Bombing Parties

The following special bombing parties, in addition to any others that may be found necessary, will be organised by Brigades, the organisation to include the replenishment of bombs:

(a) By 2nd Infantry Brigade

(i) To bomb down the enemy's front and support lines, to meet a sim-ilar party from the 15th Division bombing upwards
(ii) To bomb up the enemy's front and support lines, to meet a similar party from the 1st Infantry Brigade bombing downwards
(iii) To bomb down the North Loos Avenue trench to point 39 (Loos-La Bassée road), where a barricade will be constructed and held.

(b) By 1st Infantry Brigade.

(i) To bomb down the enemy's front and support lines, to meet a sim-ilar party from the 2nd Infantry Brigade bombing upwards.
(ii) To bomb down the trenches 16-81 and 52-31 (German trenches immediately east of the Loos-La Bassée road). OC Green's Force will arrange to obtain his own information as to when the bombing parties at (b) and (d) above have met.

4   Gas

The best wind for the gas is 4 to 5 miles per hour. Thus during the last 2 minutes of smoke discharge the last of the gas will have travelled 250 yards. There is therefore no fear of our own men running into the gas before reaching the German trenches.

There is no danger in following up the gas in the open, but as trenches, dugouts, and cellars, in the German lines will probably be found full of gas, these must not be entered without lowering smoke helmets.

All available Vermorel Sprayers are to be pushed up immediately behind the assaulting troops with a supply of solution to refill them. Special parties are to be organised for the purpose in 1st and 2nd Infantry Brigades, and in Green's Force, and a proportion told off to accompany the special bombing parties.

The last two minutes of the gas and smoke discharge will be a smoke discharge only. During the last minute of this, the Infantry will get out of their trenches and move forward under cover of the smoke which is harmless, ready to launch their assault.

Previous to the attack, troops should be warned that no food or water found in the German trenches after the gas attack should on any account be used, as the gas may, in all probability, have a poisonous effect on both.

5   Movements

As soon as the German front system of trenches, which lies near the crest of the ridge, has been taken, all movement of supporting and reserve troops, within our own trench area, will take place across the open, wire being freely cut along our back lines two nights before the assault. Similarly, the attacking troops will advance direct on their objectives moving rapidly in extended order across the open. In the case of the special bombing parties referred to in paragraph 3, it is left to the discretion of the Officers in charge whether to bomb from inside or outside the trenches attacked.

Battalion commanders are to impress upon all their Officers, and the Officers to their men, the necessity of rapid forward movement, irrespective of whether troops on their flanks are being temporarily held up. If full advantage is to be taken of the gas the attack must be in the nature of a rush through, and as much ground made as possible before the enemy can recover his morale, or man his second line trenches east of the line Puits 14 bis-Hulluch. At the same time no mention is to be made of the fact that gas is to be used until Battalions are actually in the trenches.

6   Special Bombardments

When any special bombardment is asked for, it is to be understood that normally it will continue from the first to the last gun for half an hour, of which the last five minutes will be intensive. The Officer asking for it should invariably specify the time at which he wishes it to cease. It will cease at this hour precisely, irrespective of whether the time of receipt of the message by the battery has enabled it to last the full half hour or not.

An Artillery Officer will be attached to each Infantry Brigadier, and to OC Green's Force, who will be in direct communication with the commander of the Artillery sub-group affiliated to these formations.

In addition, Artillery Officers will be sent forward with (though not attached to) such Battalions as may be at the moment be found convenient, to keep their sub-group commanders in touch with the situation.

7   Wire Cutting

Numerous gaps in the wire along our whole front line will be cut during the night before the assault. As this is all French wire, the portions removed should be placed so as to conceal as far as possible the fact of its having been cut.

8   Information

Attention is invited to the importance of getting back information to Brigade and Divisional Commanders. Brigadiers will arrange to send back a report every half-hour, even if the information in it is of a negative character. Additional reports will of course be sent in the event of anything of importance occurring between the half-hours.

Information by aeroplane
As an additional means of procuring information use will be made of ground signals, which will be observed and transmitted by aeroplane to a wireless receiving station, situated near the Divisional Report Centre in Mazingarbe.

The following signals only will be used:

(a) By the 1st Infantry Brigade

(i) The figure V (inverted) pointing towards the enemy to indicate that our troops have captured Hulluch
(ii) The figure V pointing away from the enemy to indicate that our troops have been driven out of and are no longer holding Hulluch.

(b) By the 2nd Infantry Brigade

(i) The figure T to indicate that our troops have captured Puits No 14 bis
(ii) The figure T (inverted) to indicate that our troops have been driven out of and are no longer holding Puits No 14 bis.

These signals will consist of strips of white sheeting 8' x 2' and will be carried and laid by the Headquarters of a particular Battalion, to be detailed by the Brigadier, near his Brigade Headquarters.

9   Communication

All communications from Advanced Divisional Headquarters to the Divisional Battle Station, and throughout the trench area are to be tested every hour during the night preceding the assault, and every half hour from 5.00 a.m. up to the time of the assault. A diagram showing all communications in the 1st Divisional area has been issued to Brigadiers and to OC Green's Force.

10   Maps

All messages and reports will refer to either the 1/10,000 sheet 36c NW, or to the 1/40,000 sheet 36b and 36c, or to the 1/20,000 sheet 36c NW.

11   Time

The official time for the assault will be taken from the watches of the gas company representatives in the front line trenches. Brigadiers will be responsible that the watches of all commanders are synchronised with those of the gas company.

12   Veterinary

Units are to be warned that contagious disease is known to be rife among the enemy's horses. Captured animals, other than those required immediately to replace casualties, must not therefore be retained.

1st Division HQ	W.G.S. Dobbie, Captain,
18th September 1915	General Staff, 1st Division

These then, were the detailed tasks for the 1st Division, with the interesting comment 'under gas', in that there is no danger in following up the gas cloud in the open assuming the wind is in the right direction. Anyway the gas was released on time and Rawlinson was an interested spectator on the 1st Division front, from his vantage point on top of a Fosse about three miles from the front line. He later recorded: "The view before me was one I shall never forget. Gradually a huge cloud of white and yellow gas rose from our trenches to a height between 200-300 feet, and floated gently towards the German trenches. It was a wonderful sight." But once again circumstances were to put a spanner in the works. The wind, which was blowing ever so slightly from the south, pushed the drifting cloud more in a northerly direction along No Man's Land rather than eastwards towards the German lines. The British front line from the area of the Northern Sap to the Vermelles-Hulluch road bulged eastwards in a small salient, so that the area held by the 2nd Brigade faced south-east. This meant their area lay directly in the path of any gas blown northward from the 15th Division area, which is precisely what happened when the wind veered to an almost southerly one. Gas and smoke from both the 1st Division's area and that of the 15th Division began to drift back across the 1st Divisions trenches. The gas was quickly turned off but not before a number of casualties had been suffered by the 2nd Brigade. The two leading battalions from the 2nd Brigade, the 2nd King's Royal Rifle Corps (KRRC) and the 1st Loyal North Lancashires both had about 200 men incapacitated by the gas. The majority of those affected had been destined to be in the leading wave so the second wave had to be told they were now first off. Then around 6.20am the wind again changed direction to a south-westerly one and so the cylinders were turned on again. The time for the actual assault was therefore delayed by four minutes to allow the cloud to drift away from the British lines. The leading waves crossed into No Man's Land at 6.34am.

For a few moments there was no German reaction, but then the leading men were spotted by two German machine gun positions, which were situated about 50 yards in front of the main German line. One was by Northern Sap and the other south of Lone Tree. They had escaped destruction during the artillery bombardment and were able for a time to cause considerable havoc on the leading waves. It was also discovered that due to clever siting of defensive positions the barbed wire was virtually undamaged and worse still, it was over ten yards in depth. All efforts by men from the Loyals to cut the wire were unsuccessful and the entire advance of the 2nd Brigade stalled minutes after setting off. The report from the Loyal North Lancs War Diary gives some idea of the extent of the casualties in front of the German wire that morning:

> Colonel Sanderson and the Adjutant, Captain Dever, were wounded, also Second Lieutenant Goldie who was with them was killed. Officer casualties; 9 killed, 5 wounded, 2 missing. Captain Faulkner, Lieutenants Levesey, Wharton and Healey all killed right on the German wire. Lieutenant Warborough, Machine Gun Officer, took his two guns practically up to the German wire, he was killed. Lieutenant Gardner, the other Machine Gun Officer, went out on left flank with his two guns, nearly all his team was gassed and he carried a gun out himself with two men. He was gassed but came back to get ammunition and was told by the Doctor to return to the rear, but he went and got more ammunition.

This hold-up also gave time for the defenders to man their positions and also allowed reinforcements to arrive. These extra men who did arrive were from the 157th Regiment coming from Southern Sap and from North Loos Avenue on the 15th Division front. This movement of men probably helped the 15th Division gain their objectives, but stopped the 2nd Brigade. Again the leading elements of the attackers were in a difficult position under fire close to the barbed wire, unable to go forward or back. The follow-on waves faired little better, taking up position behind a crest in No Man's Land roughly in the middle of the open ground. Then around 7.30am the smoke and mist cleared, making the prospects for an attack even more unfavourable. Nevertheless in the finest traditions of the British Army attempts were made to rally the men but it was hopeless and attempts were made to crawl back to the British front line. The CRE 1st Division, Lieutenant-Colonel C. Russell-Brown said later:

> In my opinion this chlorine and tear-gassing of the 1st Division had a very stupefying effect on the troops engaged in the attack. The two brigades making the attack had distant and divergent objectives, and in my opinion this initial gassing did much to spoil the impetus of the attack and later to make the men slow in re-forming.

The War Diary of the 2nd KRRC recorded that: "On reaching the German wire it was discovered that it was not cut, being low and wide. During the fierce

Looking towards Hulluch from the Grenay Ridge, the area of the 1st Brigade attack.
(IWM Q43119A)

fighting the Battalion was compelled to retire in order to reorganise." One of the survivors of the original attack from A Company, Rifleman G. Peachment, noticed his Company Commander, Captain G. Dubs, lying wounded near the barbed wire some 15 yards from the German lines. Peachment crawled forward to assist him and despite the intense fire and shelling, tried to bandage his wounds. While he was doing this Peachment was wounded in the chest by shrapnel from a bomb, Dubs was also hit in the chest by a bullet. In spite of his wounds Dubs was attempting to drag Peachment into a shell-hole when he received a fatal gunshot wound to the head. Rifleman George Peachment was 18 years and 4 months old and his courage was recognised by the recommendation for a Victoria Cross. His citation read:

> For most conspicuous bravery near Hulluch on 25th September 1915. During very heavy fighting, when our front line was compelled to retire in order to reorganise, Rifleman Peachment, seeing his Company Commander, Captain Dubs, lying wounded, crawled to assist him. The enemy's fire was intense, but, though there was a shell hole quite close, in which a few men had taken cover, Rifleman Peachment never thought of saving himself. He knelt in the open by his Officer and tried to help him, but while doing this he was first wounded by a bomb and a minute later mortally wounded by a rifle bullet. He was one of the youngest men in his Battalion and gave this splendid example of courage and self-sacrifice.

George's body sadly was not recovered and he was posthumously awarded the Victoria Cross and he is commemorated on the Loos Memorial to the Missing at Dud Corner CWGC Cemetery. He had only joined the Army in April 1915,

View from Bois Carré Cemetery towards the Double Crassier. (Geoff Parker)

Looking in a south westerly direction from Bois Carré towards Fosse 5. (Geoff Parker)

which must prove that the number of pre-war Regulars in the Battalions had been dwindling away.

It would be best to leave the 2nd Brigade here as the shattered remnants of the two attacking battalions struggled to get back to the British front line, and return to them in a while. On the left of the 2nd Brigade was the 1st Brigade. Their commander, Brigadier A. Reddie, again opted for a two-up attack. He chose his two junior units, the 8th Royal Berkshires and 10th Gloucesters, for the initial assault. The gas was marginally more effective here but again the main problem was the German defences. On the crest of a ridge facing the two battalions were the remains of two small copses. These were La Haie in front of the Berkshires and Bois Carré in front of the Gloucesters. Although they had been shelled and did not really present a problem to get through, the Germans had positioned saps in the woodland and placed machine guns in them. Regrettably the barrage had not destroyed them and they caused severe casualties, especially in the Gloucesters. A further hazard was the German tactic of firing shells into the gas and smoke cloud in the hope that the explosions from this fire would disperse the gas. In spite of severe casualties the Gloucesters managed to neutralise the machine gun post in Bois Carré and captured the German front line trench. They were temporarily stopped here under heavy small arms fire from the German support trench about 80 yards from the Gloucesters. However they rallied themselves and pushed on and managed to take the support line with a few Germans fleeing towards Hulluch. This success was however achieved at a terrible price, only around sixty men remaining standing.

Here are some comments from soldiers of the 10th Gloucesters about their experiences on the 25th September. First, Private W. Jennings:

> The gas caused a lot of trouble and men were lying in the trench bottom foaming at the mouth. On the whistle we climbed out of the trench up stepladders. Our own barbed wire was supposed to have been cut during the night by Sappers, but the only gap I could see was on my right. Private Taylor was next to me and as he tried to pass through the gap he was shot dead. I crouched to see how I could get through, but a bullet shattered my rifle and took my left thumb and forefinger. Another bullet grazed my chin and tore a hole in my gas helmet. Someone crouching on my left was also hit and fell. I bent down to help him but an NCO ordered me back into the trench. I tore off my gas helmet and splashed some water from the trench bottom onto my bleeding chin, not realising I was breathing in gas lying in the trench. I crouched there, shocked and dazed, until a soldier of the Black Watch came by and put a field dressing on my hand. He had moved off along the trench a little way when a shell exploded, knocking me down and killing the Scotsman.

Private W. Collins:

> I was detailed to act as bayonet man to the bombing section of Number 4 Company because the Sergeant said I was "strong in the arm and thick in the head." I was to rush into the German trench after the bomber had thrown his bombs and mop up. We reached the German barbed wire in front of their parapet; it was still there, undamaged. We couldn't get through it so we lay down in front of the wire. A German machine gun was firing over our heads, they were so close we could hear them chattering away between bursts. It was lucky for us. Some of the Battalion got through the wire further along and the Germans surrendered.

The Battalion War Diary records that in some cases the bayonet men had to fight without the help of the bombers, the poor quality of the British bombs being to blame. It said: "Their bombs in the main refusing to explode, the Brock lighters having got wet with the rain that fell in the early morning, nevertheless the attack was pushed home with the utmost resolution."

Below are some accounts from men who managed to reach the outskirts of Hulluch but when there became casualties from the increasing German resistance. Corporal A. Carter:

I was lucky really. I got into the German trenches unscathed with the few survivors of the Battalion. The Germans had made off to a village not far away called Hulluch. We were ordered to dig in and repulse any attacks the Germans might make, but at about 6pm I felt my rifle fall from my fingers. I looked down and to my amazement saw I had been shot through the hand. Strangely I didn't feel a thing at the time.

Private R. Fennell:

I did not lose much blood but I knew right enough the moment I was hit, for the pinging pain was different to anything I have previously experienced. What hit me was no doubt some broken bits of metal contained in a shell from a field gun about 4 inch in diameter, which on striking the ground bursts and whoever is in the neighbourhood has to look out. It came over my head sideways, I did not see it, but immediately on bursting I felt the twinge in my right side and on my left leg and foot. It travelled right through the thick of the leg, grazing the bone. Of course, I was done for as regards advancing because I could not keep up, and as there was no way of doing it, I had to walk back absolutely alone. When I could not walk, I crawled and when I could not do that, I sat down and by perseverance and covering a distance of four miles, several hours later I reached a dressing station.

Finally Private J. Groves:

My brother Fred and I were in Number 3 Company and we hadn't got far across No Man's Land when a shell dropped amongst my section. The blast knocked me unconscious and shattered my rifle and entrenching tool but leaving me only scratched. When I came around it was late in the afternoon and I made my way forwards to find the rest of the Battalion. Eventually I found them defending some captured trenches. Only three of my section were left and the Battalion had lost so many men there was only one man every 20 yards of trench. I later heard that poor Fred was dead.

Unfortunately Fred Groves' body could not be found and he is now commemorated on the Loos Memorial to the Missing. He was aged 28. The unit's War Diary briefly summed up the difficulties by saying:

The assault was carried out in three lines, frontage being Bois Carré inclusive to point 39 in G.17.d. The attack was delivered at 06.30 a.m. with the accompaniment of gas and smoke. The wind was not favourable with the result that from the start several men were affected. Notwithstanding this drawback the three lines moved forward punctually to the moment, machine guns accompanying.

The Germans' wire entanglement, which had been torn into gaps by bombardment, proved a considerable obstacle. The wind proving more favourable to the enemy than ourselves, in the smoke, direction was not properly maintained, but deflected to the right. Heavy resistance encountered at the support and reserve German works, at the first, the enemy eventually evacuation these positions, and retreated towards Hulluch. Our bombers suffered severely, their bombs in the main refusing to explode, the Brock lighter having got wet with the rain, which fell in the early morning. Nevertheless the assault was pushed home with the utmost resolution over the second German line into the third, and up the flanking communications trenches to eastwards.

The 8th Royal Berkshires, who had the benefit of several rehearsals on ground similar to their attacking area, managed to rush La Haie Copse and enter the German front line trench without such severe losses as the Gloucesters. This Battalion, one of the first New Army units into action on the Western Front, perhaps heeded the old Army maxim of 'Prior Planing and Preparation Prevents Poor Performance', in that nearly every aspect of the attack was looked at. This unit's War Diary records:

Bois Carré Cemetery. Situated on the Loos-La Bassée Road, in an area that was on 25th September 1915 No Man's Land. A number of casualties from the 8th Royal Berkshires are buried here. This cemetery suffered considerable damage as the War progressed and a large number of the original graves were lost. (Geoff Parker)

The smoke helmets issued are going to be troublesome in the attack and I am arranging to have them pinned down to the coat behind with a safety pin and have some elastic let in to draw them close round the throat, as there would not be time to let them down in a charge on to a trench and tuck them in the coat.

Here is an account from a Royal Berks soldier, Private H. Rowland, about the last few hours before the attack:

We advanced 6.30 Thursday night (23rd September) from the reserve trenches into the second line of trenches, which were a foot and a half deep in mud. We were all wet through but we Tommies did not mind that. We were all cheerful. After remaining in the second line until the following evening we went into the firing line. We all heard that the following morning there was going to be the biggest charge of the war made and we were to help the first line of attack. After we had settled down to the best of our accommodation (it was about 12 midnight), we managed to get a little sleep, having our blanket to roll in, taking sentry duty in the trenches by turns.

It was 3.30 the next morning when the order came along to stand to arms. The day of the great advance had arrived and we were all ready and cheerful waiting for the order which would make the great difference to the war. It was at 6 o'clock that the order came to fix bayonets, which was done in great silence broken by a terrible bombardment of the enemy's trenches which were 250 yards away from ours. Then the enemy replied. The din was fearful: shells dropping everywhere; shrapnel flying; gas shells bursting. It was really indescribable. We were all wound up to kill all the Germans in the world.

An unnamed Corporal from the same unit recalled:

Two platoons each of A, C and D Companies were in the first line when the charge was made. We had orders to go over the parapet at about 6.30am on Saturday; this everyone mounted and went forward. The enemy did not fire until we reached the firing line. Then they opened a terrific fire with machine guns and rifles. For a short period the fighting was of a severe character, but our superiority was so pronounced that the Germans decided that further resistance was useless and they either tried to make good their escape or surrendered. A large number were taken prisoner. At this juncture I was wounded. The enemy appeared to have been taken completely by surprise.

Private H. Rowland continues his account with:

Then came the order "Charge!" Over we went, hundreds and thousands of us, yelling like madmen. Then came my first sight of death in battle. A shell burst a few yards from me killing my Officer and nine men. I felt a pang of sorrow go through me when my Officer dropped; he was liked by everyone. My blood roused, I went like mad towards the first line of the trenches we had to capture, but the Germans had all fled, leaving their dead and dying behind them.

So far so good, the 8th Royal Berks had advanced through La Haie and managed to capture the German front line trench, despite heavy losses caused by the unbroken German barbed wire defences, which had come through the British bombardment relatively unscathed. The 8th Royal Berks had so far advanced about 400 yards. The time was now here for an attempt on the next objective, an unnamed soldier from the Royal Berks recalled:

> Immediately the first line of the enemy trench was taken, the Royal Berks and the other Regiments supporting them made a charge to the second line. As soon as we got over their parapets the Germans started retiring down their communication trenches as fast as they could.

The second line was captured without too many problems and the advance continued beyond the second line such that by around 8.00am, the third line, Gun Trench, had been reached - an advance of around 1,200 yards.

Here are two accounts of the events that happened in and around the third German line:

> But on reaching the third line the Germans put up stubborn resistance. They replied with heavy fire and the fighting was very severe, but by the aid of our reinforcements we were able to become masters of the situation. By this time their casualties had been very heavy. There is no doubt that the 8th Royal Berks made a very fine charge and we had earned encomiums of many who were in a position to judge our excellent work.

And:

> The Berkshires showed great dash and tenacity. We were met with terrible machine gun fire and the Tower Bridge on our right, played the deuce with us. It was enfilade fire that we had to endure and some of our men say we were fired on from the back. However we achieved our objective, though many of our comrades fell during the day. The Officer of my Platoon was Lieutenant Gentry-Birch, who is very popular, hard working and a good commander. We were all glad to hear that he came through unscathed. Second Lieutenant Rouse had a terrible wound in his right arm, but I saw him drag one of our fellows into safety.
>   I think it was about 10 o'clock when, owing to the mist and smoke, a part of the Regiment became separated from the main body. I and others joined with the Gordons who were immediately on our left. The Germans were cowards when it came to close quarters and cried out "Bon Comrade." It was of course necessary to bomb out of the trenches those who would not surrender. Lieutenant W. Hobbs was our Bombing Officer. He was killed during the day.

Hobbs has no known grave and is commemorated on the Loos Memorial to the Missing. The 8th Royal Berks had now made steady progress so that a distance of over 1,200 yards had been advanced into enemy territory. The poplar trees along the Lens-La Bassée road could be discerned about 500 yards ahead. This is what the 8th Royal Berks War Diary has to say:

> The fire of our artillery lifted and the Battalion advanced in quick time to assault the first line enemy trenches. The advance was opposed by heavy artillery and machine gun fire, while the wire in front of the German trenches was found to be scarcely damaged, and it was in cutting a way through this obstacle that most of the Regiment's heavy casualties occurred. Shrapnel and machine gun combined to play havoc in our ranks, and an additional disaster was the blowing back of our gas, by the wind, into our own ranks.

After a struggle the German first line was penetrated, and the trench was found to be practically deserted, the enemy, apparently, having deserted it, leaving behind sufficient men to work the machine guns. Mainly overland, but with some men working in the communication trench, our line advanced successively to the second and third German lines and met but slight opposition.

Meanwhile the 1st Cameron Highlanders, who had been following behind the Royal Berks, now took over the attack through Gun Trench (where three field guns were captured) to the Lens road. Here a halt was called and after a quick reorganisation, several small scouting parties were sent out in the direction of Hulluch. It is possible that at least one party got through into Hulluch, but most of them did not, being held by barbed wire defences outside the village. Indeed the War Diary of the 1st Camerons records a message sent to 1st Brigade HQ timed at 9.10am: "One Company reports that a small mixed party of our Brigade have captured a trench close to Hulluch. Enemy reported to be retiring there." There were now troops from three units facing Hulluch, but it was decided that there were insufficient numbers to attack at the moment, so it was a case of waiting until the 2nd Brigade and Green's Force advanced on the right hand side. It might then be possible to organise a combined attack against the positions around Hulluch.

It is now best to return to the 2nd Brigade with the remnants of two shattered battalions getting back as best they could after their mauling in No Man's Land. In spite of this disaster, around 7.30 am, the Brigade Commander, Pollard, hearing of the success of the 1st Brigade, ordered forward some more troops. These were the 2nd Royal Sussex Regiment supported by two companies of the 1st Northamptonshire Regiment, and they were tasked with attacking (again) the German front line. He did intend these new troops to carry forward with them the remnants of the 1st Loyal North Lancs and the 2nd KRRC. The attack went in and again the lack of reliable information caused difficulties and confusion. For unknown reasons it spread round that this second assault had been successful and around 8.00am Pollard sent a message to his Divisional HQ saying: "2nd Brigade at first held up, but Sussex have now got through into German trenches." The GOC, Major-General A. Holland, believing the Germans to be totally routed and on the run along the whole of his Divisional front, was galvanised into action and issued a string of orders. To try and get support to the men of the 1st Brigade near Hulluch as quickly as possible, he ordered the 2nd Brigade to "push on with all speed." Green's Force, from its position near Le Rutoire, was ordered to move across the open to the British front line and support trenches near Lone Tree and to await orders there. The Divisional reserve, the 3rd Brigade, also situated near Le Rutoire, was ordered by Holland to follow up close behind Green's Force.

Then at 9.01am, a report from the 2nd Brigade reached Divisional HQ which said that the earlier report was false, and that the second attack, just like the first, had been halted by stiff German resistance south of Lone Tree. Holland's orders caused problems too for Green's Force. Small arms fire directed at the units of the 2nd Brigade also caused casualties amongst the ranks of Green's Force as they advanced across the open to the front line trenches. The second wave of the 2nd Brigade consisted of the Northamptonshires on the right and the Royal Sussex on the left. It is most likely both battalions suffered from the effects of the gas cloud as they waited in the front line while the attack by the first wave went in. As we have seen, the first attempt failed and so a second assault was ordered.

Just after 7.30am the men of the 2nd Royal Sussex and the 1st Northants together with a few men from the 1st Loyal North Lancashires left the trenches and attempted to take the German front line trenches. It was a brave try but again it failed in the face of heavy rifle and machine gun fire. The barbed wire was as before still uncut and no progress could be made. It is a bit of a cliché to say 'uncommon valour was a common virtue', but the bravery of the old sweats of the senior Division cannot be faulted. As well as Rifleman Peachment, three other men from the 1st Division were awarded the Victoria Cross for their actions this day.

The survivors of the 1st Northants were forced, due to the weight of German fire, to lie down in whatever cover they could find in No Man's Land for some

Headstone of Captain A. Read VC, killed on 25th September 1915 and now in Dud Corner Cemetery.
(Niall Cherry)

hours, during which time they suffered considerable losses. As their War Diary records:

A second attack was then ordered, the Sussex to advance on the left, centre on Lone Tree. The Battalion, less A Company and parts of B, who were used for carrying ammunition, to attack on their right. The attack commenced about 9.00 a.m.. The men went forward well. D Company were able to get close to German wire entanglement which was found to be uncut. C Company having a wide open piece of ground to traverse were unable to get so far forward and had heavy casualties. Lieutenant Jockey being mortally wounded. The line was unable to advance close enough to cut wire and remained lying out in open for two hours. Sussex on our left being in same predicament. This limited attack stood no chance of success, by now the smoke and gas had dispersed during the delay.

Sgt Harry Wells VC headstone at Dud Corner Cemetery. (Niall Cherry)

It was during this period that Captain A. Read of the 1st Northants won his VC. The unit's War Diary records:

Captain Read had very gallantly gone out to rally a party of about 60 men of different units who were retiring disorganised owing to the gas drifting back. The men were led forward again by him and took up a position south of Lone Tree, where they maintained themselves for some hours- Captain Read was mortally wounded during this time.

His body was later recovered and he now lies at Dud Corner CWGC Cemetery, his VC was gazetted on 18th November 1915. Part of his citation read:

Though partially gassed, rallied, several times, parties of different units which were disorganised and retiring. He led them back to the firing line, and, utterly regardless of danger, moved freely about encouraging them under a withering fire. He was mortally wounded whilst carrying out this gallant work.

On the left of the Northants were the 2nd Royal Sussex, at the appointed time they went over the top into a melee of gas, smoke, bullets and artillery fire. They discovered like everybody else that the German wire was uncut. The Battalion War Diary records: "All our Officers and Men who had reached or got close to the wire were either killed or wounded." At this point Sergeant H. Wells literally stepped forward, taking command after his platoon commander had been killed, and led them forward to within 15 yards of the German wire. About half of his platoon had been either killed or wounded, and the survivors literally clinging on for dear life, as

Captured German trench with the barbed wire relatively well cut. (IWM Q28969)

part of his VC citation states: "With the utmost coolness and bravery Sergeant Wells rallied them and led them forward." Even fewer were still surviving, but Wells standing up, urged them to attack again and was shot and killed in the very act of attempting to urge his men forward to the assault. His citation also said: "Finally, when very few were left, he stood up and urged them forward once more, but whilst doing this he was killed. He gave a magnificent example of courage and determination." He was recommended for a Victoria Cross and this was gazetted posthumously in November 1915. His body was also recovered and is at Dud Corner CWGC Cemetery. After the war in 1919 a survivor of Loos, Major F. Wilted, wrote:

> Owing to the wire being entirely uncut, the assault failed, the Battalion losing 19 officers and nearly 600 men in less than 15 minutes...Sergeant Wells, three times rallied his men and led them against the wire under close and continuous machine gun fire. During the third attempt Sergeant Wells and practically all the survivors of his platoon were killed.

Wells had originally joined the Army in 1904, serving for six years. He was recalled to the Colours in August 1914 and obviously did very well, quickly reaching the rank of Sergeant.

Perhaps here is a good place to briefly divert from the story of the Victoria Crosses to relate an entry from the diary of Private F. Colvin of the 2nd Royal Sussex:

> Saturday 25th September. We arrived in the trenches about 12.45am, took up our position and found the best place where we could to advance. The day for the great battle arrived. It was a very nasty wet morning, our artillery started bombarding and clouds of gas was sent over from our trenches. One could not see anything more than 50 yards to the front. All our boys seemed quite happy and cheerful, about 6.00am we received our orders to charge, over we got, and advanced about 400 yards only to be met, by clouds of gas and a murderous rifle fire from the Germans. Our men were falling fast, some gassed, some shot, and some almost blown to pieces.
>
> We were held up here for several minutes owing to the gas, we had already lost about four out of ten of our officers. We received orders from our officer to make another dash. We had only got about five yards when our sergeant fell (gassed) and then our officer followed him - shot. We had then five officers left but we did not mean to be beaten although it seemed impossible to advance any further, but it had to be done, so again we made a dash and got just in front of that German trench; and were held up again by gas and the rifle fire was worse than ever - it was murder. Men were falling like corn being mown down. We received orders to retire and had only just started to do so, when a sharp knife seemed to go in my back and right leg. I was wounded and helpless and lying near the German trench with our dead and wounded, but however I managed to get back to the British trenches, there I received assistance.

Private Colvin was wounded badly enough for him to get shipped back to Lincoln, where he had several operations on his leg before being passed fit and transferred into the Machine Gun Corps.

Finally, there was Private H. Kenny of the 1st Loyal North Lancashires. Private Kenny had taken part in the initial attack, survived this and was one of the lucky ones who also returned unscathed to the British front line. He on his own initiative went out into No Man's Land on six occasions, each time bringing back with him a wounded man. Whilst helping his sixth wounded man over the parapet, Kenny was hit in the neck, which caused him to be invalided home. His VC was not gazetted until March 1916. He again had been a pre-war Regular and had been recalled in August 1914. He certainly appeared to bear a charmed life as he had been at Mons, the Retreat from Mons, the Marne, the Aisne, the defence of Ypres, La Bassée and Neuve Chapelle before Loos.

So just to recap, the 2nd Brigade (at least, 4 battalions of it) had been virtually wiped out, held up on the barbed wire, with the 1st Brigade waiting for reinforcements near the village of Hulluch, Green's Force taking casualties before they had even reached the British front line and the 3rd Brigade waiting in Reserve. Meanwhile the German defenders opposing the 2nd Brigade now began to move northwards along the stretch of their 'own' lines that had been passed over and left vacant by the advancing troops of the 1st Brigade. Around 9.00am they were roughly in line with Bois Carré and had also reoccupied the sap leading into the copse. This of course had the effect of threatening the rear of the three battalions positioned along the Lens road facing Hulluch. The Brigade Commander, Reddie, therefore diverted his reserve unit, the 1st Black Watch, from reinforcing the troops near Hulluch to a new task. He now ordered them to advance to the east of La Haie copse, and then swing south, attacking down on either side of the German front and support trenches with the intention of stopping this northern German advance.

The leading company came under heavy small arms fire from the area of Bois Carré so that only around 30 reached the German front line. Here they quickly constructed a defensive position and blocked the trench, ready to stop the German advance. The situation was now becoming difficult, it was a case of success in some areas and failure in others. The reports reaching the Divisional Commander confirmed that the attack of the 2nd Brigade had definitely failed. However to the north and south of it, the German front line defences had been breached. To the south, the 15th and 47th divisions were reporting success and pressing forward to their objectives with, as we have seen, Loos village reported to be taken. It became clear to Holland that the general advance would soon be in danger because of the large gap of around 2,000 yards between Puits 14 bis and Hulluch, caused by the failure of his 2nd Brigade to get forward. Given these circumstances it appeared to Holland that it might be practical to move both Green's Force and the 3rd Brigade round either north or south of the 2nd Brigade, and then into a position to cover the gap along the Lens road between 1st Brigade and 15th Division. However, it was known that the survivors of the 2nd Brigade were still lying close to the German wire, unable either to go forward or back. It was hoped that in the very near future the small number of German defenders (according to intelligence) would surrender if a further attack by the 2nd Brigade went in, combined with a two company group from the 12th HLI from the 15th Division. This group from the HLI were believed to be bombing their way northwards from Loos Road Redoubt to Northern Sap. Green's Force was therefore ordered to make yet another frontal attack on the left of the 2nd Brigade, whilst the 3rd Brigade were told to move north of a gap in the German defences near La Haie, to reinforce the right flank of the 1st Brigade. It would perhaps be useful to look at the actions of the men from the 12th HLI before going back to Green's Force and the 3rd Brigade.

The party from the 12th HLI were deployed, with A Company entering the German front line in the area of Loos Road Redoubt and proceeding to bomb their way up the front and support trenches towards their B Company. This company had the job of bombing up Southern Sap (well in a south-easterly direction) to join up with A Company. Southern Sap was a particularly tough nut. The wire in front of it had not been a target during the preliminary bombardment, hoping that surprise would be the sledgehammer to crack it. Intelligence had believed it to be a trench but in fact it was only a very shallow excavation and the men were faced with trying to cut wire with their left flank completely exposed to fire from positions from the north. This was due to the failure of the 1st Division's attacks. The casualty figure was extremely high - over 90% of the officers and 60% of the men - but they still managed to make it to the junction of Southern Sap and the German front line. The remnants of these two companies managed to make an advance northwards of about 100 yards, where a shortage of bombs brought a halt to their progress.

Holland's orders which were sent off by runner at 9.10am, did not actually reach Lieutenant-Colonel Green until 10.55am. It was not till after noon that the London Scottish and the 9th Kings reported that they had received the orders and were ready to go on the offensive. Holland's orders contained the following instructions:

> Green's Force: It is essential that the 2nd Brigade should get forward without delay. Push on your two Battalions for all you are worth so as to capture the Germans in front of it. 3rd Brigade: You are to send three of your battalions north of Green's Force to cross the German empty front line trench about La Haie copse, and thence march south-eastwards to the gap on the Lens roads, where you will support the right of the 1st Brigade in their attack on the southern part of Hulluch.

Broken down, these orders (for the case of Green's Force) instructed an attack with one battalion either side of Lone Tree. The King's and the London Scottish therefore attacked side by side, with Lone Tree being the aiming point for the inner flanks of both units. Before both battalions had reached the intact barbed wire defences they were met by a hail of small arms fire. Every attempt to get forward and cut the wire ended in failure. The troops attempted to find what cover they could and return fire when possible. Some solace was given by a solitary machine gun brought across No Man's Land by some men from the 9th King's, and plans were made to try and send a company from the London Scottish in a flanking attack. Generally though, the situation was one of stalemate, and at around 1.00pm for once a senior commander made a bold decision. Major-General Holland decided to abandon attempts to take the German positions by frontal assaults, and to send those men he had spare round through the gap made by the 15th Division to the south. He therefore instructed the 2nd Brigade to:

Collect all available men of your Brigade, leaving only sufficient to hold the line. Move to the Vermelles-Loos road and across the German trenches at the Loos Road Redoubt. Then wheel up to your left and attack along line North Loos Avenue and Loos-La Bassée road, so as to get behind the Germans holding up your Brigade.

To assist the 2nd Brigade in this plan, they were allocated the 1st Gloucestershires, then in Divisional reserve. As it turned out, the 2nd Brigade had been so depleted during the morning attacks that the Gloucesters were tasked with this operation on their own.

Meanwhile the reserve brigade, the 3rd, after receiving their orders made relatively slow progress and around 10.30am, Brigadier Davies reported back saying:

Munsters have been ordered to advance north of Bois Carré, and when through German trenches to wheel half right and attack in support of 1st Brigade. Welch follow in support, with orders to push through southern end of Hulluch. South Wales Borderers will be ready to support Welch.

As you might imagine the situation was somewhat confused but orders are orders and the 3rd Brigade went on the attack.

The leading unit, the 2nd Munster Fusiliers, under the command of Major A Gorham only numbered around 250; this was due to their mauling at previous battles and the fact that replacement drafts had been slow in reaching them. They had been leagured around Le Rutoire Farm in the morning of 25th September, until around 10.45am, when they received orders to proceed to the front line north of Bois Carré. This entailed a move of about a mile across ground broken up with old and new trenches, shell holes and barbed wire. Originally an attempt was made to move up the communication trenches, but as these were choked with gassed and wounded men, Major Gorham gave the order to advance cross-country with predictable results. Two of the companies (but really just over two platoons) lost their bearings and moved to the right, and became mixed up with the left hand side of Green's Force. But this force was virtually annihilated trying to get across No Man's Land. The remainder of the Battalion reached the front line opposite La Haie, but had been so delayed waiting and looking for the lost two companies, that the 2nd Welch, who although in support, managed to get in front of the Munsters. Even so, the Munsters advanced, crossed Gun Trench and occupied a position facing Hulluch. Meanwhile the Welch had left the area of Le Rutoire around 11.00am, and were able to move unmolested across No Man's Land in the area north of La Haie copse. They passed through the deserted German front line and they arrived at Gun Trench virtually intact at 2.00pm as the following comment from their War Diary records:

We moved off from Le Rutoire in extended order two companies leading and two behind, fully imagining that the Munsters' were in front. We came under heavy fire immediately from the Germans who were by the Bois Carré but they did no damage. We then crossed over the German first and second lines, not losing anyone.

Around this time some Germans from the 157th Regiment indicated their willingness to surrender:

Suddenly the fire from our right slackened and it at last stopped altogether and a German bearing a white flag came towards us. He was sent by the Germans holding out to arrange their surrender. We then captured 160 men and 5 officers.

As there was no sign of the 2nd Munsters, the CO of the Welch, Lieutenant-Colonel Prothero, ordered his Battalion to wheel half right, continuing the advance down into the valley in the direction of the junction of the Loos-Hulluch and Lens-La Bassée roads north of Chalk Pit Wood. Here they hoped to meet the right flank of the 1st Brigade. This movement took the Battalion to the rear of the German positions south of Bois Carré. These were the positions that were holding the 2nd Brigade and Green's Force up, and the Germans here tried to do a 'Gloucesters' and fired back to back. Nevertheless the Welch kept on going and at around 2.30pm the Germans here surrendered, the prisoners numbering about 160 officers and men. After a brief pause to reorganise and sort the prisoners out, the Welch pressed on and later halted and went firm on the Lens-La Bassée road south of Hulluch. The area seemed completely empty and apart from the odd round of small arms fire from Hulluch deathly quiet. The CO, Lieutenant-Colonel Prothero, could see no friendly troops on either flank. So he decided to sit tight and wait for further support before advancing further. He weakened his force (quite rightly in the author's opinion) by sending a company to attack the Germans still believed to be holding up the 2nd Brigade and Green's Force. The Battalion settled down facing east along a section of the Lens-La Bassée road. Then, from out of nowhere, contact was gained with troops from the 1st Brigade situated about 500 yards to the north. The South Wales Borderers, who had followed behind the Welch, were ordered to occupy the German support trench, east of La Haie, later being brought forward to the Lens-La Bassée road. The movement of the company from the Welch, threatening the rear of the Germans holding up Green's Force, forced them also to surrender. Another 400 or so prisoners were taken by the London Scottish and 9th Kings. These men from the 157th Regiment must be credited with delaying the centre of the 1st Division's attack and probably stopped a decisive breakthrough in the area of Hulluch. It again proves that in defence, even when vastly outnumbered, disciplined troops can punch well above their weight.

Also around this time, a counter-attack from the reserve battalion of the 157th Regiment was launched on the men of the 1st Brigade along the Lens road. This battalion had been sent forward in the morning from its reserve position near Pont à Vendin to try and bring some relief to their colleagues in Lone Tree Trench. After advancing through Hulluch, the Germans drove back the small number of British troops in and around the village, but failed to push the 1st Brigade back and their attack was easily repulsed. They then took up defensive positions in and around the village of Hulluch.

Meanwhile the survivors of Green's Force and the 2nd Brigade were now relatively free to advance into the German rear. Estimates gauge the group as about 1,500 strong. They were looking into the wide expanse of the Loos valley and it was decided that the flank manoeuvre by the 1st Gloucesters was unnecessary. However it was getting late in the day and it started to rain, but through the gloom about a mile ahead the Lens road could be identified. Beyond it, on the northern slopes of Hill 70, the two immediate objectives: the wooded copses of Bois Hugo and Chalet Wood. By around 5.20pm the group had reached the Lens road, their right flank resting on Bois Hugo, where the 1st Northamptonshires met the 6th Cameron Highlanders. The Germans were unable to get many reinforcements to this area and apart from the counter-attack previously mentioned, left the British unmolested. This breathing space gave them the chance to reorganise and dig in. The 2nd Brigade and Green's Force were therefore able to consolidate their positions around the Bois Hugo, their right flank was on the northern edge of the wood, about 200 yards east of the Lens road. Although not in physical contact with the 15th Division situated at the southern edge of the wood, they sent out regular patrols to maintain communication. The left flank was close to the Lens road, about 300 yards north of the Chalk Pit. Their support line was based on the Lens road itself and their reserve, the London Scottish, was in the area of the Chalk Pit itself. It should be remembered though that all of these units had suffered a severe mauling earlier in the day and were probably most grateful for the relative quiet and calm of the latter part of the day. However the large losses meant that the fronts occupied by all the sub-units of the 1st Division were shorter than had been expected and there was a gap of over 1,000 yards between the inner flanks of the two parts of the 1st Division. The 1st and 3rd brigades were of course further north opposite Hulluch.

Because of a lack of communication, so it seems now, Murphy's Law came into play. It took quite a time for some patrols from the 2nd Brigade to find the 1st and 3rd brigades. Also the two brigadiers near Hulluch, Reddie and Davies, having received no word of the whereabouts of Green's Force or the 2nd Brigade, and having toured their fronts, believed they were in danger, isolated in an exposed position. They thought they had a right flank up in the air, and so decided to swing their centre and right hand side back and occupy for the night a German communication trench known as Alley 4, to the east of the Lens-La Bassée road. It should also be noted that the combined strength of these two brigades was less than 2,000 men from around the 7,000 who started the day. This left these brigades in contact with the men of the 7th Division at the junction of the Vermelles-Hulluch and Lens-La Bassée roads and their right flank in Alley 4 running towards Lone Tree.

But this withdrawal of the right flank increased the gap between the two parts of the 1st Division to around a mile. It is one of the tragedies of Loos that no one in High Command realised there was this large gap. It appears that all the three brigades informed Divisional HQ of their positions around 5.00pm on the 25th. At 6.22pm, 1st Division HQ informed IV Corps that Green's Force was in contact with the right of the mixed 1st/3rd Brigade Group which was not actually true. It is normal in the British Army for a commander to go forward and visit his subordinates at least once a day, and Rawlinson visited his three divisional commanders between 7.00 and 8.30pm. He was not told of the gap (or so it appears) when he

Table 4.4
1st Brigade 1st Division casualties, 25th September

8th Royal Berks	493
10th Gloucesters	459
1st Camerons	387

1st Black Watch	278
Total	1617

Table 4.5
2nd Brigade 1st Division casualties, 25th September

1st L North Lancs	489
2nd Royal Scots	481
2nd KRRC	460
1st Northants	298
Total	1728

Table 4.6
3rd Brigade 1st Division casualties, 25th September

2nd Welch	311
1st Gloucesters	124
1st South Wales Borderers	121
2nd Royal Munsters	120
Total	676

Table 4.7
Green's Force 1st Division casualties, 25th September

London Scots	260
9th Kings	235
Total	495

visited Major-General Holland. There was a chance to rectify this ever-increasing problem when Brigadier Davies reported at 9.10pm in a message to Divisional HQ the new positions of the 1st and 3rd brigades. This message is given in records as being received at 10.35pm, but the significance of its contents appear to have been overlooked. No reports were made to IV Corps and the actual situation on the ground differed greatly to what Rawlinson and Haig believed. This situation was going to cause tragic consequences on the following day.

However just to tie up the loose ends for the 1st Division, they had suffered heavily and the casualty figures were as follows:

This then was an overall casualty total for the day for the 1st Division of 4,516. Not for the first time in the Great War there were a lot of men wounded out in No Man's Land, together with many dead. It was the small medical resources attached to each unit that had to go out and try to collect those men they could. Here is a comment from Lance Corporal Clifford of the 10th Gloucesters:

At Loos, I acted as a medical orderly and stretcher-bearer. On the battlefield we had a terrible time telling whether a man was dead or just unconscious. You see, most of them were wearing their gas helmets, and we couldn't see their faces, so we had to go to each one and take off these gas helmets. Many were dead, and we marked their bodies by sticking their rifles, butts upwards, in the ground at their side. I think most of the casualties were caused by the machine guns.

Additionally officer casualties were high and the War Diary of the 10th Gloucesters contains the following comment: "The Officers fell, as the position of their bodies showed, leading their men, 14 out of 21 were lost. The bodies of our dead indicated how they had died, with faces to the enemy."

The day of 25th September ended with much thinking to be done by Haig and his senior commanders. Success had been gained in some areas (at a great cost) and total failure in others. It is a maxim that sometimes the most difficult day of a battle is the second one, with the commanders having to decide what to do with their reserves and with their plan for the first day not having been achieved. This is true of Loos on the evening of 25th September and decisions made in the next few days were to have far-reaching consequences.

5

Overnight 25th/26th September and the efforts to reinforce I and IV Corps

The Germans were probably far more adept at the use of counter-attacks than the British in the Great War and it was inevitable that sooner or later these would be launched. Prior to the attacks the Germans had harassed the British in their new positions with artillery and small arms fire. On the I Corps front attention was particularly centered on the Quarries and Fosse 8, positions held by men from the 7th and 9th divisions. Indeed a full-blown counter-attack was launched around 1.00am on the 26th September from the area of the Vermelles- Hulluch road towards Fosse 8. It is believed this attack consisted of troops from the 117th Division supported by the 26th Reserve Brigade. This attack was skillfully carried out and the Germans were among the British troops without many even realising they were there. The left prong of the German attack bumped into the 'new positions' of the 20th Brigade near the junction of the Vermelles-Hulluch and Lens-La Bassée roads. After a brief fight the defenders, mainly from the 2nd and 6th Gordons and 8th Devonshires, fell back towards Gun Trench. It had been decided to put Gun Trench in a state of defence and act as a fallback position for the advanced one. Some German troops following close on the heels of the men from the crossroads, did manage to enter Gun Trench. After a fierce hand-to-hand fight they were driven back with heavy losses. Men from the 2nd Borders, 2nd Bedfords and 6th Gordons were prominent in this fight. The 'front line' was now settled on Gun Trench.

However, a more important German success was achieved at the Quarries. The furthest forward British position was in a rough and ready trench about 200 yards forward of the Quarry. This was held by a mixed bag of troops from the 1st South Staffs, 2nd Green Howards (who had relieved the 4th Camerons) and the 2nd Queens (these troops coming from the 21st and 22nd brigades). The second line position was actually in the Quarries. Regrettably though, no contact had been established with any supporting troops. The 9th Division on their left were about 500 yards away. To assist their counter-attack the Germans softened the defenders at the Quarries up by the liberal use of gas shells. It must be said here that the technology for chemical warfare was far more advanced in the German Army than the British. Gas shells were still some months away for the British. Around 1.00am orders were received for the 21st Brigade to be temporarily withdrawn, to reorganise in the rear with a view to taking up the attack again at dawn. With perfect timing, the cards turned in the Germans favour, as while the men of the South Staffs were forming up to withdraw, the German attack came in. They had infiltrated in between the gap between the Quarries and the 27th Brigade. They entered the area from the side and rear. It is reported that their arrival was totally unexpected. The GOC of the 27th Brigade, Brigadier Bruce, who had visited the Quarries to use a field telephone to report back, was captured in the signals dugout. There was some

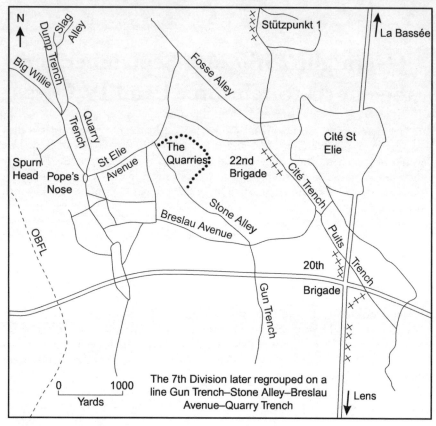

OBFL   Original British Front Line
+++   Furthest positions reached by 7th Division

The Quarries were lost around midnight/1am on the night of 25th/26th September

Map 9: 7th Division in the Quarries area, 25th/26th September 1915

confused fighting over the next few minutes but at the end of it, the Germans un-questionably had retaken the area. However further attempts to advance were stopped by men from the 2nd Green Howards and 1st South Staffs, who had man-aged to escape, firing from the original German front line about 600 yards west of the Quarries.

This report, from Captain Philpot of the 2nd Queens, is probably the only surviving account of the loss of the Quarries and the capture of Brigadier Bruce:

> Shortly after 11pm somebody looked into the dug out and stated that all the troops in front of us had retired at the double, and that our troops were being bombed out of their trench by Germans following up. The Germans bombed the Queen's from both flanks in the trench.

Some dozen of us, comprising a General, the CO, the Adjutant, four company officers and myself, together with the RSM formed up in the Quarry. The first German we saw was promptly shot and we then dispersed a party on our right flank, about 40 yards away. A party on our left flank was similarly fired on and scattered, when turning about we saw the enemy behind us. These we drove back with rifle and revolver fire, and after engaging the other parties of the enemy, it was decided to make a dash for it. When I left the Quarry, the Germans were about 15 yards away, and I saw two men fall in front of me killed. I think they must have been the General and the CO as they are the only two now missing.

Brigadier Bruce was captured alive and spent the rest of the war in captivity.

Meanwhile the right hand unit of the 27th Brigade, the 12th Royal Scots, which had also been subjected to shelling and sniping, heard the sounds of battle coming from their right rear. In the absence of the Brigade commander it was agreed by the Battalion's CO to withdraw back to the original British trenches, regain contact with the 7th Division and reorganise. This is what happened, meeting up with units of the 21st and 22nd brigades. To the area south of the Quarries elements of the 2nd Wiltshires and 2nd Bedfords held the line from Stone Alley to Breslau Avenue. The rest of the night was spent in these positions. But the loss of the advanced position and the Quarries completely upset the plans for the next day's operations. Artillery observation positions gained at such a cost during the 25th had been lost, which also meant the gunners had to return back to their old firing positions, as in some places they were exposed to small arms fire at very short range. There was not a battalion in the 7th Division that had not suffered heavily;

View from Gun Trench across the 20th Brigade sector. (IWM Q 41991)

nine of them had lost their commanding officers. It was clear that if the Quarries were to be retaken fresh troops must be found to do the job, even more would be needed if Cité St Elie was to be added. It would not be the job of the 7th Division to attempt this but it was given to the 9th Norfolks of the 71st Brigade from the 24th Division, who had been lent to the 7th Division. The first effort to retake the Quarries was made around 6.00am by the Norfolks. Dead tired from its approach march, its attack was immediately stopped by heavy German fire. The wisdom of sending totally inexperienced troops into such a situation can be gauged by the casualty figure of 13 officers and 409 men for about five minutes 'fighting'.

The 4th Camerons from the 7th Division had been nominated to launch this counter-attack but the arrival of the Norfolks meant they stepped aside. It is worth recording that the Camerons, in spite of their efforts on the 25th, were probably in a better shape to carry out this attack than the Norfolks. The survivors of the Norfolks fell back to Quarry Trench to lick their wounds. The right prong of the German attack centred on Fosse 8 and this was successfully repelled. It was somewhat fortunate that just before the attack went in the thousand or so survivors from the 26th Brigade, were being relieved by men from the 73rd Brigade from the 24th Division. This Brigade, although inexperienced in combat, were almost at full strength (4,000 men) and were a welcome sight to the Jocks of the 26th Brigade. The 73rd Brigade had been handed over to I Corps in Haig's orders on the morning of 25th September. General Gough had placed it under the command of 9th Division and it was decided to assemble them in the old British trenches west of the Hohenzollern Redoubt. Again this unit suffered travel difficulties and although the journey was about four miles the leading units did not reach this area till after 4.00pm on the 25th, the rear of the column about 7.00pm.

While this Brigade was sorting itself out, the 26th Brigade requested urgent assistance, as it appeared Fosse 8 might fall without reinforcements. Gough decided to use the entire 73rd Brigade there and informed Major-General Thesiger that help was on its way. It was also suggested that these new troops be used to replace the tired men of the 26th Brigade. A staff officer from HQ 9th Division and some officers from the units of the 26th Brigade were detailed to help these relatively inexperienced battalions across to the area of Fosse 8. For the record, the units of the 73rd Brigade were all New Army - 12th Royal Fusiliers, 9th Royal Sussex, 13th Middlesex and 7th Northamptons. The journey involved crossing five lines of German trenches and all the associated obstacles. One of the troops involved in this movement was Private G. Marrin from the 13th Middlesex. Here is his account:

> We marched straight into the battle. By the time we got into the front line we were right by the coal mine, Fosse 8, on the left, that's where the Scots got slaughtered, yes, because we saw these men lying around and coming in wounded - thousands of them. The whole thing was an absolute shambles. We were frightened out of our lives. It was terrible. It was our first experience of warfare, and there was machine gun fire and shelling, and everything seemed to be exploding everywhere. You just didn't know what was taking place. Then we got somewhere - they said it was in the line. We didn't know. You were facing one way and they said "That's where they are," but you didn't know. You put up rifle fire but you didn't know what you were shooting at. You'd no idea what

you were doing or supposed to be doing. It was just a continual bashing of gun-fire. Terrifying. You couldn't think. We were scared out of our wits.

It took until nearly 10.00pm for the leading men, again tired from the previous days movement, to reach Corons Alley Trench north-west of the Dump at Fosse 8. The arrival of the 73rd Brigade here was a lengthy process taking over three hours. So it was around 1.00am on the morning of 26th September in the pouring rain when German soldiers were spotted around 100 yards away from the British positions. Hurried fire orders were shouted out and the Germans were cut-down, with only a few Germans from the 91st Reserve Regiment actually getting into the British trenches. Those that did were dealt with by cold steel. The area then went quiet, allowing the 26th Brigade to withdraw back to the old British front line. This meant the 73rd Brigade assumed responsibility for the area of Fosse 8 down to Fosse Alley with three battalions in the front line: 7th Northants, 9th Royal Sussex and 12th Royal Fusiliers. About half of the 13th Middlesex were positioned as a right flank guard in Slag Alley, the old German communication trench south of the Dump, to connect with the 27th Brigade in Big Willie in the old German front line. However it had been a difficult baptism of fire for the men of the 73rd Brigade and no punches were pulled in one of the entries in the War Diary of the 9th Royal Sussex about this day: "It is regretted that before being launched into such a desperate action steps had not been taken to accustom the men to war conditions."

This then virtually leaves the whole of the I Corps actions on 25th September covered and we will now look at the events further south in IV Corps. Just a final point to remember for the I Corps area was the total lack of success in the extreme north by the 2nd Division.

In the southern sector, that of IV Corps, there was better news. The 15th Division had, during the day of 25th September, taken Hill 70 and the London Territorials had done well on the right flank. As usual the question was, could this success be reinforced?

Virtually the only reserves available to Rawlinson were the 62nd Brigade from the 21st Division and these only late in the day on the 25th. Rawlinson placed them under command of the 15th Division with the intention of supporting and if necessary relieving the men on Hill 70. Again the situation facing these virtually raw troops was a difficult one. They had been located in the village of Mazingarbe before around noon on the 25th receiving orders to head for the front. The Brigade Commander, Brigadier Wilkinson, was given orders along the lines of: "If, when you reach Loos, you find Hill 70 abandoned, you are to retake it and then press forward to Cité St Auguste." Wilkinson having no more information than this and no knowledge of the ground could do little more at his Orders Group than point out Hill 70 on a map and tell the unit COs: "We do not know what has happened on Hill 70. You must go and find out: if the Germans hold it, attack them; if our people are there, support them; if no one is there, dig in."

By now it was around 3.00pm and Wilkinson decided in the first instance to only send two battalions forward. The units selected were the 8th East Yorks and the 10th Green Howards. Apparently, on the approach march at Noeux les Mines they were stopped by a Redcap. He advised the units that from this point onwards, the battalions must advance in open order with gaps between sections. It is believed that in their inexperience they obeyed these instructions further slowing progress. The other two units of the Brigade following in behind the others were the 12th and 13th Northumberland Fusiliers. Around 4.30 p.m., the two lead units were marching down the Lens road in fours with a hundred yards between platoons and reached the crest of the slope leading down into the Loos valley. After crossing the original British front line, they left the road and headed cross-country towards the Loos Pylons. Around this time they came in direct line of sight of some German artillery in Cité St Pierre with inevitable results. Many casualties were suffered particularly amongst the transport column, which was following the men. Things now started to go from bad to worse, trying to navigate from a 1/100,000 map (roughly 2½ miles to the inch) and without guides, across unknown ground the advance lost direction. Instead of heading towards the village of Loos and asking which piece of high ground was Hill 70, the two leading units headed towards Lens along the western side of Loos village and the Loos Crassier. They soon came across the men from the 20th Londons who were defending the old German communication trench about 200 yards north of Chalk Pit Copse. The commanding officer of the 20th Londons, Lieutenant-Colonel Hubback, tried to stop their advance but as the men were in an extended line it was a difficult job. It is believed that around this time the senior commanders of the 63rd Brigade finally received some decent information when Brigadier Wilkinson met the Brigade Commander of the 141st Brigade (the 20th Londons were one of his units), Brigadier Thwaites. He was on his way to visit his battalions and they bumped into each other at a small estaminet at the North Maroc-Loos and Béthune-Lens crossroads, and explained the layout as best he could. This was to say that his Brigade had occupied and was holding from Chalk Pit Copse to the south-east end of Loos Crassier and that Hill 70 was to the north-east of the Crassier. But it was just too late, and German infantry in the southern part of Chalk Pit Copse opened up on the 62nd Brigade, and both the 8th East Yorks and 10th Green Howards suffered heavy casualties. The men fell back in disarray. Attempts were made to steady the men and reorganise. From now on the 62nd Brigade started to be used in penny packets and for a variety of tasks. Some men were sent to man a gap near the Loos Crassier, others went to reinforce the 20th Londons. Others went back to the Lens road and returned to the Grenay-Loos crossroads (behind the lines of the 141st Brigade) and were mistaken for a German patrol and fired on by the rearguard of the 10th Green Howards. Confusion reigned for a while until order (of a sort) was established. The remnants of the Green Howards positioned themselves in and east of the Loos Cemetery, while the 8th East Yorks together with some men from the 19th Londons dug themselves in next to the 20th Londons. They extended the line of troops over and beyond the Loos Crassier.

Meanwhile the other two battalions of the 62nd Brigade with the Brigade commander in tow had navigated correctly and arrived relatively unscathed in Loos village. The Brigade commander, Brigadier Wilkinson, reported in at 45th Brigade HQ located in Loos and was asked by Brigadier Wallerston to relieve men on Hill 70. Wallerston expected Wilkinson's men to relieve those battalions of the 44th and 46th brigades, which had not already been relieved, by men from the 45th Brigade. But of course the 62nd had only two battalions present in Loos, so Wilkinson decided to only send the 12th Northumberland Fusiliers to Hill 70 and even then just two platoons to test the water as it were. When they confirmed everything was ok, a further two platoons were sent forward. Meanwhile the arrival of the Fusiliers on Hill 70 was seen by the 9th Black Watch and 10th Gordon Highlanders as the signal for them to retire, which they promptly did. This at that time just left one company of Fusiliers there and they were instructed to remain in position and await developments.

The other unit from the 62nd Brigade still in Loos (13th Northumberland Fusiliers) was sent around 11.30pm to report to the 46th Brigade "believed to be a 1,000 yards north-east of Loos-Haisnes road". They eventually ran into the 12th Highland Light Infantry from this Brigade, and as the CO knew where his Brigadier wanted these reinforcements, he was able to point them in the right direction. Soon three companies were digging in along the Loos-Hulluch road. The remaining company was sent to support an isolated 12th HLI platoon on the extreme left flank near the Lens road south of Chalet Wood.

Again the arrival of these 'fresh' troops was mistaken for a general relief and many men from the 46th Brigade began retiring. Again it is fair to say that chaos reigned and the British front line here (if only the Germans had known!) was very thinly held.

However, there was some good news for the British, in that two German counter-attacks in the area were repulsed. The first was directed against the 7th Royal Scots Fusiliers (on the right of the 45th Brigade) below the summit of Hill 70 on the eastern side of the Loos Crassier. A second and heavier one was made from the direction of Cité St Laurent against the same unit also failed. The Scots Fusiliers had been greatly helped by the 11th Motor Machine Gun Battery, which had been brought into the area late on 25th September.

At daybreak on the 26th the situation had not altered much around Loos and Hill 70. The 47th Division was still holding the ground it had gained the previous morning, forming a defensive flank between the Double Crassier and the Loos Crassier looking towards the north-eastern suburbs of Lens. The 45th Brigade from the 15th Division, together with two battalions of Northumberland Fusiliers, was positioned on the western slope of Hill 70. Further to the left were men from the 15th Division holding as far as the western edge of Bois Hugo. At the Bois Hugo the 63rd Brigade had relieved units of the 1st Division and their front extended up to the Chalk Pit. But there was of course the gap in the front that has previously been mentioned. On the IV Corps front there was a gap between Chalk Pit Wood and Hulluch. At Hulluch the 3rd Brigade had retired back to Alley 4 Trench. The final counter-attack of this night was made against the South Wales Borderers situated on the left frontage of the 1st Division in Gun Trench. Behind the Welshmen were three abandoned/captured German artillery pieces, which it had not been able to move. The CO of the unit, Lieutenant-Colonel Gwynn, rightly guessed that the Germans would try and retake them. A party of around 300 Germans came forward, some calling: "Don't shoot, we are the Welch." The Borderers had laid an almost perfect ambush with machine guns on the flanks allowing crossfire, their discipline was excellent and fire was only opened up at the last second. The Germans were virtually wiped out, with only a few Borderers wounded. This ended the nighttime manoeuvring for position. The BEF was now set for a second surge on the morning of the 26th. The only topic left to look at now are the German movements during the 25th September and the night of 25th/26th September.

The day of the 25th September caused the Germans many anxious moments, the front line defenders had in many places been overwhelmed by the weight of numbers thrown against them. It had also been doubtful whether the few immediately available reserves would have time to reach and man the second line defences before they were reached by the advancing British. It will come as no surprise that it was a race that the Germans won. At certain locations such as Bois Carré and Lone Tree in the middle sector, the stout resistance put up by the defenders probably broke the impetus of the advance. However it is certainly no exaggeration to say that nearly all the available soldiers, even the cooks and bottle washers, were sent to the front. It is recorded in a diary of a captured German artillery officer that there was also panic in the rear areas. This extract concerns the German IV Corps HQ at Douai (about 12 miles back): "There were at 4.00pm 25th September endless convoys of wagons formed up in double lines ready to march away, and the wagons of the Corps Headquarters were also awaiting the order to move off. It was a sad picture of retreat." The 91st Reserve Regiment marching to the sound of gunfire also found the transport ready to withdraw east and reported in their War Diary: "Something extraordinary must have happened. There was talk of the successful attack of the British after the gassing of our line, that had been shot to pieces by the bombardment of the previous days."

The Germans proved in the Great War (as they did in the Second World War) that they were masters of improvisation and reacted quickly. Local reserves were soon warned to move, before receiving orders to do so. Early in the afternoon of the 25th a battalion from the 26th Regiment arrived from its rest area at Annay to strengthen a perceived weak point either side of Stützpunkt IV. The reserve battalion of the 11th Reserve Regiment moved up from Wingles into Cité St Elie during the late morning and occupied positions in front of it for the rest of the day. The reserve battalion of the 16th Regiment, together with the 11th Jäger Battalion, took up positions in Cemetery Alley Trench immediately after the Jocks of the 9th Division had advanced through Fosse 8. But later in the day, it took part in a counterattack which forced the Jocks back from Pekin Trench (opposite Haisnes) to Fosse 8.

These then were the deployments of the local reserves, and the only other formed bodies of men immediately available to reinforce the sector under attack were those in the German 6th Army reserve, these units being the 8th Division from IV Corps near Lille and the 2nd Guards Reserve Division of X Reserve Corps situated near Douai. Soon after, news had arrived of the British advance through the German front line between Loos and Auchy the reserves were warned to be ready to move. With admirable thinking it was decided to attack the flanks of the gaps first. To plug this gap and start applying pressure initially nine infantry battalions, closely followed by seven more, were sent from north of the La Bassée Canal and Douai to the northern part of the gap near Haisnes. A further six battalions were sent to the southern gap around Bois Hugo and Cité St Laurent, these units moving from the area of Lens.

The 8th Division was ordered to mobilise its 93rd and 153rd regiments to help with the defence of Lens. They were swiftly moved by train and vehicle to a

Panorama from the north-west of Loos looking towards Cité St Auguste.
(IWM Q41998)

place called Billy Montigny (about three miles from Lens), marching the rest of the way by foot. Contrast this with the protracted journey of the 21st and 24th divisions. Both regiments were sent to take up defensive positions: the 93rd Regiment going to the area of Cité St Laurent and during the night taking up a position between Hill 70 Redoubt and the Loos Crassier, the 153rd Regiment moving to the area of Cité St Auguste and Bois Hugo. In this way therefore the southern flank of the battlefield (in German eyes) had been secured. These two units together with local reserves now formed a strong defensive position from the Loos Crassier across Hill 70 (including the Redoubt) through to the eastern end of Chalet Wood and Bois Hugo.

Looking at the northern sector reserves were also sent here. Two reserve brigades (the 26th and 38th) from the 2nd Guards Reserve Division were moved from the rear areas during the late afternoon/early evening of the 25th September. Two complete regiments (the 15th Reserve and 91st Reserve) moved one from each of these two brigades quickly to the front by train. The 15th Reserve Regiment was moved to Allennes, about seven miles east of La Bassée. The 91st Reserve Regiment was deposited even closer at Meurchin three miles east of Hulluch. In spite of their other problems it seems the Germans were still able to move these units even closer to the sound of gunfire by vehicle rather than foot. The remaining two regiments from these brigades, the 55th and 77th Reserve regiments, were moved to the area of Wingles and Douvrin, acting as close support. The Germans in both World Wars, as previously stated, were masters of creating *ad-hoc* forces or *Kampfgruppen*. Such a group was formed in the late evening of the 25th by a

Colonel Staubwasser of the II Bavarian Corps from mixed troops who arrived from a neighbouring Army Group by rail. It was immediately formed and put into the line at Haisnes. In addition a battalion of the 55th Regiment was sent from their position north of La Bassée to a village further south by vehicle and to act as VII Corps reserve. It is believed that, in all, an additional 22 battalions were moved into the Loos sector on 25th September and by the morning of 26th September it is believed the new German line was more strongly held than the original German front line at the time of the British attack. Perhaps the only advantage the British had (on paper) was that their artillery strength was still far greater in number than their counterparts, but would this count for anything?

It appears that by nightfall on the evening of 25th September, any fears that the German senior commanders had of a complete breakthrough by the BEF were abating at a rapid rate. North of the La Bassée Canal appeared to be 'All Quiet on the Western Front', while south of the canal between Haisnes and Loos, the initial successes had not been followed up beyond the Lens-La Bassée road and virtually none of the second line positions had been seriously threatened. The advance across Hill 70, threatening Lens had been halted by the reserves of the 7th Division and further south the assault by the French 10th Army against Vimy Ridge was in German eyes little more than a feint. This attack had been repulsed and indeed troops were moved northwards from there.

I am sure Haig would have been more than a little surprised if he had known that the first orders for the German fight-back had been issued as early as 3.00pm, a little more than eight hours after the initial attack. The orders issued by the commander of IV Corps, General Sixt von Armin, envisaged two simultaneous attacks directed inwards from the flanks of the gap. In the north, the 117th Division augmented by the 2nd Guards Reserve Division was to attack from Haisnes and Cité St Elie on a frontage Fosse 8 to the Quarries to Gun Trench. In the south the 8th Division was to assault Hill 70 and carry on to Loos.

In the northern sector the attack as we have seen went in around midnight, directed towards the Quarries and Fosse 8. Moving in a south-westerly direction from Cité St Elie/Haisnes area the 15th Reserve Regiment attacked Gun Trench. The 3rd Battalion of the 91st Reserve Regiment together with elements of the 11th Reserve Regiment assaulted the Quarries. Finally the attack on Fosse 8 was entrusted to the 1st Battalion of the 91st Reserve Regiment, together with elements of the 2nd Battalion and men from the 55th Reserve Regiment. As we have seen the northern attack managed to penetrate as far as the Quarries, but stout resistance held up further progress. There were more difficulties with the southern attack, as we shall soon see. This is now an opportune moment to draw to a close the actions during the day of 25th September and the night of 25th/26th September. The question now was, who would get the upper hand on the morning of the second day?

6

Behind the British Lines

It must have been very difficult for the British senior commanders to grasp exactly what had happened on the battlefield of Loos on the 25th September. The plan must be said to have achieved some initial success, in that in numerous places things had gone well. The 47th Division in the extreme south had done their task well and formed the defensive flank, facing Lens. The 15th Division had captured the village of Loos, advanced through the village, seized Hill 70 and carried on past it, albeit in the wrong direction. The 1st and 7th divisions had reached the Lens-La Bassée road. The 9th Division had taken the Hohenzollern Redoubt, Fosse 8 and the Dump and then gone further into the German rear near Haisnes. The only note of caution was the 2nd Division, who had failed to gain any ground at all. Everyone else had gained possession of the German front line and positions beyond it. The question was, could these gains be consolidated and indeed improved upon? In an ideal world fresh troops would be required, close up and ready to press on to exploit any gains and there were two corps in reserve under the control of the Commander-in-Chief Field Marshal Sir John French. It is calculated that the losses of the 1st Army for the 25th September were around 500 officers and 15,000 men, approximately one-sixth of the entire strength deployed.

It appears there was communication between French and Foch on the evening of 25th September, during which Foch decided he was going to carry on with his attack, which forced the British to carry on with their attack, which as you will recall was, in theory, subsidiary to the French effort. If the attack was to continue and as the original orders stated, Sir John French was to "act vigorously", it was essential that fresh troops would have to take up the mantle. Haig as Army commander had included in his plans XI Corps acting as the immediate reserve to his two corps, I and IV. This is why he put all his divisions in the front line and assured his senior commanders that "ample reserves would be ready immediately behind them to carry on the advance." XI Corps consisted of the Guards, 21st and 24th divisions and also in reserve was the Cavalry Corps (1st, 2nd and 3rd cavalry divisions). Sir John French had told Haig that two divisions of the General Reserve would be in the area and placed under his command when required, but - and this is the important point, they would remain under French's personal command and released only when French considered it appropriate. This was pointed out in a letter to Haig from GHQ on 7th August which stated: "The troops available for the operations will be those of your own Army, plus the Cavalry Corps and two divisions held in General Reserve under the orders of the Commander-in-Chief."

Even more alarming was the decision by French prior to the battle that he would keep the whole of the General Reserve near Lillers until released by him. Haig expressed his opinion in forceful terms that this was too far back, Lillers being sixteen miles by road to Vermelles. General Foch backed up Haig by suggesting that the reserve should be about 2 kilometers (1¼ miles) behind the corps reserves. As there were no corps reserves it made all the more sense to have Sir John's men close in support. Joffre apparently wrote that if "Sir John kept his reserve divisions too far back they would run the risk of arriving too late to exploit the successes of the leading ones. It is indispensable that these divisions are put, before the attack at the absolute disposal of General Haig."

Haig also pointed out that he had based his plans on at least two divisions being readily available as reinforcements for his Army, and if held 16 miles away they would not, at the earliest, reach the battle area until the evening of the first day. Haig was also mindful of experience gained the hard way earlier in the year at such places as Neuve Chapelle and Festubert. Events had proved that attacking troops quickly became exhausted and shown how soon fresh divisions are required to carry the assault forward. An additional point was the need to take immediate advantage of any initial success, as previous battles had shown that the Germans had always managed to get some of their reserves to the attacked area within about four hours, man their rear defences and bring the attack to a grinding halt. For all these reasons, Haig urged Sir John French to move forward two divisions from XI Corps, so that they were located near Vermelles, around 2,000 yards back by dawn on the day of the actual assault. Haig, according to the post-war Official History, was supported in his view by Lieutenant-General Haking, the commander of XI Corps. He believed a gap might well occur between I and IV corps into which his Corps would have to step. He thought his best position would be to deploy his divisions between Mazingarbe and Vermelles but early in the morning. However he knew that Sir John French intended his Corps to be held under his control until the last moment. As the Official History puts it, "His position was a most embarrassing one". It appears that in spite of all these reasons for having the reserves close at hand to exploit any success and beat the German reserves to the area, Sir John just said he did not agree and would keep his men in the Lillers area until the battle had developed sufficiently to enable him to decide if and where to commit them. He stamped his authority on this messy situation in a GHQ Order dated 18th September 1915:

> The Cavalry, Indian Cavalry and XI Corps will form the General Reserve at the disposal of the Field Marshal Commanding-in-Chief. Separate instructions will be issued for the concentration of these troops. The 2nd Army will keep one division in Army reserve west of Bailleul to reinforce either the 1st or 2nd Army as the Commander-in-Chief may decide.

But he clouded the issue by then going on to say:

> Once the enemy's defences have been pierced a situation must be created in which manoeuvre will become possible, and to do this the offensive must be continued with the utmost determination directly to the front in the first instance. It must be impressed on commanders that to delay the advance in order to work outwards to the flanks will give the enemy time to re-establish his front. The advance must be made in depth so that rapid manoeuvre may be possible.

All of this is fine, but given the experience of the previous attacks in 1915, the reserves needed to be immediately available to press on with the attack especially as it was envisaged that the BEF would be operating deep in the enemy rear. The day after these instructions, Haig wrote to French formally repeating his request for the General Reserve to be positioned closer to the front and asking that the leading units of the two divisions be on the line Noeux les Mines-Beuvry (about 2¾ miles back) by daylight on the 25th September. Perhaps it was an un-written request but fairly obvious that they be ready to move, but rested and fully briefed on their likely tasks. Sir John French did not waste much time in firing off a reply, which again must have caused confusion, as he said to Haig: "Two divisions of the XI Corps will be assembled in the area referred to in your letter by daybreak on the 25th September." One can imagine that an army commander re-ceiving such a message as this would assume that it was likely that the reserves would be ready to move in support of their orders. But Sir John in his final in-structions said that whilst they could move, they were to remain under his con-trol until released. He tried to justify this in a despatch of 15th October 1915 in which he said: "In view of the great length of line along which the British troops were operating, it was necessary to keep a strong reserve in my own hand. The XI Corps was detailed for this purpose."

The move of XI Corps started during the morning of 24th September when at a conference the Corps commander informed his senior commanders what was planned. Haking warned that the units might be cut off from their logistical sup-port until the night of 26th/27th September. To alleviate these losses, each man was to carry his pack and greatcoat together with some additional rations. These ra-tions consisted of one iron ration and an extra cheese ration, a haversack portion of bread and cheese and a tin of pea soup. The men were warned to be careful with this food, as it was unclear whether the catering staff would be able to meet up with their units on 26th/27th September.

As it was, it took until 7.00pm on the evening of the 24th (when it was now dark) for the leading units to begin their move towards their pre-allocated posi-tions. This move, varying between 7 and 11 miles, could normally be expected to take around 4 hours, which ought to have allowed them the chance of getting some rest before being launched into the assault the next day. The march as it turned out took at least double this time for most of the sub-units. Indeed the Corps com-mander Haking later wrote in a report about this move:

> I am of the opinion that the delay was caused chiefly by their own indifferent march discipline, especially as regards first-line transport. These divisions only received their transport just before leaving England, the drivers were not well trained, and the march discipline of these new divisions, though good when marching without transport was certainly not good when marching with it, and constant halts and checks occurred.

Is this criticism fair? At the time it certainly was an easy scapegoat to put for-ward. However at least one unit on the march reported in its War Diary that it was held up for over 90 minutes by the unit in front of it. This hold-up apparently oc-curred because the horses struggled to get up a small hill. It was suggested that night work was more tiring to horses than men, as they rarely rest properly in day-light. It also seems strange to blame the march discipline of the 21st and 24th divi-sions when there were no previous adverse reports when moving through rear areas. Perhaps it is also worth mentioning that for a lot of the New Army divisions, training in Britain due to a shortage of weapons consisted of route marching.

In the author's opinion, the real cause of the delays was the lateness of the move and then sending the men to the front via roads that were inadequate. A catalogue of disasters can be traced. On the narrow French roads, the units found motor and horse transport moving away from the front and they had to literally force their way past them. Poor staff work, for example, also came into play. The Gonnehem-Chocques road, designated as a 'down' road, was used by the 24th Division as an 'up' route. This 'road' was only three or four feet wider than a column of fours with a deep ditch on each side. It is fairly obvious to say that for most of the time the men were in single file, again slowing progress. At every crossroads there seemed to be a traffic jam. The Official History written in the 1920s stated that it was like trying to push the Lord Mayor's Procession through the streets of London without clearing the route and holding up other traffic. Delays were also experienced at the numerous level crossings such as at Chocques (many medical facilities were based here), Marles les Mines and Place à Bruay. The 64th Brigade was delayed for around two hours due to a train accident at Place à Bruay and then for nearly an hour at Marles les Mines. These problems cannot be laid at the door of these divisions, indeed they had been told by XI Corps that arrangements with the French railway authorities had been made and they need not anticipate any delays. The only problem was that the French railways did not run to an XI Corps timetable. But without doubt the most farcical incident occurred on the outskirts of Béthune, where an officious military policeman stopped the men of the 72nd Brigade entering the town because the Brigade commander did not have a pass. Added to this, some map reading errors and loss of direction meant it was a recipe for disaster. With the benefit of hindsight it is easy to say that errors made in other theatres were being repeated. Here I am thinking of the landing at Suvla Bay on Gallipoli in August 1915, when units were only told of their role in the landings when on the boats to the Peninsula.

In spite of (or because of) these difficulties the units of the 21st and 24th divisions arrived in their allocated positions between 2.00 and 7.00am on the morning of the 25th, many just collapsing in fields close to the road. The divisions were spread out anything from five to eight miles behind the front line. It must have been difficult to rest as it was raining on and off and there was noise from the artillery bombardment.

Meanwhile Sir John French had decided to move what I will call, in modern day terms, his Tactical HQ, to a chateau near Lillers, around 20 miles away from his Main HQ at St Omer. A move of this kind is fine provided adequate communication is available. It appears that his only means of communication with Main HQ was by dispatch riders and the French telephone system. There was no communication by wire with his army commanders.

Around 7.00am on the 25th when favourable reports from I and IV corps about the attack started to arrive at 1st Army HQ, Haig decided to send a staff officer by car to inform Sir John of the success of the initial attack, and to urge the release of XI Corps from the reserve. Additionally around 8.45am another message was sent saying that "The reserve brigades of the I and IV corps have either reached the German front line trenches or were on the move there. Could XI Corps be placed at my disposal and pushed on at once?"

How did Sir John react? Haig (and others) of course, felt that the 21st and 24th divisions should have moved forward at 6.30am and already valuable time had been lost. Having received several reports of progress by the I and IV corps and 1st Army, Sir John French decided to move the divisions forward at 9.30am, with the following order being issued:

> 21st and 24th divisions will move forward to 1st Army trenches as soon as situation requires and admits. On arrival there they will come under the orders of 1st Army. Arrange move in communication with 1st Army accordingly. Guards Division will move up to ground vacated by 21st Division. XI Corps less 21st and 24th divisions will remain in General Reserve.

Now once again there is controversy over the timings of these instructions: GHQ records state this message was timed at 9.50am and received by Haig at 10.02am and that at "about 11.30am" Sir John visited Haig and informed him he "would arrange to put XI Corps (less the Guards Division) under his orders." Sir John then went to visit Haking at Noeux les Mines where he states he arrived at noon. The XI Corps War Diary records that the Commander-in-Chief gave his orders about the move at 12.03pm. At 1.20pm, HQ XI Corps reported to HQ 1st Army that 21st and 24th divisions were now under their command and marching to the areas ordered, but were delayed (once again) on the roads. According to the Official History, in Sir John's post-Loos despatch dated 15th October he reported: "The 21st and 24th divisions were put at the disposal of the GOC 1st Army at 9.30am, who at once ordered the GOC XI Corps to move them up in support of the attacking troops." These comments were the subject of a protest by Haig to GHQ, the repercussions of which will be told later. The 21st and 24th divisions were ordered to assemble as soon as possible on the line Mazingarbe-Vermelles on either side of the Béthune-Lens road. The 24th would support I Corps and 21st Division IV Corps. Again Murphy's Law came into play and soon after the 21st Division started its move forward, it was ordered to stop to let an ammunition supply convoy cross its path.

Perhaps jumping forward a bit, Haig in his eagerness to get his 'reserves' into the battle, in the late morning, warned his two corps that help was on the way. Gough in I Corps was advised that the 24th Division would be his, and he proposed to use it to continue the attack through and beyond Haisnes. Rawlinson in IV Corps was given the 21st Division. With the benefit of hindsight it is easy to see that things were not going well in all areas, but in 1915 many commanders were reliant upon very sketchy reports and sometimes these were optimistic or just plain wrong. Haig, some miles behind the front, received encouraging reports, such as that the 15th Division had taken Hill 70, the 7th Division was in Cité St Elie and one of the brigades from the 1st Division was in Hulluch. Haig must have felt the desired breakthrough had been achieved and around 10.30am he ordered his only reserve unit (at that time) forward. This was the 3rd Cavalry Division and they were ordered to move to the Corons de Rutoire near Vermelles. This was in readiness to move forward through the infantry and capture the high ground between Harnes and Pont à Vendin as soon as Cité St Auguste had been taken.

It appears that there was always a place for the cavalry to have a starring role and, on paper, win the glory. Every time they were called forward their starring role was relegated to a walk-on part, for example, the cavalry at the Somme in 1916 and Monchy-le-Preux in 1917. In any case, the GOC of the 3rd Cavalry Division, Major-General Briggs decided to investigate for himself and visited the HQs of three of the infantry divisions - the 1st, 7th and 15th. The reports he gathered from these HQs in his opinion were nowhere near as favourable as had been depicted. He therefore left liaison officers at these HQs with instructions to report back to him any favourable opportunities for his force. The fog of war again came into play in the early afternoon, when Haig, believing an attack was going in against Cité St Auguste, ordered the 3rd Cavalry Division forward. Briggs continued to stick to his guns and advised Haig that the current situation was not favourable but that he would go forward when opportunity existed.

In spite of this Haig still believed that the attack was going well and was convinced that the German defences were on the point of breaking down completely. He therefore had no reservations at 2.35pm, when he sent an order to General Haking concerning the 21st and 24th divisions. Haig told Haking to: "Push forward at once between Hulluch and Cité St Auguste and occupy the high ground between Harnes and Pont à Vendin, both inclusive, and secure the passages of the Haute Deule Canal at these places." It seems Haig believed the cavalry had already gone forward and the units of XI Corps could relieve them, so the cavalry could move towards Carvin. For his part, Haking believed that his flanks would be secure, as he had been passed reports that I Corps had entered Hulluch and IV Corps had captured Hill 70. Following on the order from Haig, Haking issued his own orders to these units. He ordered the 21st and 24th divisions to move forward across the open ground between Loos village and the Vermelles-Hulluch road and to "secure the crossings over the Haute Deule Canal at Loison sous Lens, Harnes and Pont à Vendin." He instructed them that their first objective would be the high ground just in front of the Canal. The 21st Division was to advance on an approximately 1,000 yard front between Fosse 7 (on the Béthune-Lens road) and the Vermelles-Loos track, the 63rd Brigade in the lead with the 64th Brigade in support. The 24th Division was again given a frontage of around 1,000 yards between the Vermelles-Loos track and the Vermelles-Hulluch road, the 72nd Brigade leading with the 71st Brigade in support. Note here that each division had 'lost' one of its brigades on temporary detachment to I and IV corps. It appears now that these orders led to the impression that the Germans had been routed and little or no organised resistance would be met in this advance. It seemed that little more was required than a long march chasing a retreating enemy. These orders seemed to confirm to the senior commanders of these two divisions what they had been told a few days earlier. At a briefing before the attack they had been told by the Chief of the General Staff, that in no conceivable circumstances would they be used unless and until the Germans were absolutely smashed and retiring in disorder. Haking confirmed this when he told them to carry greatcoats and extra rations and be prepared for a long march. These 'conditions' would have been ideal if they had been adhered to as these two divisions had never been in action before or even held the line. As it was they were sent into a difficult situation over unknown ground with little information.

Perhaps it would be advisable to take a small step back and review the movements of the units of the 21st and 24th divisions before the 2.35pm Haig order.

Around 10.30am, both divisions were instructed by Corps HQ to move to their as-sembly positions behind Vermelles. It was a move of about six miles but still took over four hours to achieve, due to clogged roads with stores going forward and wounded coming back. Here are some of the sub-units journeys to the front: The 63rd Brigade left its overnight position at Houchin at 11.15am and did not reach Mazingarbe (four miles away) till nearly 3.00pm . The 64th Brigade, due to a com-munication foul-up, received their order late, so left Hallicourt around noon and took over four hours to move the seven miles to Mazingarbe. In the 24th Division, the leading units of the two brigades reached their positions near Noyelles around 3.00pm but the rear parties were still over two miles away.

Meanwhile Haig's 2.35pm order, although given to liaison officers from the divisions almost straight away, did not reach the actual fighting troops till 5.00pm. It is worth recording too that many of the men had not had a hot meal for many hours, but in spite of this the units did start to deploy. However, at the end of the day (literally), as dusk approached, General Haking telephoned HQ 1st Army to say that his units had not fully deployed and reported a delay. This was around 6.00pm. Haig's Chief of Staff, Major-General Butler, after a consultation, in-formed Haking that it was deemed inadvisable for the advance to go beyond the Lens-La Bassée road that night. He did suggest that patrols be sent out towards the Haute Deule Canal to prepare the ground for a general advance the following morning. Haking was questioned as to the state of his divisions and he apparently answered that the men were tired but ready to carry out the planned operation. Perhaps some useful insights on the state of the men can be gauged from two com-ments. First, a report from the Assistant Provost Marshal: "The men appeared to be very tired, and many complained that they were dead beat owing to the succes-sion of night marches from St Omer." Secondly, the War Diary from the 103rd Field Company RE recorded: "25th September. 11.45am Marched out. No ra-

Table 6.1
March timetable from the War Diary of 103rd Field Company R.E.

20th September 1915	Eperlecques to 21st September 1915 Wittes
21st September 1915	Wittes to Lieres
22nd September 1915	Lieres to Allouagne
23rd September 1915	Rest Day
24th September 1915	Allouagne to Noeux les Mines
25th September 1915	11.15pm Noeux les Mines
25th September 1915	01.20p.m. Noyelles les Vermelles

tions received. Arrived Annequin 3pm . Marched out to attack still having had no food. Men dead tired with long night marches and continuous checks to columns on march."

Here is an account of the march up by a private from the 12th Northumberland Fusiliers, Harry Fellows. His unit was in the 62nd Brigade of the 21st Division:

View westwards from Bois Carré with the village of Philosophe in the centre distance.
(Geoff Parker)

The name of the place where we eventually finished our five night trek is still a mystery to me, but when some big guns commenced firing immediately behind our bivouac area, it became obvious that we were near the front line. There was no sleep that day! During the late afternoon we received the order to "Fall in by companies" and our Company commander, Captain Graham Pole addressed us. He told us that we were going to take part in a battle that had commenced in the early hours of that morning and which, it was hoped, would result in a breach in the German lines. Several divisions had taken part and a Scottish Division was now on the outskirts of the mining town of Lens. We would be going forward that evening to relieve them. I can still remember the cheers. Little did we know what was before us.

During the early evening we were issued with a bread and cheese ration, with special orders not to eat it until ordered. Shortly afterwards we received the order to "Fall in" as a Battalion and after the usual inspections, we marched off. On the line of march it was the custom of our CO, Lieutenant-Colonel H. Warwick, to change the leading Company of the Battalion and now it was my C Company that had this honour. Our field kitchens and cooks had been taken away from us, otherwise the whole of the Battalion transport was following in the rear.

When ambulances and walking wounded began to pass us going towards the rear we realised that we were getting near the scene of action and we passed through a built-up area along the Lens road called Philosophe. By this time it was quite dark. After Philosophe and Quality Street came our passage through the old trench system. In a hollow to our left front some enemy shells were bursting and in the light from these we saw some buildings which afterwards turned out to be the village of Loos. It appeared to be so far away to our left that it seemed we must bypass it. However, we were getting nearer all the time and presently we were at its outskirts and owing to shell holes in the road and fallen masonry progress was reduced to a crawl. It must have taken my Company an hour to pass through the village and we suddenly came to a full stop, afterwards finding that the head of the Battalion had been halted by the front line. It was obvious that someone had blundered and we had to wait for things to be sorted out.

We will return to Harry Fellows later, on Hill 70. A final comment comes from an officer with the 21st Division's pioneers, Lieutenant N. Dillon of the 14th Northumberland Fusiliers:

Nearing Vermelles I was sent ahead as a scout to try and find our billets. I seem to recall we were under artillery fire and the night was spent in a ploughed field with no kit. The following morning while some of the officers were gathered round a small fire trying to warm up a bit, the Company second-in-command came along and said he had had a bit of bladder trouble in the night. He said he was too cold to stand up and he had just rolled over and let fly where he was. We thought nothing of this, till the Company commander came along and he said, "It must have been wet last night. I was lying in a furrow next to Jones and my trousers are completely soaked." We all said, "There's been no rain." But he still didn't work out what had actually happened and I certainly didn't tell him!

While this move forward was going on at 6.10pm, HQ XI Corps issued new orders, which stated:

Leading brigades 21st and 24th divisions will gain the Hulluch-Lens road as the first objective. Be prepared to continue advance if moon gives sufficient light. The right of the 72nd Brigade and left of 63rd Brigade will be directed on the Hulluch-Loos, Lens-La Bassée crossroads. GOC's 72nd and 63rd brigades should consult at junction of Loos-Haisnes road and Lone Tree-Hulluch track at 1.00am regarding arrangements for further advance.

Obviously these orders did not take into the account the conversation (and decision) between Haking and Butler, so a contradictory set of orders was issued, timed 8.17pm:

21st and 24th divisions will secure and entrench the line from Hill 70 to west end of Hulluch, linking up with the troops of IV Corps on the right and I Corps on the left. This operation to be completed as soon as possible. Having gained this line, the 21st Division will send strong patrols to reconnoitre the canal bridges at Pont à Vendin. If these localities are found to be unoccupied, each division will send forward an advanced guard during the night to secure them. During the night both divisions will bring up their artillery and be prepared to continue the attack at daylight tomorrow with the original objectives. I and IV corps on the flanks are making similar preparations for an attack at daylight along their respective fronts.

These orders were received by both formations after 2.00am on the 26th September. So in spite of these orders the two divisions were still acting on previous instructions and began to form up for the supposedly unopposed advance to the Haute Deule Canal. In their inexperience the decision was taken to use the same daylight plan, but now to be carried out in the dark. To add to command and control problems it was now beginning to rain heavily. In view of previous difficulties with moving by road, the units now went cross-country. On the 21st Division front, after moving initially by road to the area of Fosse 7, the lead brigade, the 63rd, moved out on a compass bearing on a two battalion frontage with each battalion in company lines. This was around 9.00pm, with the supporting brigade, the 64th, about 30 minutes and a 1,000 yards behind them. It was probably around 10.00pm when the lead unit of the 24th Division, the 72nd Brigade, began to deploy near Le Rutoire Farm, with their support unit, the 71st Brigade, to its left rear.

It was completely dark when the two lead brigades set off on a compass bearing of 112º (basically in a north-easterly direction) and headed across a stretch of open ground approximately three miles wide towards the Lens-La Bassée road. At times there was reasonable visibility due to a clearing of the mist and illumination from various fires burning in Loos as a result of German shelling. Progress is always slower at night and this was reinforced when the British and German trenches were crossed. There were few bridges over the British lines, narrow gaps that were difficult to find in the German wire and often just one wooden plank to get over the German trenches. It is reckoned that it took the leading brigades nearly two hours to pick their way through all the obstacles and form up again on the other side.

It was decided to leave the men's large packs here for the transport to pick up later. The area of the Loos-Haisnes road was not reached till after midnight. Around 1.00am on the morning of 26th September the GOC's of the two leading brigades (Nickalls and Mitford) did meet up at the allocated position as ordered. Here Mitford (72nd Brigade) reported that a patrol from one of his units, the 8th Royal West Kents, had approached Hulluch (which they had been told had been entered by British troops), and had come under small arms fire. It was decided to send a staff officer to the 3rd Brigade, who were meant to be on their left, for news. Miraculously the officer not only managed to find the 3rd Brigade HQ and get information but also was able to find his way back to the two brigadiers. He returned with a message from Brigadier Davies, who confirmed that Hulluch was in German hands, and said that the situation was understood by his Divisional (1st) and Corps staffs. He also gave the news that his Brigade had been told to stop in its current location (the German communication trenches) west of the Lens-La Bassée road till daylight, when further orders would be forthcoming. In spite of this news Nickalls and Mitford decided to continue the advance across the Lens-La Bassée road and through the German second line positions. To protect this movement, as they had no knowledge of the strength or location of the enemy (except in Hulluch), it was agreed to send one battalion to take Hulluch or at least its southern edge. The unit detailed for this task was from Mitford's Brigade, the 8th Royal West Kents. They were ordered off on this task soon after 2.00am. However, just after they had departed, new orders arrived from 24th Division, which were as a result of Haig's 8.17pm order of the previous day. These ordered Mitford to halt west of the Lens-La Bassée road, maintaining contact with the 3rd Brigade on his left and the 63rd Brigade on his right. Upon receipt of these orders Mitford decided to leave his Brigade where it was and advised Nickalls of his position, meanwhile the move on Hulluch was cancelled and the

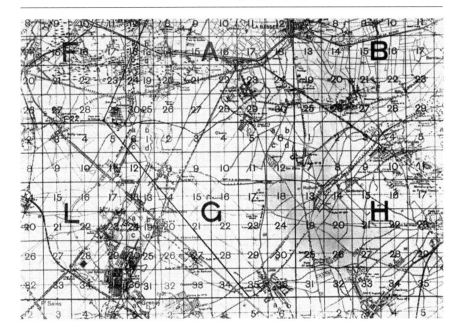

The Battlefield of Loos. (IWM Q 37755)

Royal West Kents were directed to occupy some empty trenches near the Lens road. All four units of the 72nd Brigade began to dig in, using whatever implements were to hand. The Brigade was deployed two up, two back. The 8th Royal West Kents and 9th East Surreys were forward with the 8th Queens and 8th Buffs in support. However just before dawn the units were withdrawn to the support trenches of the original German front line and to the communication trench known as Alley 4 leading towards Hulluch.

The support brigade for the 24th Division, the 71st Brigade, spent the remainder of the night in the original British front line opposite Lone Tree. But its cohesiveness and effectiveness was greatly affected during the early hours of the 26th when Brigadier Shewen was ordered by HQ 7th Division to detach one of his battalions to attack and retake the Quarries. Therefore around 1.00am the 9th Norfolks were sent off to carry out this task. Confusion continued to reign as the 9th Division also asked for support in retaking the Quarries and the 8th Bedfords were sent to assist them. In the darkness and confusion they were unable to join up with the Norfolks and later in the morning of the 26th returned back to the Brigade.

Meanwhile, what of the other leading unit the 21st Division's 63rd Brigade? After the meeting at Lone Tree, Brigadier Nickalls returned to his HQ and ordered the advance to continue. The 8th Lincolns and 12th West Yorks were in the two up mode with the 8th Somerset Light Infantry and the 10th York and Lancasters two back in support. His Brigade was virtually on their own and on reaching the area of the Loos-Hulluch road they came under small arms fire, believed to come from Chalk Pit Wood. Fortunately a patrol from the West Yorks had ascertained that Chalk Pit Wood was in British hands. The Brigade War Diary reports:

No information had been received that the position of the Chalk Pit was in oc-cupation of our own troops. Luckily, no unfortunate results took place, which might very easily have occurred with new troops advancing to a position at night, which was not known to be in our possession. It reflects great credit on the officers concerned, who kept their men so well in hand. The absence of in-formation of what was happening elsewhere was nothing short of disastrous, as no one knew what anyone else was doing.

It is likely that this fire came from Hill 70 but can there be a more damning report in a formation's War Diary about the situation regarding battlefield information? The author cannot recall seeing anything similar. As it was the 63rd Brigade managed to join up with the 2nd Brigade around 3.00am in the morning of 26th September. This was east of the Lens-La Bassée road, north of the Chalk Pit towards Bois Hugo.

The men of the 2nd Brigade and its commander Brigadier Pollard were proba-bly very relieved to see the 'reinforcements' arrive, as they had had a very trying 24 hours, suffering, as we have seen, over 1,500 casualties. The two brigade com-manders met and discussed the situation. Pollard was all for Nickalls men taking over his positions. Indeed it had been stated in the operational orders that the 21st Division should have relieved the 2nd Brigade and Green's Force during the night 25th/26th September. This was included in IV Corps orders, but this does not seem to have been realised by XI Corps HQ. Nickalls said that as far as he was aware he was still under command XI Corps and had not received any orders re-garding any relief. Nevertheless he accepted the situation and took over the posi-tion. This allowed the battered survivors of the 2nd Brigade and Green's Force to be relieved and allowed them to withdraw to the British lines, although on the way German artillery observers spotted them and fire was brought down, causing more than 50 casualties. Meanwhile Nickalls told his men that these positions were a temporary one and he expected them to be moving forward soon. Around 8.00am a message arrived from 21st Division HQ reporting that a general attack had been ordered for later that morning. We shall return to this formation later.

This then left the 63rd Brigade, the most advanced, with the 12th West Yorks north of Bois Hugo and east of the Lens road, and, to the left, the 10th Yorks and Lancs north of the Chalk Pit along the Lens road. Three companies of the 8th Lin-colns were along the southern edge of Bois Hugo, with the other one situated on the northern side. Two companies of the Somerset Light Infantry were acting as brigade reserve positioned in Chalk Pit Wood. The other two companies, with the CO, had suffered from a navigation error and went too far south and at dawn found themselves mixed up with men from the 15th Division near Hill 70.

The other part of the 21st Division, the 64th Brigade, was positioned behind their sister brigade with the 14th and 15th Durham Light Infantry in a German communication trench along the Grenay-Hulluch road. The other two battalions, the 9th and 10th Kings Own Yorkshire Light Infantry, were about 500 yards be-hind in a trench along the Loos-Haisnes road. It is worth remembering that these positions had only been reached about 3.00am. So we have seen that although not actually involved in combat, the men from the 21st and 24th divisions had under-gone an eventful night with little opportunity for rest. Back at 1st Army HQ Haig had believed that most of them, having only moved a couple of miles to the Lens-La Bassée road, were getting as much rest as possible. He intended to use them as his spearhead for the continuation of the attack later on the 26th September.

7

The Second Day - 26th September

At dusk on the 25th September at HQ 1st Army, Hinges, General Haig had to issue his orders for the following day. He was not helped by the lack of accurate information, or perhaps more correctly, his misunderstanding of the situation. It is probably fair to say that he was unaware of the heavy losses or the gap in the 1st Division's frontage, but from reports reaching him and others, he believed that the Germans had been driven back from their main line of defence. These reports suggested that the Germans were almost a broken force and only holding a weak line between Cité St Auguste and Haisnes. Haig was, for most of the war, a great believer in the 'big breakthrough' and a war of mobility. He probably believed a determined assault by 'his' reserves, the 21st and 24th divisions, south of Haisnes would prove decisive. If they broke this weak defensive position, he believed they could turn the whole German positions and perhaps even take Lens. But as we have already seen the 21st and 24th divisions had endured far from an uneventful night on 25th/26th September.

Perhaps more worrying, with the benefit of hindsight, was the failure of the French 10th Army attack, and it was far from clear whether they this would continue. As we have seen, the Germans had decided to ignore the French Army in the area of Vimy Ridge. Even more dangerous for the British was the dogleg in the front line. The French would need to advance more than three miles to bring their front into line. Until this was done any new breakthrough by the British north of Lens would run the risk of developing into an isolated position with a large vulnerable southern flank. This would mean using nearly 25% of the available troops (47th and 15th divisions) as flank guards. However in spite of these reservations it was thought that if the offensive was continued, British success would make the French task easier south of Lens, so it was decided to continue with the attack on the 26th September.

Therefore at around 9.00pm Haig drafted orders for the following day which were sent out to his formations at 11.30pm on the 25th September. These said:

> Following attacks will take place tomorrow - 26th instant - after an adequate artillery preparation. IV Corps with one brigade of 21st Division (XI Corps) will attack the Redoubt on Hill 70 at an hour to be arranged by GOC IV Corps. 1st Division of IV Corps will attack Hulluch at 11.00am. I Corps will attack Cité St Elie at 11.00am. XI Corps (less one brigade attached to I Corps and one brigade to IV Corps) will attack the German second line between Hulluch and Cité St Auguste at 11.00am and push on and secure the high ground between Harnes and Pont à Vendin. The I and IV corps should communicate direct so as to render the attacks on Hulluch and Cité St Elie simultaneously. No 1 Group HAR will support the attack of the IV Corps and XI Corps. No 5 Group HAR will support the attack of the I Corps. The I, III and Indian corps will continue to operate in such a manner north of the Canal as to pin the enemy to his ground and prevent him despatching Reserves south of the Canal.

As Haig explained to the three corps commanders at a 9.00am meeting on the morning of the 26th, the idea behind these orders was to continue with the advance and to push the 21st and 24th divisions through the perceived thin German crust between Bois Hugo and Hulluch and then on to the banks of the Haute Deule Canal. The flanks of this advance were to be secured in the north by the 1st Division, who were to take Hulluch, and by units of I Corps, who were to simultaneously attack Cité St Elie. In the south, the 47th Division was to maintain its positions, while the 15th Division, supported by the 62nd Brigade, was to take Hill 70 and establish a defensive position there. This, then, was the plan of attack for the morning of the 26th September, though as we can see most of the attention was on IV Corps, as relatively more success had been gained in the southern sector than the northern. In the early hours of 26th September the two corps commanders most involved, Rawlinson and Haking, met to plan the actual assault for Hill 70 and Hulluch and the German positions in between. They quite rightly decided that since an advance by the 21st and 24th divisions beyond the Lens-La Bassée road would be in open view of the Germans still entrenched in Hill 70 Redoubt, it would have to be neutralised first. It was therefore decided that the troops holding the western slope of Hill 70 would have to attack the Redoubt at 9.00am, leaving them two hours to gain possession of it before the main attack.

The 15th Division was ordered to carry this out and their orders timed at 5.00am on the 26th September stated:

> The 45th and 62nd brigades will attack Hill 70 at 9.00am today. 45th Brigade will attack from the west, with its left on the track from Loos through the Hill 70 Redoubt to the Lens-La Bassée road. The 62nd Brigade will attack from the north-west with its right on the same track. The attack will be preceded by an hour's intense bombardment by all available guns, and artillery barrages will be established on the enemy's trenches south and east of Hill 70 during and after the attack. Hill 70, when taken, will be strengthened and held to cover the advance of the 21st and 24th divisions against the enemy's positions between Cité St Auguste and Hulluch. 44th and 46th brigades will remain in their present positions ready to support the 45th and 62nd brigades, respectively if required. Before the bombardment of the Hill 70 Redoubt begins the infantry will be withdrawn to a safe distance. 45th Brigade will keep touch with the left of the 47th Division throughout.

There are some useful points behind these orders that bear thinking about. There was an attempt to coordinate the fire of fifteen batteries of the 1st and 15th divisional artillery. Later, the guns of the 47th Division were added to this number. But they were hampered by a lack of ammunition. In addition, the reserves for this attack on Hill 70 were the remnants of the force that had already been up the hill on the previous day. Nevertheless, orders were orders. Soon after receipt of them, the two brigadiers, Wallerston and Wilkinson, met at HQ 45th Brigade and thrashed out a plan. As the 45th Brigade was at this moment positioned around the track leading to the Redoubt (which had been nominated as their left hand flank) it was not considered practical to move the Brigade to the south side of the track. The two brigadiers therefore opted to launch the assault from their current locations. Therefore, the 45th Brigade was to make a frontal assault astride the track directed at the Redoubt and the summit of Hill 70. It was decided to use the three units already in the line: the 7th Royal Scots Fusiliers on the right bypassing the southern flank of the Redoubt and against the southern face of the summit, the 11th Argyll and Sutherland Highlanders against the centre of the Redoubt, and the 13th Royal Scots were left with the northern face of the Redoubt and Hill 70. The 62nd Brigade's orders were somewhat vague in that they were "to move up from Loos and act in immediate support."

As it was, the orders did not reach the individual battalion commanders until (in most cases) 7.00am, although later times are recorded. Indeed, some units of the 11th Argylls, 13th Royal Scots and 13th Northumberland Fusiliers did not receive them until after the artillery barrage had started. Perhaps barrage is the wrong word to use, as most of the guns assigned to the 15th Division were limited to firing at the rate of two rounds a minute. It also appears that no orders were given to soften-up the German second line positions behind Hill 70 Redoubt, which had appeared to be instrumental in repelling the attack on the previous day. Finally, a number of rounds fell on British trenches, which caused casualties, particularly amongst the 13th Royal Scots, probably having a detrimental effect on their later performance. At 9.00am, after some early morning mist had cleared towards the end of the barrage the attack went in, under a clear line of sight from the Germans positioned along the crest of Hill 70. The Redoubt and the immediate area had been reinforced during the night and the artillery barrage had had little effect, but nevertheless men from the assaulting battalions managed to get a toehold on the outer defences, using the bayonet to good effect. Further fierce fighting ensued and a number of Germans completely abandoned the position, although a few defenders continued to man the Keep in the centre of the defences. The 45th Brigade tried to press round the flanks of the Redoubt, but heavy fire from both sides and from artillery firing from Lens and Cité St Auguste broke up each attack. Casualties were heavy and eventually the survivors were forced to withdraw behind the crest-line. The following two comments from the War Diaries of units involved in this attack are worth relating. First, the 13th Royal Scots:

> At the time fixed for the assault the Regiment to advance in lines of two platoons, order of companies, A, B, C, D, MG; D Company to bring up entrenching tools and entrench the position. The time at our disposal for issuing orders and forming and direct detailed scheme of attack was much too short. The enemy's artillery started shelling Loos and part of Hill 70 at 8am. At 8.30am our own guns so effectively shelled B Company that they were unable to get into position, and any attack by this Company was out of the question. A Company was unable to advance owing to the guns not having cut down the German wire in front, which at this spot was particularly strong. Major MacPherson and Captain Robertson were killed immediately, they got out over our parapet in front of C Company, and then the whole assault fizzled out, it was not likely that guns, which had not registered, would accomplish in half an hour what four days bombardment and forty minutes of gas was considered necessary for on the 25th.

7th Royal Scots Fusiliers:

The Loos-Vermelles road on the 27th September 1915, with destroyed transport from the 21st Division. (IWM Q17373)

Assault delivered by our first line at 9.00am failed, our guns firing short caused some men on left and centre of line to turn. The line was rallied, advanced again but could not capture redoubt. Casualties heavy.

The remaining elements of the 62nd Brigade, the 12th Northumberland Fusiliers and the 10th Green Howards, who were acting in support, now arrived in the area. They had moved up from assembly positions east of Loos, to the left and right respectively, of the Loos-Hill 70 Redoubt track. They were about 300 yards behind the 45th Brigade. But unfortunately bad luck (and perhaps bad planning) came into play. These two battalions had only been given small-scale maps, on which Hill 70 was only marked by a contour ring. Loos Crassier, which was not marked on the maps, was mistaken for Hill 70. Fortunately they had only gone a small distance off track when the error was discovered, probably when men from the 45th Brigade helped out. But it was not a good start. They now went through the 45th Brigade (taking some of them forward in the attack), and advanced towards the Redoubt and over the crest-line. Again, this latest attack was unsuccessful. A few surviving officers tried to rally the troops for a second attack but many were soon shot and their efforts came to naught. An example of this is the 10th Green Howards - both the CO, Lieutenant-Colonel Hadow, and his second-in-command Major Dent were shot and killed trying "to urge the men forward by their own example." Two other senior officers from this unit were also killed, so it is little wonder that soon after 10.00am the vast majority of the troops were back in the relative shelter of the western slope of Hill 70, exactly where they had started from. Here is an account of this attack from Private Harry Fellows, who was a member of the 12th Northumberland Fusiliers:

As soon as the first streaks of day came we began to see where we were: at the bottom of a gentle slope, with the enemy entrenched along the crest. Thus we had our introduction to the famous, or infamous, Hill 70. The absence of small arms fire during the night was easily explained when we saw the mass of barbed wire the enemy had been stringing under cover of darkness. The trench which the Scots occupied was about 4 ft 6 ins deep and 2 ft 6 ins wide with all the earth thrown to the front to form a parapet and one could see that it had been hastily dug since it was in a straight line, in fact it was little more than a slit trench. It still remains a mystery to me why the enemy did not open fire on us: we were crowded in the trench and along the rear, in full view, and men were still walking about on the road. Having no watch I could not be sure of the time but it was early in the morning when the order was passed for "Numbers One and Two on C Company's Lewis gun to go to the transport for the gun and ammunition." Looking along to the left I saw my mate get out of the trench and I joined him in walking along the parados and out onto the road. Passing along the village street it soon became evident that the night's shelling had done the place no good. Fallen masonry was quite abundant, but we did not find great difficulty in passing through. As soon as we got clear of the street we met our oppos from B Company. They were empty-handed and we could see from the looks on their faces that they had bad news for us. One of them said: "If you are going to get your gun, forget it. The transport is a shambles. Dead men and mules are lying all around, mixed up with damaged limbers. Some men are there shooting the badly wounded mules and trying to clear up the mess."

Later, one of our transport drivers told me: "We were standing in a group on the road discussing the Battalion hold-up when a single shell, aimed for the road, scored a direct hit on the ammunition limber. Bullets were flying around like hail, men were falling and some mules stampeded. After the panic had subsided we sorted the wounded men from the dead and, taking the wounded with us, we got the hell out of it."

We could do no other than go back the way we had come and on reaching the end of the road near the pit-head we found that our CO had established his HQ where the Battalion had come to a halt. The Adjutant, RMO and RSM were with him and, as we approached, the adjutant called out: "To which Company do you belong?" and I replied "C Company, Sir." "Wait a little while. The CO has a message for you." My oppo, Tip Henson, a Geordie from Ashington, walked on towards our trenches and out of my life, I never saw him again. [Note that 13599 Private Harold Henson's date of death according to the CWGC is 25th September 1915, he has no known grave and is commemorated on the Loos Memorial to the Missing.] After a while the Adjutant gave me a slip of paper from an ordinary Field Message pad on which was written: "The CO wishes the attack to be carried out with the bayonet in the approved Northumbrian manner." The Adjutant told me to take it to Captain Pole, the message was not signed or dated but I remember those words as I remember the Lord's Prayer, and this was the first intimation I had that we were going to attack. I had not seen Captain Pole since we had been led into the trench during the night, now I had to find him.

As I walked along the parados I could plainly see that events had been moving during the time I had been away. All the men crowded together, along with those of our men in the trench, were standing with bayonets fixed. It was useless trying to get into the trench as it was so solidly packed. Then our lads began to climb out and go forward as fast as their cumbersome equipment would allow. The men at the back dropped into the places which had been vacated and then climbed forward. Suddenly realising the Captain must have gone forward, but not comprehending that the message I had for him was now out of date I scrambled across, still intent on finding him. The whole slope in front of me and as far away to the left as one could see was crowded with cheering men moving forward as fast as they could. And still the enemy had not fired a shot. It seemed like they had gone home.

The leading men would have been about 100 yards from the German wire, and I was about the same distance from my starting point when all hell was let loose. As if from some predetermined signal the enemy machine guns opened up with a murderous fire, both from the front and enfilading fire from some buildings which had been out of sight behind some trees. Men began to stumble and fall, then to go down like standing corn before a scythe. The cap from the head of the lad in front of me flew from his head and he fell - I stumbled over him - and even to this day I feel no shame when I say that I stayed where I was: my face buried in the grass, and never had the good earth smelled so sweet. I was 19 years old and no hero - just a scared teenager who had no wish to die and, after seeing all that devastation in front of my eyes, I was frightened. The firing seemed to go on for hours. I afterwards learned that it was not even ten minutes. Bullets were cracking overhead and then it ceased as abruptly as it had commenced.

After a few more minutes I rose to my knees and should I live to be a hundred I shall never forget the sight that met my eyes. The whole slope was one mass of prone figures; some even lying on top of one another. The Germans still held their fire and soon there was some movement. Men began to get to their feet, others rose only to fall back again, whilst others limped and some even crawled. Many, like the lad I had stumbled over, would never move again. Many men, even though wounded themselves, were helping their wounded comrades back. Still the Germans held their fire. Some months later the German commander of this particular sector was reported to have said: "My machine gunners were so filled with pity, remorse and nausea at the Corpse Field of Loos that they refused to fire another shot." Assisting a lad who had a bullet wound in his foot, I arrived back in the trench near where the Scots had their machine gun. They had stayed behind in the attack, having obviously been mauled during the previous day's fighting. One of the team offered me his water bottle: water was extremely scarce. I still remember the emotion in his voice as he said: "Ye nae had a chance."

There was plenty of room in the trench now and we set about the task of trying to sort ourselves out. There did not seem to be any officers or NCOs left and being with the Scots our companies were all mixed up and we wondered what the immediate future held for us. With the exception of a few rifle shots in the distance and the welcome sound of a few of our shells passing over, everything had gone ominously quiet again and it was nerve racking to hear the cries of the men lying wounded on the slope. Even if the Germans had allowed us to help them - which I believe they would - we had no stretchers. Ours had gone back with what was left of our transport and the Scots had used all theirs up with their own wounded during the previous day's fighting. I learned afterwards that a Field Ambulance Company went in that night, but I am afraid that many would have died before then.

The problem of what was to happen to us was partly solved during mid-afternoon when the Scots heard that they were to be relieved that evening by a Battalion from the Guards Division, and it was fully solved a little later when the word was passed down the line for "All Northumberlands to make their own way back and rendezvous at the Old Brewery in Noyelles les Vermelles." On receiving this order we made our way through the village and across the old trench system, singly or in small groups. On reaching our destination we were met with the heartening sight of our field kitchens in action and we were soon sipping hot tea, which tasted like nectar. We certainly looked a very bedraggled lot with three days growth of beard and as we had no sleep for a similar number of days we were out on our feet. Looking around I was pleased to see that Captain Pole was safe and remembering the message I still had for him I handed it to him with an apology for the delay. After reading it he said, with a tremor in his voice: "It doesn't matter now. But isn't that just what we tried to do?"

As well as suffering from small arms fire this abortive attack on Hill 70 also seems to have suffered from an artillery bombardment with the German artillery throwing in the odd gas shell for good measure. The withdrawal mentioned above, and that of the Green Howards, left a thin line of men from the 45th and 46th brigades holding a reverse slope position on the west side of Hill 70. However one unit was not impressed with the attack by men from the 21st Division as the following comment appears in the 13th Royal Scots War Diary:

About 11.30am the situation became further complicated by the 21st Division advancing to the attack. They crossed the Loos-Hulluch road and established a firing line from which they proceeded to pour a heavy fire into the left of the 45th Brigade and Hill 70 causing heavy casualties. However by establishing some machine guns near Puits 14 the enemy came to the assistance of the 45th Brigade by enfilading the 21st Division, causing the latter to retire.

Other areas close to Hill 70 seem to have seen little action and the 20th Londons supported by the 8th East Yorks continued to hold a position astride the Loos Crassier, while Chalet Wood continued to be held by Scottish troops from the 15th Division, mainly the 6th Cameron Highlanders. Because Hill 70 had not been taken it would have been considered wise by most people to cancel the attack by the 21st and 24th divisions, but regretfully this did not happen. General Haking decided not to change his plan in any detail. Perhaps he was under the impression that when the 1st Division had captured Hulluch, and then broken through the German second line between Bois Hugo and Hulluch, it might be possible to outflank Hill 70 and roll up all the positions there. But just to be on the safe side in case any of these attacks failed, he sent orders to the Guards Division (timed at 10.05am) to move forward to the original British trenches south of the Vermelles-Hulluch road. As will probably be no surprise, some of the units did not receive notification of this move till about noon.

The 21st and 24th divisions were ordered to attack German positions over ½ mile east of the Lens-La Bassée road along a small crest known as the Cité Ridge. This meant they would have a long advance over a barren and virtually open landscape with the prospect of fire being directed on them from Hill 70, Hulluch and the Bois Hugo. Additionally, the German defenders on the Cité Ridge had spent the night of 25th/26th September strengthening their positions there, mainly by adding barbed wire. On the morning of 26th September it was around 20 feet deep and about 4 feet high. Already positioned along the line of assault were some German strongpoints - Stützpunkt III, IV and V, all containing a number of concrete machine gun positions. It is useful to bear in mind that although these positions were probably not as strong as the front line ones, they had not been subjected to the four day artillery softening-up barrage, nor was there enough chlorine gas to act as a substitute for the guns. The German garrison on this sector on the morning of the 26th amounted to about six battalions: one battalion from the 157th Regiment in Hulluch, one battalion of the 26th Regiment holding the area between Hulluch and Stützpunkt IV, three battalions of the 153rd Regiment south of Stützpunkt IV through Bois Hugo to Cité St Auguste and one battalion of the 22nd Reserve Regiment in the village of Cité St Auguste. It is probably true to say that there were more defenders on the second day than the first and also the attackers had fewer cards to play with. All in all, the plan for these two divisions was a very difficult one for them to achieve, especially as they were virtual 'new boys' on the battlefield. It was very different from chasing a demoralised enemy, as they had been told their role would be.

The artillery units of the 21st and 24th divisions were combined under the control of Brigadier C. Alexander, CRA of the 21st Division, with a preliminary barrage lasting one hour. However they were helped by the support of 1st and 15th brigades RGA of No 1 Group Heavy Artillery Reserve, even though they only had 200 rounds of 6 inch and 90 rounds of 9.2 inch. The plan was for the field batteries of the two divisions, under the cover of darkness, to move forward to reach a position behind Lone Tree Ridge before dawn, between the Béthune-Lens and the Vermelles-Hulluch roads. The move forward was fraught with difficulties, the artillery from the 24th Division were already in action away from the area where they were meant to be forming up. Additionally it had been decided to use Le Rutoire Farm (one of the only recognisable places on the plain) as a meeting point for all the Division's transport. Therefore a mass of intermixed vehicles was causing traffic jams there, leading to delays for the batteries. As a result, many of the guns did not reach the position till after dawn. A thick mist did not help matters. When the mist cleared, around 9.00am, most of the guns found themselves about 1,000 yards from where they should have been. Instead of being on a reverse (eastern) slope, they were on a forward (western) slope west and south-west of Le Rutoire. The guns themselves were virtually exposed to German view from Haisnes and Hulluch, and almost immediately artillery fire was brought down on them, which continued throughout most of the morning. It was considered too late to try and alter the battery positions, so the barrage went in as best it could. It comes as no surprise to report that the barrage was spasmodic and had virtually no effect on any of the German positions.

The infantry of the 21st and 24th divisions had their own ordeals to get through. The troops had endured a sleepless and trying night on the 25th/26th, on top of several night marches over the previous days. They had received little, if any, hot food and drink. Hardly any information had been provided to the command structure of the units and virtually none as to the general situation and exact positions of the various battalions. A more unfavourable set of circumstances for an attack could scarcely be provided.

Additionally, the late hour of the attack at 11.00am gave the Germans the opportunity of, what could be described as 'getting their retaliation in first'. On the 21st Division frontage they launched a counter-attack from the south-east before the 21st's attack. In fact this counter-attack had been postponed from the previous day as the reinforcements had arrived too late. As it was, during the night of 25th/26th September small parties of German infantry moved from Cité St Auguste into the wooded areas of Bois Hugo and Chalet Wood. Early on the morning of the 26th September they were reinforced by the best part of four battalions - three from the 153rd Regiment and one from the 106th Regiment. Bolstered by these reinforcements the small number of isolated British positions were easily overwhelmed and the whole of Bois Hugo and Chalet Wood were occupied. These put the forward elements of the German forces bordering the Lens-La Bassée road, where they were in the middle of the 63rd Brigade from the 21st Division. Regretfully the 63rd Brigade had not occupied Bois Hugo in any strength when it relieved men from the 2nd Brigade. The War Diary of the 12th West Yorks gives an explanation for this:

A Scottish Regiment of the 15th Division (6th Cameron Highlanders) was in possession of Puits 14 bis and our 62nd Brigade had been lent to the same Division for a fresh attempt on Hill 70. It was the knowledge of all these troops on the south side of the wood which influenced the Battalion commander in not extending his line into the wood and so protecting his own flank with his own men. A sergeant and 12 men were sent into the wood in front of the right of the line.

Unfortunately it is not recorded what happened to these 13 men but one suspects their options were severely limited when they were discovered by the Germans. As soon as the mist cleared around 9.00am this large body of Germans began to make their presence in the area known. A particular unit to suffer a lot of casualties were the 8th Lincolns, who were forced back to the area of the Lens-La Bassée road. There is an interesting account regarding this from a company commander. It comes from Major L. McNaught-Davis, of D Company from the 8th Lincolns, concerning not only the actions of the 26th but beforehand as well:

24th - overnight in a field about two miles from Vermelles. Next morning at dawn, everything pointed to the fact that a great undertaking was involved, there being exceptional aerial activity and heavy gun fire, huge sausage shaped balloons ascended for reconnoitering, transport, guns and motor cyclists and vehicles dashed along the roads, even Tommy became affected with the general bustle, and excitement. As things grew more lively he began to give vent to his feelings, and wanted to know when we are going to get a move on, he had not long to wait! At 11am we received a telephone message to the effect that the

Highland Brigade had secured the first two lines of the German trenches with the aid of gas, and the bayonet, and were attacking the third line. At the same time an order to move in the direction of Vermelles which was still being shelled by the enemy, and who seemed bent on taking revenge out of the church steeple, which although full of holes and still standing, would take but very little more pummeling to bring it down. Just beyond we encountered men of the Scottish regiments who were struggling in wounded, they had evidently had a great fight, mostly being pretty badly mauled. This was my first experience of war after 25 years of Army service, I had always been abroad at the time of our previous wars. It was now 5pm, and it had taken us from 11am that morning to traverse two miles, there being a continuity of halting which became monotonous. We now proceeded to take up our positions along the main road behind the first line of trenches which had been occupied by the enemy that morning, here the congestion of traffic was very bad. Artillery, ammunition columns, engineer field service units and pontoon troops were densely packed in the highway and it was some considerable time before our Division managed to get through.

At 7pm we left the roadway and took up a position in the line of trenches, where we halted till about 9pm, it was now pitch dark and drizzling with rain. Here I received a message from the Colonel stating that only four officers in-

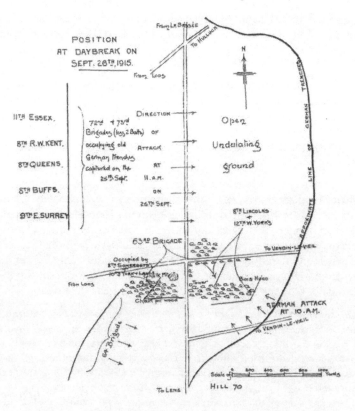

Map 10: 72nd and 73rd Brigade attack, 26th September 1915

cluding myself were to go into action. I detailed two to fall out and return to Headquarters.

After that we moved forward to the open country in lines of platoons, the rain was now very heavy and the men were pretty well wet through. We now came under howitzer and heavy artillery fire directly we advanced, and although shells fell all around us we managed to survive. After having gone about a mile, machine guns opened fire from a wood on our right front, and now being in extended order the only thing to do was lie down, and by constant rushing and crawling get over the open ground as quickly as possible. It was here my second-in-command Captain Harrison was hit in the leg but managed to trudge gallantly on.

I would like to point out here that we only had a vague idea of our objective, and only a compass bearing of 30° had been given to march on - our orders were to advance through the line of our own troops holding the front line of trenches and continue the attack, and these orders were admirable had it not been so late in the day, but the attack had now been launched since 6am and it was now nearly midnight.

No effort had yet been made to dislodge the machine guns in the wood, and later they ceased fire, and it was then that a rest was made till early morning about 3.30am when the firing recommenced from the wood and we withdrew under cover of dead ground and shell holes, some of them being regular pits of chalk of which the ground was composed of here. Shortly afterwards we were ordered to go forward to occupy the trenches occupied by the Highlanders the previous day which were only a few yards away.

Why we did not attack then I am at a loss to understand, but the orders were to wait until 10am, and just before, this was countermanded till 10.30, this lapse must have given the enemy the very opportunity he wanted to reor-

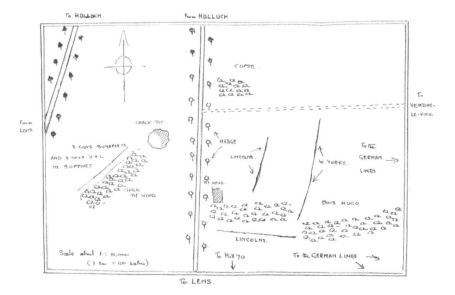

Map 11: 8th Lincolns around Hill 70, 26th September 1915

ganise his forces and strengthen his position. About this time the enemy commenced to shell us, their infantry joining in with rifle fire and although not heavy, several shells fell in the wood perilously near our men who were on the edge of it, finally the fire got heavier, the machine guns again joining in the melee and giving considerable trouble. There appeared to be no continuity of line beyond the right of the wood, and of this I am convinced of, had there been we should not have been outflanked.

The Germans however managed to find a gap and drove our men from the wood and trenches on the right inflicting many casualties including six officers, two being company commanders, the right flank being turned and in the open, and only part of the original line on the left being held.

It was also at this juncture that the Colonel, who had been badly hit, shouted for an officer and hearing this I left my Company and rushed out into the open, twice rallying the remnants of those retreating from the wood and got them further forward to the attack, our men fighting splendidly, being full of spirit and only wanting the opportunity to get to grips with the enemy. It was very difficult to get a view of the attackers, they having a splendid screen in the foliage and thickness of the wood. Major Storer was killed and the Colonel again hit, also Captain Jacques of the Yorkshire Regiment who had retired to us in the final rush of the attack and who died at my side.

I very shortly after got a bullet in the head and although nearly blinded by the blood, kept conscious and made for the trench about 12 yards away, wriggling on my stomach. I shall never forget it, the explosions of gas, shrapnel and other projectiles, and the groans and cries of the wounded and dying as they were hit were fearful. It was now 12.30pm and still no reinforcements, for which I had sent back messages for. I had hopes when I first dropped into the trench of waiting until dark and trying to get back, but when the artillery range gradually decreased and the shells dropped nearer and nearer the edge of the trench, I began to give up all hope of ever getting out alive, expecting each shell to drop in on top of me and end it all, but about 5pm the firing ceased. I suppose most of the men in the open were practically annihilated by then, and the Germans surrounded us with machine guns. I was then assisted from the trench practically helpless, and a good thing I showed signs of life as they had been prodding every corpse with their bayonets. We few survivors were all rounded up and marched to Lens. Here my wounds were dressed and I was inoculated against tetanus.

Major McNaught-Davis did recover from his wounds but was destined to spend the rest of the war in various German PoW camps.

Meanwhile, we must return to the overall situation for the 63rd Brigade. To try and protect the position Brigadier Nickalls ordered forward two companies from his reserve (8th Somerset Light Infantry), situated in the Chalk Pit to try and hold a line along the southern edge of it facing Bois Hugo. He also sent orders to the 10th Yorks and Lancs then located along the Lens road north of the Chalk Pit, to move two companies across to the southern edge of Chalk Pit Wood facing south-east, to prevent any German movement across the Lens road from either Chalet Wood or Bois Hugo. Due to a misunderstanding nearly all the unit (four companies) went not only into Chalk Pit Wood, but through and beyond it, where they came under German fire from positions near Bois Hugo and Chalet Wood.

Needless to say heavy casualties were caused amongst these inexperienced troops. Realising he was rushing headlong into a crisis, Nickalls wrote a hurried order timed at 8.53am to the commander (Brigadier Gloster) of the 64th Brigade behind him, asking him to send one of his units to reinforce his right flank which was under attack. Gloster acted quite quickly and sent the 14th Durham Light Infantry forward in the direction of Puits 14 bis and Bois Hugo. Whilst the British commanders were doing this, a German counter-attack from their positions between Cité St Auguste and Hulluch started. Carried out by the 117th Division, their orders stated:

> The line Fosse 8 mine dump-Quarries has been captured. Gun Trench, west of Hulluch has been reached by parts of the 15th Reserve Infantry Regiment. The 8th Division in its attack on Loos has reached with its right wing the strip of wood north-west of Puits 14 bis, and a position about 200 yards east of Loos. The general direction of attack of this Division is westwards.

Around 9.30am German artillery began to bombard the positions of the 63rd Brigade in and around the Chalk Pit and Chalk Pit Wood. After about 30 minutes of artillery fire, German infantry was seen to be advancing from the direction of Stützpunkt IV across the open ground north of Bois Hugo. This threatened the open left flank of the 63rd Brigade, north of the Chalk Pit. However men from the 12th West Yorks, supported by artillery fire, easily stopped this attack. This is what the 117th Division orders had to say about this attack:

> The 233rd Infantry Brigade will prepare one company for attack from the second position with its left flank on Stützpunkt IV. The object of this company is to close the gap between the 26th Reserve Infantry Brigade and the 8th Infantry Division, and it will drive back any British troops east of the La Bassée-Lens road, where it will dig in. Its further progress will be dependent on the 26th Reserve Infantry Brigade and the 8th Infantry Division.

A further report comes from the actual formation nominated to carry out this task, the 26th Regiment:

> The company was to advance to the Lens-La Bassée road, dig in and remain there, so as to close the gap between the 26th Reserve Infantry Brigade on the right and the 8th Division advancing through Bois Hugo on the left. At 10.15am, the company advanced in widely extended lines, the left from Stützpunkt IV, and the right from Fosse 18. On reaching the road it was attacked by about two British battalions, who advanced to within about 70 yards, when it was decided to fall back on the second line trench. This was done with considerable loss, with the British following close behind.

This movement, in practical terms, was a feint, designed to draw the attention of the 63rd Brigade from other areas, and it succeeded. The main German attack was coming through the Bois Hugo. Around 10.30am the forward positions of the 12th West Yorks, north of Bois Hugo suddenly came under enfilade fire from the eastern edge of the wood. They were taken completely by surprise and suffered many casualties and it is stated the majority of them then left the trenches and ran back towards the Lens road. The attack, as so often happens in war, came at a time when one side is temporarily at a disadvantage. In this incident, it was the British turn to suffer, as the attack came in when the CO, Lieutenant-Colonel Leggett, was on his way to Brigade HQ and had just been wounded by shell fire. Other efforts by senior members of the 12th West Yorks to rally the men failed, often being picked out as commanders by German riflemen and paying the ultimate price. The Brigade commander, Nickalls, heard the sound of battle very close by and was himself on the way to the front line to assist with command and control but was killed almost immediately. Brigadier Nickalls has no known grave and is commemorated on the Loos Memorial to the Missing Panel 2. He was 51 years old at the time of his death.

Perhaps the loss of all of these senior commanders did not help these inexperienced troops (and officers) and the West Yorks continued their retirement across the Lens road and past the southern edge of Chalk Pit Wood. As so often happens the sight of these retreating men caused others to move as well. The 10th Yorks and Lancs, in their positions in front of the wood, got up as the retreating West Yorks reached them and joined them heading westwards. A few survivors from the 8th Lincolns, finding German troops behind them, managed to escape, but as we have seen a lot were surrounded and alone. By all accounts this withdrawal was a somewhat orderly affair rather than a headlong flight, and it must have been very difficult for these untried and untested men to have been faced with so different circumstances than what they had been led to believe - chasing a routed enemy who was now chasing them! It appears that the two companies from the Somerset LI located in the Chalk Pit maintained their positions. Now there was stroke of luck for the British, for as the German infantry appeared from Bois Hugo in one great mass, several heavy artillery shells fell amongst them, these caused numerous casualties, causing them to withdraw into the tree-line. It is an interesting scenario to wonder what would have happened had the Germans followed on the heels of the 63rd Brigade, bearing in mind that their commander had only just been killed. I suspect a retirement of several miles would have occurred and again one wonders what this would have done to the career of Douglas Haig?

It must have been a very confused situation and this is demonstrated by the post action report from the CO of the 10th York and Lancasters, who wrote about his unit's actions on the 26th September:

> The Regiment would form reserve with 12th West York Regiment to an attack on Hulluch-Lens road. Then orders to move more to the north and take up an entrenched position on the Hulluch-Lens road facing east were received. The line when taken up extended from Red House by Chalk Pit east of square wood. On arrival I reported to the Brigadier. Though entrenched one had to keep down, as sniping was persistent from direction of Hill 70 or square wood.
>
> About 8.30am a verbal order came for two companies to attack square wood. B and C companies were detailed for the purpose and I took the two companies personally. As the other side of the wood was reached, a very heavy machine gun fire from concealed positions drove us back. After being driven out of the square wood fell back on southern road Loos-Hulluch. Rallied at this place together with a number of the Scotch Brigade.
>
> After the sunken road was held for some time it was seen that the position was untenable as guns placed in the vicinity north east of Benefontaine raked the road. A Lieutenant-Colonel in the Scotch Brigade considered that this line

should move back into the southern most German trenches. On this retirement as no reports were received, we had no means of communicating with troops on the left, the Colonel made the above decision under very heavy machine gun and gun fire. This movement was taking place when Captain Foster Divisional Staff suggested a rally on a line parallel to a track running north-east. Other lines were formed in rear. After the first line had passed through, this line advanced and eventually became part of the firing line with objective square wood in H 258. This attack met with strong opposition from machine gun fire from concealed guns. Another rally was made in the sunken road, southern road Loos-Hulluch and this was eventually evacuated as in the preceding case. By this time the Regiment had lost a good number of officers and Men.

While all of these small withdrawals were going on, the unit from the 64th Brigade, the 14th Durham LI, which had been sent forward at Brigadier Nickalls's request to support his right flank, was also suffering misfortune. This Battalion was advancing from the area of the Loos-Hulluch road towards Bois Hugo, and mistakenly opened fire on retiring British troops, believing them to be advancing Germans. However the error was soon realised and they continued to head towards Bois Hugo. Soon they came under heavy enfilade fire from German positions and suffered serious casualties. The list included the CO, Lieutenant-Colonel A. Hamilton, his Adjutant, all four company commanders and over 200 men. Needless to say, the advance petered out. Meanwhile a few minutes later at 11.00am, according to orders, the 15th Durham LI went forward. Again they were met with an image of wounded men heading west to the rear areas while they headed east. Again, this unit suffered heavy casualties, including the CO, Lieutenant-Colonel E. Logan, killed. It appears a few small parties did make progress, some reaching the lower slopes of Hill 70, but as on many occasions before they were beaten back. Thus the attack of the 21st Division was far from being a coordinated effort, and really cannot be classed an as attack at all. The two brigades involved gained no ground and all suffered heavily. Would its sister New Army Division, the 24th fair any better?

To recap, the 24th Division's orders had been to "attack the German second line between Hulluch and Cité St Auguste at 11am and push on and secure the high ground between Haisnes and Pont à Vendin." The 72nd Brigade had been nominated as the lead unit and at daybreak on the 26th September they were located in a communication trench known as Alley 4 east of Lone Tree, with its left hand formation in contact with the 1st Division. The other two brigades of the 24th Division were located as follows: the 71st Brigade (50% of it, as two battalions were elsewhere) were behind the 72nd Brigade in the old German front line, and the 73rd Brigade were still with the 9th Division at Fosse 8. One suspects that the High Command had no real idea that instead of the 'full-fighting strength' of the 24th Division being launched on a thin-crust defence, it was in reality only 1½ brigades (6 battalions) against a defence ever-increasing in strength and depth. The situation was still one of confusion, and as on so many previous occasions, no orders had been received. So, at 5.00am on the 26th, Brigadier Mitford of the 72nd Brigade sent back a staff officer to Divisional HQ at Vermelles to report the position of both his Brigade and the 71st and to ask for further instructions. The staff officer returned nearly five hours later, just before 10.00am, with the news that Divisional orders had been sent already (according to the War Diary they arrived at

5.30pm). He therefore verbally conveyed them to Mitford, that in essence that they were to attack at 11.00am that morning, then just an hour away. The actual orders stated:

> GSO to 72nd Brigade; 26th: Following arrangements for attack. 1st Division attacks Hulluch 11.00am, 72nd Brigade to attack second line trench between Puits 13 bis and the Redoubt exclusive. 21st Division will attack on your right against Redoubt and continuation of the trench south of it to Bois Hugo. The attack will be preceded by an artillery bombardment. The attack will cross the Lens-La Bassée road at 11.00am. From 24th Division 7.10am.

In layman's terms therefore this meant the 72nd Brigade attacking between Stützpunkt IV and Puits 13 bis (Stützpunkt III), while the two remaining battalions of the 71st Brigade (11th Essex and 9th Suffolks) acted as reserves. The grandiose statement, "the 1st Division attacks Hulluch" meant, in fact, just the 2nd Welch Regiment from that formation. At a hastily convened Orders Group, Mitford chose the classic two-up, two back formation with the 9th East Surreys and the 8th Royal West Kents leading, with the 8th Buffs and the 8th Queens in the second wave. The commanders hurried back to their units and issued orders, again very hurriedly, it being reported that in some instances there was only ten minutes notice for the attack. Nevertheless the two leading battalions from the 72nd Brigade left their positions at 11.00am, and headed down Lone Tree Ridge into the Loos valley. The appearance of this organised body of men had a calming effect on the men from the 63rd Brigade and stopped any further movement westward and got them in positions facing the Germans. We shall return to the exploits of the 24th Division later after looking at the subsidiary actions, which were meant to support their attack.

On the left hand side was the village of Hulluch and for the 24th Division to achieve their objective of the high ground between Haisnes and Pont à Vendin, they would have to go past this village. Therefore the 1st Division was entrusted with taking the village. It will be remembered that the 1st Division had suffered quite severe casualties during the 25th September and even though it was an 'enlarged' Division, it had reported back that it was "not fit for much more." The attack was to be led by the 3rd Brigade, supported by Green's Force and the 1st Brigade, with the overall commander being Brigadier Davies from the 3rd Brigade. They were to be supported by the 1st Division artillery, of which one of the brigades, the 39th RFA, had moved forward during the night to a line west of Bois Carré, immediately behind the British front line. It seems that the 1st Division got their orders much earlier than other formations as during the morning of the 26th the remnants of the 1st and 3rd brigades sorted themselves out for the forthcoming attack. The 400 or so men of the 2nd Welch Regiment were positioned on the right flank in Alley 4 trench in contact with the 72nd Brigade. The 1st Black Watch and 1st South Wales Borderers (both about 300 strong) were slightly behind the Welch in Gun Trench. The other two battalions, the 1st Gloucesters and the 2nd Munster Fusiliers, were in reserve just behind these units. The rest of the 1st Division (again much depleted in numbers) were kept in support in some captured German trenches, east of Bois Carré. The envisaged divisional attack was in fact going to be carried out by less than a brigade's strength. However, events were now going to get worse. Around 10.30am the 2nd Welch reported by field telephone that the Germans were counter-attacking past the southern edge of Hulluch; in spite of this report the Welch were again told to attack as previously ordered at 11.00am. Then, for unknown reasons but probably due to a lucky artillery round, all communication by telephone was curtailed. Soon afterwards the 1st Black Watch reported the German movement and added that the Welch were not moving forward. It appears that messages were misunderstood and that everyone was waiting for the German counter-attack. Orders were therefore issued which stated that the Black Watch and the South Wales Borderers were to stand fast and only move forward when the Welch advanced. Further misunderstandings then occurred when Brigadier Davies reported to 1st Division HQ. Davies tried to get across that his attack was only temporarily postponed until the 2nd Welch moved, but staff at HQ believed the attack had been definitely postponed, so Major-General Holland fixed a 'new time' for the attack at 12 noon. Holland sent a message to Brigadier Mitford of the 72nd Brigade:

> Brigadier 3rd Brigade reports that as there was no sign of advance of 24th Division on his right he postponed his attack at 11.00am. I have brought back my guns from their first lift and have turned them on again to Hulluch till noon, at which hour precisely I have ordered attack to be launched without fail. Report also received from 7th Division that his attack on Cité St Elie has been delayed.

Due to the usual difficulties in getting messages around the battlefield, Brigadier Mitford did not receive this message till 12.10pm. It was too late, as his Brigade had already gone forward to the Lens road, taking with it the 2nd Welch, who owing to the destruction of the telephone line had not received any changes to their orders.

The 2nd Welch left their trenches at the prescribed hour with two companies in the leading wave. They immediately came under intense artillery and small arms fire losing around 100 (from a total effective strength of 400) before they had even reached the Lens-La Bassée road. Things are now a bit confused as the leading wave of the 2nd Welch could see the men of the 72nd Brigade on their right but nothing to their left. Meanwhile the Germans who had earlier in the day taken up positions near the Lens-La Bassée road suddenly withdrew back to their second line positions. The two leading companies of the Welch halted facing Hulluch unable to make any further progress. The other two companies from the Welch followed the 72nd Brigade.

The orders delaying the attack of the 1st Black Watch and 1st South Wales Borderers was received in time, so these units attacked at 12 noon. They were, as the reader will recall, to attack the western side of Hulluch from their positions north-east of Lone Tree. They had to cross over 600 yards of open ground before reaching the German positions in Hulluch. There was no artillery barrage and the results were predictable. Before they had gone less than 100 yards half of the attackers had become casualties. It was clear there was no chance of anyone reaching the village, so the attack stopped. Fortunately the two reserve battalions were not called on to continue this futile effort. Again, as so often in 1915, nothing had been gained except more work for the medical services. So the efforts to support the efforts of the 24th Division on their left hand side had failed. On their right, although elements of the 15th Division supported by the 62nd Brigade from the 21st Division were holding on just below the ridge line of Hill 70 from Loos Crassier to Chalet Wood, the summit of Hill 70 and the Redoubt were held by the Germans - the dominating features. So the essential ingredients for a successful advance against the German second line positions between Bois Hugo and Puits 13 bis were missing. In spite of these tremendous difficulties a number of the units of the 21st and 24th divisions were now moving into a 'Valley of Death' between the German flanks. During the morning of the 26th the Germans had strengthened their grip on Hill 70 and Bois Hugo and took control of Chalet Wood. The men of the 6th Camerons led by Lieutenant-Colonel A. Douglas-Hamilton made repeated attempts to retake the western end of the wood and at times savage hand-to-hand fighting took place. The Germans had men from the 106th Reserve, 153rd and 178th regiments contesting the possession of this wood and eventually the 6th Camerons were reduced to around 50 men. The Germans started to advance through the wood and the Camerons put up a stout resistance but weight of numbers brushed them aside and the Camerons were virtually wiped out and the wood lost. Lieutenant-Colonel A. Douglas-Hamilton fought to the last and was posthumously awarded a Victoria Cross. His citation read:

> For most conspicuous bravery and devotion to duty when commanding the Battalion during operations on 25th and 26th September 1915, on Hill 70. On the 26th, when the battalions on his right and left had retired, he rallied his own Battalion again and again, and led his men forward four times. The last time he led all that remained, consisting of about fifty men, in a most gallant manner and was killed at their head. It was mainly due to his bravery, untiring energy and splendid leadership that the line at this point was enabled to check the enemy's advance.

Douglas-Hamilton, the son of a Major-General, had been a Regular Officer retiring in August 1912 but was recalled from the reserve on the outbreak of the Great War. His first job was as a transport officer at Southampton Docks, but being an infantry officer had been promoted to Temporary Lieutenant-Colonel in October 1914 and appointed to command the 6th Cameron Highlanders. His body was not recovered and he is now commemorated on the Loos Memorial to the Missing. He was also one of the older casualties of Loos, at 52 years old.

Meanwhile, men from the 63rd Brigade and the 14th Durham LI (64th Brigade) moved in the direction of the Lens-La Bassée road and towards Bois Hugo and Chalet Wood, right into the fire of well dug-in Germans. Again a misunderstanding caused a diversionary effect. Some distance to the south-east a number of troops could be seen on the slopes of Hill 70. It was believed that all the British troops had withdrawn from these positions and therefore they must be Germans. In fact they were men from the 45th, 46th and 62nd brigades. The sight of these men attracted the attention of the leading waves and they veered away from an easterly heading to a south-easterly one, heading for Hill 70. This took their route across the faces of the Germans in Bois Hugo and Chalet Wood, who wasted no time in pouring fire into the Brigade. It says much for the courage of these men that they got within a couple of hundred yards of the enemy before the weight of fire forced them back.

It was now the turn of the only virtually intact units of the 21st Division to be brought into the action. These were the 9th and 10th King's Own Yorkshire Light Infantry from the 64th Brigade who had spent the morning up to that point positioned along the Grenay-Hulluch road. Around the time that the men from the 63rd Brigade (and the 14th Durham LI) were struggling back, Brigadier Gloster was talking to the COs of the two KOYLI battalions. Gloster was thinking that nothing would be gained by throwing these two units into the 'Valley of Death' and that it would be best to hold the positions they had and wait for reinforcements. However a staff officer from 21st Division HQ was present and argued for an attack. Things are a little unclear as to how it happened but the 9th KOYLI left their positions and advanced. Gloster reacted quickly, and told the CO of the 10th KOYLI (Lieutenant-Colonel Pollock) to support them. But Gloster did try and limit any advance by saying "not to advance beyond the Loos-Hulluch road, and to occupy the trenches there." Survivors from the previous attack joined the ranks of the KOYLI in the advance eastwards. The orders from Gloster only reached, it seems, two companies of the 10th KOYLI who stopped at the correct place.

HQ 64th Brigade's War Diary has this comment:

It has not yet been discovered who ordered them forward. It was impossible to stop them, and with a few hurried verbal instructions their CO ran off after them. But practically they went off without orders. The 10th KOYLI were hastily ordered to follow in support, and their CO was ordered not to go beyond the Loos-Hulluch road. There was no prospect of two battalions succeeding where many had failed, and it was hoped merely to restore morale by ending up in advance of some kind, and then dig in near the road beyond which further advance seemed impossible.

It is fair to say that the rest of the attack was a disjointed one and again the magical effect of Hill 70 came into play, as the majority of the men again headed up its lower slopes. Once again they came under heavy small arms fire from the areas of Bois Hugo and Chalet Wood, causing heavy casualties. Again the attack was broken and men streamed back as best they could, but this time many went back to the original British front line trenches. The German 106th Reserve Regiment had this to say about the attack:

Near 12 noon masses of infantry, estimated at about a division, began to advance in about 20 waves on a front between Loos and Chalk Pit Wood moving in a southerly direction towards Hill 70. Simultaneously the British troops entrenched opposite Hill 70 Redoubt opened a heavy covering fire. The advancing masses were nevertheless taken under fire by the machine guns and rifles in Hill 70 Redoubt, and effectively enfiladed by those of the 153rd Regiment and a company of the 106th Reserve Regiment which had advanced during the morning through the woods east of Puits 14 bis and occupied the line of the Lens-La Bassée road, between Hill 70 and Puits 14 bis. The effect of this fire from two sides was very considerable, whole lines being mown down by the machine guns. The enemy fled back in confusion towards Loos. Later he attacked in a similar manner against Hill 70 and against the 153rd Regiment in position along the Lens-La Bassée road. He was easily and completely repulsed, his advance being again taken under concentric fire from Hill 70 Redoubt and from the Lens road.

Unfortunately all these moves and counter-moves were unknown to the two battalions of the 71st Brigade and the entire 72nd Brigade from the 24th Division as they advanced eastwards. Though they came under fire from both artillery and small arms fire they continued to move steadily up the open slopes of the Loos valley. But before they reached the Lens-La Bassée road, the right hand unit, the 9th East Surreys, in its efforts to maintain contact (as ordered) with the 21st Division, was drawn away to the right. This meant they crossed the road immediately north of Chalk Pit Wood. Then it continued along the northern face of Bois Hugo, coming under intense fire and therefore straying into the 21st Division's area. The left-hand battalion, the 8th Royal West Kents, together with men from the 2nd Welch, continued on track, straight for its objective, across the junction of the Lens-La Bassée and Grenay-Hulluch roads towards the southern edge of Hulluch. There was a small success here now, in that some Germans who had been part of the earlier counter-attack from Stützpunkt IV were forced to pull back to their second line positions and suffered around 200 casualties. However this is as about as good as it got. As soon as the Royal West Kents and the Welch crossed the Lens-La Bassée road they came under fire from what appeared to be all sides. They struggled on for another 300 yards or so. The situation was now one of what a brigadier in the Second World War called "a grossly untidy situation." It had been planned that an attack would go in by two divisions on a front of about a mile. The reality was about 2½ battalions separated by about 700 yards. Fortunately Brigadier Mitford realised this and tried to contain the situation. The 8th Buffs were sent in on the right, north of Chalk Pit Wood to try and fill the gap here. Additionally, as the Royal West Kents and the Welch were suffering casualties and virtually stalled by fire from south of Hulluch, the 8th Queens were also ordered forward. Their role was to "fill gaps and prolong the line to the left." Shortly afterwards the 11th Essex were sent forward to support the Royal West Kents and the Welch, with the 9th Suffolk being moved to a support position behind the middle sector of the attack. These reinforcements gave the attack of the Royal West Kents and the Welch a fresh impetus. It also gave encouragement to the right hand unit, the 9th East Surreys, who had been hanging back under fire from Bois Hugo.

Here is a short comment from an officer of the 9th East Surreys, Captain B. Fenwick, who was taken prisoner at Loos and provides information on the difficulties faced by the East Surreys when they did close with the Germans:

> I myself was stopped about 20 or 30 yards from the German wire but even there I could easily see that the thing was an impossibility. When I was afterwards taken in I saw that not a strand of the barbed wire had been cut by the artillery. In depth I should judge it about 30 feet, but it is difficult to say exactly. The woods on the right and behind were also heavily wired and untouched.

It is difficult to picture the scene now, but there were now parts of five infantry battalions all concentrated together in a relatively small area. They were doing their best to get forward into an area dominated on three sides by German fire. As well as small arms fire, there was heavy artillery fire coming down, thinning the ranks of the attackers. Men from the 72nd Brigade managed to reach the crest of a small ridge and could see about 30 yards away the formidable barbed wire defences in front of the German second line position and beyond that the actual defenders themselves. It is believed that over the next hour small parties managed to get within about 50 yards of the German second line positions but the wire had not been touched by any artillery bombardment and efforts to cut the barbed wire with cutters was a suicidal task. On the left the rear half battalion of the Welch had managed to advance against the German positions between Hulluch and Puits 13 bis and managed to seize a section of German trench, another small isolated success but there were no other troops available to consolidate or exploit this gain.

The 9th Suffolk and the 11th Essex, having been ordered forward at 11.25am, headed across the Lens-La Bassée road in an attempt to reinforce the 72nd Brigade. They also came almost immediately under heavy fire from the area of Hulluch. The 9th Suffolks managed to get about 200 yards beyond the road before the advance was checked. Part of the 11th Essex (its left hand side) veered towards Hulluch and made a brave attempt to reach the village but was forced to seek shelter in a sunken lane south of the village. The remainder of the 11th Essex moved according to their orders in the general direction of Stützpunkt IV. Some of the men reached the barbed wire and met up with some men from the 8th Queens. A report from the German 26th Regiment stated:

> The Battalion Staff was on the left flank, south of Stützpunkt IV, whence we had a wonderful view. The English attacked in whole hosts and with great dash. Our men fired standing up as fast as they could pull their triggers. No Englishmen got through the wire entanglement, and the ground in front was covered with bodies.

The situation was now similar to the previous day with parties of British soldiers trying to find what cover there was in front of the German uncut wire, which was impenetrable. Fortunately there was a belt of long grass, which did give some sort of cover, but any attempts to try and cut the barbed wire did bring down retaliation from the Germans. The survivors here could see on their right hand side the men of the 21st Division falling back and on their left, the fire (and German hold on Hulluch) showed no sign of slacking. More worryingly, there seemed to be no way forward and no sign of any help coming. It is reported that some officers felt they should remain where they were and wait for support, others could see no way out except withdrawing, as they had done all that could be reasonably expected of them. Three of the Battalion COs had been killed: Romer of the 8th Buffs, Fairtlough of the 8th Queens and Radclyffe of the 11th Essex. Two others had been wounded: Vansittart of the 8th Royal West Kents and Brettell of the 9th Suffolks. It is interesting to note the ages of the three dead COs: Romer was 61 years old and his rank was given as a full Colonel with the decorations of CB (Companion of the Bath) and CMG (Companion of the Order of St Michael and St George), Fairtlough was 54 and again a CMG, while Radclyffe was 50 but held a DSO. None of their bodies were recovered and all three are commemorated on the Loos Memorial to the Missing.

Here is an account from Lieutenant-Colonel Brettell CO of the 9th Suffolks:

> I had a leg broken by a machine gun bullet fired from the direction of Hulluch which apparently was in German hands, and judging from the stream of bullets striking the ground just before I was hit showed that this gun or guns was or were enfilading the attacking lines. I got into a shell hole and faced the German

position. Shortly afterwards a shell burst behind me, a bullet struck me in the left shoulder. It was a direct hit and could not have come from enfilading guns.

I turned round, and shortly afterwards another shell burst in front of me, I put my hand up in front of my face, back of hand next to my face, and I received a shrapnel bullet in my hand, two others in my legs and one in my left foot. My position in the shell hole was about 25 yards beyond the Loos-Hulluch road on the lower slopes of Hill 70.

It appears someone shouted "Retire" and parties of men began to withdraw, although some did not and were later killed or taken prisoner. The withdrawal for a time went well, until about 700 yards from the Lens-La Bassée road the men nearest Hulluch were mown down by machine gun fire. The line broke, with some men making for the sunken lane south-west of Hulluch. The 24th Division was now a shattered force, the only organised body left being the Divisional Pioneers, the 12th Sherwood Foresters. They were sent up to Lone Tree Ridge to stabilise the line and stop stragglers going back too far. The 2nd Welch, with the survivors of the morning's exertions situated in two locations (some in a German trench east of Hulluch and the rest to the west of the village) noticed the general withdrawal going on, so decided to join in and ended up in the trench from where they started. The 2nd Welch was now down to less than 200 all ranks and this story was repeated round the units of the 21st and 24th divisions, as we shall see later. While the withdrawal was going on, it appeared that the men of the 63rd and 64th brigades also decided it would be a good time to leave the area opposite Chalet Wood. So around 1.30pm, a mass of troops were falling back on a large front between the Vermelles-Hulluch and the Vermelles-Loos roads. It is likely the most organised body of men still forward were the survivors from the 45th and 46th brigades on the northern slopes of Hill 70. Opposite Bois Hugo men from about two companies of the 8th Somerset LI still held a tenuous grip in the Chalk Pit. Close by in some trenches just north of the north were some men from the 12th West Yorks, 8th Lincolns and 10th Yorks and Lancs. Additionally, it is believed that there were still around 300 men in front of the barbed wire belt that had stopped the advance of the 24th Division. These men, although isolated, probably drew a lot of attention from the Germans which meant the others who did manage to retire got away relatively unscathed. The retreat of the 24th Division was observed by the 2nd Welch. The post-war Official History comments that the troops "began to fall back steadily, without panic and at even pace, towards the Lens road." The 2nd Welch War Diary gives an alternative view:

But suddenly to our amazement and disgust the whole Corps on our right turned round and bolted in a wild panic. The men threw away their rifles and equipment and ran back across the valley and disappeared over the crest of the hill over which they had advanced so magnificently. In this rout they all bunched together and so made a good mark for the German shrapnel and machine guns in Hulluch and consequently lost twice as many as they did advancing. We were left with two companies opposite Hulluch, an impossible situation to remain in as we had both flanks in the air and had no support, so we retired slowly but naturally losing heavily. Eventually the remnant of us, some 150 men with seven officers, arrived in the trench we started from. Here we remained in comparative quiet.

Uncut German wire in front of one of their positions. (IWM Q28970)

However there were still some men in position under the barbed wire belt in front of the German trenches. One of these was Sergeant A. Saunders of the 9th Suffolks. Saunders was a platoon sergeant and after his officer had been wounded in the approach march he took charge of two machine guns and some men, and attempted to provide support to the attack. As the remnants of the 9th Suffolks were withdrawing he continued to fire a machine gun and as his citation said: "continued to give clear orders, and by continuous firing did his best to cover the retirement." Mixed up in this attack was a junior officer from the 6th Cameron Highlanders, Second Lieutenant Christison (later to became General Sir Philip Christison). In his memoirs written many years later the story emerged of Saunders's gallantry. In the afternoon of 26th September Christison was lying wounded in a shell-hole when the 9th Suffolks passed through his location. For a time things seemed to be going well, but then the Suffolks doubled back under German fire leaving him alone. In Christison's own words:

> But one stout fellow, Sergeant A.F. Saunders, refused to retire. He had a Lewis gun he had picked up with a full drum on it. He crawled over to me and said he'd stay and fight. He made to crawl over to the next shell-hole and, as he did so, a shell landed and blew part of his left leg off about the knee. I crawled over and got him into the shell-hole putting a tourniquet on his leg and giving him my water bottle as his was empty. I crawled back to my hole and a few minutes later saw a fresh wave of German troops advancing, there seemed to be no point in opening fire as there were, perhaps, 150 enemy advancing rather diagonally across our front. To my amazement, I heard short sharp bursts of Lewis gun fire coming from the shell-hole to my right; this was Sergeant Saunders, more or less

minus a leg. The Germans were taken by surprise and bunched, so I joined in and between us took a heavy toll and the rest retired out of sight. I took down Sergeant Saunders number, name and regiment. Stretcher bearer parties from the RE got me and Sergeant Saunders on stretchers, but shells dropped close and we were abandoned. We were lucky a stretcher bearer party from the Scots Guards picked us up and got us to an Advanced Dressing Station, where emergency surgery was carried out. Sergeant Saunders, now without a leg, was awarded the Victoria Cross, while I was given the Military Cross.

Saunders had served in the Royal Navy for 15 years reaching the rank of Petty Officer before being discharged. He decided to join the Army when war broke out in August 1914 and was promoted to sergeant within the first four weeks. Fortunately Saunders survived his ordeal but was medically discharged from the Army in 1916.

The stragglers who did get back and those who were collected together by Brigadier Mitford were positioned in Alley 4. This consisted of small elements of every battalion from the 72nd Brigade, 11th Essex, 9th Suffolks and 2nd Welch, supported by the 12th Sherwood Foresters. It is fortunate that the Germans did not launch a coordinated counter-attack here, as I doubt whether the few defenders would have been able to stop them. As it was many men from the 21st and 24th divisions had gone a long way past these men and were back behind Lone Tree Ridge. It appears around 2.00pm that a sort of unofficial truce was called by the Germans around Hulluch as medical personnel went out trying to treat and collect wounded. Perhaps under cover of this truce word was sent to the 8th Somerset LI in the Chalk Pit to get back to British lines, which they in fact managed to do. This then virtually was the last action of the 21st and 24th divisions.

It would now be useful to look up the chain of command at Corps and Army.

Not for the first time in the Great War the news that the attack had not gone to plan was greeted with disbelief at XI Corps HQ in Noeux les Mines. It was not until a written report from a staff officer of the 24th Division which arrived at Corps HQ around 4.00pm that it appears the worst was known. This staff officer had been sent forward to try and ascertain the correct situation, as conflicting reports were (as usual) being received. This note written to General Haking bluntly stated that on reaching Lone Tree he had met hundreds of men coming back. General Haig happened to be present at XI Corps HQ at this time, and as usual looked on the bright side, and tried to dismiss this report, although soon afterwards other reports confirming the withdrawal arrived. Haig immediately decided to 'reinforce' the situation by deploying the Guards Division to restore the situation. It must be remembered that at this moment the Guards Division was on the move forward from Noeux les Mines and Houchin. In theory the Guards Division was the only reserve available to the whole BEF in Flanders. Haig again had to ask Sir John French for their release from GHQ control and this time it was forthcoming relatively quickly. To their credit it seems both Haig and Haking realised that the line was only very thinly defended and Haig ordered Haking forward to the 21st and 24th divisions HQs. At both these HQs, situated at Philosophe and Vermelles respectively, he gave orders that the original German front line between the Béthune-Lens and Vermelles-Hulluch roads had to be held at all costs. He also relayed the news that the Guards Division was on its way and would relieve both divisions in the line later that evening.

The most immediate task was to try and get some of the troops back to strengthen up the line and staff officers were sent out to round up stragglers. As immediate support the Royal Engineer field companies of both divisions (who had not been used in the original attack) were ordered forward to bolster the line. It must be remembered that in the British Army nearly everyone is an infantry soldier first and a specialist second, so they were a welcome addition in numbers. It is good to report that in nearly all cases when challenged by an officer, the stragglers were ready and willing to go back into the trenches. The British Official History uses the words "Sheep without a Shepherd." One large party with only one or two junior officers present made it all the way back to Le Rutoire, where they said they had been told to concentrate. On being told by a Brigadier from the 1st Division that they would be more useful in the front line, they turned round and went back. The words of a Tommy come to mind: "We'll be all right now that we have got some orders." At the front line Major-General Forestier-Walker (GOC 21st Division) took personal control of the defence. After a few hours confusion, slowly some order was being brought to the front in this area. It was certainly a tough baptism of fire for the 21st and 24th divisions. One of the soldiers mixed up in this attack was Private E. Glendinning from the 12th Sherwood Foresters (who were the pioneers for the 24th Division). He later recorded:

> Withdrawing across No Man's Land was an amazing sight, like a flock of sheep lying asleep in a field. It became evident that the stretcher bearers had been unable to cope with the large numbers of wounded and some men were crying out, begging for water, they plucked at our legs but we were told to ignore them. In the years that followed this incident has always haunted me.

Meanwhile, back at Hill 70, the small group of men holding on here, for reasons that are not clear, withdrew back to British lines. Again the British Official History says the message, which brought this about, cannot now be discovered, nor can its origin be definitely cleared up. What is known is that around 3.00pm an order was sent from 15th Division HQ to its sub-units and the 62nd Brigade (then under command 15th Division) that all stragglers should be collected to hold the old German front line under command of the GOC 45th Brigade. It is possible that this message may have been sent by runner or by telephone to Loos for forward transmission to the HQ of the 45th Brigade. It appears that the message was brought by a soldier from the Divisional Signal Company and given to an officer in the thinly held line of the 45th and 46th brigades on the western slopes of Hill 70. This message stated that the line of the old German trenches between the Vermelles-Hulluch and Béthune-Lens roads was to be held. From their relatively high position on Hill 70 men to the north could be seen withdrawing: these of course were the troops from the 21st and 24th divisions. The message was first given to the CO of the 11th Argyll and Sutherland Highlanders, Lieutenant-Colonel McNeill. It was now a time for what I call a 'three and four pence' message to come into play. McNeill declined to take any action on receipt of this message as it was apparently incomplete and did not bear any signature (at least the part of it he received). He forwarded it and also a summary of its contents and instructions by two different runners to the CO of the 13th Royal Scots, Lieutenant-Colonel Maclear. It was sent to him as he was thought to be the senior officer present.

Maclear was indisposed when the messages arrived so they were both taken to the last remaining CO on the hill, Lieutenant-Colonel Henning of the 7th Royal Scots Fusiliers. He quite rightly decided to ignore the first message, as there seemed no reason for a withdrawal. However when the second message (the summary) arrived, he looked upon it as confirmation of the first orders not a duplicate. A local commander is sometimes in a difficult position when given some orders he feels uncomfortable with, but he must remember that he doesn't always see the bigger picture and this is probably what made Henning's mind up for him to a point. It is further alleged that Henning sent a runner back to Brigade HQ asking for another confirmation and also to request ammunition and food, but the runner came back saying that Brigade HQ had gone back to Vermelles. This must have tipped the scales in favour of the messages and Henning therefore issued orders for a withdrawal from Hill 70. These orders were acted on by nearly all the troops on and near Hill 70 including men around Chalet Wood. By around 4.00pm the withdrawal was in full swing.

Up on the hill Private R. Dunsire of the 13th Royal Scots noticed a wounded British soldier lying between the opposing troops, waving an arm as if requesting help. In spite of heavy German small arms fire Dunsire crawled out and took him back to the safety of the British lines. Shortly after this Dunsire heard another man asking for help, it was ascertained that he was considerably closer to the German lines than the other soldier, but again, Dunsire went out and returned safely with him. It is recorded "How he managed to escape without a scratch was a mystery,

British troops returning from the line. (IWM Q 60742)

for the earth was madly dancing to the continuous thud of bullets." Dunsire was recommended for a Victoria Cross and the award was gazetted on 18th November 1915. Sadly Robert Dunsire was wounded near Hulluch in January 1916 and died of his wounds on the 30th of that month. He was buried in Mazingarbe Communal Cemetery Grave 18. He was aged 24 at the time of his death.

Another small incident comes from Piper Tom Wallace of the 11th Argyll and Sutherland Highlanders who remembered the following:

> When we retired off Hill 70, and going back for roll call, we had to pass through the artillery lines someone shouted, "Give us a tune, Jock," but I said "Give me a lump of ham first." I got the ham, they got their wish - *Scotland the Brave*.

Even so, a certain number of men remained in trenches on Hill 70, especially in the lower line. The GOC of 46th Brigade, Brigadier Matheson, was surprised at this withdrawal and he hastily sent a party of about 3 officers and 100 men who he had collected up to the lower trench line of Hill 70. Two companies of the 9th Gordons, the 15th Division's pioneers, who were in Loos strengthening the defences, were also collected and sent forward to reinforce the line. It seems that later much effort was spent trying to get to the bottom of this mystery, and it seems that the only conclusion was the total exoneration from blame of the several officers who were present on Hill 70. I suspect that even if the withdrawal had not taken place, it would have been an impossible job for the 15th Division to remove the Germans from the commanding positions they held. If it had suited them they would have soon forced the British back a little. It certainly would have been easier for the German artillery to shell the British positions than vice versa. The 47th Division in the area of the Loos Crassier remained in their positions in spite of an order being received from the 15th Division advising a withdrawal. The units involved (the 19th and 20th Londons) passed the information to Brigadier Thwaites who said there was to be no withdrawal and that all positions gained were to be held at all costs. Fortunately Thwaites was in the happy position of knowing that (for him anyway) reinforcements were on the way. Two regiments from the 6th Cavalry Brigade acting as infantry had been ordered up.

The situation in the area of Hill 70 during the late morning had been causing General Rawlinson some concern and he had asked for reinforcements "in the event of any serious developments." At this time the only 'spare' organised body of men Haig possessed was the 3rd Cavalry Division. Therefore around noon the GOC of this Division, Major-General C. Briggs, was ordered to "place a cavalry brigade at the disposal of IV Corps." It should be understood that a cavalry brigade is not of the same strength as an infantry brigade. A cavalry brigade only had three regiments (battalions) in it, and the total strength would be around 2,000 men as opposed to 4,000 in an infantry brigade. For unknown reasons only two of the three units of the 6th Cavalry Brigade were ordered forward. Therefore the 1st Royal Dragoons and the 3rd Dragoon Guards left their horses near the Corons de Rutoire and went forward on foot to the original British front line, between the Loos Road and Lens Road Redoubts, and then further eastwards to the original German front line. Around 3.30pm, when Rawlinson received news that the positions on Hill 70 had been vacated, he directed Brigadier Campbell (GOC 6th Cavalry Brigade) to move to Loos with two of his regiments of cavalry and hold the village at all costs. So the 1st Royal Dragoons and the 3rd Dragoon Guards moved forward with the pylon towers being their direction markers. On the western outskirts of Loos they ran into men from the 45th and 46th brigades (about 400 strong) retreating after leaving Hill 70. On being told that the orders had been wrong, they turned round and went back through Loos towards the positions on the lower slopes of Hill 70.

These men must be given every credit for their actions on both the 25th and 26th September. It must be borne in mind that apart from a few days' experience in the trenches this was their first time in action, they performed well and bore changing circumstances very well. It must be said that they had behaved in the finest traditions of the British Army, and I suspect many pre-war Regular units would have been proud of their exploits.

By around 8.00pm on the evening of the 26th this mixed bag of troops was in position, with the 3rd Dragoon Guards on the right in the area of the Loos Crassier, the groups from the 15th Division in the middle and the 1st Royal Dragoons on the left. The Germans, for their part holding the Redoubt and the crest of the hill, decided to ignore the movements of these troops and also the strengthening of the defences in and around Loos. Meanwhile just a little further north

The Corons de Rutoire, where numerous different troops were billeted in September and October 1915. (IWM Q 17376)

the withdrawal of the troops from the Chalk Pit and Chalet Wood enabled the Germans in the increasing darkness to venture out from the shelter of Bois Hugo. It was a clever tactical move as instead of heading westwards they moved northwards along the Lens-La Bassée road, cutting off the retreat of the troops west of the road. Thus around 500 men were now trapped, mainly from the 24th Division but including men from the West Yorks, Welch and Lincolns. Facing an attack on two fronts they had no choice but to surrender. The bag of prisoners included 18 officers including 2 COs, Lieutenant-Colonels Vansittart and Prothero. Once this force had been mopped up the Germans moved forward to a position along the Lens road between Hulluch and Bois Hugo where they dug in for the night.

The only movement left to cover in this immediate area was around 11.30pm when Major-General Briggs was ordered by General Haig to make his utmost efforts to proceed to Loos with the remainder of his Division and take command there. Again the instructions were given that under no circumstances was the position to be abandoned! The 3rd Cavalry Division arrived in Loos around 3.00am the following morning, which allowed the 15th Division to be finally relieved and the battered and exhausted survivors were sent back to Mazingarbe to reorganise and hold a roll call. This must have been a grim and sad affair as the following table relates:

Table 7.1
Casualties suffered by the 15th Division for the period 25th to 27th September

	Officers	Other Ranks	Total
44th Infantry Brigade			
10th Gordon Highlanders	19	495	514
7th Cameron Highlanders	11	320	331
9th Black Watch	8	205	213
8th Seaforth Highlanders	7	200	207
Total	45	1220	1265
45th Infantry Brigade			
11th Argyll & Sutherland	15	611	626
13th Royal Scots	13	609	622
6th Cameron Highlanders	13	600	613
7th Royal Scots Fusiliers	10	598	608
Total	51	2418	2469
46th Infantry Brigade			
8th KOSB	15	509	524
12th Highland LI	10	440	450
7th KOSB	6	307	313
10th Scottish Rifles	5	216	221
Total	36	1472	1508

Divisional Troops

9th Gordon Highlanders	9	737	746
Attached Royal Artillery	3	43	46
Attached Royal Engineers	6	112	118
Attached RAMC	1	12	13
Total	19	904	923
Grand Total	151	6014	6165

After relieving the Jocks of the 15th Division, the dismounted troopers of the 3rd Cavalry Division started on the job of sorting out the village, collecting the dead and putting the village into some sort of state for defence. There was also a number of Germans still in the village and they were routed out. It is believed that a German telephone operator was found in one of the pylons sending messages back.

It is now appropriate to return to the Guards Division, who we last mentioned on the way to the front around 4.00pm. Some hours later they were digging in north of Loos village along Lone Tree Ridge in an effort to stabilize the front. It would be beneficial to review the movements of the Guards Division over the previous couple of days. The movement up on the 25th September had been carried out in similar conditions to those that had faced the 21st and 24th divisions. As the British Official History says:

> The confusion and congestion of the traffic on the roads had been appalling; all sorts of transport, ambulance wagons, troops including cavalry, were encountered, endeavoring to go in all sorts of directions, and there were not sufficient staff officers and police to enforce even the arrangements planned. Heavy rain added to the difficulties and discomfort of the march, and, although the brigades of the Guards Division moved off very early, from 5.30am onwards, it was 8.00pm before they began to reach their destinations, and midnight and after before they were all in. Even then they found Noeux les Mines and Houchin crowded and no billets reserved for them.

These movements, of course, all took place on the 25th. On the following day, at around 1.00pm, the 1st Guards Brigade left Noeux les Mines heading for Vermelles, the 2nd Guards Brigade left Houchin at 2.00pm to head for Corons de Rutoire. The 3rd Guards Brigade was in reserve and left Haillicourt (about four miles west of Noeux les Mines) heading for Sailly Labourse. Again these movements were hampered by difficulty in moving along congested roads and it is reported that the Germans fired gas shells into the British rear areas causing further delays and confusion. As previously stated, around 4.00pm on the afternoon of the 26th the Guards Division was placed under command of General Haig. But it was some hours later before the 1st and 2nd Guards brigades actually reached an area closer to the front.

It is believed that the 2nd Guards Brigade reached the Corons de Rutoire around 6.00pm and the 1st Guards Brigade got to Vermelles around 8.00pm. For a while confusion reigned, as at neither place could any HQs of any formation be found, or indeed no one could find exactly where the front line was. However, after a while, order of some sort was restored and around midnight on the 26th both bri-gades moved forward to the area of Lone Tree Ridge and started relieving the troops there. The 1st Guards Brigade was on the left including Lone Tree in its sec-tor, with the 2nd Guards Brigade on the right with Loos Road Redoubt as its ful-crum, the 3rd Guards Brigade remaining in reserve around the Corons de Rutoire. Then around midnight the forward units were sent even further eastwards to re-lieve men from the 72nd Brigade and other units in Alley 4. This meant that the line held by the Guards ran from the north of Loos village (where they were in con-tact with men from the 6th Cavalry Brigade) along the North Loos Communica-tion Trench to Northern Sap through Alley 4 towards the Lens-La Bassée road where the right flank of the 1st Division was.

Behind the sector held by the Guards Division, the survivors of the 21st and 24th divisions were being directed to the villages of Noyelles and Sailly Labourse. The roll calls of the units from these divisions again must have been a grim affair, because as we have seen casualties amongst both divisions were high. In the 21st Division the losses amongst the brigades were as follows: 62nd Brigade - 73 officers and 1,423 men, 63rd Brigade - 71 officers and 1,314 men, and the 64th Brigade - 37 officers and 1,023 men. Broken down by units the losses were as follows:

Table 7.2
21st Division casualties, 26th September

	Officers	*Men*	*Total*
62nd Brigade			
12th Northumberland Fus	22	459	481
13th Northumberland Fus	17	379	396
8th East Yorks	21	299	320
10th Green Howards	13	286	299
Total	73	1423	1496
63rd Brigade			
Brigade HQ	2	1	3
8th Lincolns	22	444	466
10th Yorks and Lancs	14	305	319
12th West Yorks	16	298	314
8th Somerset LI	17	266	283
Total	71	1314	1385
64th Brigade			
Brigade HQ	1	0	1
15th Durham LI	12	450	462
14th Durham LI	17	220	237
9th KOYLI	2	214	216
10th KOYLI	5	139	144
Total	37	1023	1060
Grand Total	181	3760	3941

If we add in the losses of the Divisional Troops of 17 officers and 93 men, we get a casualty figure for the 21st Division for their first day of action of 4,051. Meanwhile the figures for the 24th Division are as follows:

Table 7.3
24th Division casualties, 26th September

	Officers	Men	Total
71st Brigade			
11th Essex	18	353	371
9th Norfolk	13	202	215
9th Suffolk	7	137	144
8th Bedfords	2	49	51
Total	40	741	781
72nd Brigade			
8th Royal West Kents	24	556	580
8th Buffs	24	534	558
9th East Surrey	15	462	477
8th Queens	12	427	439
Total	75	1979	2754
73rd Brigade			
Brigade HQ	3	0	3
9th Royal Sussex	18	361	379
7th Northants	11	366	377
12th Royal Fusiliers	12	263	275
13th Middlesex	10	160	170
Total	54	1150	1204
Grand Total	169	3870	4059

Again if we add in the losses of the divisional troops of 18 officers and 121 men we get a casualty figure for the 24th Division for their first day of action of 4,178. Both of these are about 33% of the division's total strength. The performance of both these divisions was the subject of much debate over the next few weeks, and this will be discussed in a later chapter. Nevertheless, I feel it would be good to re-count a small comment from the AA and QMG of XI Corps-Brigadier R. Ford:

> On the morning after the debacle, while in bed (Ramsay GOC 24th Division) tendered me his resignation, which the Corps commander readily accepted. He (Ramsay) was entirely unfitted to command a division and knew it, and it is a pity those who put him in that position did not take the trouble to find out.
> The great reason for the discomfort of the men, first line transport amongst the fighting troops, loss of touch by the cookers etc, with the units, was due to the total inefficiency of the two AA and QMG of 21st and 24th divisions. Both elderly, and with Indian experience only, knew nothing of their

Major-Gen. Sir T. Capper, CO 7th Division.
(Histed.)

job, and I was instrumental in having both instantly removed together with the GOC Division.

The only action left to cover now is the actions of the I Corps north of the Vermelles-Hulluch road. In orders given by Haig, they were to attack Cité St Elie at 11.00am on the 26th September. To protect the flank the 2nd Division was ordered to defend its original positions. You will recall they failed to make any progress in their initial attack, but they were ordered to provide some units for an attack in another area. This force was commanded by the CO of the 1st King's, Lieutenant-Colonel B. Carter, with three battalions in 'Carter's Force': 1st KRRC, 1st Royal Berks and 2nd Worcesters. They were meant to be in the 7th Division's area by 7.00am on the 26th but did not reach Vermelles until 10.00am. But, as sometimes happens in war, the opposing side did not adhere to the plan. The failure to recapture the Quarries during the early hours of the 26th of September led this plan to be looked upon as impractical. There was a low rise here and as long as the Germans held this area an advance past its southern edge against Cité St Elie was tantamount to suicide. So it was decided to get Carter's Force to attack the Quarries. The attack ran into difficulties before it had even really started, reasons being the state of the trenches after the recent heavy rain, and empty and leaking gas cylinders lying in the trenches. The time of the attack was moved back to 3.30pm. The orders for the attack stated:

G.58, Carter's Force will at 3.30pm attack the Quarries from approximately the line G.11, B.34-G.5, D12; 9th Division will assist this advance by a movement from Fosse 8, the details of which will be communicated later. The attack will be preceded by a bombardment of heavy artillery and field artillery lasting one hour, the last five minutes of which will be intensive - the 20th Brigade (7th Division) will furnish an engineer party, consisting of one section, to assist in the consolidation of the Quarries when captured. The heavy artillery will lift off the Quarries at the hour, the field artillery will be detailed to continue firing till two minutes after the assault has been launched, when a barrage will be fired north-east of the Quarries.

The 1st Royal Berkshires by now had been given alternative orders and were heading towards the Hohenzollern Redoubt, leaving the 2nd Worcesters to be the spearhead of the attack with just two companies (A and C) of the 1st KRRC in support. Then at 3.30pm the attack was postponed for another hour as the Worcesters found it very difficult to move up the communication trenches, apparently being hindered by the five boxes of bombs per company they were carrying and leaking gas cylinders which affected some men who had to be left behind. However by 4.15pm they had reached the front line and at 4.30pm the signal was given for the attack to start. The 2nd Worcesters moved forward in four lines, each containing half a company (each line had two platoons from two different companies, followed by the other two platoons in the next line). In the first wave were C and D companies with A and B in the second line. The advance was carried out at the double until the first German trench was reached, in which to their surprise they found some troops from the 9th Norfolks. They, of course, had been lent from the 71st Brigade (24th Division) to the 7th Division and were still in position after their abortive attack earlier in the day. Nevertheless, the Worcesters got over their surprise and carried on towards the German positions, very few casualties had been suffered between the British lines and the old German line, but as they now approached the German positions things began to change. Rapid rifle and machine gun fire now poured into the advancing troops and casualties were heavy. The Worcesters managed to reach an old half-dug German trench where the first wave took advantage of what little cover there was and started to return fire on the German trenches about 200 yards away. It was impossible to get any further forward and as darkness fell, this position was consolidated and this work continued throughout the night. The second wave halted about 50 yards behind the first and began digging in. A bombing attack was organised to clear a communication trench called St Elie Avenue which went back to the German lines. This was successfully done and the trench was blocked to form a defensive position.

During the attack the Worcesters had drifted somewhat to the right and therefore to fill in the gap the two companies of the 1st KRRC were moved up to the left of the Worcesters. It must be said here again that communication was difficult and erroneous reports were sent back including one that alluded to the Quarries being taken. When darkness fell therefore Carter's Force was entrenched some 200 yards west of the Quarries, then through Point 22 to Points 78 and 90, with contact either side with the 21st and 22nd brigades.

The 7th Division assisted in this operation with bombers from the 20th Brigade attacking a communication trench, while the 2nd Royal Scots Fusiliers in

Breslau Avenue would give supporting fire. When the attack went in the 20th Brigade's bombers worked their way towards the north-west corner of the Quarries but were unable to dislodge the Germans from their positions. Also mixed up in this attack was the GOC of the 7th Division, Major-General Capper, who, if accounts are correct, was in the leading wave of the Worcesters and was wounded by the side of a platoon commander. Unfortunately, his wounds were quite serious and he died the following morning. This death was recorded in the Division's War Diary: "All those who knew him will mourn the loss of a gallant soldier who, by his courage and devotion to duty, set a splendid example to every officer, NCO and man in the 7th Division." Capper was originally commissioned into the East Lancashire Regiment, and was a holder of the KCMG, CB and a DSO. He died at a Casualty Clearing Station (CCS) at Lillers and is buried in the CWGC plot in the Communal Cemetery there.

The efforts of Carter's Force to reach the Quarries, although unsuccessful, did gain a message from General Gough which said: "Please express my pleasure with Colonel Carter's Brigade for their gallant attack on the Quarries, and convey my appreciation to them, especially the Worcesters, and hope they will continue to maintain all they have won." The price was heavy. The 2nd Worcesters casualty figure for the 26th September was 13 officers and 275 Men, this included all the company commanders killed or wounded. The RMO Captain E. Carrington RAMC was killed gallantly attending the wounded under fire. Edward Carrington was 26 years old at the time of his death. had previously won a MC, and is now buried at Vermelles CWGC Cemetery. He was the son of Sir John and Lady Carrington. The Battalion Padre also got a mention in the Worcesters War Diary: "Captain the Reverend R.J. Stewart, Chaplain to the Forces, and attached to the Battalion, was present during the operation, and rendered valuable assistance in attending the wounded." The 1st KRRC got off very lightly, only suffering 1 man killed and 1 officer and 10 men wounded.

Finally, for this day, the French 10th Army were continuing their attack but were unable to make any progress of real importance, and consequently their efforts did little to assist the BEF. I will not go into much detail here except for a few comments. At 8.50am on the 26th, General Foch directed the commander of the 10th Army not to attack until he had reestablished order in his divisions, and relieved those which had suffered most heavily. Meanwhile Joffre, the Commander-in-Chief, had different ideas, stating that: "We must not think of forcing the crest of Vimy Ridge." It seems his eyes were elsewhere (i.e. Champagne) where "fruitful results seem to be offered." Foch was directed to "go cautiously with the IV, XVII, XII and III corps and support the British offensive with the left wing of the 10th Army." The French did put in some attacks around noon but only made some small, localised gains. At 5.25pm on the 26th, having heard from Sir John French that the British right was hard pressed and might suffer defeat unless the left of the 10th Army acted quickly and with energy, General d'Urbal set about forming a new reserve by ordering the withdrawal during the night of a regiment from each division of the IX and XVII corps. Later that evening he ordered that the offensive be continued north of Arras at dawn on the 27th. However Foch later issued orders that the 10th Army was to economise on artillery expenditure, and to bring the 152nd Division from IX Corps out of the line. He also persuaded Joffre to cancel his original orders for taking two divisions from the 10th Army, and instead the 6th Army was instructed to produce them. So as we can see the French Army did very little to help Haig on the 26th September, which as previously stated, meant the Germans were able to concentrate their efforts on the Lens area. Thus ended the actions on the second day of Loos, 26th September.

8

The Guards go in - 27th September

On the morning of the 27th September the only real 'fresh' troops able to carry on the attack were the men from the Guards Division, although in theory the situation (on paper) was not too bad. Although Hill 70 had been lost on the 26th and the counter-attack on the Quarries had failed, the arrival in the front line of Carter's Force, the Guards Division and the 3rd Cavalry Division had made the position relatively secure against a German counter-attack. But the capacity of the 1st Army to maintain a vigorous offensive was questionable. Some of the other troops were not in a very good shape either. The men from the 73rd Brigade of the 24th Division, holding the eastern end of Fosse 8 while attached to the 15th Division, had received very little logistical support for about 48 hours i.e. food and water. It must have been a salutary experience for these totally raw troops and their GOC Brigadier R. Jelf wrote the following in a report dated 26th September:

> No communication of any kind had been established with my battalions either by wire or orderly, and I attribute this to the fact that all battalions and the Brigade staff were quite ignorant of the rudiments of what to do in the trenches, how communications were established, the method of drawing rations, etc, they never having been in trenches in their lives before. And I can confidently assert, after many months of trench warfare, that it would have taxed to the uttermost the resources of any Regular battalions with plenty of experience behind them, to have kept themselves supplied, under similar conditions.

During the afternoon of the 26th September the trenches either side of the Three Cabarets, a road junction at the eastern end of the group of houses north of Fosse 8, were under heavy bombardment from the German artillery. The exhausted troops in the trenches found it a very trying experience and probably were close to breaking point. It must have been a difficult position also for Brigadier Jelf, as he had only assumed command of the Brigade on the 26th, after their original GOC Brigadier W. Oswald was sacked. During the night of 26th/27th the trenches east of The Dump and the communication trenches leading forward to them from the area of the Hohenzollern Redoubt were under near continuous artillery fire. An especially heavy 'morning hate' of this sector also began at dawn, as a prelude to an attack directed against the left hand side of the 21st Brigade in Stone Alley. The Germans managed to gain a tenuous hold in Stone Alley but were later driven back by a counter-attack from the 2nd Wiltshires, who had been nominated as the local reserve for the 7th Division. It is also worth noting here that the second-in-command, Major C. Forsyth, was leading this unit because the original CO, Lieutenant-Colonel B. Leatham, had been killed on the 26th. Leatham, aged 34, was originally commissioned in the Green Howards and the holder of a DSO. He is now buried at Vermelles CWGC Cemetery. This is how his death was recorded in the unit's War Diary: "In the early hours of the morning the CO Lieutenant-

Major-Gen. G.H. Thesiger, CO 9th Division. (Russell)

Colonel Leatham received a bullet wound in the chest and died almost immediately."

Soon after this the Germans launched another attack towards the junction of Fosse and Slag Alleys. It is believed around 1,000 men crossed No Man's Land in the night and waited within rushing distance of the trenches. This attack, carried out by the 91st Reserve Regiment and the Bavarian Composite Regiment, was directed against men from the 7th Northants and the 12th Royal Fusiliers. The attack was a skillful one delivered against tired inexperienced men and the Germans bombed their way northwards forcing the Northants back into the Corons de Pekin, north of The Dump. They exploited this gain by taking control of The Dump itself, establishing several machine gun positions, which were able to dominate the 600 yards of open ground between here and the Hohenzollern Redoubt. Around midday more German soldiers crossed over to this position and a further attack developed southwards along Slag Alley towards The Dump. Weight of numbers forced the Royal Fusiliers back till they ended up south of The Dump. The next part of the German plan was to organise an attack against the Hohenzollern Redoubt. Brigadier Jelf considered it would be impossible to try and retake The Dump given the exhausted state of his Brigade. He decided to withdraw his men from the area of the Corons. They also gave up Fosse Trench and Dump Trench and regrouped along the eastern face of the Hohenzollern Redoubt. As is usual bad news travels fast and the GOC of the 9th Division, Major-General Thesiger (remember that the 73rd Brigade was part of his command), went forward to investigate the situation in the area around Fosse 8. However on reaching the eastern side of the Hohenzollern Redoubt, he, together with two of his staff officers was killed. Major-General G.H. Thesiger, originally commissioned into the Rifle Brigade, the son of a retired Lieutenant-General, was aged 47 at the time of his death, and had probably been destined for high command. Regretfully his body could not be found after the battle and he is commemorated on Panel 129 of the Loos Memorial to the Missing.

Haig heard of the loss of Thesiger when he was visiting I Corps HQ and ordered Major-General E. Bulfin, the GOC of the 28th Division, to take over command of the 9th Division's front. The 28th Division has not been mentioned before, so now is a good time to note their history. Almost the last of the old Regular Army, the 28th Division was formed from units recalled from the far-flung corners of the Empire. These units came from Egypt, India and Singapore and together with the 27th and 29th divisions were formed from the last Regular units returning to the UK. The 29th Division under the command of Hunter-Weston went to Gallipoli, while the 27th and 28th divisions went to the BEF. Badly mauled at Ypres in May 1915 both divisions were in rest around Bailleul when the call came for the 28th Division to move to Loos. Bulfin arrived at the 9th Divisional HQ around 3.00pm and almost immediately he was ordered by Corps HQ to initiate a counter-attack by the 26th Brigade and retake Dump and Fosse Trenches. It had been envisaged that the 85th Brigade from the 28th Division would do this but as usual they had taken far longer than expected to reach the scene of the action. The British Official History records:

> The 28th Division, after its tremendous losses in the Second Battle of Ypres, 15,533 of all ranks, had a fortnight's rest, leaving the 85th Brigade in the line. It then on the 14th June took over a sector of the Ypres front, St Eloi and afterwards Wytschaete. There it was relieved on the 20th-22nd September by the 2nd Canadian Division, and moved to Bailleul in 2nd Army reserve. The original arrangements were for one Brigade of the 28th Division to move by motorbus, one by train and the third to march. At the last moment, however, GHQ were unable to arrange this, and the whole Division marched.

There are two significant points worth commenting on from the above: the first is the casualty total for Ypres of 15,533. This is, of course, more than the entire strength of the Division! It would be interesting to know in September 1915 how many actual 'Regulars' there were in the ranks. Secondly, the comment that even GHQ was unable to produce a train or trains and motor vehicles. Perhaps the answer is that the BEF, although increasing in 'bayonet' strength, was failing to keep pace in the administrative tail.

Meanwhile back at Loos, the 26th Brigade prepared for another attack, although whether it was in a fit state to do so is debatable. It had suffered heavy casualties in the earlier days of the fighting and on the morning of the 27th sent detachments from the 8th Black Watch and 5th Camerons to assist the 73rd Brigade. It therefore left the Brigade only about 600 strong - less than a battalion in strength! In spite of their small numbers they left the original British front line trenches and advanced. Suffering heavily from artillery and small arms fire, the leading waves were able to reach the eastern side of the Hohenzollern Redoubt, but could not get any further forward towards Fosse 8 due to the weight of fire.

Nevertheless their arrival in the Hohenzollern Redoubt did bring some relief to the men of the 73rd Brigade who were running short of munitions and for the time being the position here was strengthened. It is worth adding at this point that the 26th Brigade suffered, in the first three days at Loos, losses of 79 officers and 2,100 men.

The Germans were now attacking from both sides of The Dump towards the Hohenzollern Redoubt. Additionally, men could be seen digging in on The Dump. There was much close quarter fighting now, and again a Jock stood out for his bravery - Corporal J. Pollock of the 5th Camerons. It is recorded that Corporal Pollock from C Company was one of a number of men sent forward to reinforce the Redoubt, where the 73rd Brigade was having a torrid time. The arrival of these reinforcements rallied the defenders and they were able to halt the German attacks after several bombing fights. Then around midday a large party of German bombers approached the Redoubt using Little Willie Trench. Corporal Pollock, having sought permission from an officer, climbed out of the trench alone and walked along the enemy parapet with the utmost coolness and disregard of danger to bomb the German party in Little Willie from above. He carried his grenades across to the trench under heavy fire and worked his way along it hurling bombs at the enemy. The Germans were taken completely by surprise and were held back for about an hour by this single-handed act of bravery. Pollock remained untouched during this time, although under heavy small arms fire, and was only wounded in the arm when jumping down into a British held trench. For this act of great gallantry he was awarded a Victoria Cross. He was later commissioned into the Cameron Highlanders in 1916 but was invalided out of the Army in 1917 due to a training accident.

A comment from the 13th Middlesex's War Diary gives an idea of the difficulties sustained by the men in the front line in exposed positions:

> Owing to the isolated position of the men in the front trenches, it was impossible to pass up supplies, except by night. On the Sunday and Monday nights a small quantity of water, biscuit and ammunition was sent from the companies in support trenches to those in front, but these men would have suffered much more severely if it had not been for the kindness of the 2nd Queen's Regiment who generously shared with them what rations they had.

However the loss of the ground around The Dump and Fosse 8, together with the failure of Carter's Force to retake the Quarries and the retirement of the 73rd Brigade to the Hohenzollern Redoubt had several consequences for the troops in this sector. It left exposed the key flanks of two units from the 27th Brigade (the 6th Royal Scots Fusiliers and the 10th Argyll and Sutherland Highlanders). These units were currently positioned in Fosse Alley, where they had been since the previous night in an attempt to protect the right flank of the advance of the 73rd Brigade. But now on the afternoon of the 27th their positions were literally raked with German small arms fire from end to end, and shortly afterwards the softening up parties of bombers advanced along the Alley from both ends (The Dump and the Quarries). The position became untenable as many casualties had been taken and the men had to fall back to Quarry Trench and Big Willie which had been part of the original (25th September) German front line. It was another example of what has been known in the Army as 'A come as you are party', meaning an attack carried out with limited resources and support and with little or no planning rather than an all-arms, coordinated, combined attack. Just to jump ahead slightly in order to finish the story of Fosse 8: there was an effort in the early hours of 28th September to retake the position. HQ I Corps ordered that the 85th Brigade from the 28th Division be given this role. Instructions were given (whilst on the march) for them to relieve (it thought) the 9th Division and the 73rd Brigade in the Hohenzollern Redoubt area to attack the Fosse. But again things went wrong, the Brigade commander (Brigadier C. Pereira) and his Brigade Major were both wounded early on. In spite of the best efforts of the officer who took command (Lieutenant-Colonel A. Roberts from the 3rd Royal Fusiliers) it was a very confused situation. It was not helped by severe congestion in the trenches and the conditions underfoot were treacherous. By 6.00am in the morning of the 28th only two battalions from the Brigade were in a position to attack, but it was deemed to be too late and the attack was cancelled. In fact, this should be called the 'second' attack as an earlier one had been made at 2.30am by a unit from Carter's Force, the 1st Royal Berkshires. They had been digging trenches for most of the 27th September so they were probably not in the best physical shape. As it was, the distance between the trenches was around half a mile, but again no proper reconnaissance had been carried out, and the ground was unknown to the unit. An additional problem was that the ground was cut up by shellfire and interspersed with trenches and barbed wire. However, it was hoped that the bright moonlight would help navigation and Lieutenant-Colonel Carter decided to lead the attack. What was seen as a favourable moon for the attackers was also a favourable one for the defenders. The leading waves were spotted after they had travelled less than 400 yards and heavy German fire rained down on them. It says much for their fortitude and courage that they got as close as to within 70 yards of the Fosse. But they could get no further forward. Again the supporting lines were able to actually reach the Dump only to be quickly driven off it by the Germans. Casualties had been heavy: 13 officers (including the CO and second-in-command) and 288 men again killed or wounded. Daylight was approaching and Lieutenant-Colonel Carter called a halt to any further attacks and the 1st Berkshires returned to the original British front line. During this attack a further action was deemed worthy of an award of a Victoria Cross, that to Second Lieutenant A.B. Turner. The Battalion's War Diary records:

> Owing to the bright moonlight the enemy saw us approaching. When we were 400 yards from our objective (Fosse 8) they put up Very lights and kept up a continuous fire on us from our right front - this grew heavier as we got nearer.

As stated before, the attack was halted short of the slag heap with part of C Company and D Company in the most advanced British positions. The Germans started bombing down a communication trench towards the Royal Berkshires positions. Second Lieutenant Turner volunteered to lead a fresh attack when the unit's bombers could make no progress against German bombers down Slag Alley. It is recorded that Turner virtually single-handedly drove the Germans back about 150 yards throwing his bombs incessantly with dash and determination. His citation concluded: "His action enabled the reserves to advance with very little loss, and subsequently covered the flank of his Regiment in its retirement, thus probably averting a loss of some hundreds of men." Sadly Turner, after seeming to bear a charmed life, was hit in the abdomen by a bullet, but was able to make it back to the unit's RAP. From here he was put in the casualty evacuation chain and ended up at No 1 CCS at Chocques, where he died of his wounds on 1st October aged 22. Alexander Buller Turner (a relative of another VC winner, General Redvers Buller from the Zulu Wars in 1879) now lies at Chocques CWGC Cemetery Plot 1 Row B Grave 2. The attack achieved nothing except more work for the medical services. We must now turn to look at the actions of the Guards Division south of the Hulluch road.

General Haig's orders for the 27th September, issued at 11.30pm on the 26th before Fosse 8 was lost, but with the knowledge that the German 2nd Guards Reserve Division was in the area, gave instructions for the "holding of the line and the pulling out of a new General reserve." This meant that the XI Corps was to secure the line between Loos and Hulluch by using the Guards Division, and use the time gained to reform the 21st and 24th divisions. The IV Corps was made responsible for Loos, with the 3rd Cavalry Division being allocated to Rawlinson for this role, until an infantry unit could relieve them. Additionally IV Corps was to hold the line between the left of the Guards Division and the right flank of I Corps. It was decided to send the shattered remains of the 15th Division back to Noeux les Mines to become the General Reserve. Finally in I Corps, it was intended for the 1st Division to be returned to IV Corps with the 7th Division taking over responsibility for their section of the line. Also the 9th Division to retire to Béthune to become part of the General reserve as soon as it had been relieved by men of the 28th Division then on their way to the Loos sector. There was a special mention in these orders for the GOC of XI Corps to submit a plan for the capture of Hill 70 on the afternoon of the following day. This was because the Hill 70 Redoubt now dominated virtually the whole of the Loos valley. The words 'prior planning and preparation prevent poor performance' come to mind but this is easy to say nearly 90 years on.

After a brief discussion the GOC XI Corps (General Haking) and the GOC Guards Division (Major-General The Lord Cavan) decided on a simultaneous attack on Hill 70 from the north and west directions. Haig approved this plan, but to achieve this some preliminary movements needed to be carried out. The first was a movement by the 2nd Guards Brigade eastwards from North Loos Avenue across the Loos valley and the Loos-Hulluch road against Puits 14 bis and Chalk Pit Wood. From there it would pass through the small pieces of woodland, Bois Hugo and Chalet Wood. Once these positions had been secured they would wheel southwards so they were facing Hill 70. The other part of the assault from the west was due to be carried out by the 3rd Guards Brigade; they had to move forward from Vermelles during the afternoon of the 27th where they had been held in reserve. They were instructed to time their attack from the west with the attack by their sister brigade from the north. The 1st Guards Brigade, positioned to the left of the 2nd Brigade, was to move from Alley 4 Trench and secure the line of the Lens-La Bassée road when they had confirmed that Puits 14 bis and Chalk Pit Wood were occupied. The start time for the 2nd Guards Brigade was timed to be at 4.00pm after an artillery bombardment of the key positions that were due to be attacked.

Strangely, the barrage was timed to begin at 12.30pm and was due to last for 2½ hours to be carried out by the IV Corps artillery supported by No 1 Group HAR. Then after a gap of 40 minutes there was to be a 20 minute 'hurricane' bombardment by the Guards Division artillery finishing at 4.00pm. One assumes this was intended to lull the Germans into a false sense of security and man their front line positions and then be caught by the second barrage. It was a tactic that had been used in Gallipoli on the Manchester Infantry Brigade's front during the Third Battle of Krithia in June and perhaps information was being exchanged. As additional supporting measures, the 47th Division was to try and capture the whole of Chalk Pit Copse and a small amount of chlorine gas (virtually the last of it for the time being) was to be discharged on the 2nd Division front near Cuinchy between the Vermelles-La Bassée road and the canal.

Around 2.00pm on the afternoon of the 27th news reached 1st Army HQ of the loss of Fosse 8. Sir John French had just left to visit General Joffre in an attempt to urge him to lean on the French 10th Army commander to carry on with his offensive. Haig for his part went forward to visit two of his corps commanders. He first visited I Corps HQ and saw Gough and then moved to IV Corps HQ, arriving there about 3.00pm. After a brief discussion with Rawlinson, he telephoned Haking to ask whether it would be possible to cancel or stop the Guards Division attack. Haig was now thinking along the lines that the position around Fosse 8 made the situation a potentially dangerous one. Haking expressed the view that it would be virtually impossible to inform the leading battalions from the 2nd Guards Brigade, but there would be time to get a message to the 3rd Guards Brigade who were then moving from Vermelles towards Loos. Given these circumstances Haig now decided that the attack was to become a limited one, and not to go beyond the line Hill 70 - Puits 14 bis - Chalk Pit Wood. Lord Cavan quickly sent instructions to his brigade commanders. This now had the makings of a disaster. Due to Haig's limitation, the attack of the 1st Guards Brigade was stopped and the assault southward from Chalet Wood towards Hill 70 was abandoned.

Meanwhile the 2nd Guards Brigade had settled into its positions in North Loos Avenue, on the western slope of the Loos valley with its objectives about a mile away on the other slope. The entire advance was going to be carried out over completely open ground, so to cover the northern flank of the attack support was enlisted from the 1st Guards Brigade. They were ordered to lay a smoke screen south of Hulluch and also to put down covering fire on the German trenches near there as well. For once something went well and around 4.00pm aided by a westerly breeze an effective smoke screen lay over a large area south of Hulluch. It is reported that decent visibility in the area between Hulluch and the Bois Hugo did not return for 40 minutes. The German artillery shelled the cloud and the infantry poured small arms fire into it, believing no doubt that it was full of advancing troops. With its northern flank obscured by smoke, the advance of the 2nd Guards Brigade across the valley was carried out very rapidly and with very little losses. The 2nd Irish Guards were the leading troops with Chalk Pit Wood as their first objective. Slightly behind them and to their right were the 1st Scots Guards heading for Puits 14 bis as soon as the Chalk Pit had been taken. Around 4.45pm the 2nd Irish Guards were in Chalk Pit Wood and were hidden from view by the surviving foliage from the main German positions in the Bois Hugo. Soon afterwards the left

The 1st Welsh Guards moving off from Vermelles for the attack on Hill 70 27th September 1915. (IWM Q 17374)

hand part of the attack took the Chalk Pit itself. The 1st Scots Guards now moved forward heading for Puits 14 bis. In the excitement their left hand side passed through the 2nd Irish Guards in the Chalk Pit, taking a lot of the Irish Guards with them. As the Official History puts it, before

> Leaving the cover of the wood the mixed-up units headed towards the Lens road, but before they had reached it, heavy small arms fire was poured into the massed ranks of Guardsmen from the Bois Hugo. The commanding officer of the 1st Scots Guards, Lieutenant-Colonel S. Godman, was wounded with 11 other officers killed or wounded and around 350 men also killed and wounded.

In spite of these losses a small party of Scots Guards did manage to reach the area of the Puits 14 bis. This however was as good as it got and just before 5.00pm the majority of the Irish and Scots Guards were withdrawing back in some confusion. It is alleged that someone, perhaps a German soldier, shouted "Retire" in the area of the Chalk Pit Keep and the order was repeated and acted upon. Some men stayed in the Chalk Pit and Chalk Pit Wood but others went as far back as the Loos-Hulluch road before the situation could be stabilised. Then fortunately around 5.15pm the 1st Coldstream Guards came up in support of the Irish Guards and took the men who had gone back to the Loos-Hulluch road forward once again. Again it was relatively easy, and a line was reestablished along the eastern edge of the Chalk Pit. Help was also at hand for the Scots Guards left in Puits 14 bis as two companies of the 3rd Grenadier Guards managed to reach them. They had suffered heavy losses in advancing up the slope to the Puits, but a small number managed to join forces with the Scots Guards and reinforced them in the buildings they were occupying. However, so intense was the small arms fire coming from the area of Bois Hugo on other parties trying to reach the Puits, these efforts were abandoned. It was decided instead to extend the current positions from the southern end of Chalk Pit Wood towards Loos. As it was now rapidly getting dark it was relatively easy to entrench this new line. Also, during the hours of darkness the remnants of the 1st Scots Guards and 3rd Grenadier Guards, all under the command of Captain J. Cuthbert, were able to slip away from their isolated position in the Puits and get back to British lines.

The 3rd Guards Brigade due to capture Hill 70 from a westerly direction, left its positions around Vermelles at 3.00pm and moved towards Loos village using the Vermelles-Loos road. On reaching the area of the Loos Road Redoubt they deployed into open formations and advanced across country. The only problem with this was it was broad daylight and soon after cresting the ridge of the Loos valley they were in clear sight of the Germans. Artillery fire was quickly called down upon them and it is recorded there were numerous casualties, including many animals from the transport sections. What they were doing here is a bit of a mystery, but present they were and they suffered accordingly. Nevertheless the Guards carried on towards Loos village eventually reaching some communication trenches, which gave them some protection on their journey into Loos. The 4th Grenadier Guards who had been leading came into the village from the north-west while the 1st Welsh Guards came in from the west.

Here are two accounts from Guardsmen with the 4th Grenadier Guards. First, Guardsman W. Jackman:

> Getting nearer our destination we kept seeing wounded chaps passing us and when we saw a lot of Highland regiments, they had aprons over their kilts, so we knew we were getting nearer to the firing line. My Company was Number 1 Company, leading, and we went up from Vermelles over a ridge. It was like a big valley. In front of us was Hill 70. Then we came under fire. Well, I didn't understand it was fire! It was like a lot of whips cracking. Then the order came get into artillery formation. Well, artillery formation is about ten feet between each soldier, and we went down in line like that, straight down the hillside, and it was a most eerie affair because it sounded like whips cracking, and then you'd see the man on your left, just flop down and that was that.

Secondly, Guardsman W. Spencer:

> Well, I wasn't really frightened to tell you the truth. We were all marching in fours, you know, the same as we might do in England. Then all of a sudden, when the first shell burst near the road as were marching up, we all deployed left and right of the road and spread out, and we kept on marching. Some were knocked out, but we kept on going and we did feel a little excited but not frightened - that's the impression it gave me. As a matter of fact, I was a bit disappointed with the first two shells. I thought they'd make a bigger explosion. But I found out afterwards it wasn't always the ones that made the most explosion that caused the most damage. We advanced roughly a mile and then we saw some old trenches which had been previously occupied by British troops that had gone forward and they were mostly Scotsmen who were laying about on the ground and I always remember two who were actually hanging on the barbed

wire. In kilts too. That's very vivid in my memory. We paused by those trenches and then went forward again and our Battalion went straight forward for the town of Loos.

The other two units of the Brigade, the 2nd Scots Guards and 1st Grenadier Guards, halted in Cemetery Trench, situated west of Loos, which they then shared with men from the 18th and 23rd Londons. Amongst the shells thrown at the Guards by the German artillery were a number of gas shells, which caused some important casualties amongst the command elements of the 4th Grenadier Guards incapacitating the CO and his Adjutant. In the resulting confusion one half of the Battalion working its way round the northern side of the village lost touch with the remainder. This northern element then got mixed up with men from the 2nd Guards Brigade and ended up attacking Puits 14 bis. When the mix-up was sorted out the GOC 2nd Guards Brigade, Brigadier J. Ponsonby promptly hijacked these two companies and ordered them to go firm on the Loos-Hulluch road to defend his right flank. Therefore there were only the elements of two companies from the 4th Grenadier Guards to lead the attack and in fact, due to losses, it was really only about a company strong. Fortunately, the GOC of the 3rd Guards Brigade, Brigadier J. Heyworth, was close by and he quickly ordered forward the 1st Welsh Guards to carry out the attack, in conjunction with the Grenadiers but positioned on their right. It was a historic moment as this was the first ever attack for the newly formed Welsh Guards. They had only been formed in August 1915 from Guardsmen with a Welsh background serving in the other four Guards regiments. The attack went in as dusk was falling around 6.00pm.

In describing this attack I hope the reader will understand if I borrow a few lines from the British Official History mentioning Hill 70: "From the summit, the lower part of Hill 70 is dead ground, the chalk slope being convex." This meant that for the first few minutes the oncoming attackers were out of sight of the defenders but the higher they got up the heights, the closer they were to danger. When nearing the upper slopes heavy machine gun fire swept the waves of attackers, and after a few short rushes trying to get closer to the German positions no further progress was possible. From the positions of the Guardsmen lying down on the upper slopes through the growing gloom they could see thick belts of barbed wire in front of the German lines. The defenders had not wasted their time up on Hill 70, any movement seemed to bring down a hail of fire. A point had been reached beyond which it seemed further progress was impossible and suicidal. The CO of the 1st Welsh Guards, Lieutenant-Colonel W. Murray-Threipland, up with the leading waves shouted out that they were on no account to try and get any further forward and to dig in where they were. These advanced positions were probably no more than 25 yards from the Hill 70 Redoubt.

Some time later, possibly around 10.00pm, the 2nd Scots Guards arrived, having moved from their position in Cemetery Trench. The CO of this unit, Lieutenant-Colonel A. Cator, decided that a position about 25 yards from a German one would be impossible to hold once daylight arrived, so he instructed his men to dig in on a terrace about 100 yards away from the Redoubt. It was decided to withdraw the Guardsmen from the advanced position to this one further back during the night and this manoeuvre was successfully carried out. Much of the night was spent digging and wiring in this new position. The 'new' line consisted of the

Guards Division being in contact with troops from the 3rd Cavalry Division on their right, who in turn had contact with the 47th Division in the area of the Loos Crassier. However on the left of the Guards Division it was not so stable, parties of Royal Engineers and pioneers sent up to work on the 2nd Guards Brigade front found a gap between them and other troops on the Loos-Hulluch road. The situation was stabilised by bringing up the 2nd Coldstream Guards from the 1st Guards Brigade to plug this gap and during the night began to dig a new trench line from Alley 4, south of Hulluch, towards the 2nd Guards Brigade in Chalk Pit Wood.

Some other minor points also need to be covered here. At Cuinchy, where a gas diversion and attack was due to go in, the result was virtually useless. The attack was timed to go in at 5.00pm after the gas discharge. Those positions that did have gas cylinders were allocated them about 7 per emplacement. The attack was made between the Vermelles-La Bassée road to the Canal and was carried out by the 6th and 19th brigades from the 2nd Division. The gas discharge failed to make any impression on the Germans, who used fires on the parapets of their trenches to disperse the gas. Additionally, the wind direction was variable and rain was falling. Another attack on The Quarries by Carter's Force was ordered for 4.00pm but the units involved had trouble concentrating for the attack, and so shortly before Zero Hour the time was moved till 5.30pm. After the failure of the gas both attacks were abandoned. Obviously the front line trenches were crowded with men and perhaps the Germans were able to observe the mass of men in them. The Germans started firing *Minenwerfer* bombs at the British trenches. One of these mortar bombs landed in a trench occupied by men of the 1st Hertfordshire Regiment (a Territorial Force unit) but did not explode. Corporal A. Burt ran to the bomb, wrenched out the fuze and threw it over the parapet, probably saving the lives of around 20 men. His bravery was recognised and he was later awarded a Victoria Cross, although as his citation says: "He had opportunity of taking cover behind a traverse and did not know if the bomb would explode."

Further south in the 47th Division area, they were ordered to capture a German strong point known as Stützpunkt 69, astride the Lens-Béthune road and Chalk Pit Copse. For once the preliminary bombardment went well, a very effective three hour barrage was fired by the 40th Howitzer Battery commanded by Major Pollard. The effects of this artillery fire were contained in an account by a German Officer from the 26th Regiment:

> There were no deep dugouts, only shelters in the side of the 200 yards of trench. I myself was buried five times, several others had their skulls broken open by the splinters of hard chalk caused by the shells bursting in the trench itself. The sight of the agony all along the trench was terrible; one man near me had his head blown off, another was cut in two pieces in the middle, and another was blown right out of the trench in pieces. By the time the infantry attack was made, most of the trench had fallen in.

This is, I feel, a most interesting account as it shows what could be achieved. It is reported that the fire of this Battery was controlled by Brigadier Thwaites (GOC 141st Brigade), from a house at Valley crossroads, which had clear observation of the German trenches to be attacked. It was his Brigade that was supplying most of the troops for this attack and the 20th (Blackheath and Woolwich) Londons supplied most of the bayonets supported by bombers from the 17th, 19th and

23rd Londons. For the uninitiated, a howitzer is an artillery piece that should allow the shells to drop nearly vertically from the top of their trajectories and so smashes down with devastating effect, similar to a mortar. The attack was entirely successful, the assaulting troops, led by bombers moving in from both ends of the copse, annihilated the Germans here. It was a similar story at the Stützpunkt and by 7.30pm both objectives were completely in the hands of the 47th Division. The casualty figure was just 2 killed and 14 wounded, while over 150 dead Germans were found. During the night a new trench was dug along the eastern and southern edges of Chalk Pit Copse, joining up with the line previously held. Incidentally, this remained the front line for almost the next three years. Additionally the German communication trench leading to Cité St Pierre was blocked. This now meant that although two days late, the 47th Division could say they had taken all their original objectives.

It is also worth recording that back at 1st Army HQ in the late evening a report was received, which caused great excitement. From somewhere an 'intercepted' German message was relayed. This contained the news that the "British Guards had attacked north of Lens and had broken through, and that the wireless station, then at Loison, behind Lens was falling back four miles." General Haig ordered Rawlinson, if the report was true, to send forward at once from Loos the 3rd Cavalry Division, supported by infantry to occupy Vendin le Vieil, Annay and Pont à Vendin before daylight. To make sure of what he needed to do, Major-General Briggs sent these orders on at least six occasions by six different special messengers. Briggs, because he had liaison officers with the Guards Division, was able to disregard these orders and sent back word that the Guards Division had been unable to break through. As we have seen, with the exception of the small success by the 47th Division in Chalk Pit Copse, it was not a good day for the 1st Army.

During the 27th September fresh German reserves arrived in the area. Three battalions of the Guards Corps were positioned near Wingles on the Hulluch front, acting as support to the 117th Division. A Guards Field Artillery Regiment was also sent up to the area behind Hulluch. The Germans were also thinking of launching a counter-attack but circumstances went against them. The German 6th Army history records that it was the intention of the commander to use the Guards Corps to retake Loos village and the original front line positions on Lone Tree Ridge. Urgent appeals for reinforcements from the 4th Army holding Vimy Ridge that had arrived during the day frustrated this plan, and the Guards Corps was sent piecemeal into the battle area instead of being used for one big effort. For this reason the counter-attack was postponed.

Meanwhile, what were the French 10th Army up to further south around Arras? During the morning of the 27th General d'Urbal decided to make his greatest effort on his left flank. At 9.30am he moved the French 154th Division to the command of XXI Corps and later a colonial Spahi Brigade. The XXI Corps was the extreme northerly corps of the 10th Army and therefore closest to the BEF. He also reinforced the XXXIII Corps and ordered as many heavy artillery batteries as could be spared from south of the River Scarpe to Bully Grenay to neutralise the German guns at Angres and Liévin. General d'Urbal fixed the time for the attack at noon but later postponed it to 2.00pm when it did go in. Neither the XXI nor the XXXIII Corps made any significant progress. The attack was called off by d'Urbal following General Foch's instructions about an hour after it started. Further attacks on the northern part of Vimy Ridge were postponed till the following day.

Some of the units involved in the defence of Loos during this period belonged to the 6th Cavalry Brigade from the 3rd Cavalry Division and here is an account from the GOC of the Brigade, Brigadier D. Campbell, in a letter written to his family shortly after the battle:

> I am writing this from a veritable shell-trap of a town, or rather large village of Loos. We had an awful day yesterday from shells and gas. However, to start from the beginning, I was sent for, and ordered to take two regiments and occupy the German front line trenches to cover the retirement from Loos. I moved up to the German front line, which was being heavily shelled. They were an awful sight, the trenches and all round being strewn with dead Germans and British - it was a horrible sight - horrible! Having got my men out (only about 450), I went back half a mile to the telephone. On arrival, I got an order to send my two regiments into Loos. I rang Briggs up and explained that the General who had been holding Loos was now with me at the telephone and that he informed me that to the best of his belief all his men had left Loos. I asked him to cancel my orders as it seemed madness to send two regiments 460 strong to hold a place probably occupied by the Germans and requiring a Garrison under most favourable circumstances of at least 2,000. Briggs agreed, but said the order was direct from Army HQ and he had no power to cancel them. He advised me to go back to the German front line, see what the situation looked like, and use my own discretion.
>
> I went back as hard as I could, sweating like a pig. Arriving at the front line, I saw infantry pouring up the hill from Loos in disorder. I, however, saw what looked like some men in the town. I ordered my two regiments to advance at once, which they did under heavy shellfire. I watched them into Loos, and then went and telephoned that my men had entered the town. On arrival at the telephone station I received an order from Army HQ - "Brigadier Campbell will take over command of all the troops in Loos and will hold it at all costs." I went back again as hard as I could go, and got down into Loos after dark. With great difficulty, I got in touch with the OC Royals (Dragoons) and the OC 3rd Dragoon Guards, and found ALL the troops consisted of my 400-odd cavalry and, with the exception of about 200 Gordons, about 400 absolutely demoralised infantry. The Gordons were full of heart, but very beat and starving. I made the best disposition possible, being considerably assisted by finding that my right flank was protected by troops under a Brigadier Thwaites (GOC 141st Brigade) who seemed a really stout-hearted man.
>
> I had all sorts of odds and ends under my command, and all the officers came to explain that they had only a few deadbeat men, and it would be much better for them to go back and collect more! I agreed, but I said I could not spare a man, and I showed them how impossible it was as I received five separate copies of the same order - "Brigadier Campbell must on no account leave Loos, which must be held at all costs." After receiving the fifth copy, I replied: "I have now received five separate copies of Order No .... I have no intention of leaving Loos, but the troops at my disposal are quite inadequate for holding Loos in the event of a serious attack."
>
> This had the desired effect, and Briggs to whom I reported the situation and who thoroughly agreed with me, arrived about 2.00am, with four more reg-

iments, about 1,000 men. With this addition things looked much rosier, and we were soon in a position to give the Bosche a real hotting-up if he came on. The situation was now practically saved, and there were two howitzer batteries (British) and two field artillery batteries (British) which had been abandoned in the immediate vicinity of Loos, and also there were several German guns in the town itself as well as any quantity of equipment, all of which would have fallen into German hands again if we had not managed to retrieve the situation.

On Monday the Guards were ordered to make an attack, and one brigade advanced through Loos. The attack started at 4.00pm and the shelling was something terrific. No words can describe the noise. The Germans concentrated a terrific fire on Loos, especially on that portion where Brigade and Divisional HQs were. The shriek and whistle of the shells through the air mixed with the cries of men wounded, and then - the gas. It is the first time I have experienced gas, and the warning cry, "Gas" gives one a curious feeling - a feeling that one was about to experience something one had not met before. We all put on our helmets, and not withstanding these I found the sensation very trying. The air was thick with gas from gas shells, and the smell of the chemicals in the helmet was very trying - one longed to pull one's helmet off, and yet one knew one dare not. However, the gas passed off, and about 6.00pm things quietened down. We had a fairly quiet time till 4.00pm the next day, Tuesday, when another attack took place, and the scene of the day before, with the exception of gas was repeated.

The 27th September is also noteworthy for two deaths. Although not recognised as significant at the time they have probably attracted more attention than any other casualties at Loos. First, was Captain The Honourable Fergus Bowes-Lyon, son of the 14th Earl of Strathmore and Kinghome of Glamis Castle, Forfarshire, an old boy of Eton and the 2nd Black Watch (with service pre-war in India) and at the time of his death a member of the 8th Black Watch. He had survived the attacks of the 26th on the Hohenzollern Redoubt on the first two days of Loos, but his luck ran out on the 27th. Aged 26 he was posted missing presumed killed in the Hohenzollern Redoubt area, his body was never recovered and he is commemorated on the Loos Memorial to the Missing. Fergus Bowes-Lyon's sister later became better known as the wife of King George VI and later as Her Majesty Queen Elizabeth The Queen Mother, before her death in 2002. After the wedding ceremony to Prince Bertie at Westminster Abbey in 1923, she placed her wedding bouquet on the tomb of the Unknown Warrior in memory of her brother.

Secondly, Lieutenant John Kipling, the beloved son of the (at that time) English-speaking world's arguably most famous author Rudyard Kipling. Rudyard Kipling had pulled strings to get his son a commission in the 2nd Irish Guards. Kipling, by all accounts, was devastated by the loss of his son and tried to find out what had happened to John after he was reported 'missing' on 27th September. For some time after Rudyard Kipling frequently visited hospitals where wounded Irish Guardsmen were recovering in the hope of finding news. There was one report that "John was seen to fall, get up and go into a small shed which was almost immediately surrounded." On the 27th December a friend of the family, Rider Haggard, spoke with two young wounded Guardsmen by the names of Franklin and Bowe. Bowe stated he was within 40 yards of John Kipling when they entered the wood near Givenchy where he vanished. Franklin expressed the view that he was either blown to bits by a large shell or taken and murdered in the German lines. Rider did not apparently relate this second comment to Rudyard Kipling. Then Frankland wrote to Rider stating that his friend Bowe had now remembered more:

> He saw an officer who he could swear was Mr Kipling leaving the wood on his way to the rear and trying to fasten a field dressing round his mouth which was badly shattered by a piece of shell. Bowe would have helped him but for the fact the officer was crying with the pain of the wound and he did not want to humiliate him by offering assistance. I shall not send this to Rudyard Kipling - it is too painful.

Later Rudyard Kipling wrote the Great War History of the Irish Guards and in the introduction penned an almost personal eulogy for John:

> And there were, too, many, almost children, of whom no record remains. They came out from Warley with the constantly renewed drafts, lived the span of a Second Lieutenant's life and were spent. Their intimates might preserve, perhaps memories of a promise cut short...in most cases the compiler has let the mere fact suffice; since to his mind, it did not seem fit to heap words on the doom...

In his book on the Irish Guards he briefly said, when recounting the attack of the Guards Division on 27th September:

> The attack of the 1st Scots Guards on Puits 14 bis in their rush took with them some few Irish Guardsmen with Second Lieutenants W H Clifford and J Kipling of No 2 Company ... together this rush reached a line beyond the Puits, well under machine gun fire ... Here Second Lieutenant Clifford was shot and wounded or killed - the body was found later - and Second Lieutenant Kipling was wounded and missing.

Later in his book he summarised the casualties of the Battalion from 25th to 30th September 1915: 324 casualties of which 101 were missing. He said: "Of their officers, Second Lieutenant Pakenham-Law had died of wounds; Second Lieutenants Clifford and Kipling were missing...it was a fair average for the day of a debut."

Rudyard Kipling mourned the loss of his son deeply and although he tried hard to trace John he failed. In 1917 Rudyard was appointed as a Commissioner for the Imperial War Graves Commission and was asked as 'the soldier's poet' to compose a suitable form of words for the headstone of the unidentified bodies. He came up with the simple, yet deeply moving 'A Soldier of the Great War Known Unto God.' Here the story ends until June 1992 when the Commonwealth War Graves Commission announced that John Kipling had been 'found'. A grave in St Mary's Advanced Dressing Station Cemetery, Plot 7 Row D Grave 2, was that of John Kipling and the headstone bearing the words 'A Lieutenant of the Great War Irish Guards Known Unto God' was being replaced by one bearing John Kipling. It is now probably the most photographed headstone in the Loos sector. The author has had a number of discussions with fellow WFA members regarding the most photographed headstone on the Western Front, usually a subject for lively debate. The answer often seems to be Captain Noel Chevasse VC and Bar at Brandhoek New Military Cemetery. Other people who come into the frame are

View across No Man's Land from St Mary's ADS Cemetery towards Ninth Avenue and Bois Carré Cemeteries. (Geoff Parker)

Lt J Kipling headstone at St Mary's ADS Cemetery alongside the road from Vermelles to Hulluch. It takes its name from the fact that an advanced dressing station was established in the old front line after 25th September. It contains nearly 1,800 graves, of which less than 10% are known. (Keith Harris)

Wilfred Owen at Ors, Henry Webber at Dartmoor Cemetery on the Somme and, as my (nameless) friend said, "the guy who is to the left of Chevasse at Brandhoek". How did John Kipling come to be found? For a more detailed explanation I would point the reader in the direction of the book *My Boy, Jack?*, but a brief synopsis follows. A CWGC worker in the early 1990s had been checking the documentation of 'unknowns' that seemed there may have been a chance of identifying. A body was found in September 1919 in grid square G25 C 6 8 with no identification save that to indicate the man was a Lieutenant from the Irish Guards. The 2nd Irish Guards only lost three subalterns on 27th September and as it was believed the other two (Pakenham-Law and Clifford) were either known to have been buried in a garden well away from 'Kipling's' grid square (Pakenham-Law) or was last seen heading towards the Bois Hugo which was grid square H25D or H25C (Clifford). Therefore the CWGC worker deduced that neither of the two could be the body in St Mary's ADS Cemetery. There are some discrepancies in this theory (in the author's opinion), in that Kipling's body was found in G25, which according to the trench maps is nowhere near Chalk Pit Wood, although H25 was. John Kipling was last seen alive badly wounded near this wood.

John Kipling considered himself a Second Lieutenant in a letter home on 16th July, yet he was promoted Lieutenant on 7th June and as such was recorded on the Memorial to the Missing and the new headstone. He even asked in a letter home to his father for a new identity disk on 19th September (eight days before his death) saying 'Second Lieutenant'. It seems that the major part of the case for 'the prosecution' for changing the headstone revolves around the assumption that Kipling was a full Lieutenant, yet he considered himself a Second Lieutenant just before his death. The War Diary of the 2nd Irish Guards also called him a Second Lieutenant, as the following entry for 27th September shows:

> Meanwhile 1st Scots Guards had come up partly round and partly through the right flanks of 2nd Irish Guards and had captured Puits 14 bis. Second Lieutenants Clifford and Kipling and some few Irish Guardsmen had also gone forward with this party and had reached a line just beyond the Puits buildings. While there according to the evidence of 6846 Corporal Rossiter (Number 2 Company) and 5824 Private Power (Number 2 Company) Second Lieutenant Clifford was shot and wounded or killed. Also while there according to the evidence of 5838 Private Green (Number 2 Company) Second Lieutenant Kipling was wounded. These two officers were subsequently missing, for shortly before 5.00pm the men in and beyond the Puits commenced to retire and fell back into and through Chalk Pit Wood in some confusion.

I will leave it to the reader to make up his own mind. There is a final twist in the tail of this story, in that Pakenham-Law's date of death was originally recorded as 27th August 1915 not 27th September 1915. As a result of this slip-up his name was originally on the Le Touret Memorial to the missing, which bears the names of those with no known grave prior to the Loos battle. When the error was discovered the CWGC removed his name from the Le Touret Memorial and placed his name on the 'Addenda' panel at Dud Corner. Thomas Pakenham-Law was also recorded as a Second Lieutenant and died at the age of 36, surely one of the oldest subalterns at Loos.

9

A Pause for Breath

The GOC of the Guards Division, Major-General The Lord Cavan, who had spent most of the 27th in his Advanced HQ at Le Rutoire farm (it shows how barren the landscape was that so many units/HQs at some stage passed through this farm), visited in the evening the HQs of the 2nd and 3rd Guards brigades. He did this to make himself fully aware of the details of the days fighting and also to discuss future operations and the morale of his units. He saw with his own eyes that for the moment no good purpose would be served by attempting to launch a fresh attack on the strongly held German positions on Hill 70. But he did give orders that every effort must be made to strengthen the forward line on the lower slopes of the hill. In fact the decision of whether to launch a further attack on the 2nd Guards Brigade front for the capture of Puits 14 bis was taken out of Cavan's hands, as the order for a renewed attack here came from Haig and 1st Army HQ. The aim was presumably to finish the task that had originally been given to the Guards Division and to secure the Lens-La Bassée road. With the benefit of hindsight it is difficult to see how an attack on a strongly defended position by a brigade operating alone should be more successful than it had proved to be when part of a large combined attack the previous day. It is easy to see now that the attack by the Scots Guards on the Puits had failed due to the inability of the artillery to knock out enough of the German machine gun positions.

Anyway after being ordered by 1st Army HQ to carry out the attack, orders were issued at noon on 28th September to Brigadier J. Ponsonby (GOC 2nd Guards Brigade) instructing him to attack the Puits at 3.45pm that day. The attack was to be preceded by a bombardment of the Puits and some nearby buildings by some heavy artillery batteries. For the final five minutes the Divisional artillery were to join in with a 'hurricane bombardment.' The attack was to be launched from the southern edge of Chalk Pit Wood.

As soon as he received this order, Brigadier Ponsonby sent a message back to Major-General The Lord Cavan stating that in his opinion the attack had little chance of success. The message never reached its destination, and although Ponsonby was anxious to postpone the attack till darkness had fell (his preferred option), as he received no word back he felt (like many others during the Great War) that he had no option but to carry on. He gave the leading position to the 1st Coldstream Guards then currently in the Chalk Pit. The CO of this battalion, Lieutenant-Colonel A. Egerton, was told that after taking the Puits he was to push on the railway line south of the Puits and then go firm there. As support the Coldstreams were allocated all the available machine guns with their fire concentrated on Bois Hugo. To their right the 2nd Irish Guards were also in support, laying down covering fire also on the Bois Hugo. At the appointed hour the Coldstreams went forward into a hail of small arms fire literally from three sides - left, right and front. In spite of the unbelievable weight of fire some men led by Lieutenant C. Riley and Second Lieutenant O. Style actually managed to reach the

Puits. Meanwhile as well as the small arms fire the Germans had called down a fierce artillery barrage and casualties began to mount. In the face of this most unfavourable situation Brigadier Ponsonby ordered the attack to be halted. It is recorded that 9 officers and 250 men were killed or wounded in the attack. Of the men to make the Puits only three returned, all of them wounded. Fortunately the Germans did not follow up with an immediate counter-attack so a quiet night was spent collecting the wounded and consolidating the position.

The War Diary of the 1st Coldstream Guards recorded the following entry for 28th September:

> They were met, almost before they got out of their trenches, by a terrific machine gun fire which enfiladed them from three sides (chiefly from Bois Victor Hugo). They were absolutely mown down. Two officers, Lieutenant Riley and Second Lieutenant Style, with eight men reached the objective, which they found not held by the enemy but only enfiladed by yet another machine gun. Lieutenant Riley (wounded) and two men got back. The men behind behaved splendidly, as not only were they subjected to this enormous enfilade fire but also to a most terrific bombardment by 8" shells and shrapnel and every kind of heavy gun fire which was most accurate. Meanwhile Number 3 and 4 companies doubled forward to Chalk Pit Wood under fire.

The GOC of the Division Lord Cavan later wrote that his plan was "faulty in the light of knowledge gained since of the enemy's position, in that our artillery preparation was too much centred on what we believed to be the strong points, whereas they were about 100 to 200 yards further east."

But as usual, behind the scenes there were political manoeuverings going on, as Sir John French during the night of 27th/28th September informed General Joffre that he had virtually no reserves left and the right flank of the 1st Army was exposed. He further advised that he was of the opinion that unless General d'Urbal attacked quickly and vigorously, the BEF would be forced to call a halt to its offensive. Joffre responded saying he did not know the exact situation to make an immediate decision but nominated Foch to look into the matter and decide what could be done. On the morning of the 28th General Foch visited the BEF's Advanced GHQ at Lillers, and it was agreed that the French would take over some British sectors. Between the 28th and 30th September it was planned that the French 152nd Division would relieve the 47th Division south of Loos. This would then free them up act as a reserve, but with the proviso that the BEF should make their best attempt to take Hill 70 and attack towards Pont à Vendin. Also later in the day General Foch decided to relieve two divisions on the right of the French 10th Army by two other divisions and to send them then to the Loos sector. This meant the French 10th Army on their northern boundary would be responsible for Loos and Hill 70. These movements would free up several formations then in the Loos sector to form a reserve. As well as the 47th Division, the 2nd Brigade from the 1st Division (who had relieved the 3rd Cavalry Division in Loos) and the 2nd and 3rd Guards brigades would become available. Other moves were also afoot in that during a visit to Haig by Sir John French, Haig was informed that the 21st and 24th divisions would be withdrawn for further training and that their replacements in XI Corps would be the 12th and 46th divisions. Both of these divisions were currently part of the 2nd Army in the Ypres Salient and would need to be brought south. The 12th Division left Bailleul on the 28th September and the 46th Division on the 1st October started its move south. Haig was buoyed by the prospect of some 'fresh' troops and this coupled with the planned reduction of his front called a conference at Vaudricourt with his three corps commanders. The subject with the benefit of hindsight almost unbelievably was a 'new' plan to break through the German positions and advance to the original 25th September objective, the Haute Deule Canal. The plan was now for the XI Corps (but with the Guards, 12th and 46th divisions) to punch a hole between Hulluch and Cité St Auguste push on immediately to the canal at Pont à Vendin and seize crossings there. Rawlinson's IV Corps (1st, 15th and 47th divisions) were to protect the right flank towards Hill 70, pending the arrival of the French troops, and press on towards Loison two miles east of Cité St Laurent. Finally Gough's I Corps (2nd, 7th and 28th divisions) were if possible to protect the left flank by taking Hulluch and then sending two brigades forward to Wingles. The unanswered question must be, why did they think that this attack would succeed when previous, better supported, attacks had failed? The author does not know the answer to this question, so will leave it open for debate.

Meanwhile while this conference was going on, the French 10th Army had one of their best days, elements of the 6th Division reached the highest part of Vimy Ridge (point 140) in the German third line. This was a big setback for the Germans and forced them to divert the major part of the Guards Corps to Vimy. This corps had been intended to be used against the BEF in the Loos sector but was given a new role. Then General d'Urbal suggested that the 152nd Division be used to exploit this success, but he was forbidden to do this by Foch, as this Division was earmarked to relieve the BEF's 47th Division. It is worth adding here that although the French managed to consolidate their gains during the night of 28th/29th September, Foch considered it an appropriate moment to suspend the offensive and prepare a new general attack again in conjunction with the BEF. There was another conference on the morning of the 29th at which Foch and French agreed that they would go back on the offensive on the 2nd October. This would also give the French 10th Army a brief chance to regroup after losing over 36,000 men in their recent attacks. Joffre approved this course of action and another ongoing French offensive in Champagne was also stopped on the 30th September. As the British Official History describes it:

> No account was taken of what the Germans might do during the interval thus allowed them in which to improve their defences on the fronts attacked and to bring up reserves; nor was any suggestion made to shift the point of attack to other sectors behind which no German reserves were already accumulated.

Just because the offensive had been temporarily halted, this did not mean the casualties stopped. On the 29th September the 1st Coldstream Guards in the area of the Chalk Pit suffered heavily at the hands of German artillery. The CO, Lieutenant-Colonel A. Egerton and his Adjutant, Lieutenant the Honourable D. Browne (son of the Earl of Kenmare) were both killed by the same shell just outside Battalion HQ. Their Brigade commander, Ponsonby wrote: "The Coldstreams Guards have lost a most valuable Commanding Officer in whom all ranks had the greatest confidence." Browne must also have been an able officer if he was the

The infamous Double Crassier; it was a lot smaller in 1915 than today but still gives commanding views of the surrounding country. (IWM Q 37910)

Adjutant at the age of 21. They are buried side by side in Vermelles CWGC Cemetery Plot VI Row G Graves 6 and 7. In all the 2nd Guards Brigade between the 26th and 29th September suffered casualties of 42 officers and 1,266 men killed, wounded and missing, while the 3rd Guards Brigade for the same period had figures of 27 officers and 674 men. On the evening of 29th September the 3rd Guards Brigade positioned on Hill 70 and Loos was relieved by the 142nd Brigade from the 47th Division and they were detailed to hold the position until relieved by French troops. This left the front line in this area held by the 140th and 142nd brigades with newly arrived troops from the 12th (Eastern) Division on their left. Then on the evening of the 30th the 140th Brigade was relieved by the 152nd French Division who assumed responsibility for the front as far north as the Lens-Béthune road. The 142nd Brigade held the front for three days and during this time the Bombing Officer of the 22nd Londons, Lieutenant Baswitz explored some apparently abandoned dugouts in No Man's Land on Hill 70. In one he found six Guardsmen guarding two captured Germans. They had been there apparently for four days. Baswitz brought them all back to the 47th Division's lines. When the Londoners did leave the line they were all reunited in villages south-west of Béthune whilst they reorganised for a few days.

On the 30th October detailed instructions were issued for the forthcoming offensive towards the Haute Deule Canal. Amongst other things, these included the digging of a new trench parallel to the Lens road between Chalk Pit Wood and Alley 4. It was intended to be a jumping-off point. men from the Guards Division dug this new trench on the night of 30th September/1st October. It apparently took until nearly 4.00am to finish the trench and almost immediately the Guards were relieved by elements of the 12th Division. The 1st Guards Brigade moved to Mazingarbe and the 2nd Brigade went to Verquiqneul. Over the next few days the 35th Brigade (from the 12th Division) finished the trench system begun by the Guards by digging communication trenches, dugouts and crossing places. It is worth adding here that the sector was not a quiet one as the artillery were constantly exchanging barrages. The most notable casualty must be Major-General F.D.V. Wing, the GOC of the 12th Division. A shell killed him during the afternoon of 2nd October whilst in the area of Fosse 7, which was being used as the Divisional Advanced HQ. Originally commissioned into the Royal Artillery he was 54 years old at the time of his death and he was buried in the Noeux les Mines CWGC Cemetery Plot I Row K Grave 15. The following comment is taken from the War Diary of the 12th Division for 2nd October:

> The night was quiet and there was little hostile shelling. The front trenches were shelled intermittently throughout the day. The Chalk Pit and locality about Lone Tree were more heavily shelled. The Advanced Report Centre, being surrounded by batteries, came in for some heavy shelling during the afternoon. At 3.45pm General Wing and his ADC Lieutenant Tower, were killed whilst crossing the road outside the Report Centre.

Meanwhile the French appeared to be having some difficulties over the relief of the BEF in the southern areas of Loos. The operation should have started on the 28th September and been completed by 30th September. In fact, the operation did not start until the 30th when the French 17th and 152nd divisions started relieving British troops. The transfer was not effected till the night of 2nd/3rd October when the French Army finally held all the ground up to the Puits 14 bis track. The French commander, General d'Urbal, gave as reasons for the delay factors such as bad weather and the mass of traffic that delayed the movement of his IX Corps. Indeed he reported during the night of 29th/30th and again on the morning of the 30th that he would not be in a position to restart offensive operations until the morning of 3rd October, 24 hours later than planned. Therefore General Foch visited Sir John French at his HQ at Lillers on the morning of 30th September to inform him of the 'new' French plan. Instead of a disjointed attack as on 25th September (attacks going in with a six hour difference) it was intended to be a simultaneous attack by the BEF's 1st Army and the French 10th Army. It was planned to take advantage of a salient in the German front line. The attack was to be in a south-easterly direction heading towards Loison and Pont à Vendin on a three mile frontage. At the same time the French IX Corps was to attack and try and enlarge the foothold on Hill 70. At this meeting it was decided to launch this attack on the 4th October.

Once again it was almost a case of the BEF being forced to fight over ground it was not happy with. At a conference between Foch and Sir John on the 1st October, Sir John expressed doubts as to whether the BEF's part of the attack could be effectively carried out until his flanks were secure. By this he meant that he needed the whole of Hill 70, Fosse 8 and the Quarries to be in Allied hands. He stated that the attacks on these positions should precede the general attack, with Hill 70 being the responsibility of the French IX Corps and the other two to be looked after by the British. General Foch in a counter-move suggested that it would be impossible for the IX Corps to maintain complete control of Hill 70, as it would be exposed to artillery fire from two sides if the attack was an isolated one. It was finally agreed at this meeting that an attack against Fosse 8 should go in on 4th October with a 'demonstration' by artillery against the positions on Hill 70 on the same day. The actual date of the attack on Hill 70 was again moved back a day to 5th October when the IX Corps would completely wrest control of the heights from the Germans. Joffre who arrived at the meeting towards the end agreed with these plans, and did his best to support it by agreeing to make additional artillery ammunition available to the 10th Army.

However, all of these plans were somewhat undermined by the fact that the Germans still dominated Hill 70 with its relatively good views of the surrounding area and also the even more dominating position of Fosse 8. German observation posts on the Dump overlooked the ground to the south as far as Vermelles, and beyond the Vermelles-Hulluch road; and those on Hill 70 covered much of the ground in the British area south of that road. It is also worth advising that the British troops were often in badly sited positions and under easy German observation hence artillery fire. Indeed German observation was so good it was virtually impossible to get artillery pieces in the right places without bringing down heavy fire on them. In consequence the effects of the preliminary softening-up of the German positions may be described as negligible. As a result of all these problems it was Sir John French's turn to talk to the French. He advised Foch that as the preliminaries for the operations against the Quarries and Fosse 8 could not be completed until the 5th October, the main attack would have to be put back a day. I suppose given all their delays and postponements the French had little choice but to agree.

It is worth adding here that there were several moves played out before the general attack went in. Several attempts were made by the 1st Army to recover the Dump and Fosse 8. One of the most savage and costly was the attempt on the morning of the 28th by the 28th Division. The assault started at 9.30am led by the 3rd Royal Fusiliers from the 85th Brigade supported by the 2nd Buffs, 3rd Middlesex and 2nd East Surreys. Later on in the day two further battalions from the 83rd Brigade were thrown in (1st York and Lancaster and 1st KOYLI) but very little progress was made. The German positions were just too strongly held and sited. Many of the COs were killed, indeed the casualty figure for the day was high and when a new brigade commander arrived in the evening of the 28th his men were in the same positions they had started from, except that the Germans had managed to pinch a toe hold in both Little and Big Willie. The following comments are all taken from Battalion War Diaries for this period and they give an understanding of the difficulties encountered.

2nd Buffs:

General Pereira and Captain Flower (Brigade Major) accompanied the Buffs. The communication trenches were so congested with troops that the Buffs quitted them and reached their appointed positions being shelled heavily en route. On arrival a Platoon of D Company charged the enemy and accounted for a score. Captain Flower was wounded and at about the same time General Pereira was wounded.

2nd Buffs:

The companies filed up the trenches and suffered many casualties en route from shell fire. The congested state of the trenches due to dead, wounded and units waiting to be relieved admitted very slow progress. One position whence one Company was to attack was in possession of the enemy, and these circumstances prevented the companies taking up their approximate positions until after 10.00am.

2nd Buffs about the 10.00am attack:

B and C companies followed by A Company charged across the open and were greeted with the fire from machine guns massed on either flank, also shell and rifle fire. Eleven machine guns, at least, were counted firing from the Miners' Cottages and Slag Alley. B and C companies - every man cheering- gained the edge of the Dump and, clambering up the crumbling slopes of the 30 foot high Dump gained the summit. The Dump was then plastered with shells of all descriptions from our own guns and those of the enemy and the attack was broken. The companies crossed the large expanse of the Dump summit and attempted to reach the enemy in the trenches at the foot. It was a hopeless task and those who attempted it were shot or grenaded. The companies reformed and returned to the original trenches, leaving over 100 men killed or wounded on the Dump.

3rd Middlesex attack on Dump Trench 28th September:

Considerable progress was made when bombs ran out and urgent appeals were made for more. The Battalion then began to suffer considerable casualties from a heavy attack with bombs by the enemy. The narrow trench then became congested with wounded, men of other units who were on their way out of the trench and also the Buffs who had to give way on our right. The CO then gave the order to withdraw slowly. This operation was most difficult, the trench being a narrow one and seven feet deep. We were enfiladed on both sides by machine gun fire and it was impossible to show a head over the parapet.

The following day was also a difficult one for the 28th Division particularly the 85th Brigade who seemed to be under attack most of the day but managed to hold on. This is part of the entry for the 29th September from the 3rd Royal Fusiliers War Diary:

On the morning of the 29th the Germans attacked Little Willie and North Face and after a heavy fight were only kept out by Number 4 Company coming up in support of the East Surreys. Number 2 Company also advanced to straighten up the line, but could not go far as the right was turned there by the Germans bombing down South Face. Shelling was fairly heavy that afternoon and the heaviest attack of all took place down South Face and the Middlesex evacuated Big Willie, leaving the flank of Number 2 Company in the air. The Germans bombed down Western Face driving Number 2 Company back to almost the head of the communication trench leading back form the supports.'

Help was at hand for the hard-pressed Fusiliers from C Company of the York and Lancasters who launched a counter-attack. Their War Diary states:

At 5.00 pm there was a sudden panic in the Redoubt and about 50 men rushed over the top into our trench. The order was given to fix bayonets. About 5.30 pm Captain Lucas gave the order to charge. The left flank put out of action a bombing party which was stationed at the corner of the Redoubt and a communication trench.

Additionally two men from the 28th Division distinguished themselves on this day and were later awarded the Victoria Cross for their actions. The first went to Second Lieutenant A. Fleming-Sandes of the 2nd East Surreys and the other to Private S. Harvey of the 1st Yorks and Lancasters. As previously stated, the fighting in and around the Hohenzollern Redoubt and the Dump during the 29th September was more or less continuous. The situation see-sawed backwards and forwards. The 2nd East Surreys were given the job of sorting out the mess and totally taking control of the Redoubt and also Little Willie (surely a job for more than a single battalion?). In this attack parties of German bombers moving up Little Willie threatened the East Surreys and the men were forced back behind a barrier thrown across a trench on the western side of the Redoubt. Further progress by the bombers was halted by a group of men led by Second Lieutenant Jannson, who led them out of the trench into the open and, firing from prone positions, they poured fire into the Germans in their trench, both inflicting and suffering heavy casualties. At this critical time some men on the right hand side of the Redoubt began to withdraw, exposing a gap. Into this vital position came Second Lieutenant Fleming-Sandes and a party of men, having been sent forward with a supply of bombs. At this point the Germans launched a fresh assault and Fleming-Sandes jumped up onto the parapet and began to throw bomb after bomb at the Germans, all at a range of about 20 yards away. The ferocity of the attack drove the Germans back, but Fleming-Sandes was hit in the right arm by a bullet, which also broke it. He continued to throw bombs with his left arm until he was hit again, this time in the face. However the defenders had been "inspired by his devotion to duty and personal courage." He was awarded a Victoria Cross, which was gazetted in November 1915. Fleming-Sandes recovered from his wounds but was not fit for active service until 1918. It might be interesting to add that even though Fleming-Sandes was in a 'Regular' Division, the 28th, he was not a true 'Regular'. When the war broke out he enlisted in a TF unit, the Artists Rifles, leaving for France in October 1914. He received a commission in France on 9th May 1915 and being posted to the 2nd East Surreys, a sign surely that the 'pre-war Regulars' were becoming thin on the ground, Fleming-Sandes survived the Great War and died in 1961.

Private S. Harvey of the 1st York and Lancaster Regiment, part of the 83rd Brigade, 28th Division, was also awarded the Victoria Cross. During the night of 28th/29th September the Battalion received orders to relieve troops who had taken part in the earlier fighting in positions near the Hohenzollern Redoubt. The trenches were somewhat congested so some men were forced to use some reserve trenches. During the early hours of the 29th A and B companies were sent forward to reinforce troops in the Hohenzollern Redoubt who were being attacked. The two companies arrived in Big Willie around 5.00am on the morning of 29th September. The Germans held several sections of trench in this area, which enabled them to launch bombing attacks at British-held areas. Then at 6.00am the Germans made a heavy bombing attack just as A Company commanded by Captain

Foster was moving up Big Willie to relieve the 2nd Buffs in Dump Trench. It is likely the Germans using information from observation posts on slag heaps to the left of the Redoubt had begun to see the 2nd Buffs starting to leave their positions and decided to launch an attack at this most opportune moment. The British troops were closely packed together and seeing the danger the OC of B Company, Captain Buckley led his bombers out of the trench to launch a counter-attack in the open. They were joined in by the Buffs and A Company but casualties were heavy. The bombs they had were quickly used up and Private S. Harvey stepped forward and volunteered to go and get fresh supplies. As the communication trench to the rear was blocked with casualties and reinforcements, he chose the quickest option going overland. Private Harvey over the next 13 hours made numerous trips in the open bringing up around 30 boxes of bombs to his comrades in B and C companies. On the last of these his luck ran out and he was wounded in the head, he was awarded a Victoria Cross for his actions and the citation included the comment: "it was mainly due to Harvey's bravery that the enemy was eventually driven back." Harvey never recovered sufficiently from his wound to see active service again but survived until he died in 1960. Harvey was a pre-war Regular, joining the York and Lancaster Regiment in 1905 and was a short man, apparently just 5 feet tall, which perhaps helped him on 29th September by being a smaller target. King George V awarded him his Victoria Cross at Buckingham Palace in January 1917, perhaps as a result of his slow recovery from his wounds.

After the intense fighting on the 29th, the following day was a quieter one but not without some attacks launched towards the 83rd Brigade. The War Diary of the 1st York and Lancaster Regiment records the following for 29th/30th September:

> About 6.00am A Company advanced through Big Willie and two platoons had entered the advance trench when the Germans commenced a strong bomb attack on the left flank. The Buffs meanwhile, were filing out and the trenches were very congested. The order was given by the Adjutant of the Buffs to about turn, but this was almost impossible owing to the congestion, although Number 4 Platoon was able to file into an empty trench to allow the Buffs to pass. Captain Buckley, in response to a request for bombs, led the bombers of B Company over the top and delivered an attack, returning when the supply of bombs was exhausted. The wounded passing down the trench made the trench more congested still and the order was given to charge. The charge was led by Major Robertson and Captain Forster and was successful in preventing the Germans coming over the top and also drove them back along their trench.

Lieutenant Coles, the OC of B Company York and Lancaster, went in search of the 3rd Middlesex in South Face Trench, they not there due to a bombing attack which had forced them back to West Face Trench, and left part of Big Willie Trench unoccupied, thus exposing the flank of the York and Lancaster, which again their War Diary recorded:

> The Germans who had evidently crept up an unused communication trench were established in Big Willie with a supply of bombs. The party withdrew to report and ordered to return with bombs. In the meantime the Germans had advanced up the trench slowly and were assisted by gas fumes which em-

anated from a burning mop shaped apparatus which had been placed on our parapet.

However help was at hand as towards the end of the day their sister brigade, the 84th, relieved the 85th Brigade. But during the day the Germans made some moves. Parties from the area of Cité St Elie captured 250 yards of Gun Trench from the 7th Division, north of the Vermelles-Hulluch road. The attack was preceded by a very heavy artillery bombardment, Gun Trench coming in for particular attention. They managed, with their higher quality HE Shells, to cut all the telephone lines from the trench. This made it difficult to bring down counter-battery fire or bombard the German positions. The barrage started around 4.30pm and lasted for 90 minutes when the barrage lifted and the German infantry came forward. Some came up the communication trench leading from Cité St Elie to Gun Trench, while others came overland. The main point of the attack was cleverly pressed home at the junction of two units, the 2nd Bedfords and the 2nd Royal Scots Fusiliers. Great destruction had been caused by the bombardment and it is recorded that the left hand company of the Scots Fusiliers had nearly all their bombs and small arms ammunition buried under debris. However the men put up a good fight causing many casualties amongst those who crossed the open ground. But in the end the German bombers forced their way up the communication trench and entered Gun Trench and forced the Fusiliers back a short distance. However a stand was made, reinforcements having been sent up, notably a weakened company from the 2nd Green Howards, followed by two more companies. On the left, the 2nd Bedfords were forced back about 30 yards due to the superior German tactics and weaponry. By this I mean the grenades or bombs, the German version being far better than the (current) British improvised 'cricket ball' bomb. The Bedfords retired to Stone Alley and then most effectively blocked the trench stopping any further German progress. But even though the Germans had been checked on the flanks, they had managed to seize a large chunk of Gun Trench and it was considered essential to recover it. Therefore the acting brigade commander of the 21st Brigade (Lieutenant-Colonel Berners) ordered bombing parties to attack from both ends while the 2nd Green Howards would advance from the support trench at the same time. Regretfully the Green Howards got caught up on barbed wire in front of the support trench. The Germans spotted them and opened up fire causing the attempt to be abandoned. Additionally the bombing parties were unable to make much headway and their supplies of bombs quickly ran out, so the decision was taken to wait for a few hours until additional bombs could be brought forward and a fresh attack organised.

The new attack went in around 1.15am on the morning of 1st October, bombing parties from the 4th Camerons having come up to help the 2nd Royal Scots Fusiliers. The Green Howards gave covering fire from the support trench and initially the attack was looking promising, as a contemporary account recalls: "The German bombs were more handier and more accurate, less liable to be made unserviceable by wet, and they could throw five to our three and throw them further." Neither the 2nd Bedfords nor the 2nd Royal Scots Fusiliers could make any progress in the face of the superior German bombing. The casualty list was growing, including Major Monteith (CO of the 2nd Bedfords). As dawn was approaching it was decided to block the trench at both ends of the lost portion and to delay any further attempts till fresh units could relieve the absolutely exhausted and seriously depleted ranks of the 7th Division. They had been in action for five days continuously, in miserable conditions and had seen around 5,500 of their comrades become casualties. The trenches were successfully blocked and I suspect the battered survivors were glad to get away during darkness on the evening of 1st October when the 5th Brigade from the 2nd Division arrived to relieve them.

The 7th Division regrouped at the villages of Les Quesnoy and Le Preol, where the long-suffering 21st Brigade were nominated as the reserve Brigade. Almost immediately they found they had been detailed to relieve units of the 2nd Division in front of Cuinchy and just south of the La Bassée Canal - no rest for the wicked! The 1st and 2nd October saw the continuation of fighting in and around the Hohenzollern Redoubt and the fighting went the Germans way, as they gained most of Little Willie and a foothold back in the Redoubt. The 28th Division, and in particular the 84th Brigade, bore the brunt of the fighting, having to put in an attack, with a very good account contained in the War Diary of the 1st Welch Regiment concerning their attack on Little Willie: "Precisely at 8.00 pm, climb over the parapet. Move forward in perfect silence, move in quick time, keep line." On the right of the attack two companies from the 2nd Cheshire Regiment were to attack a relatively new trench known as The Chord, which was described in the unit's War Diary as "a strong trench running north to south across the Hohenzollern Redoubt."

The 1st Welch got to within about 100 yards of Little Willie before they were spotted and the Germans opened fire. The Welch's War Diary reported:

> The CO's voice rang out 'Forward 41st - Get at them Welsh!' In 20 seconds there were 250 men and a proportion of the officers on the floor. The remainder were in the trench bayoneting those in there and firing at the retreating Prussian Guards.

The men of the 1st Welch had managed to capture a section of Little Willie but regretfully it was an isolated one with Germans at each end of the captured section. Worse still there was no communication trench connecting Little Willie to the British lines. Although the Cheshires captured some ditches and shell holes, the Chord remained in German hands. The following day the area was subjected to a heavy German artillery and mortar bombardment, the Welch War Diary recording:

> The enemy then opened with *Minenwerfer* shell. The shell, having reached the distance it is regulated for, drops perpendicularly down and can be seen all the way down and can be dodged. The men were now so congested that it was impossible to get out of the way. When one lands in the trench 6 men in the vicinity disappear.

Later that day the section of Little Willie held by the Welch was lost and the 1st Suffolks were instructed to retake the trench during an attack planned for 8.00pm. Difficulties in moving up delayed the attack till midnight. A request to postpone the attack was turned down by Brigade HQ and the Suffolk's War Diary retells a grim episode:

Orders were then given by Major Sinclair-Thompson to get the men out of the trenches and form up in two lines, C and D companies in the front line from left to right and covered off by A and B companies, OC B Company was ordered to take the place of D Company, whose men could not be found. A Company moved off before the other companies were ready, and the attack of the other three companies, inclined to the right. The attack failed.

The next morning the Germans again launched a fierce counter attack from the direction of Little Willie, aimed at the few remaining men from the Welch Regiment. They were driven back towards the Redoubt and then it was the turn of the 2nd Cheshires. They too were forced out of The Chord and West Face with their War Diary recording:

> The enemy broke through part of the trench occupied by the 1st Welch on our left flank and advanced with great rapidity, throwing hundreds of bombs, their bombers being supported by machine guns and riflemen. The attack came as a complete surprise.

Then in the early hours of the 3rd October the Germans put in a strong attack against the 84th Brigade holding the Hohenzollern Redoubt area and managed to retake the remainder but stout resistance kept them from also pinching Big Willie. The Bavarian Composite Regiment supported by men from the 57th Regiment and the 104th Regiment completed this attack, made from both sides of the Dump. Both of these latter two units had travelled many miles to take part in this offensive.

One of the last acts for the 28th Division was when the 83rd Brigade, commanded by Brigadier Ravenshaw, was ordered to send three battalions over the top in a counter-attack intended to retake the lost Redoubt and Big Willie Trench. It was intended to use the cover of darkness and the 1st KOYLI and 2nd East Yorks would attack the Redoubt, while the 2nd King's Own would deal with the Big Willie. There was as usual little time for planning and reconnaissance. At 4.15am on the morning of 4th October the leading waves of the 1st KOYLI crept into No Man's Land. There appeared to be no artillery support even though it had been laid on. The attacking troops were quickly spotted and the Germans opened fire. The attack achieved nothing and the casualties were heavy. The War Diary of the 2nd East Yorkshires apparently written by the CO himself for this day does little to hide his disgust.

> I attribute the failure of this attack to the following causes:
> (i) No artillery bombardment
> (ii) Complete lack of element of surprise. The Germans were well prepared, and had not been in the slightest shaken by the desultory shelling that had taken place throughout the day
> (iii) The Germans had been digging in during the day previous, and had thoroughly improved their trenches
> (iv) The relief the day before did not finish until 7pm. Company officers had only very indistinct idea of the trenches they were occupying, and none at all of the positions they were to attack.

The GOC of the 28th Division Major-General Bulfin was not quite so scathing in his report on this attack:

For information of Corps commander I beg to submit the following brief report on attack made this morning by 83rd Infantry Brigade:

The attack on the Redoubt by the 83rd Brigade took place this morning beginning with an artillery bombardment starting at 4.15am and lifting at 4.45a.m.. A copy of the orders for the attack are attached.

At 4.15am the artillery bombardment commenced and the first two lines of the attacking party left their trenches and advanced some sixty yards and lay down. Each line consisted of two platoons of the KOYLI with four platoons of the East Yorks on their right. The third line of attackers left their trenches at 4.30am and lay down thirty yards out. At 4.45am the artillery bombardment lifted and the Infantry attack was made in four lines on a front of between 350 and 400 yards. The fourth line was met with terrific machine gun fire presumably from Mad Point and were only able to leave their trenches in isolated places. The three attacking lines were very severely cut up up by machine gun, shrapnel and rifle fire.

The machine gun fire came from Mad Point, the cottages south-east of Mad Alley, the most southerly lines of cottages south-east of Corons Alley, the Dump, a point in Little Willie just east of the second N in Hohenzollern, and from an emplacement between Points 33 and 32 in the Redoubt. Rifle fire came from Fosse Trench. The attacking party got to within 30 yards of the enemy trenches but could proceed no further.

This information was collected from the GOC 83rd Infantry Brigade and from officers of the KOYLI and the East York Regiment who took part in the attack.

For their part the weary 28th Division, during its few short days in the Loos sector, suffered losses of 146 officers and 3,231 men.

The loss of the Hohenzollern Redoubt threatened the position in the salient opposite the Quarries and as this called for a bit of a re-think, Haig, with the approval of Sir John French, changed the plans again. It was decided to abandon all other attacks except those concentrating on the recapture of the Hohenzollern Redoubt and Fosse 8. To these ends the 1st Army was now reorganised. In the north I Corps had responsibility from the La Bassée Canal to the Vermelles-Auchy road. In the south IV Corps was positioned between the French 10th Army and the Vermelles-Hulluch road. Sandwiched between these two was XI Corps. These changes became effective during the night of 4th/5th October, and so the planning for the attack on Fosse 8 and the Quarries became the responsibility of XI Corps. This Corps of course consisted of the Guards, 12th and 46th divisions, which was a 'perfect' combination of Regular, New Army and Territorial Force men. The attack was to be supported by all the available artillery of the 1st Army with the additional help of a gas and smoke cloud. The 12th Division was to take the Quarries and the Guards Division was responsible for the Hohenzollern Redoubt and Fosse 8.

It might perhaps be best to jump back a little in time to outline here the plan for the Guards Division and the orders that were issued in the days prior to 5th October. On the 1st October Major-General Lord Cavan received an order from XI

Aerial view of the Hohenzollern Redoubt area. (IWM Q 44167)

Corps HQ instructing him to prepare a plan by the following day for the capture of the Quarries and to relieve the 2nd Division on the night of 3rd/4th October on the sector extending southerly from a point about 600 yards south of the Dump. At 12.15pm on the following day the preliminary instructions for the relief were issued. The 1st Guards Brigade was ordered to relieve the 6th Brigade on the left hand side with its right positioned just south of the Quarries. The 3rd Guards Brigade were to relieve the 5th Brigade south of the 1st Guards Brigade, the 2nd Guards Brigade was to remain in reserve at Vermelles. The Divisional Pioneers, the 4th Coldstream Guards, were detailed to remain with Divisional HQ awaiting further instructions. However, shortly before midnight, after consultation with the 2nd Division, detailed orders were issued from Divisional HQ, which, it was stated, would be opened at the Noyelles les Vermelles chateau on completion of the relief. As it turned out, the transfer of the units was far from a smooth one and this must have been repeated around other parts of the front. One senior Royal Engineer officer wrote:

> The parapets of the fire trenches had been freely undercut to try and afford protection against shell fire. The communication trenches were very badly damaged and battalion and brigade HQs were not very safe. The German trench mortars were very attentive and accurate.

Indeed the activities of the Germans were so aggressive that an attack warning was issued during the actual transfer of troops. Major-General Lord Cavan issued special instructions to Brigadier Feilding (GOC 1st Guards Brigade) warning him to take every possible precaution against an attack as his troops were approaching the German trenches south of the Quarries and to attempt no offensive operation until he was firmly established in the line. He also instructed both brigades to have parties of bombers in readiness during the actual hand-over and emphasized the paramount importance of the troops quickly getting to grips with the construction of good communication trenches with the least possible delay.

Around 6.00pm on the evening of 3rd October the 2nd Division reported heavy shelling of the British positions just north of the Vermelles-Hulluch road. As soon as this message was received at Divisional HQ, the 3rd Guards Brigade, whose units were still in the area of Sailly-Labourse were ordered to remain there until further orders were received. A report about an hour later said the situation had stabilised and so orders went out for the relief to carry on. This was duly done and the 3rd Guards Brigade assumed responsibility for their sector at 3.00am on the 4th October, the 1st Guards Brigade relieving the 6th Infantry Brigade a couple of hours or so earlier. During the early hours of the 3rd October the Germans succeeded in retaking the Hohenzollern Redoubt, which materially changed the situation on that part of the front. As we have seen, the loss of the Redoubt made the left flank of the line somewhat insecure, and the proposed attack on the Quarries was shelved. The men's efforts were directed towards strengthening the positions they held and it also meant a readjustment of the line. Therefore the XI Corps handed over to the IV Corps the sector it was holding from Loos on the French left to a point about a mile north of the eastern edge of the village. The XI Corps thus now released took over a section from I Corps from the left of the line held by the Guards Division to the Vermelles-Auchy road, which runs north of Fosse 8. Of this sector the southern portion was allocated to the 12th Division and the northern part from just south of the Quarries to the Vermelles-Auchy road by the Guards Division. It was decided that the front held by the 12th Division would be supported by the artillery from the Guards Division, the 12th Division and the 7th Division (less one Brigade RFA), while the Guards would be supported by the guns of the 28th Division and the one brigade from the 7th Division.

It may be of interest here just to briefly relate the memories of a soldier from the 9th Royal Fusiliers part of the 36th Brigade from the 12th Division about his thoughts on hearing of the attack at Loos and his movements to the area. These notes come from an interview conducted with C. Quinnell in 1975. I feel we can forgive him the odd wrong date that slipped in:

> On the afternoon of the 25th September 1915 we were taken out of the line at Houplines and a very interesting Army communication was read to us stating that our troops had that morning broken through the German lines at Loos. We gave three cheers and we were greatly excited because close by some buses were drawn up and we were told to get in them and we had the one and only ride on a bus in France that afternoon. We were taken down to a place about 15 miles behind the line at Loos and there we debussed and had a forced march up to the battlefront at Loos. We were met by a sergeant of the Grenadier Guards in the village of Vermelles and he was the guide who was going to take us to our new position. We were taken into the reserve line that had previously been occupied by the Germans, so of course the trenches were facing the wrong way. The fire step was looking towards the British lines so it meant a lot of digging.
>
> After we'd been in the line actually in front of the village of Loos, or the ruins of Loos, we were moved along the front line 1½ miles to 2 miles away north,

in front of a village called Hulluch. Now at Hulluch the Germans hadn't been rooted out of their trenches there, and both sides fought like wildcats over silly bits of trench, you would have thought they were inlaid with diamonds the way they fought. But one particular evening at dusk the Germans bombarded our front line and we knew an attack was coming but we had orders not to open fire until we got the order. Well, in the dusk we could see the Germans forming up in a fold of the ground, we could just see their heads and the bayonets of their rifles.

   After a while these Germans marched up to us in columns of four and then a machine gun on our left opened up so without waiting for any order everybody opened up rapid fire.

The orders from XI Corps outlining these moves, reached the Guards Division HQ around 9.00am on 4th October, while they were positioned at Noyelles, and at 6.00am on the following day the detailed instructions for the moves were issued. The 3rd Guards Brigade was warned that it would be relieved that night by the 37th Brigade from the 12th Division and take over billets currently occupied by the 2nd Guards Brigade. The 2nd Guards Brigade would relieve the 83rd Brigade (28th Division) then positioned around the Vermelles-Auchy road. The 1st Guards Brigade would extend their left so as to join up with the right flank of the 2nd Guards Brigade. By 4.15am on the 6th October these various reliefs and moves had been successfully carried out and Divisional HQ moved to Sailly-Labourse.

   Hand in hand with these moves was the need to make preparations for the gas and smoke cloud for the forthcoming attack. Detailed instructions with regard to the preparations for the installation of the gas cylinders, allocated at 120 per attacking brigade, were issued. Also covered were the construction of jumping-off trenches and the method by which the cylinders were to be moved to the front line trenches. On the 25th September (or even before that date), the movement of the unwieldy heavy cylinders had been the reason for much cursing by the infantry, who often ended up carrying them. These new instructions hoped to avoid any unnecessary congestion in the communication trenches. However the shortage of actual routes to and from the front line, and the constant work to keep them open due to artillery and trench mortar fire, was a severe blow to the plan. Indeed there were numerous problems in completing all the necessary work so that the attack was postponed till the 9th October, with the attempt to recapture the lost section of Gun Trench being undertaken on the 8th October.

   These delays caused concerns amongst the French High Command, especially Joffre, who wanted to renew his attack in Artois and Champagne on the same day as the BEF. However Joffre was apparently reassured by an intelligence report that due to the activity in the Loos sector, the Germans could not withdraw any troops from there to send to Champagne. It also showed that intelligence indicated there were now over 150 German artillery batteries on the French 10th Army and British 1st Army fronts. It was believed there had been 108 on 25th September. The preliminary bombardment for the French attack in Champagne had already started when Sir John French on the 5th October stated that the BEF's attack must be postponed from the 6th to the 9th October. General Joffre resigned himself to the inevitable and wrote back saying he regretted the delay but recognised the reasons that lay behind it. As it was, the French attack went in on the 6th October, after a five day bombardment which virtually used all the available French artillery ammunition. The gains as a result of this attack were limited to one or two very localised successes. Meanwhile on the Artois sector bad weather had greatly interfered with French preparations and on 5th October General d'Urbal advised that due to the bad state of the ground, any forward movement would be impossible for several days. Then on the night of 5th/6th October the commander of the French III Corps reported that the divisions in his control were so badly worn out by recent fighting and hardship caused by the bad weather, that it was necessary to relieve them. General d'Urbal, for unknown reasons, agreed to this, but it seems that it would take until the 9th October for the infantry to be relieved and 11th October for the artillery. He ordered the relief to be carried out before informing General Foch, and as a result the attack of the French 10th Army was again postponed until the 10th October.

While all of these plans, counter-plans, moves, counter-moves, cancellations and postponements were being argued and discussed the Germans got their retaliation in first. On the afternoon of 8th October they launched a counter-attack between the Double Crassier near Loos and the La Bassée Canal. The British Official History records that the Allies had no warning of this attack. The Royal Flying Corps had reported a certain amount of train movements during the preceding week; but no signs of increased traffic on the roads had been seen. It is likely that the bad weather hampered the British and French more than the Germans and they took the advantage of the lack of aerial reconnaissance and bombing to move their forces in unnoticed. Even so not everything went to plan on the German side. This counter-attack, intended originally for the 27th September and to be carried out by the Guards Corps, had been delayed for several days. It had been the intention to retake Loos and the area around Lone Tree much earlier but the use of some of this Corps' formations against the French on Vimy Ridge had put paid to an early attack. So it was not until the 6th October that sufficient forces could be assembled north of Lens to retake the positions lost on the days following 25th September. The attack was planned for the afternoon of the 8th, and it appears that the French on Hill 70 reported that passages had been cut in the German barbed wire there. This was nearly always a give-away that an attack was imminent. Unfortunately it seems that this information was not acted on or widely distributed. At noon a heavy artillery bombardment started on the Allied positions from the La Bassée Canal southwards to opposite Lens. It increased in intensity culminating in a peak between 3.00 and 4.00pm, when the German infantry left their trenches to carry out an attack on the sector Double Crassier through Hill 70 to Chalk Pit Wood. The aim was to occupy Loos village and the neighbouring trenches as a springboard to retaking their original line.

The assault was carried out by twelve battalions from the 7th and 8th divisions, either side of the Lens-La Bassée road, in the extreme south of the French sector (the left and centre of the German attack). It only met with a limited success and resulted in the Germans taking only a small section of trench. The German troops attributed their failure to the fact that the gunners had failed to destroy the French barbed wire, which they were able to reach but not penetrate. Does this sound familiar? The success they did gain was a length of about 400 yards of trenches between the Double Crassier and the Lens-Béthune road. An attack was carried out by battalions from the 153rd and 216th regiments slightly further north against the British 1st Division in the Loos-Puits 14 bis-Chalk Pit area. The 9th King's, 2nd Royal Munster Fusiliers and the 1st Gloucestershires held the front line here. It is reported that the artillery barrage was quite successful here causing heavy losses in both the front and support lines, but there were survivors and they took heavy revenge on the advancing German lines. The Germans managed to get within 40 yards of the British positions before the weight of fire stopped the attacks. It is therefore worth remembering that the Germans had just as much trouble in attacking as the Allies. In no position were the Germans able to enter a trench held by the 1st Division, a notable success for the British.

As well as the attack near Loos, a subsidiary attack was made in the area held by the 2nd Guards Brigade, also launched at 4.00pm. The main point of the attack was directed against a narrow salient in the line just south of Big Willie, where the track leading from Le Rutoire to the Loos-Haisnes road crossed the front line. The German intention was to drive the British from this position and so straighten the line. Battalions from the 55th, 77th and 97th regiments carried out the attack. It was led by bombers advancing down the trench that led from the southern face of the Hohenzollern Redoubt and also from the communication trench that ran south and east of the British position. Two companies from the 3rd Grenadier Guards held the line here and they were faced with being attacked from three sides. The Germans managed to drive the Grenadiers back and it was looking like developing into a very dangerous position for the 2nd Guards Brigade, as the War Diary of the 3rd Grenadiers relates:

> The enemy bombers rushed our left flank and came bombing down the line. They surprised and surrounded our own bombers, killing most of them, including Lieutenant Anson. A machine gun crew, commanded by Lieutenant Williams from the Battalion, were also killed and three successive machine gun sergeants. The two companies who occupied the finger, numbers 2 and 3, were ordered to retire down the communication trench and make way for bombs and bombers who were hurried up from the support companies.

Into the breach, literally, to save the situation stepped Sergeant O. Brooks of the 3rd Coldstream Guards. The 3rd Coldstreams positioned on the right of the Grenadiers had suffered a brief set back when some Germans managed to gain a brief foothold in one of the advanced saps before being bombed out, but now came to the aid of their comrades. On his own initiative Sergeant Brooks followed by a small number of bombers and some riflemen began bombing down the new German trench. According to reports a fierce fight went on for some 45 minutes and ended with the party of men led by Sergeant Brooks regaining control of the trenches lost by the Grenadiers. It is believed that the Coldstream Guards in this one afternoon used over 500 bombs. Sergeant Brooks was awarded a Victoria Cross for his actions this day, the citation mentioning "his absolute fearlessness, presence of mind and promptitude." Brooks was a pre-war Regular who had served his time and was on the reserve in 1914 and then recalled to the Colours. The award was gazetted on 28th October 1915 and presented to him on 1st November 1915 in somewhat unusual circumstances. Brooks was taken to a hospital train at Aire Station, on which King George V was a patient, after suffering a bad fall from his horse. The King was confined to bed but wanted to present the award himself, and so Brooks had to kneel in the carriage while the King tried to pin the medal on. It is reported that he was unable to get the pin through Brook's thick khaki uniform jacket.

Other Guardsmen came into this particular area, notably No 1 Company of the Grenadier Guards and two companies of the 1st Scots Guards, and consolidated the position. Later the German bombers attempted to cross the open ground to the south of the Dump but they were mown down by machine gun fire. It is also reported that the guns of the 3rd Brigade RFA wrought havoc in the communication trenches leading to the Hohenzollern Redoubt. The position was further stabilised when Lieutenant-Colonel Corry (CO 3rd Grenadier Guards) ordered the blocking of the northern end of the trench and forming of a defensive front running in a north-easterly direction from the Le Rutoire-Haisnes track. Meanwhile on the front held by the 2nd Coldstream Guards (on the right flank of the 1st Guards Brigade), there was also a heavy attack from German bombers but they were unable to shift the Coldstreams from their positions. The fighting went on till dusk when the Germans withdrew. The conduct of the Guards was recognised by a telegram from Sir John French to Lieutenant-General Haking which said:

> I have once more to express to you, and the troops under your command, my deep appreciation of their splendid conduct yesterday in the severe repulse inflicted upon the enemy's violent attack all along your line south of the La Bassée Canal. Please communicate this to the troops.

There was a final British move to be carried out in the early evening and this was in the area of Gun Trench. Here at 6.15pm in a prearranged attack (before the German one), the 37th Brigade on the right of the 12th Division, made an assault on the 250 yards of Gun Trench north of the Vermelles-Hulluch road still in German hands. The plan called for simultaneous bombing attacks from both ends. This meant the bombers had to come from Stone Alley and the southern part of Gun Trench, coupled with a frontal assault from the support trench. This attack was carried out by the 6th Royal West Kents and they initially managed to gain a foothold in the German section but were unable to maintain their grip due to losses and a shortage of bombs. The casualty figure was 5 officers and 103 men. The bombing attacks from the flanks failed due to being met by parties of German reinforcements that were heading for the front line along communication trenches. The fighting was all over soon after dark and the position in Gun Trench remained unaltered.

Just to end this chapter it may be of interest to relate the tactics of the German bombers at this time and some comments from the German side of the attack.

> The bombing party was arranged as follows: two to four bayonet men in front, followed by three bombers, one to throw, the second to prepare the bomb for number one, and the third to keep handing bombs up to number two, the three men being trained to interchange their positions as they got tired or casualties occurred. The three bombers were followed by thirty bomb carriers, who kept passing the bombs along from the rear and acted as reserves. The attack was protected by covering fire from machine guns directed along the flanks of the communication trenches. The bayonet men in front were to deal with a rush down

the trench. The bombers received an ample supply of bombs from the carriers and were themselves relieved by men drawn from the carriers as necessity arose. If attacked with bombs, the German bombing party withdrew until the enemy supply of bombs was exhausted; they then immediately pressed forward again.

The British copied this formation (once they found out what it was) but amended it, as normally two men armed with Lewis Guns followed the bombers.

This is what the German 57th Regiment reported about their attack of 8th October:

About 4.30pm the barricades of the sap were broken down and the attack began. At the head of each of the two columns that were to storm along the saps was a strong party of bombers, followed by men carrying filled sandbags ready to make a barricade whenever necessary. Behind was a detachment with rifles and hand grenades who were to search and clear any enemy dug outs and defend the barricades. At the tail of the columns were reserve bombers for replacing casualties in the front bombing party. At first the attack in the western sap went well, but was checked by the explosion of a mine which killed and wounded a number of the bombing party in front. A heavy and effective machine gun fire from a gun in the sap beyond the mine, and fire from a trench mortar compelled this column to withdraw step by step with the enemy in pursuit, back to its sortie position. The attack along the eastern sap was held up by the same explosion and the enemy, counter-attacking shortly afterwards, forced back this column also with heavy losses to its sortie position. The attack by the 117th Division, further south, with which it had been intended to join hands, likewise had no success.

10

The Hohenzollern Redoubt - Again

The German attack on the 8th October obviously delayed the preparations for the proposed attack on 10th October but did not postpone it. Over the nights of 10th to 12th October the gas cylinders were moved up to the front line and the date for the attack was now set at 13th October. General Foch, on hearing this news, decided that the French 10th Army should attack the crest of Vimy Ridge without waiting for the British. It was also agreed that 'simultaneous and combined operations of the two armies shall be carried out later', whatever this was meant to encompass. As it was, the French plan was changed, in that their IX Corps would not now attack Hill 70 but only try and retake the section of trench lost near the Double Crassier on the 8th October. The attack by the French 10th Army went in on the 11th October and had disappointing results. The men of the IX Corps were stopped at the German barbed wire and failed to reach their initial objective. Some formations of IX Corps did not even attack and only in one area was a small gain made. Foch blamed indifferent artillery preparations. Nevertheless Foch decided that the French attack would be renewed at the earliest possible opportunity, as the 10th Army, although very close to the crest of Vimy Ridge, would have a very tough time spending the winter being overlooked by the Germans. His commander, Joffre, was of a different opinion. The shortage of artillery shells, particularly for the heavy guns meant that any considerable offensive operations in both Artois and Champagne could not be contemplated. Joffre therefore issued instructions that any forthcoming offensive operations be limited to the IX Corps helping any British attack by an artillery demonstration only as previously planned. This then marked the virtual end of the Battle of Loos as far as the French were concerned. On the 15th October General d'Urbal instructed his units "to consolidate the ground won, and to create a strong defensive organisation with a view to a future resumption of the offensive."

Meanwhile the preparations were proceeding for the British attack. By 6.00am on 11th October 840 gas cylinders had been moved up to the front line sector then held by the Guards Division. On the previous day orders had been issued by XI Corps stating that the 12th and 46th divisions would relieve the Guards Division on the night 10th/11th October. The orders also outlined the objectives and scope for the forthcoming attack. The overall aim of this offensive was (again) to reach the line Henin-Pont à Vendin. As the first stage in this forward movement the IV Corps was tasked with taking a line along the Lens-La Bassée road. The I, III and Indian corps were ordered to support this attack with a smoke cloud and harassing fire. The XI Corps was to establish a strong defensive flank to the north of IV Corps to bring about the capture of Fosse 8 and the Quarries, and after this to make contact with the 46th Division on its left and IV Corps on its right, then send out strong patrols towards Cité St Elie. The aim was to see if the village was still held by the Germans. The 46th Division were to capture Fosse 8 and the Dump (and of course the Hohenzollern Redoubt which was in front of them), and then to

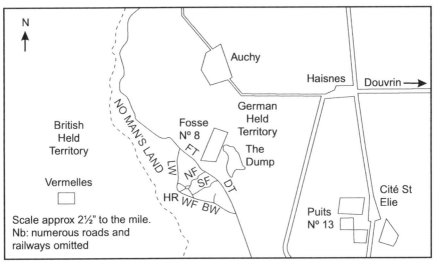

HR Hohenzollern Redoubt (the area bounded by
  Fosse and Dump Trenches and Big and Little Willie)

NF	North Face	DT	Dump Trench
SF	South Face	BW	Big Willie
WF	West Face	LW	Little Willie
FT	Fosse Trench		

Map 12: The Hohenzollern Redoubt area

consolidate a line north and north-east of the Corons de Maron, and in the process gain contact with the I Corps and 12th Division on its left and right respectively. The Guards Division were ordered to arrange for the protection of both these attacks by discharges of gas and smoke. This comment does surprise me a little as it now seems that 'ordinary' soldiers were being allowed to deploy the gas and smoke cloud rather than the specially trained Royal Engineers personnel. There were full instructions issued for the guidance of those from the Guards Division left behind in order to carry out the release of the gas and smoke. But before these reliefs could take place the Guards Division was called on to attempt to improve the situation in Big Willie. The 2nd Grenadier Guards held the old German trench system in Big Willie for a short distance beyond the road that passed south of the Dump, the left hand side of the Grenadiers front ending in a barricade. On the other side of the barricade were the Germans. The Germans in this area held a short length of communication trench and a portion of fire trench running south from it formed a kind of small salient in the Guards positions which was known locally as 'The Loop'. This position was a thorn in the side of the Guards as it was able to fire into the reverse parts of British trenches and also to put down enfilade fire on other parts of the trench system. The 2nd Grenadier Guards after a bombing attack on the night of 10th October encompassing severe hand-to-hand fighting in which 60 Grenadiers were lost, captured The Loop and a section of trench beyond it, and also held it against a determined counter-attack at dawn on the morning of 11th October.

On the 11th October misfortune also befell the 1st Irish Guards when a shell landed close to the HQ dugout. It seriously wounded the CO, Lieutenant-Colonel G. Madden, his Adjutant, Captain The Lord Fitzgerald and the Padre, Father Gwynne. Lieutenant-Colonel Madden sadly died over a month later on 12th November, and interestingly is one of the few Great War dead to be buried near his home. He is the only Great War soldier buried in the Church of Ireland churchyard of his home village of Currin in County Meath, Republic of Ireland. Perhaps he died whilst on a spot of leave from a military hospital on the mainland, or perhaps his family was able to pull some strings.

On the afternoon of the 12th, after a heavy two hour artillery bombardment, German infantry tried to retake the lost positions. As usual bombers led the attack but the 2nd Grenadier Guards put up a stiff resistance and the attack was beaten back. The Grenadiers, however, suffered a further 80 casualties. It is easy to see how a battalion's strength can be eroded away even without taking part in any major attacks. In two days the Grenadiers lost the better part of a company and this at a time when experienced soldiers were at a premium. Indeed the shelling and trench mortar barrage was so severe that the relief of the Grenadier Guards by the 7th Suffolks and 5th South Staffordshires from the 12th and 46th divisions respectively, which should have started at 6.45pm, was postponed until midnight and was finally completed at 6.00am on the 13th October.

Let us just make a small diversion here, as I would like to mention the award of a Victoria Cross for actions on 11th and 12th October. This went to Acting

Forward sap in Big Willie Trench manned by men of the 1st Scots Guards October 1915. (IWM Q 17389)

Sergeant J. Raynes of A Battery, 71st Brigade RFA attached to the 15th Division. For several days before the 11th October this battery had been firing at German positions from several different locations. They first started firing from close to Fosse 7, then moved into Loos village and finally, as a result of counter-battery fire, moved out onto the Loos plain near some dugouts. Here again they were subjected to counter-battery fire including gas shells that caused a number of casualties. When the order to cease-fire was given, Raynes found out that his friend Sergeant J. Ayres had been wounded. He ran to where Ayres was lying, about 40 yards away and bandaged his wounds before moving him a little way to a position where he thought he would be safer before returning to his gun which was being ordered back into action. Again the fire from the 71st Brigade attracted German fire and it was so intense that another ceasefire was called. During this lull Raynes, assisted by two gunners (both killed shortly afterwards), carried Sergeant Ayres back to the Battery dugout. On arrival here the area was subjected to a further gas attack and being unable to find Ayres's smoke helmet, Raynes gave his own to his wounded friend. Raynes then went looking for another smoke helmet but suffered from the effects of the gas and lapsed into unconsciousness for a short while before coming round. Upon his return to the dugout he found that it had been blown in and he began to try and dig the trapped men inside it out. Sadly Ayres and a number of others were dead but two of the men inside were alive. The story does not end here as on the following day the Battery moved to a house on Quality Street. The Battery commander later reported: "A large projectile landed on the house used as our cookhouse and completely wrecked it burying sixteen of my own men." Sergeant Raynes was amongst those buried and remarkably dug himself out even though he was bleeding from a cut head and wounded in the leg. He then proceeded to dig out the Battery Sergeant Major, Warrant Officer Austin, who was severely wounded and then Raynes carried him to a nearby aid post. He then returned to help with the rescue operation before having his own wounds dressed. After this he reported back for duty with his Battery, which was again being heavily shelled. He was recommended for a Victoria Cross by his Battery commander who recorded later that on the 12th October: "He was obliged to send to the dressing station the whole of the personnel at that time with the firing battery. Only seven men survived to the end of the engagement." Sergeant Ayres was buried in Fosse 7 CWGC Cemetery near Marzingarbe. John Raynes had served as a Regular for eight years as a gunner before leaving in 1912 to join the Leeds City Police until the outbreak of the Great War, when he was recalled. It is probably fair to say that this exposure to gas caused him problems in later life, as he was forced to retire from the Leeds Police in 1926 as he was paralysed, becoming bed ridden in later years until his untimely death in 1929 at the age of 43.

Meanwhile the day of the new attack the 13th October arrived and by all accounts was a bright autumn day. This day also had historical significance, as it was the day that news was received that on the previous day Edith Cavell, the head of a training school for nurses in Brussels had been shot by the Germans. She was a British citizen placed on trial by the Germans on the charge that she had harboured escaped and evading British and French soldiers, and Belgians civilians of military age assisting them to escape from Belgium. She was found guilty and executed by firing squad. Also on this day Britain severed diplomatic relations with Bulgaria as a prelude to declaring war on the 15th October.

The preliminary bombardment began at noon and was due to last for two hours. It was carried out by the following British artillery pieces: 54 heavy howitzers, 86 field howitzers and 286 field guns with a further 19 batteries (approx 60 guns) allocated for counter-battery work. At the same time the French IX Corps artillery made its demonstration by firing at German positions on Hill 70 and in the Bois Hugo. The XI Corps was faced with attacking the Hohenzollern Redoubt and then pushing on through to the Quarries and Fosse 8. As a supporting operation the IV Corps were to take and consolidate the line of the Lens-La Bassée road between Chalk Pit Wood and the Vermelles-Hulluch road. This would have the effect as those famous oft repeated words, of 'straightening the line in order to facilitate the preparation of a further offensive against the German second line position at and south of Hulluch.' As on 25th September the attack was to be preceded by a gas and smoke cloud. This was timed to start at 1.00pm at three locations: in the 2nd Division area between the La Bassée Canal and the Cambrin-La Bassée road, on the 46th Division front between the Hohenzollern Redoubt through Mad Point to the Vermelles-Auchy road. Finally in the 1st Division sector south-west of Hulluch. The total number of gas cylinders carried up to the front line trenches was 3,170 of which only 1,100 were discharged. This is perhaps because of the use of 'untrained personnel' and lessons learnt from the 25th September. The Chief Gas Officer Colonel Foulkes arranged for the cylinders to be grouped in a denser concentration and ordered their discharge two at a time.

One of the Special Company officers Lieutenant Lievens had without authorisation cobbled together rubber pipes and a four-way connection system and used it on the 25th September with great success. They were pieces of rubber hose used for connecting one end of the pipes to the gas cylinder and the other end to the parapet pipes. The order now came from Foulkes to Lievens to go and get enough supplies to re-equip the entire Special Companies. Armed with only verbal instructions from Foulkes, Lievens was despatched to England to procure the necessary raw materials to replace the ineffective and unwieldy metal fittings. As early as the 28th September the materials were being turned into new pipe kits. The method was as follows: the rubber tubing was cut into suitable lengths and then binding the hose to metal sockets with copper wire. One end was a spigot for connection to the gas cylinder and the other went to the parapet pipe. These were quickly tested under high pressure and proved far superior.

Other changes included having four men instead of two in each emplacement and that Section officers must assume ultimate on-the-spot responsibility for the order to discharge. There was planned to be ten cylinders in each emplacement hopefully in a sap ahead of the fire trench. The first four cylinders were discharged two at a time in order to catch the Germans with a strong concentration of gas when they were adjusting their respirators, and the last four when the 'life' of their respirators had in theory expired, the other two were to be discharged at equal intermediate intervals. The gas was to be stopped at 1.50pm, ten minutes before Zero Hour, and the smoke continued in that interval. It was also written into the plan, the idea of a flexible Zero Hour and that the infantry would either wait for a more favourable wind (if it was not satisfactory) or go without the gas and smoke cloud.

Opposite Cambrin in the northern sector, the wind died away just before Zero Hour, and this time section commanders from the 186th Company counter-manded the discharge order. In other areas such as opposite the Hohenzollern Re-doubt conditions could be described at noon as marginal, but within an hour or so, conditions turned very favourable with a 5 mph wind blowing from the south-west. At the appointed time the valves were opened and in almost textbook fashion the gas cloud headed towards the German lines. A soldier from the Royal West Kents in the 12th Division described what he saw:

The gas attack was on and I saw it rise from those cylinders, form into a white cloud, and this cloud rose to about 6 to 8 feet from the ground. The whole lot joined up together, and with a west breeze behind it, just went towards the German lines.

Despite this almost perfect discharge, trenches still filled with gas and it is said that on the 13th October the cloud did not even provide the limited assistance it had given on the 25th September. It probably served as more of a warning to the Germans than causing them any harm. It also had its dangers to the British as the following comments by an infantry soldier, Fred Hunt, illustrate:

We were crowded together in trenches near Hulluch like herrings in a box, shoulder to shoulder, so congested that it was almost impossible to get your hand in your pocket, then we realised the gas was coming back on us, but we were so tightly packed together it was impossible to take precautions. I passed out from the effects of it and I woke up in hospital.

The other action encompassed the dangers of blow-back but also, for the sol-dier involved, gained him the award of the only Victoria Cross to a member of the Specials. On 13th October Corporal J. Dawson from the 187th Company was, po-sitioned virtually opposite the Hohenzollern Redoubt. It appears that whilst the wind was virtually perfect the technology let the men down. The trenches were crowded with the attackers of the 46th (North Midland) Division making move-ment difficult, so Corporal Dawson climbed up onto the parados and walked back-wards and forwards along the trench in order to be able to give better instructions to the sappers under his control and also to move men away from areas of the trench line that were thick with gas. In spite of the new hoses, the problem of leak-ing cylinders and valves had not been solved. Dawson then found three leaking gas cylinders, which he got out of the trench and rolled them away some distance and then fired bullets into them in order to release the gas. All of this was done under heavy small arms fire and the obvious danger of poisoning from the chlorine gas. Without his prompt action it is likely many men in his sector would have suffered from the effects of the gas. His courage was noted and culminated in the award of a Victoria Cross in December 1915. Dawson was a Scot who gained a degree in chemistry at Glasgow University and then became a teacher. On the outbreak of was he joined the Scottish Rifles and went to France in early 1915. When the Army was looking for men to join the gas units, his degree in chemistry was noted and he was compulsorily transferred to the Royal Engineers. He was later granted a com-mission and even stayed in the Army after the war. He also served in the Indian

Army from 1929 before retiring with the rank of Colonel in 1948 and died in 1967.

Meanwhile, returning to the events of 13th October on the IV Corps sector, the 1st Division was to capture a 'new' German trench. This had been dug along the Lens road from the junction of the Loos-Hulluch and Lens-La Bassée roads, northwards towards Hulluch, a length of around 1,400 yards. After capturing this they were to consolidate this trench and then extend it to an existing one that led south to the Chalk Pit. The actual task was given to the five battalion strong 1st Brigade supported by the 2nd Brigade, who were positioned in the old German trenches. The 3rd Brigade in the trenches to the right of the 1st Brigade were told not to advance but would hold a line through Chalk Pit Wood to the Loos-Puits 14 bis track. The distance between the opposing lines was around 300 yards and as usual there was very little cover except for the gas and smoke screen. The spearhead of the advance consisted of strong bombing parties and they soon disappeared into the thick dense cloud. It is believed that the contents of 310 gas cylinders was discharged together with many smoke candles and at first things went well. The appearance of the cloud was (as usual) greeted by heavy small arms fire but this gradually died down, and the leading waves were able to get to within 50 yards of the German trenches when unfortunately the smoke began to clear. As visibility improved more and more fire was brought down on the men of the 1st Brigade but nevertheless they managed to reach the belts of barbed wire in front of the German defences. Again it had been hoped (planned) that the artillery would be able to either cut passages in the wire or destroy it. In neither option was much success obtained. Attempts were made to cut paths through with wire-cutters but it was a suicide mission in the face of the heavy German fire. The bombers soon used up all their grenades and suffered heavy casualties when German bombers counterattacked. The attack virtually ground to a halt in front of the German barbed wire.

The following is the story of one of the five units mixed up in this attack, the 14th London Regiment, otherwise known as the London Scottish. The CO of this unit, Lieutenant-Colonel Lindsay, realised that the artillery would probably have a difficult job in cutting the wire and so ordered that D Company be given all the available wire-cutters, as they were the leading company. The other companies were deployed as follows: A Company to be close behind D Company ready to rush through the gaps cut in the wire, B Company was to remain in the front line trench until this was done and then advance through A Company and take the German second line, C Company was to remain in reserve in the support trench. D and A companies advanced with the greatest bravery but floundered on the barbed wire and most of the commanders became casualties, the rest taking what cover they could. The rest of the 1st Brigade faired a little better. It is reported that the 1st Black Watch (at least, a few men from them) managed to get into the German positions but were soon overwhelmed. Then the fog of war came into play and conflicting messages were received, some of which seemed to indicate that everything was going well and that A Company of the London Scottish had breached the wire. Later a message from an A Company Officer, Captain Sayer, reached Battalion HQ, reporting that the attack had been a total failure. C Company remained in the support line and under cover of darkness that night the shattered survivors returned to the British lines. On the following morning the London Scottish were withdrawn from the lines to recuperate. It is recorded that of the 12 officers who took part in the 13th October attack 5 became casualties, including all those who had joined as Battle Casualty Replacements for officers lost on 25th September. Perhaps one of the sadder casualties from the London Scottish on this day was Private G. Ford. He had been a former Captain in the unit but had resigned to join the priesthood. He rejoined as a stretcher-bearer on the outbreak of war. Guy Ford, aged 38, has no known grave and is commemorated on the Loos Memorial to the Missing.

The final effort in this area was on the night of the 13th October when the 2nd Brigade were ordered forward to attempt the same attack as the 1st Brigade except under the cover of darkness. However due to transport problems they were unable to get into the front line trenches and reorganise for this attack in time so it was cancelled. This day's effort cost the 1st Division around 1,200 casualties. The 10th Gloucesters (another unit in the 1st Brigade) suffered around 150 casualties, the majority killed.

Further north on the front of the XI Corps, the attack in the Quarries area was delivered by two brigades from the 12th Division. On the right hand side the 37th Brigade was detailed to make another attempt to retake the 'lost' section of Gun Trench north of the Hulluch road and the additional objective of gaining a presence in the eastern corner of the Quarries. On their left the 35th Brigade was nominated to seize the Quarries and consolidate a line from the eastern corner northwards towards Fosse Alley to gain contact with the 46th Division attacking there. There was no gas support on this sector, just smoke candles and grenades. The only reason why gas was not used here that I have been able to ascertain was due to its shortage. The production of poison gas was still in its infancy in Britain and the two offensives of the 25th September and 13th October must have stretched resources very thin indeed.

The attack on the right hand side of the sector of the 37th Brigade was relatively successful. The smoke screen was very effective and the distance between the front lines was somewhat shorter than elsewhere, just over 100 yards. It was the classic two-up attack with the 7th East Surreys and the 6th Royal West Kents being given the leading positions. The 12th Division was of course a New Army Division and this was virtually their first taste of action, but they performed well in places. They were able to storm the 250 yards of Gun Trench that had previously given so much trouble and capture some Germans. The 7th East Surreys, although heavily counter-attacked, managed to fill in 50 yards of the communication trench leading to Cité St Elie so as to block it. On the left hand side of the 37th Brigade sector the 6th Buffs had further to travel and the smoke screen was less effective. When moving across the open ground south of the Quarries they came under heavy small arms fire from a position known as 'Gun Trench Extension' which led to the Quarries itself. This trench was virtually untouched by the artillery bombardment and as it had only been dug relatively recently its actual position was a little vague. The Germans here extracted a heavy price from the Buffs and in a few minutes caused 9 officers and over 400 men to become casualties. The attack here petered out having gone less than 100 yards from the starting point, obviously they failed to get anywhere near the German positions.

One other unit from the 37th Brigade involved was the 6th Queens, although in a reserve capacity. This is a comment from the 6th Queens War Diary:

> At 2.00pm the East Surreys, on the immediate right, assaulted the German trench between G.12 B.22 and G.12 D.57 and got into it. At 4.30pm after repeated appeals for assistance from the Company of the East Surreys in the German trench, one Platoon of A Company, under Lieutenant Pike, and one section of D Company were sent to its assistance. The Platoon of A succeeded in blocking the German communication trench and held it. B Company, which was at the disposal of the Officer Commanding 7th East Surrey Regiment, was sent to support him at 4.30pm, and two platoons of this company moved into the three foot trench behind the captured German trench, while two were kept in reserve. Our machine guns made good practice on some of the enemy who were running out of the trench when the East Surreys advanced. During the whole afternoon and evening the enemy kept up a lively artillery fire on our trenches, but did not do much damage. Second Lieutenant Mann, who had been sent to act as Liaison Officer between the Buffs and the right of the 35th Brigade, did very good work. The casualties in the Battalion were 1 man killed and 15 NCOs and men wounded.

On the other part of the 12th Division's sector, the commander of the 35th Brigade, who was tasked with taking the Quarries, threw all his four battalions in at once. On the left were the 7th Suffolks and the 9th Essex, and on the right the 7th Norfolks and the 5th Royal Berkshires. The smoke screen regretfully was not as thick here and failed to hide the movements of the Infantry from observation by Germans from the Dump. The Brigade was subjected to heavy fire from the front and sides coming from Slag Alley and the Dump, causing many casualties. However there was some success. A group of about 60 men from the 7th Norfolks led by Captain Ottar managed to gain a foothold in a trench to the left of the Quarries, which was not the intended objective but often in battle any gain will do. A runner managed to get back with the message that the 'objective' had been reached and that immediate support was required. The reinforcements were mainly A Company from the 5th Royal Berks commanded by Major W Bayley but did include some men of the 7th Norfolks. Unfortunately they also suffered numerous casualties from the trenches, which the Norfolks had been unable to seize. Thankfully the commander of the 5th Royal Berks saw the situation was pretty well up and took the decision not to send any more across, but this was of course too late for A Company, which was all but wiped out. The second-in-command of A Company, Captain F. Mount, was one of the early casualties and was initially posted as missing, and the CO of the unit, Lieutenant-Colonel Foley, wrote to his wife a few days later:

> It is with the greatest regret I write to tell you that poor Frank is missing and I fear that there is very little hope of his being alive. The Regiment was ordered on the 13th inst. to follow the Norfolk Regiment in the attack. The Norfolks attacked at 2.00pm. When I arrived with Major Bayley and his company the Colonel of the Norfolks informed me that they had suffered very heavy casualties but had reached the German trenches and were badly in need of reinforcements. I accordingly despatched Major Bayley with his Company to reinforce the Norfolk Regiment. Major Bayley and your husband led the attack in the

most gallant manner. Unfortunately before they reached the trench, the Germans had retaken it and brought a very severe machine gun and rifle fire to bear on them and very few of them got anywhere near the trench. Though search parties have been sent out to try to find the bodies only the body of Mr Reiss has been found, and one of the two men looking for it was killed while doing so, and the other man wounded. I can hold out little hope of your Frank being alive.

Sergeant E Lane from the 5th Royal Berks was involved in some fierce fighting as he described later:

Having got to the German trench, I was immediately confronted by the enemy and hand-to- hand fighting ensued for some time. I ended up with a bayonet wound in my mouth and my front teeth knocked out. Nevertheless I had the satisfaction of disposing of my opponent whom I believed to be an Uhlan, in as much I was able to get his spiked helmet and his Iron Cross from under his top pocket lapel. The helmet was covered with a green cover and numbered 233. We were beaten out of their trench later that day and I lay in a shell hole in No Man's Land amid white chalk until the early hours of the next morning when I was able to crawl back to our trench. Stretcher-bearers took me to safety and eventually I was sent home on seven day's leave.

It seems that help was on hand to some degree from a special group drawn from the four battalions known as the Brigade Bombing Party. The 5th Royal Berks contributed five groups drawn from all companies to this force under the overall command of the Bombing Officer, Lieutenant R. Pollard. He personally led one group forward and as they set out they had to negotiate their way over the dead bodies of other men from their unit who had been killed by a German shell that landed in their trench. A machine gun opened fire on the group from the right hand side and Lieutenant Pollard was wounded in the face along with several other members of the party. Undaunted they carried on and reached the first German barricade. The bayonet group went over first, closely followed by Pollard carrying bombs. On the other side they were faced with a barbed wire entanglement protected by an eighteen inch high earth bank. The best way to get forward was to take off their webbing and packs and crawl beneath the wire, pushing their bombs in front of them. Then they were able to start lobbing bombs. At this point the party came under small arms fire and Lieutenant Pollard was hit a second time, before insisting that he be propped up on the parapet and continued throwing bombs. His men wanted to carry him back to get medical attention but he refused saying, "No! Fire on lads." Soon after this he was wounded for a third time, this time fatally. One of the men under his command, Lance Corporal C. Goddard, removed Pollard's watch so it could be sent to his family. Regretfully Roger Pollard's body could not be recovered and he is therefore commemorated on the Loos Memorial to the Missing. His gallantry was recognised with the award of a posthumous Mention-in-Desptaches, which perhaps seems a little harsh, but I suspect no other senior officers were present to recommend anything else.

It is recorded that the Royal Berks were using two types of bombs, labelling them 'lemons' and 'cricket balls', both taking their names from the shape of them. It is reported that the pins of many of the lemon bombs were rendered unserviceable by knocks received on their journey up to the front line. The cricket ball type required a striker but none had been provided so the men could not use them. Eventually the supply of lemon bombs ran out and in response to urgent shouts four men from another unit appeared, one of whom had the necessary striker so the attack could continue with cricket ball bombs. Despite this extra effort the position could not be held due to counter-attacks coming in from the Germans, so orders were given for the battered survivors to withdraw to the British lines.

An insight into the feelings of an officer with the 5th Royal Berks both during the attack and before it comes from Captain P Gold, who was second-in-command of B Company in October 1915:

A meeting was called by the Brigadier of all officers in the Brigade. This was viewed with some apprehension when we found a field laid out with sandbags representing the trench we were to occupy and the German trench which it was proposed we, with the Norfolks were to capture. An elaborate scheme was then expounded whereby A and C companies were to open the attack; B and D companies moving up to the jumping-off position to await orders for our turn. It was a long harangue by our lugubrious CO, his final words being "I should like to shake you Gentlemen by the hand as I don't expect to see any of you again." With this cheerful farewell we departed to brief our NCOs and men in preparation for the morning of 13th October.

We were promised an intense bombardment which would cut the German wire and stupefy the opposing troops. After a troubled night in a German dugout I was called by my batman, Bayliss, with a mug of tea laced with whisky. I emerged into the trenches to await the thunderous bombardment which would cut the wire, drive the defenders mad only to surrender in droves. Instead there was an intermittent salvo from an 18-pounder Battery bursting high above the German trenches, the Germans chuckling in their 30 foot deep chalk dugout, whilst the barbed wire was not touched and remained intact. After a few minutes a whistle sounded, the range of our guns lengthened to the support trench and the thin khaki line of A Company advanced with bayonets fixed. What followed will never be erased from my memory.

The German machine gunners having manned their trench, the steady monotonous thudding of their numerous guns commenced and our men fell in sheaves. The supports followed and suffered the same fate. B Company meanwhile had moved to the assault position and were awaiting the signal to advance when the CO, who had watched this with horror, ordered the attack to cease. I had a few minutes before been struck by a large fragment from a coal box shell on the wrist which left the arm useless and it was being attended to by a Red Cross orderly when a German whizz bang exploded behind my head and I felt a sharp stab in my right upper arm. The MO examined this and said the shrapnel bullet was still there lodged against the bone and as both arms were practically hors de combat, ordered me to find my way back to the dressing station.

A very lucky man, Pat Gold survived the war and died in 1976 aged 87.

Meanwhile the 7th Suffolks also managed to seize a length of German trench about 250 yards long known locally as 'The Hairpin'. This was situated at a right angle to the British lines along the north-west edge of the Quarries. The 9th Essex

Dud Corner Cemetery and Memorial to the Missing. Located on the main road between Béthune and Lens, on the crest of the Grenay Ridge on the approximate site of the Lens Road Redoubt. This positioned was attacked by the 9th Black Watch on the morning of 25th September 1915. It contains around 2,000 graves and 20,700 names of those who have no known grave. (Niall Cherry)

filled the gap between the Suffolks and the Norfolks, but the original aim of taking the Quarries was as far away as ever. By the end of the day the 37th Brigade was holding Gun Trench and the southern part of Stone Alley, while the 35th Brigade had taken part of the south-western edge of the Quarries and The Hairpin but at a heavy price. One of the most significant losses of this day, that probably went unnoticed at the time, was Captain C. Sorley of the 7th Suffolks. Charles Sorley had been born in Aberdeen in 1895 and was the son of the Professor of Moral Philosophy at Aberdeen University. Sorley, educated at Malborough College, had obviously inherited his father's genes and was said to be extremely intelligent. He was accepted for admission to University College Cambridge on a scholarship but decided on a gap year in 1913 in, of all places, Germany. When war was declared in August 1914 he managed to get back to England, just avoiding being interned, and enlisted in the Suffolk Regiment and was soon granted a commission. Charles Sorley arrived in France in 1915 and was promoted Captain in August of that year. He was killed somewhere in the Quarries area on 13th October and has no known grave and is therefore commemorated on the Loos Memorial to the Missing. His lasting legacy was a collection of 37 poems including one he wrote just before he was killed, *When You See Millions of the Mouthless Dead*. A book of his poetry *Marlborough and other poems* was published in 1916 and ran into four editions; it was said that he had a real gift for rhyming. Perhaps he was the first to use that well known phrase 'pale battalions', which appeared in *When You See Millions of the Mouthless Dead*.

Here are a few words about the Hairpin from Corporal C. Quinnell, who spent a fair bit of time there:

Just imagine a lady's hairpin, or long finger, a finger which stuck out into the German lines. It was enfiladed, all told it was about 250 yards long. In the winter time the soil there was clay and in parts chalk, but as the weather deteriorated so the trenches got more and more sodden with water until if you had a long period of rain the trenches just became ditches, and that's where the thigh boots that we were issued with came in very, very handy. Ordinary Wellington boots weren't high enough, the water would come over the top of them.

A final comment here is the entry in the 12th Division War Diary for 13th October which even though written in the normal guarded language paints a difficult situation for the front line troops:

Operations commenced at noon with heavy bombardment by artillery as prearranged. At 12.10pm the German artillery replied by placing a barrage with gas shell on the Hulluch road in squares G.11.C and G.12.C. The Hulluch Road, Breslau Avenue and old German trenches were heavily shelled. The front trenches were also shelled, especially about G.12.A.54. The smoke curtain commenced at 1.00pm. It was very effective on the 37th Brigade front but less so on the 35th Brigade front. At 2.05pm the 7th East Surreys took Gun Trench G.12.D.47 to G.12.B.22. This they commenced consolidating though heavily counter-attacked with bombs. The 6th Buffs attacked the German trench from G.12.B.22 to G.12.A.99. The southern face of the Quarries was left unattacked and this enabled the German to pour a murderous enfilade fire with machine guns on the Buffs with such results as to stop the attack about 100 yards from their parapets. Only a few survivors managed to get back. The 7th Norfolks gained the south west face of the Quarries. The bombers of the 5th Berkshires failed to reach G.12.A.46 and assist the 7th Norfolk right, and the latter running short of bombs were forced to get back to their trenches. The 7th Suffolks attacked the north west face of the Quarries and with their bombers assisted the Norfolk left. This attack was very severely dealt with by enfilade fire from machine guns. The bombers reached G.6.C.13 and held on. All gains are being consolidated. The 9th Fusiliers in reserve to the 35th Brigade were ordered up at 5.00pm. Though communications held nearly throughout the day, information from the Front was very meagre and inaccurate. This points to the necessity for a thoroughly organised system for gathering information as to the situation from time to time. The 6th Buffs and 7th Norfolks suffered severe casualties. The shelling was very heavy along the communication trenches and rendered movement and communication difficult.

This left the 46th (North Midland) Division with the unenviable task of attacking the fearsome Hohenzollern Redoubt, Fosse 8 and the Dump. This Division relieved the Guards Division in Big Willie and the trenches behind it on the night of 12th/13th October, and as said before it was not until 6.00am that the relief was finished. This was just about in time for them to attack but left little time for preparation, although this had been realised in the few days beforehand by sending nearly all the officers and some NCOs on a visit to the front line trenches. This gave them the opportunity of at least seeing the ground over which they had to attack. Admittedly it was of little value, but it was better than nothing, as had

The attack on the 13th October 1915. A gas and smoke cloud can be seen in the centre and left of the picture. Fosse 8 is just visible behind the shrapnel shell burst in the centre, with the Hohenzollern Redoubt this side of Fosse 8. (IWM Q 29002)

The Dump from the original British front line. Big Willie and Dump Trench are visible from the chalk lines in front of it. (IWM Q42190)

been the case with the 21st and 24th divisions a few days earlier. After looking at the ground the GOC of the 46th Division, Major-General E. Montagu-Stuart-Wortley, was of the opinion that the best course of action was to proceed, as in siege warfare, by bombing attack and taking the objective piece by piece. He was overruled and the general plan of attack was broadly similar to that used by the 9th Division on the 25th September.

If I may I will pause to give the reader a brief recap about the Hohenzollern Redoubt and Fosse 8. This is what an officer wrote about these two places shortly after war in 1919:

> The Redoubt was one of two outstanding positions of the line between the La Bassée Canal and the slopes of Grenay, near the town of Lens. It stood out from the German front line some 500 yards, comprising a honeycomb of trenches and machine gun emplacements, and being defended, in addition to its own natural strength, by heavy firing, and by water lying between the German and British trenches. The other position was Fosse 8 - a great black slag heap. This mass, some 60 feet in height, lay about 600 yards within the German lines. It, also, was consolidated with a network of trenches, concrete machine gun emplacements and strong shelters for the gun crews during bombardments. On the north end of it stood the Engine House and Power Station, now converted into a formidable fortress and affording a perfect field of fire through its loopholed walls, whether for rifle or machine gun. Its cellars provided stout shelter for supports. The position, even more advantageous; in fact, to those holding it than it seems to be on paper, had long been a bone of fierce contention.

It was now the turn of the men from the North Midlands to have a go at this task. The following is their operational order:

46th Division Operational Order No 20
October 10th 1915

1   The XI Corps is to attack and capture the Quarries and Fosse No 8, in order to establish the left flank of the 1st Army and render a further advance in conjunction with the French possible. The line to be established is G.12.d.39-G.12.b.22, G.6.c.82 and 45-G.6.a.42-A.29.d.25 NW. Corner of Corons de Maron-A.29.c.1.6-A.28.d.49 and along Auchy Les-La Bassée-Vermelles road to our present front trench A.28.c.33.

The task of the 12th Division is to capture the Quarries and establish the above line as far north as the track at G.5.b.68. The task of the 46th Division is to capture the Hohenzollern Redoubt and Fosse No.8, and establish the above line from the track in G.5.b.68 to our front trench at A.28.c.33. The attack will take place on the 13th instant. The Infantry will assault at 2pm watches will be synchronised under Divisional arrangements on the morning of the 13th.

2   The 46th Division will assemble for the attack in accordance with instructions for assembly to be issued separately.

3   The distribution of the Division for the attack will be as follows:

Right Attack

Commander - Brigadier E. Fathom, CB
137th Infantry Brigade ("The Staffordshire Brigade")
100 Grenadiers 139th Infantry Brigade
2 Sections Divisional Cyclist Company
2nd Field Company RE.

Left Attack
Commander - Brigadier G. Keep
138th Infantry Brigade
1st Battalion Monmouth Regiment
125 Grenadiers 139th Infantry Brigade (25 to be attached to 1st Monmouths)
2 Sections Divisional Cyclist Company
1st Field Company RE.

Divisional Reserve
Commander - Brigadier C. Shipley
139th Infantry Brigade (The Sherwood Foresters Brigade) (less 225 Grenadiers)
1 Platoon Divisional Cyclist Company
2 Troops Yorkshire Hussars

The Brigadier commanding 139th Infantry Brigade will detail one battalion to be at the disposal of the Brigadier commanding 137th Infantry Brigade; and one battalion to be at the disposal of the Brigadier Commanding 138th Infantry Brigade.

RE reserve under C.F.D.
1st Field Company RE

Artillery
The attack will be covered by the Artillery as follows:
(a) Three groups of Heavy Artillery under the Corps commander.
(b) One group of Divisional Artillery (6 brigades 18 pdr and 1 Brigade 4.5" howitzers) under the CRA 28th Division and at the disposal of the GOC 46th Division.

FO officers will accompany the Battalion commanders of assaulting columns as under:
Right Battalion 137th Brigade FOO of 22nd Brigade RFA now with Right Battalion 1st Guards Brigade
Left Battalion 137th Brigade FOO of 22nd Brigade RFA now with - Left Battalion 1st Guards Brigade
Right Battalion 138th Brigade FOO of 3rd Brigade RFA now with Right Battalion 2nd Guards Brigade
Left Battalion 138th Brigade FOO of 146th Brigade RFA now with Left Battalion 2nd Guards Brigade.

And will be attached to Brigade Headquarters as follows:

137th Brigade Headquarters FOO of 22nd Brigade RFA now with
1st Guards Brigade Headquarters
138th Brigade Headquarters FOO of 36th Brigade RFA now with
2nd Guards Brigade Headquarters.

4   The attack will be carried out as follows:

(a) Artillery

(i) The Heavy Artillery bombardment is now in progress and is being
directed against the enemy's guns, machine gun emplacements, observation stations, trenches (both front line and in rear) and strong
points such as the Pentagon in A.29.c.53 and the houses in A.28.d.28.

(ii) There will be an artillery bombardment of the position to be assaulted by every available gun in the Corps commencing at 12 noon
on the day of the attack. This bombardment will last two hours. From
1 to 1.50 gas and smoke will be employed, the smoke being continued
till 2, at which hour the infantry assault will commence. The Heavy
Artillery from 1 to 1.10 will bombard the Coron de Pekin, Coron de
Maron, Pentagon Redoubt and the north-east end of the Dump, and,
for the remainder of the smoke and gas period, will devote its attention to counter-battery work and to bombarding the enemy's approaches and communication trenches and the likely positions of his
reserves. During the assault the Divisional Artillery will form a barrage
from about A.30.c.72 along Pekin and Cemetery Alleys to Mad Alley
and Mad Point, the Heavy Artillery assisting on the Cemetery, Lone
Farm and the houses near Mad Point. This barrage will continue from
2.0 to 4.0, after which fire will be lifted from Mad Point and the
houses near it to the trench A.28.c.48-A.28.b.17, and a slower rate of
fire maintained throughout the night.

(b) Infantry

The infantry will assault as follows:

The dividing line between the right and left attacks will be G.4.b.60-
right edge of village east of Corons Alley, Pentagon Redoubt,
A.29.c.53 (latter to right attack).

1) Right Attack

The 137th Brigade from the old British front trench between
G.10.b.98 and G.4.d.26 and assembly trenches in rear will assault at
2pm with their left directed on the north-west corner of the Dump.

1st Objective: Track crossing Fosse Alley at G.5.b.68-G.5.b.39 and
A.29.d.22 to Pentagon Redoubt at A.29.c.53 (inclusive). The assault will
pass straight on without pause to the far side of the Dump. Bombing par-

ties will be told off by the commander, Right Attack to bomb along the following trenches as they are successfully reached by the assault.

(i) South Face

(ii) Fosse Alley to join up with the left of 12th Division about the track at G.5.b.68.

(iii) Trench running towards Three Cabarets from A.29.d.22.

Bombing parties will also be organised to deal with Dump Trench and Slag Alley and with machine gun emplacements and other defences found in the Dump and clear them of the enemy. Dugouts must be cleared by bombing, and the greatest care taken that none are left unsearched.

2nd Objective - A.29.d.25 - Three Cabarets, north-east edge of Coron de Pekin-west edge of Coron de Maron-Railway A.29.c.16 (exclusive).

2) Left Attack

The 138th Brigade from our front trench between G.4.d.26 and G.4.a.72 and assembly trenches in rear will assault at 2pm with their right directed on the north-west corner of the Dump.

1st Objective - Pentagon Redoubt, A.29.c.53 (exclusive)-A.29.c.16-28.d.63 and 43-first 'i' of Little Willie to our present front trench at A.28.c.51.

The assault will pass straight over the Hohenzollern Redoubt without pause. The 1st Battalion Monmouth Regiment will follow immediately in rear of the assault, and will occupy the Redoubt, clear it of the enemy, and organise it at once as a strong supporting point with all-round defence. They will connect the Redoubt to our present front line by Big Willie and the trench running through the first 'e' of Hohenzollern.

Bombing parties will be told off by the commander, Left Attack to bomb along the following trenches as they are successfully reached by the assault, particular attention being paid to the clearing of dugouts.

(i) Trench leading north-west from north-west face of the Hohenzollern Redoubt. This must be cleared back to our present front line

(ii) Little Willie

(iii) Fosse Trench

(iv) Trench running north-west through A.28.d.68.

(v) Trench running to A.28.d.49.

(vi) Trench running north from A.29.c.16.

(vii) Trench running north-east towards A.29.c.69.

2nd Objective - Railway A.29.c.16 (inclusive)-A.28.d.49. Mad Point-front trench at A.28.c.33.

If possible both assaults will be pressed straight through to second objective, which will be immediately consolidated. If the assault is checked at the first objective, immediate measures will be taken to consolidate the position won, and a further attack will be organised against the second objective, which in its turn will be consolidated as soon as secured, in order to obtain two good strong lines of defence. The first essentials of consolidation are wire along the front and the establishment of a fire trench. Machine guns must be brought up as quickly as possible to points whence their fire will cover the front and flanks during consolidation. A smoke curtain will be established to cover the work of consolidation. Instructions are attached-Appendix B.

Distinguishing Flags
5   Infantry will carry 3' square screens divided diagonally into red and yellow, to mark the position of the firing line.

Bombing parties will mark their positions in captured trenches by red flags 18" square.

Allotment of Communication Trenches
6   Main communication trenches are allotted as follows:

1. In

137th Brigade

Gordon Alley to junction with Hulluch Alley-Hulluch Alley to G.10.b.89 and thence to G.5.c.57.

138th Brigade

Bomb Alley and Left Boyau.

2. Out

Both brigades

Central Boyau and Central Trench

3. Evacuation of wounded.

(i) Haywards Heath and Barts Alley (stretcher and walking cases)

(ii) Central Boyau and Central Trench (walking cases only).

After the capture of the enemy's position, Slag Alley, North Face and Corons Alley will, as far as possible, be reserved for IN traffic and South Face and the trenches between the Dump and the village for OUT traffic.

Dress and Equipment

7   Troops will carry greatcoats and waterproof sheets in the attack, but not packs. All men in the front trenches must have their smoke helmets on before the gas cylinders are opened at 1pm. The assaulting troops will wear a smoke helmet (old pattern) and carry a tube helmet in addition. The smoke helmet will be worn on the head tucked in at the back of the neck in such a manner that it can easily be pulled down and adjusted on encountering gas. Every man will carry 220 rounds of ammunition (Grenadiers 100 rounds), his iron ration and 2 empty sandbags. One Vermorel Sprayer per Company will be carried forward, and, if possible, four gallons of solution in addition.

Depots
8   Depots of grenades and engineer material and food will be formed as detailed in Appendix C.

Communication
9   Every endeavour will be made to maintain communication with Battalion and Brigade Headquarters by carrying forward telephones and wire with the attack and by running. In addition, the OC Divisional Signal Company will arrange for visual signalling to be established from south of the Dump to a suitable point or points in our present system of trenches, informing all concerned as to the arrangements made.

Prisoners Of War
10   Prisoners of War will be immediately disarmed and then collected in batches of 50 to 150 and passed back by units to the road junction G.2.d.60 north-east of Vermelles, whence they will be forwarded under escort of the Yorkshire Hussars to Divisional Headquarters. officers and if possible, NCOs must be kept separate from their men. Escorts for prisoners should be on the following scale:

   For 50 prisoners 10 NCOs and men

   For 100 prisoners 15 NCOs and men

   For 150 prisoners 20 NCOs and men.

   Prisoners should be collected and sent back in as large parties as possible in order to economise escorts. Infantry escorts before returning from Vermelles to their battalions, will report to their Brigade Headquarters in case they may be required to carry up stores, water, etc.

Medical
11   A Collecting Station will be established at Barts G.3.c.66, to which all wounded will be taken or directed if able to walk. From here wounded will be taken to an Advanced Dressing Station at the Chateau, Vermelles, G.8.c.38, whence they will be evacuated by Motor Ambulance.

Carrying Party
12   The CRA will arrange for a carrying party of 5 officers and 250 men to be at the Advanced RE Park, The Brewery, Vermelles at 5pm the day of attack.

Headquarters

13   Advanced Divisional Headquarters will be at house in Sailly Labourse on the main Béthune-Loos road in L.3.b.

P. Game Lieutenant-Colonel, G.S. 46th Division.

In essence, these orders produce the almost obligatory two-up brigade attack with one in reserve. The two leading units were the 137th and 138th brigades, with the 139th in reserve. The day after the Divisional Order was issued the Brigade Orders were issued and here is the one for the 137th Brigade:

Operational Orders No 22.
By
Brigadier E Feetham CB, Commanding
137th Infantry Brigade.

11.10.15

1   These orders are issued with reference to 46th Divisional Operational Order No 20, 6 copies of which have been issued to each Battalion. Map references are the same.

2   Paras. 1,2,3 and 4 (i) require no amplification. As regards 4(ii) the Brigade will advance without checking on to the second objective: it will only cease its advance at the first objective if it is found impossible to reach the second. The advance will be in four lines:

The 5th and 6th South Staffs Regiment with their left directed on the centre of the Dump will assault the right portion of the objective allotted to the Brigade; The 5th and 6th North Staffs Regiment with their right directed on the centre of the Dump will assault the left portion of the objective allotted to the Brigade.

The two companies of the 5th North Staffs Regiment detailed for the first line will advance at 2.5pm having previously under cover of the bombardment, left their trench and passed through the remains of the wire in front of them; the two companies of the 5th South Staffs Regiment detailed for the first line will similarly get through the wire in front of their trench and advance in line with the two companies of the 5th North Staffs Regiment as they come level with them; the two companies of the 5th South Staffs Regiment and the 5th North taffs Regiment detailed for the second line will advance 50 paces in rear of the first line.

The following bombing parties will follow the second line and will bomb trenches as follows, care being taken that any of the enemy secreted in dugouts are bombed:

I. 6th South Staffs Regiment - Slag Alley

II. 6th South Staffs Regiment - Dump Trench from 5.A.6.0 in a north-westerly direction

III. 5th South Staffs Regiment - Fosse Alley to the south-east from G.5.c.39.

IV. 5th South Staffs Regiment - Trench running from Three Cabarets from G.5.c.39.

V. 6th North Staffs Regiment - Big Willie starting 2pm

VI. 6th North Staffs Regiment - Trench running north from 5.A.6.0.

VII. 5th North Staffs Regiment - Dugouts, if any, on the Dump

VIII. 5th North Staffs Regiment - Trench running from G.5.a.53 to the Pentagon.

Numbers VI and VIII bombing parties will then bomb up trench running from Pentagon to Coron de Pekin. The two companies of the 6th South Staffs Regiment and the 6th North Staffs Regiment detailed for the third line will follow the second line at 200 paces distance, and will carry shovels, picks and sandbags; the shovels, picks and sandbags are being arranged in loads, and must be drawn from the Brigade RE Dump early on the morning of the 13th; loose shovels and picks are also being placed in the Assembly trench of the third line, and as many as possible must be carried up.

The fourth line will at once follow the third line and occupy Dump Trench on the frontage allotted to the Brigade. They will carry up to it SAA and all available trench stores and bombs left in the Assembly Trenches of the Brigade, and will send up parties with wire, pickets and sandbags for the consolidation of the line forming the objective of the Brigade.

All officers must take compass bearings of the line of their advance in case the Dump should be obscured by smoke at the moment of their advance.

3   Reference para.6, the allotment of communication trenches comes into force after the relief is complete on the night 12th/13th.

4   Reference para. C and Appendix C, the Brigade RE Trench Dump is about G.10.b.49 not G.10.b.89; additional wire-cutters can be drawn there.

5   Reference Appendix B, para.1, officers commanding battalions will arrange for orders to light up the smoke arrangements to be conveyed to the men of the Guards in charge of them by their own Battalion officers; the smoke will not be made if the wind is unfavourable.

Reference para.2 of Appendix B, the officers of the 139th Brigade in charge of the 139th Brigade Bombers will arrange for parties of bombers to carry up the fumite and lachrymatory grenades, if they are received, behind the third line, and for them to be thrown as necessary during the consolidation. Two 4" mortars will also be available for this purpose, the personnel being found by the RA.

6   All SAA boxes in the Assembly Trenches must be placed in conspicuous positions near, but not actually in the communication trenches.

7   The 6th Battalion Sherwood Foresters will come under the command of GOC 137th Brigade at 12 noon on the 13th inst. The Battalion will be located in the following trenches:

(a) Trench from Junction Keep to Central Keep exclusive.

(b) The trench from G.9.b.82 to G.9.b.79.

(c) The trench from G.10.a.79 to G.4.c.23.

The OC Number 2 Section 46th Divisional Signal Company will arrange for telephonic communication with Headquarters, 137th Infantry Brigade.

8   One Section of 2nd Field Company RE will follow the third line of the Right Attack, and one Section the third line of the Left Attack. Their first duty will be to block trenches leading to the enemy after they have been cleared by the bombers, and secondly, to assist in the consolidation of the position by wiring.

9   The Brigade Machine Gun Officer will arrange to send up eight machine guns to cover the consolidation of the line forming the objective; they will follow the third line and take advantage of the enemy's trenches where necessary and possible; the remaining eight guns will remain with fourth line, until required elsewhere.

10   The position of Brigade Headquarters will be at G.3.5.3, and officers Commanding battalions must make every endeavour to get reports sent back by telephone or runners, who should be lightly equipped; the extreme importance of timing messages must not be forgotten.

R Abadie, Major.
Brigade Major 137th Infantry Brigade.

This then gives a flavour of the tasks expected from the North Midlanders on the afternoon of the 13th October. The 138th Brigade was given the job of crossing the Hohenzollern Redoubt and taking up a line beyond the Corons north of the Dump. It was therefore intended not to attack the Dump directly but hopefully bypass it so it could be mopped up later. The gas and smoke cloud, although turned on at the correct time, seemed to have little effect on the Germans. It did not affect the level of resistance as hoped, and probably only gave the Germans warning that an attack was imminent. It is recorded that the British barrage was ineffective and the German positions in Big Willie and Little Willie were almost untouched. To make matters worse the Germans then brought down a very effective barrage on the trenches where the massed ranks of the 46th Division were waiting to go over the top. It is reported that the CO of the 6th South Staffs, Lieutenant-Colonel F. Law, sent back a message advising that to him any forward movement would be futile due to the most effective German fire. The reply came back that the attack would go in at Zero Hour. So when the whistles were blown the troops left the trenches and ventured out into No Man's Land. Almost immediately they came under heavy small arms fire and began to suffer heavy losses. This fire seemed to come from a number of machine gun positions near the foot of the Dump, and the south-east and south-west sides of the Corons. Fire also came from Little Willie and Dump Trench. One of the leading battalions, the 5th North Staffs who were tasked with rushing Big Willie, lost 20 officers (including the CO, Lieutenant-Colonel J. Knight) and 485 men in the first few minutes of the attack. Knight was 50 years old and had been a volunteer since 1883. Sadly he has no known grave and is commemorated on the Loos Memorial to the Missing. Here is an account from a member of 5th North Staffs Private J. Barlow:

> About five minutes before we charged, they opened up a murderous machine gun fire, simply sweeping our parapets. It was a mystery to us, but still we knew we had to face it in a few minutes. Just then the officers sent the word along that we must buck up, and that they were proud of us, and bid us a last farewell. We raised a cheer, and sent word back that we were proud of them, and trusted them, and would follow them anywhere. Watches were out. Two o'clock - five more minutes to go. Our sleepiness began to shake off. We felt at our bayonets, and put our smoke helmets on. Four minutes to go-three-two- "God help us"- one; "Up, lads and at 'em."
>
> Up we scrambled, bullets whistling past our ears like hailstones. Off we started. The lad on my left dropped all in a heap, without a murmur. About five more paces, the lad on my right dropped. Then they dropped all round me in twos and threes. I wondered when my turn would come, and what it would feel like when it did come. I had not long to wait. I had gone about 50 yards when bang; I got it in the leg. Just throwing my arms up in the air - bang! Copped it again in the right upper arm. Down I go. That was about seven minutes past two. A few yards away lay seven or eight pals, some dead, some dying, some gone delirious.

Private Barlow lay for several hours out in No Man's Land until he felt it safe to try and return to the British trenches, which he did safely and was put into the casualty evacuation chain, ending up with a 'Blighty one'.

It is also reported that of the two companies of the 5th South Staffs who tried to join in the attack and get forward, all who went over the parapet became casualties. Not a very encouraging start to say the least, and when the half-battalion sized groups from the remainder of the 137th Brigade (6th South Staffs and 6th North Staffs), supported by the Brigade RE unit, the 2nd North Midland Field Company RE, attempted to get across to Big Willie they suffered the same as everybody else. The 6th North Staffs War Diary has this comment about the leading wave of two companies:

> Under a very heavy rifle and machine gun fire from the enemy, which accounted for the large number of casualties in the first 200 yards of the advance. Apparently there were no company officers left with the leading two companies and the men got grouped together and suffered heavily in consequence, particularly on the left.

Someone saw sense and stopped any other troops going forward. All in all it was a very confused situation and the CO of the 6th South Staffs reported that around 3.00pm he saw signalling from the Dump asking for more bombs and small arms ammunition and later still calling for reinforcements. The only success was when an attempt was made to bomb westwards along Big Willie in the hope of joining up with the 138th Brigade and a few yards of trench were secured but that was all. The attack by the 137th Brigade virtually ended where it began.

Here are some comments from the 6th South Staffs about this attack:

As soon as the extended lines of infantry began the advance their position became clear. The enemy on the left were able to direct an enfilade fire at close range upon our men, who, advancing slowly over open ground, presented an easy target. But still the advance continued, and in orderly formation but with sadly depleted ranks the survivors arrived at their first objective, only to find that the troops whom they were supporting had been unable to make any ground owing to the breakdown of the attack on the left.

It was but the remnants of a battalion which reached Point 57 at the top of Hulluch Alley, there joining the 5th South Staffords, who had themselves suffered considerable casualties in attempting to advance on their objective. But the day's work was not yet finished, for a bombing duel was taking place where the British trenches merged with the German, and Sergeant Bratt particularly distinguished himself by leading his team gallantly and efficiently for hours on end. Other parties worked to the right flank, where a gap existed, and established communication with the adjoining Division.

This is Lieutenant-Colonel Law's report to the GOC:

At 12 noon on 13th October my Battalion was distributed in Assembly Trenches, and all RE tools and material had been served out to the third line. When our bombardment began, the enemy commenced to crump the Assembly Trenches, doing little harm. At 1.30pm I heard the enemy machine guns ranging on these same trenches for five minutes. This I reported to Brigade Headquarters, saying that I believed the fire came from the direction of the Dump. At 1.45pm they started again. I reported this, saying that more machine guns seemed to be firing, and that their fire came from the South Face trench and rear of it.

The third line moved up, in accordance with orders, and suffered heavy casualties before reaching the front trenches held by the 5th South Staffords. No information was received by me that the 5th South Staffords had not left their trenches, and, the smoke obscuring the trench, the fourth line moved up to the old British front line trench. I observed signalling from the Dump for more bombs and SAA; also later for reinforcements. At the time I took the signals to be from our advanced bombing line but I could not convince myself that they could have arrived there.

After that, all men that could be collected were pushed up into the fire trenches, which at that time were very thin in places. About a dozen men were kept back for passing bombs up the communication trenches, which had become badly blocked with wounded. The remaining signallers were sent to work the telephone of the 5th South and 6th North stations, and all remained in this position until we were ordered to withdraw from the line.

Some days later the *Staffordshire Sentinel* published the following account about the 5th North Staffs attack:

With the battle-cry of "Potters for ever!" and "Now, the Potters!" the advance started. With an amazing *sang-froid* they pushed ahead under the Colonel's leadership. With grim intent they pressed on. Men were continually falling. Before they had gone far a merciless and murderous machine gun fire started. From right and left there was a leaden hail from the quick firers, from the front there was a persistent and steady fusillade of bullets and shells. From every point there was fire. Men were falling in scores, and the destruction became heavier as they advanced. Men dropped, and mingled with the bodies of Scottish soldiers, who had been killed in the previous attacks. Even the fallen had their encouraging word to shout, "Carry on boys, I've got one."- "Good luck! I'm done."

Their spirit was indomitable. The thin khaki line became terribly attenuated, and by the time they were approaching their objective they had lost the Colonel and most of their officers. Men struggled on, but they were not sufficient to complete their mission, and they dropped into an empty trench. How even this small body came through the devastating fire is a miracle to them. There is not a single man but can tell of hairbreadth escapes. Bullet-torn clothes and equipment were the experiences of everyone. Beyond the trenches is dead ground, churned up earth of shell holes and mine craters where life cannot exist. Bullets and shells come over unceasingly, and men who in their agony raised themselves even the slightest were stricken again. There is no more noble epic of self-sacrifice than Lieutenant Mayer's heroic death. He was shot in the leg and fell, but the cries of a wounded man for water came to him. He crawled to the wounded man to give him a drink from his water bottle. As he raised the man's head in his arm he was struck again by a bullet in the head, and killed instantly. Later he was found, his outstretched arm still holding the water bottle. Another man's unselfish devotion to his officer should be recorded. Captain Ridgway fell grievously wounded, and he lay in the open exposed to the bullets, and unable to help himself. His orderly, Private Fielding, never left him. Facing, without heed of his own safety, the danger of exposing himself, he dug his Captain in, and made him comparatively safe. He then brought his Captain a drink, and then went and fetched a stretcher bearer. Captain Ridgway was brought in, but died of his wounds. Deeds of bravery and heroism were done in a hundred places, and there were many thrilling escapes. Captain Wenger found half-a-dozen bullet holes through his mackintosh, which was slung on his back, and two through his trousers. Captain Worthington had a Bible in his breast pocket, and in the enfilade fire a bullet went through it lengthwise without touching him. One man had his cap and boot heel blown off, and near him was another man saved by the wire ring in his cap.

There have been many such advances during the War, when the attack has had no chance. The men of North Staffordshire showed that that they could "do and die" like others, as their casualties proved. As given by the Divisional Report, these comprised 19 officers and 488 men. Colonel J.H. Knight was killed though there was a mystery as to how he died. There were also killed the Adjutant, Captain J.H. Fleming; Captain H.A. Ridgway, commanding D Company, Captain R.T. Johnson, commanding B Company; and Lieutenants O.W. Boddington, N. Bishop, C.A. Lowndes, H.R.G. Davies, P. Mellor and F.B. Meyer; and nine other officers were wounded. Over 700 men and officers went in to the attack, and over 500 were killed or wounded. These figures alone will show that the 5th North Staffs had not faltered, and that they had gone on until they dropped. Those who saw the advance have expressed their admiration. Men of the Guards were full of approval, and war correspondents have stated that "the advance was magnificent." Major-General Stuart-Wortley, North Midland Divisional commander, said that "the Division had behaved with distinguished gallantry, worthy of the best traditions of the British Army."

There has been much criticism on this attack. It is known now that the bombardment had been ineffective, and that the Germans were ready with their machine guns to sweep the line of advance. The gas attack, too, had failed, and no troops could have succeeded in the task. But there has never been a word of criticism of the behaviour of the officers and men. That was simply sublime.

There is a similar comment from the 5th South Staffords about the 13th October:

Number 7 Platoon on the right of B Company left the trench to form up on the parapet for the assault and was followed by Numbers 8 and 6. Captain Miller, commanding the Company, the Platoon officers of Numbers 7 and 8 and most of Number 7 Platoon were almost immediately hit by enfilade machine gun fire from the left, and the rest of the Company was withdrawn into the trench to await the arrival of the 5th North Staffs Regiment.

Having received no message that our front line had been unable to advance and not being able to see their positions for smoke, the two companies forming the third line followed the second line and suffered very heavy casualties - 18 of all ranks from A Company and 53 from C Company survived. Their fourth line, which was meant to help consolidate the positions taken, was weighed down with picks, shovels and defence stores followed a few minutes later. They had no idea that their comrades attack had failed so badly and they too took numerous casualties.

The attack was called off but as usual it was not long before the Germans launched a counter-attack and this is what was recorded in the 5th South Staffs War Diary:

A number of Germans in the South Face Trench got out of their trench and attempted to cross to Big Willie but were driven back with loss by rapid fire from Number 10 Platoon. The German bomb attack came over the second barrier into the space between the two barriers and was there engaged by our bombers who drove the enemy back again beyond the second barrier, 8696 Sergeant J Beard and 7952 Private W Barnes doing good work with the bayonet. At this point our men came under bomb fire from three directions, right, front and half left, and were forced to retire to the first barrier.

The attack was eventually driven back and the Territorials were able to draw breath and lick their wounds, as it had been a tough day.

The attempt by the 138th Brigade was made with the 4th Leicestershires and 5th Lincolnshires in the leading wave, supported by the 4th Lincolnshires and the 1st Monmouthshires with the 1st North Midland Field Company RE attached. You may wonder what these Welshmen were doing here. They were the Divisional Pioneer Battalion, thrown in to make up the numbers as the other unit of the 138th Brigade, the 5th Leicestershires, were in Divisional reserve. The attack by this Brigade had slightly better odds as they had a shorter distance to rush than the 137th Brigade. They were ordered to go in at Zero plus 5 by Divisional Order. This was so that its flanks would be covered. It reached the area of the Hohenzollern Redoubt with (in theory) fewer losses than its sister brigade. They pressed on towards Fosse Trench and heavy casualties started to be taken from small arms fire from German positions in the Corons and Mad Point. In spite of the losses Fosse Trench was reached and small groups are reported to have got even further and entered the Corons. But the success could not be maintained due to the fact that Fosse Trench was under enfilade fire from the Dump and Mad Point causing heavy losses. It is recorded that the three COs of the 4th Leicesters and 4th and 5th Lincolns were wounded. It was clear the position was untenable and over the rest of the afternoon, particularly once darkness had fallen, the battered survivors drifted back to the area of the Hohenzollern Redoubt, where the 1st Monmouths were holding the line. It was clear that in spite of all efforts the Hohenzollern Redoubt was still a tough nut to crack and was probably the most disputed piece of territory in the Loos sector, with Hill 70 coming a close second.

Meanwhile the reserve brigade, the 139th Brigade, moved up into the front line to replace the men from the two brigades that had gone over the top. At the request of the Brigade commander from the 138th Brigade (Brigadier G. Kemp) two companies of the 7th Sherwood Foresters were sent forward as reinforcements to this unit. It is reported that these two companies reached the northern part of the Hohenzollern Redoubt but were unable to maintain this position. For the next few hours there was a lot of confused fighting in the Redoubt area, which to my mind was very similar to the difficulties associated with the street fighting at Stalingrad and Arnhem. It is unclear what happened here, except that the Germans with their superior bombs held the advantage, as this was a key weapon in this enclosed form of trench fighting. After dark on the night of 13th October it was decided to evacuate the eastern face of the Hohenzollern Redoubt and dig a new position behind it, which became known as 'The Chord.' This trench, being dug by the 46th Division's pioneers the 1st Monmouths, and elements of the four Sherwood Forester battalions from the 139th Brigade (5th, 6th, 7th and 8th), were sent forward to consolidate this new position.

This was not the end of the fighting in the Hohenzollern Redoubt area but before considering this further, just a word or two about the 2nd Division who put in a limited attack to the north of the 46th Division. Here a bombing party drawn from men of the 5th Brigade led the attack. The orders for the 2nd Division were:

To form a gas and smoke curtain from its trenches at 1.00pm; to form a smoke barrage on Mad Point with trench mortars; to open machine gun fire on the opposing trenches, and finally to carry out a bomb attack at 2.00pm up New Trench to cooperate with the bombing parties of the 46th Division.

The following is a comment from the War Diary of the 6th Sherwood Foresters about the 13th October 1915:

46th Division attacked German trenches on a line from Dump Trench to north of Hohenzollern Redoubt - 137th Brigade on right, 138th Brigade on left, 139th Brigade in reserve. At 12 noon Battalion came under orders of 137th Brigade to which it was in immediate support. Artillery opened at noon - gas attack at 1.00pm. Infantry attacked at 2.00pm, A Company moved to first line trenches. B and D ordered to push on to Dump supporting South staffords but Major Blackwall found attack unsuccessful and kept them in trenches. All companies eventually in front line and immediate support trenches. Great congestion in trenches owing to evacuation of wounded and carriage of SAA and bombs.

New Trench was of course the trench dug from the British lines due east up to the centre of Little Willie. Mad Point was a small salient jutting out from the German lines just north of Little Willie. The 1st Queens and 9th Highland Light Infantry from the 5th Brigade were nominated to carry out this attack together with the Brigade Bombing Party. The 9th Highland LI was positioned on the left with the 1st Queens on the right. The plan in more detail called for the bombing of New Trench and capturing the junction of this trench with Little Willie, then to turn right (southwards) in Little Willie and join hands with the 138th Brigade coming up northwards from the Hohenzollern Redoubt; also to turn left (northwards) up Little Willie to the junction of this trench with Fosse Trench. After this to bomb eastwards along Fosse Trench until contact was made with a bombing attack completed by the 46th Division coming from a south-easterly direction. The discharge of the gas and smoke cloud started at 1.00pm but again this had no effect on the Germans except to warn them of an imminent attack. Then just before 2.00pm another smoke screen was released from an advanced sap in New Trench. Promptly at 2.00pm the Brigade Bombing Party led by Second Lieutenant Ramsey from the 2nd Ox and Bucks LI moved forward up New Trench followed by supporting

Present day view of the Hohenzollern Redoubt area. (Peter Boalch)

troops from the 1st Queens. Immediately the first party left the sap head, it came under heavy small arms fire from virtually three sides and the party was all but wiped out. The second party led by Lieutenant A. Abercrombie from the 1st Queen's had slightly better luck, in that he and only one other man succeeded in reaching the junction of Little Willie and New Trench. After a while, waiting for reinforcements that never arrived, Abercrombie sent the soldier back with a message asking for reinforcements. This man was wounded and the message was either not received or acted upon. In spite of being on his own Lieutenant Abercrombie decided to 'go for a walk' up Little Willie and after using up all his bombs and destroying a machine gun, he returned unscathed to the Queen's positions (in their original lines) and reported in. Lieutenant Abercrombie was aged 19, and had a sad end as he died on 31st December 1918 in a military hospital in the Guildford area, obviously after the war had ended. By then he was a Captain and had been awarded a DSO and MC all by the age of 22. It seems the 9th Highland LI did not even leave their trenches; the Queen's had 2 officers killed and 62 men either killed, wounded or missing. A further attack was planned for midnight on the 13th/14th October which did not actually take place until 4.00am and then failed due to insufficient preparation and a shortage of bombs.

Back on the 46th Division front the Germans started an artillery barrage on the area when they discovered the new situation. At 4.00am on the morning of the 14th they launched a counter-attack but it was beaten back by some stout defence by the 7th and 8th Sherwood Foresters. The fighting continued on and off for several hours and during this time an officer from the 7th Sherwood Foresters gained the last Victoria Cross of Loos. Captain C. Vickers was in command of D Company, who had been in the front line acting as supporting troops for the attack on 13th October on the Hohenzollern Redoubt by 138th Brigade. They remained in the trenches that night and on the following afternoon Captain Vickers and around 50 of his men were sent forward to the Redoubt area to relieve exhausted men from their own Battalion positioned in Little Willie. This was successfully carried out and Vickers took control of the fighting at a barricade at the north-west end of the Redoubt. Again the marked inferiority of the British bombs (and the shortage of them) put the defenders in a difficult position, so that after a while there were only three men left from the original party at the barricade. These three men including Captain Vickers held the barricade for several hours against repeated German bombing attacks. Whilst this small group were holding the Germans back, Vickers ordered a second barrier to be built about 30 yards behind his position. This decision effectively cut him off from any support but his valiant defence enabled the few surviving members from his original party of 50 to complete the building of the second barricade. He manned the advanced barricade on his own for a considerable time before withdrawing to the new barricade when the Germans blew the other one up. During his time at the advanced position Captain Vickers was wounded on several occasions. His bravery at the advanced outpost was recognised with the award of a Victoria Cross, which was announced on 19th November 1915. Part of the citation read "that he was during his occupancy, personally and solely responsible for maintaining a hold on the Hohenzollern Redoubt." Vickers was only 21 years old at his time, his birthday being 13th October, and his wounds were such that he was evacuated back to England for specialist care.

Table 10.1
46th (North Midland) Division casualties, 13th–15th October

	Officers	Men	Total
137th Brigade			
5th North Staffords	20	485	505
6th South Staffords	18	389	407
5th South Staffords	13	306	319
6th North Staffords	17	298	315
Total	68	1478	1546
138th Brigade			
5th Lincolns	22	461	483
4th Leicesters	20	453	473
4th Lincolns	10	387	397
5th Leicesters	12	175	187
Total	64	1476	1540
139th Brigade			
8th Sherwood Foresters	11	159	170
7th Sherwood Foresters	11	140	151
6th Sherwood Foresters	2	58	60
5th Sherwood Foresters	1	48	49
Total	25	405	430
Divisional Troops			
1st Monmouths (Pioneers)	13	147	160
Divisional Troops	10	77	87
Total	23	224	247
Grand Total	180	3583	3763

Table 10.2
Roll call taken by the RSM, 6th South Staffs, morning of 14th October

	Officers	Sergeants	Other Ranks
A	1	2	27
B	1	5	71
C	0	5	63
D	1	4	69
CO	1	0	0
Total	4	16	230
Deficit	18	9	447

He was later passed fit for duty in September 1916 rejoining his former unit and finished the war as a Major and second-in-command of the 1st Lincolns. In the

Second World War he was Deputy Director-General of the Ministry of Economic Warfare and additionally a member of the Joint Intelligence Committee of the Chiefs of staff, dying in 1982.

The action around the Hohenzollern Redoubt continued spasmodically over the next few days and although the CO of the 8th Sherwood Foresters, Lieutenant-Colonel G. Fowler, was killed on the morning of the 15th October, the serious action was over. The 46th Division had been badly mauled and a look at the following table will give an idea of how badly. Most of the losses had occurred in the first few minutes of the attack and the British Official History states: "It was long before

Table 10.3
Brigade strength, 137th Brigade, 16th October

	Officers	Other Ranks	Total
5th South Staffords	11	606	617
6th South Staffords	6	566	572
5th North Staffords	8	447	455
6th North Staffords	9	622	631
Total	34	2241	2375

Table 10.4
137th Brigade casualties for October 1915 (dated 30th October)

	Killed	Wounded	Missing
Officers	22	43	4
Other Ranks	194	927	365
Total	216	970	369

the Division recovered from the effects of the 13th October." The losses in manpower could be replaced but the performance of the Division had far-reaching consequences, which will be discussed later.

Here are a couple of tables contained in post-action reports from the 137th Brigade.

The fighting by the Hohenzollern Redoubt and in the other areas achieved nothing of any material gain except work for the medical services. What few early gains were achieved were quickly lost and to me the main reason seems to be the lack of an effective bomb. The French on the British right still had not attacked, so Hill 70 remained in German hands. IV Corps attacked for no gain and continued to hold a line of trenches west of the Lens road by Chalk Pit Wood to the Vermelles-Hulluch road. In the north I Corps positions remained unchanged from the Vermelles-Auchy road northwards to the La Bassée Canal. In the centre XI Corps had achieved small gains in the areas of Gun Trench, the Quarries and the Hohenzollern Redoubt but these did not really weaken the German hold on the battlefield.

11

Stuttering to a Halt -
October and November 1915

Even before the abortive attack of the 13th October, Sir John French had written to Haig that any actions or plans he made after he had 'secured his left flank' were to depend on the progress made by the French 10th Army. He wrote that as he understood it, the French were stalled unable to make any progress beyond Vimy Ridge and, in this case Haig's Army was not at this moment in time required to reach the objectives given to them in the orders dated 18th September. Just to refresh the reader's memory, these orders stated that the 1st Army was to seize crossings over the Haute Deule Canal and then advance beyond the Canal. How Sir John French thought they would ever get there is, I am afraid, a question that is not easy to answer. Given the small progress over the previous three weeks or so the Haute Deule Canal was about as far away as the moon. Nevertheless he did instruct Haig to continue his efforts to secure key positions that would enable the 1st Army to maintain its presence in the salient that had been pushed into the German lines in the Loos sector. Additionally they were to be ready to make further attacks when ordered, although Sir John French did make it clear that any offensive for any reason was not to be carried out unless personally approved by him.

Then, on 15th October, after Sir John had heard that the French offensive had been halted and the recent British attack had failed, he sent a further letter to Haig. In this he said that he did not now wish the operations of the 1st Army to be carried further than was necessary to secure its left flank against any German attacks from the direction of Haisnes and Auchy. He was further of the opinion that if the left flank could be secured without taking the Dump, Fosse 8 and the Quarries then Haig need not attack these locations again. Haig, in responding, would have none of it. He asserted that he considered that the Dump and Fosse 8 were dominating features, essential to the security of the area. Also, whilst he considered the Quarries of lesser importance he had already directed his staff to come up with new plans to take these three features. It seems that more than suggest plans he had already formulated them and Haig intended to operate using a series of systematic bombing assaults in a bite and hold operation (i.e. with limited objectives). At the same time he was planning the digging of jumping-off and communication trenches with a view to getting as close as possible to the German lines so they could be rushed over a very narrow No Man's Land if the bombing plan failed. The attacks were intended to be assisted by gas and smoke clouds where possible, with diversions planned on a large scale to be carried out by the Indian Corps north of the La Bassée Canal up to and including Neuve Chapelle. Haig suggested that it would take about two weeks for the preparations to be ready for this attack, mainly for the digging of all the necessary new trenches. On the 21st October Sir John replied to Haig confirming that it would be in order for him to go ahead with his proposals. In the meanwhile the Guards Division were ordered to 'keep up the pressure' with a number of bombing attacks on the Hohenzollern Redoubt and Big Willie. These attacks were made with the idea of moving steadily forwards towards Dump Trench, as this trench had been selected as the last position needed before the next big attack. Dump Trench as we can see was opposite the Dump and so would be an ideal jumping off point.

In the early hours of 14th October the commander of XI Corps decided to relieve the two brigades from the 46th Division then positioned in the front line. The 3rd Guards Brigade was therefore nominated to carry out this relief on the night of 14th/15th October. Almost as soon as the Guards were in the trenches they were given the task of capturing and holding Dump and Fosse trenches, and then to form a defensive flank facing north to cover a subsequent advance towards Fosse 8. Although the actual distance to be covered in this proposed assault was not great, it was still a most formidable task. During the 14th October the German artillery supported by mortars had systematically destroyed the remnants of a trench system, which up till that point had been part of the forward positions. Additionally this barrage caused severe damage to the communication trenches. The War Diary of the 1st Coldstream Guards records the following for 15th October:

> The state of the trenches was terrible, unburied bodies lying everywhere, and the parapets and communication trenches blown in on all sides. The trenches allotted to the Battalion were knocked about and we found dead bodies, equipment and debris of all kinds mixed together. Salvage parties worked all day. Just as much damage was done to the communication trenches as to the front line trenches.

Indeed the Brigade commander himself, Brigadier Heyworth, came forward to inspect the area and he advised Major-General Lord Cavan that he felt it was impossible to carry out an offensive operation on a large scale before 17th October. Lord Cavan agreed with this view and reported accordingly to XI Corps HQ.

In light of these considerations and other factors after a conference at the Guards Division HQ on 14th October, it was decided by Lieutenant-General Haking that it was not possible, at the present moment, to carry out all the tasks allocated to the Guards Division in one single operation. It was decided therefore to take a number of preliminary objectives by a series of bombing attacks supported by artillery and trench mortars. The 3rd Guards Brigade on the right were detailed to take the junction of Slag Alley Trench and Dump Trench, also the triangle formed by the southern face of the Hohenzollern Redoubt and the southern part of Dump Trench. The 2nd Guards Brigade on the left were tasked with attacking the northern part of Little Willie and the northern part of the Hohenzollern Redoubt. Both of these brigades were firmly entrenched in the line by the night of 15th/16th October taking over from the weakened brigades of the 46th Division. The 1st Guards Brigade had been left in reserve around Vermelles and Sailly Labourse, with one Battalion on 30 minutes notice to move.

It is reported that during the relief period, German bombers carried out three attacks on the British positions in the western part of the Hohenzollern Redoubt. All of these attacks were driven back by the Guards, but of course they added to the difficulties of the situation. The accurate German artillery fire directed against the communication trenches also greatly hindered the preparations for these planned attacks. The War Diary of one unit present reports: 'It was a very trying night for all ranks.' In spite of these difficulties the attack still went in at the appointed hour of 5.00am on 17th October, supported by a small artillery and trench mortar barrage. On the 3rd Guards Brigade front the 1st Grenadier Guards carried out the attack and 2nd Scots Guards supported by the 4th Grenadier Guards. Further over on the left in the sector of the 2nd Guards Brigade the 1st Coldstream Guards supported by the 3rd Grenadier Guards carried it out. The artillery barrage regretfully had had little effect and it had not seemed to effect the efficiency of the German machine gun fire. This, coupled with the difficult conditions underfoot, made it impossible for the Guards to reach their final objective. Around 8.00am when Major-General Lord Cavan heard of the problems, he issued orders that the attack was to be stopped and to consolidate the ground that had been gained. These small gains were of some tactical value in that they allowed the construction of barricades in the trenches leading west from Dump Trench and this ought to allow it to be easier to sap forward towards the rear of the Hohenzollern Redoubt which by now had been reduced to a mound of earth and broken sandbags. The casualty figure for this three hour attack was over 400 officers and men killed and wounded. It is reported that the two brigades used over 15,000 bombs in the few hours fighting.

It may be of interest to digress slightly here and give a description of the Hohenzollern Redoubt as described post-war by George Coppard, who was in the 6th Queen's of the 12th Division during the Battle of Loos:

The Hohenzollern Redoubt had developed a reputation as one of the worst spots in the whole of the trench system. It was at the extreme left flank of the British attack, though fierce fighting had been going on there a considerable time before the attack began. Our General Staff must have prayed that the Redoubt would be captured in the early stages of the Battle, and thus permit a further broadening of the salient which was to be driven through the enemy lines as far as Lens. But the British, with some assistance from the French, failed to reach Lens. Moreover, the Germans clung tenaciously to the Hohenzollern Redoubt on their right flank, not yielding in spite of repeated assaults against them. The territory of the Redoubt, a mass of pulverised dirt, covered no more than three or four acres, yet thousands fought and died there for months on end. There were times later on in the winter when temporarily at least things were quiet on a good length of the front, but never in the Redoubt. The place consisted of a number of huge mine craters, roughly between the German front line and our own. In some cases the edge of one crater overlapped that of another. The Redoubt was scarcely a planned military work, for it was fortuitously formed by the craters almost fusing both front lines together, so that there was in fact a more or less constant dispute for the possession of No Man's Land.

Because the front line trenches and craters in the Redoubt area were so close together, neither side used artillery. The casualty rate rose rapidly for the first hour after the capture of a crater as alarm spread to neighbouring craters and trenches. Inspired by mutual hate and desperation, the volume of fire from short-range weapons increased, creating an almost impossible demand for stretcher bearers. Crater fighters were considered to have a pretty mean chance of survival, twelve hours being reckoned as the limit a survivor could stand and keep his reason. Before starting a twelve hour shift in a crater, each man had to complete a field postcard for his next of kin, leaving the terse message "I am quite well" undeleted. What use this was I could never understand, for many a poor Tommy was dead within the hour.

According to my dictionary the definition of the word Redoubt is, 'a detached outwork or fieldwork enclosed by a parapet without flanking defences.' If this is correct, then the Hohenzollern Redoubt wasn't a Redoubt at all, for there was no enclosed parapet. A better description for it would be, 'a bloody appendage to a trench sector.' Now that I am considerably older, with time to reflect, I still cannot understand what it was all for, but I have a strong suspicion that it was allowed to develop into a prestige cockpit of no military importance. Neither the Germans nor the British had the courage to say, "Keep your blasted craters. You can have them. We will not waste any more lives uselessly in this way." In spite of the bitterness of the long drawn-out conflict, neither side secured any appreciable advantage over the other.

Meanwhile back on the Guards Division front the very small gains achieved on 17th October finally seemed to have convinced Sir Douglas Haig that it was useless to attempt the recapture of Fosse 8 and the network of defences around the Dump until the Germans had been forced out from their outer positions. Consequently Haig after receiving a report from Lieutenant-General Haking decided to change tactics slightly. This report by Haking suggested the policy of biting off the German defensive trenches by means of constant bombing attacks and persistent sapping. Haking further wrote in his report:

> I am of the opinion that before any further attack is made against Fosse 8 we must establish our line along Dump Trench and Fosse Trench. I think this can best be done by organising bombing attacks; covered by artillery fire carefully concentrated on certain definite points, and made along Dump Trench from the south-east, along South Face and North Face from the south-west, and along Little Willie from the south. An attack of this nature is somewhat slow, but it should be sure, and, with Dump Trench and Fosse Trench in our hands, with a good barrage on Mad Point and Mad Alley, we can arrange a far better assaulting line against Fosse 8 than we have at present.

It was hoped that by means of periodic bombardments of the German trenches round the Fosse and the Dump, their defensive positions and weapons would be destroyed, thus making the capture of these positions somewhat easier, well this was the plan. It probably worked to the soldiers' advantage as it stopped any thoughts of a general attack, it being the intention for the Guards Division to consolidate and reorganise this sector. The main aim was to make the line as straight as possible and as easy as possible for the 12th Division, which was to then relieve them and to carry on with operations for the recapture of Fosse 8.

This task of 'biting off' sections of the German positions in the vicinity of the Hohenzollern Redoubt was no easy one and the Guards had several difficult days to get through. On the evening of the 19th October the 1st Guards Brigade relieved the 3rd Guards Brigade, and on the 21st October, the 2nd Guards Brigade took over a section of trench from the 5th Brigade on their left. During the night of 20th/21st October the 2nd Irish Guards made an attempt to storm the trenches held by the Germans behind the west face of the Hohenzollern Redoubt. Two parties of bombers, from the north and south were used, supported by the Divisional

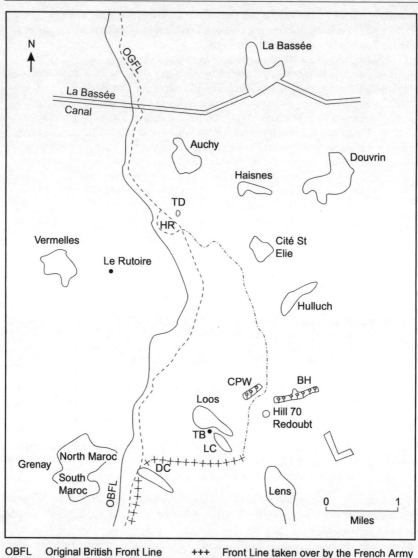

OBFL	Original British Front Line	+++	Front Line taken over by the French Army
OGFL	Original German Front Line	- - -	British Line at the end of the Battle
HR	Hohenzollern Redoubt	TB	Tower Bridge
TD	The Dump	LC	Loos Crassier
CPW	Chalk Pit Wood	DC	Double Crassier
BH	Bois Hugo		

Map 13: Ground gained during the Battle of Loos

artillery firing on Little Willie, North Face and South Face. The 2nd Coldstream Guards were to weigh in with small arms fire from the right flank. The northern group, after twice being beaten back, succeeded in its third attempt to seize the German barricade about 25 yards from their starting point and consolidated themselves there. The southern party, which initially met less resistance made a little more progress but eventually came under attack from three sides and stopped after a gain of about 50 yards. This was about the last action of the Battle of Loos as the Guards tried no more attacks because they seemed to get a lot of attention from the German artillery and bombing parties over the next few days before handing over to the 12th Division on the night of 26th/27th October.

As we have just seen, several days of strenuous effort made by the Guards only led to heavy casualties and no serious progress. Nevertheless Haig continued with his plans and decided on the 7th November as the provisional date for the next big push. But the really bad weather, notably heavy rain and accurate German artillery fire made preparations difficult if not impossible. In the light of this and therefore the possible postponement of the 7th November attack and the forecast of even more bad weather Haig wrote to Sir John French on the 4th November. In this letter he advised that he felt compelled to abandon any hope of continuing the offensive and all orders concerning the attack were cancelled. For the men on the ground this was probably the best news they had had for a long time. It had been a difficult year for the BEF, with four major attacks in the Artois area all initially achieving limited success only for things to go wrong. The same divisions were called on time after time to do more than 'their bit'. However there was a glimmer of light with the appearance of even more 'New Army' divisions over the next few months to perhaps shoulder some of the load.

The Battle of Loos had cost the 1st Army grievously, it is recorded that between 25th September and 16th October they lost 2,013 officers and 48,367 men, a total of 50,380. Of these it is thought that nearly 16,000 of these were killed or missing and were never seen again. According to the British Official History the German looses in the Loos sector between 21st September and 10th October were 441 officers and 19,395 men. The Germans unfortunately used a different method of casualty reporting so it is not possible to accurately compare the figures, but it can be seen that the British suffered about double the German casualties. Interestingly it is reported that of the total German casualty figure less than 5,000 of the total were killed. All in all this was a good result for the Germans.

The following tables may be of interest.

Table 11.1
British 1st Army casualties at the Battle of Loos 1915

	Officers				Men				
	K	W	M	T	K	W	M	T	GT
IV Corps									
15th Div	84	116	28	228	617	3503	2548	6668	6896
1st Div	79	146	21	246	756	3718	1310	5784	6030
47th Div	32	48	2	82	435	1057	256	1748	1830
3rd Cav Div	2	15	0	17	26	106	5	137	154
Total	197	325	51	573	1834	8384	4119	14337	14910

I Corps

	K	W	M	T	K	W	M	T	GT
9th Div	63	100	27	190	798	3037	2033	5868	6058
7th Div	72	129	19	220	622	2664	1718	5004	5224
2nd Div	38	90	18	146	416	1750	1065	3231	3377
28th Div	42	68	21	131	486	1884	864	3234	3365
Total	215	387	85	687	2322	9335	5680	17337	18024

XI Corps

	K	W	M	T	K	W	M	T	GT
24th Div	24	88	75	187	194	1424	2373	3391	4178
21st Div	33	128	37	198	219	2271	1363	3853	4051
46th Div	64	97	19	180	416	1893	1274	3583	3763
12th Div	40	64	10	114	541	2226	458	3225	3339
Guards Div	12	57	5	74	232	1207	602	2041	2115
Total	173	434	146	753	1602	9021	6070	16693	17446

Table 11.2
British casualties suffered during subsidiary attacks, Battle of Loos 1915

	Officers				Men				
	K	W	M	T	K	W	M	T	GT
Indian Corps									
Meerut Div	30	68	39	137	309	1926	778	3013	3150
Lahore Div	5	18	0	23	65	620	8	693	716
19th Div	15	18	0	33	107	409	123	639	672
Total	50	104	39	193	481	2955	909	4345	4538
III Corps									
8th Div	16	28	6	50	157	770	356	1283	1333
20th Div	6	13	0	19	77	311	154	542	561
Total	22	41	6	69	234	1081	510	1825	1894
V Corps									
3rd Div	37	77	21	135	368	2161	420	2949	3084
14th Div	18	29	9	56	213	1127	421	1761	1817
Total	55	106	30	191	581	3288	841	4710	4901
Grand Total	127	251	75	453	1296	7324	2260	10880	11333

Table 11.3
Total British casualties at the Battle of Loos 1915

	Officers				Men				
	K	W	M	T	K	W	M	T	GT
Grand Total	712	1397	357	2466	7054	34064	18129	59247	61713

Key: K - Killed, W – Wounded, M – Missing, T – Total, GT - Grand Total

12

Loos - A Balance Sheet.
Casualties and the Medical Services

So what can we put on the other side of the balance sheet to counter the losses of over 60,000? In material terms the 1st Army captured 53 officers, 3,100 men, 18 artillery pieces and 32 machine guns. For their part in the supporting attacks the French captured 50 officers and 2,100 nen in the Artois, and in Champagne 330 officers and 18,900 men. But again these gains were purchased at a high price, the French suffering around 48,000 casualties in Artois and 144,000 in Champagne. The gain of ground could realistically be measured in yards rather than miles. The BEF had once again proved it was possible to capture parts of the German line but the elusive breakthrough failed to materialise. Perhaps the most unrecognised part of any battle are the actions of the medical services and Loos was no exception, as it was the greatest number of casualties that they had had to deal with in the war so far.

The Royal Army Medical Corps was only a young Corps at the beginning of the Great War. It had been formed in 1898 and received a quick baptism of fire in the Boer War. When units arrived in France with the BEF in 1914, it was to a large extent still relying on practices and procedures learnt in South Africa. After some short sharp lessons in the school of hard knocks it started to evolve and settle down into a casualty treatment regime known as the casualty evacuation chain. For those unfamiliar with this term here is a brief outline of the casualty evacuation chain as it was in 1915. Basically, the chain is a system whereby casualties are moved from the point of wounding rearwards through a number of different units where their condition is assessed, stabilised and their priority for treatment determined. When a major battle is being fought it is essential that the evacuation chain runs smoothly. If any link in the chain breaks, all those units forward of the break will quickly reach saturation point and fill up and be unable to accept new casualties or treat properly those already there.

It must be said that the 'minor actions' during the summer of 1915 did not really create any major difficulties for the medical services. However it was noted that the ambulance train link did not always run smoothly and so the control of these had been simplified by the appointment of an Assistant Director Railway Transport (ADRT) to both a northern and southern line of evacuation, with whom the Director of Medical Services (DMS) of each army was in direct communication, and who was now responsible for bringing ambulance trains to the locations directed to him by the DMS. The DMS was the top man on the ground for an army and held the rank of Surgeon-General. I will talk discuss the roles of all the units in the chain in a moment but first, the casualty evacuation chain.

During the Great War on the Western Front the following chain could be typical for a Tommy wounded in a front line trench. It is also worth bearing in mind that casualties could go up the chain as well as down it.

Casualty Evacuation Chain

Point of Wounding

FEBA/FLOT

⇓

RAP

⇓

Advanced Dressing Station

⇓

Main Dressing Station

⇓

Casualty Clearing Station

⇓

Base/Stationery Hospital

⇓

Hospital Care (Blighty)

After being wounded a man would be moved from the front line, perhaps by stretcher bearers or walking by himself, and with some initial treatment by comrades or even himself he would move to his unit's Regimental Aid Post (RAP) run by the Regimental Medical Officer (RMO). This could be a dugout in a reserve trench or in an abandoned building or bunker. This is where he was first seen by a doctor and RAMC personnel and further initial treatment was prescribed. The role of a RAP was to briefly check a man's condition and dressings, carry out emergency amputations, splint fractures and do everything possible to delay the onset of shock. Apart from this, evacuation to the next link in the chain, usually an Advanced Dressing Station (ADS) would follow.

A stretcher would probably move him to here and his wounds would be inspected before moving to a Main Dressing Station (MDS), where painkillers and hot drinks would probably be given.

Links two and three in the chain were manned by personnel from the field ambulance. This was a unit of about 180 commanded by a Lieutenant-Colonel with about 10 officers. A field ambulance was a very flexible unit as it had sections (3 or 4 each with 20 men), which could form ADSs while the bulk of the unit formed the HQ and MDS. Each infantry division would normally have three field ambulances attached to it and these would be assigned one per brigade. The principal role was to accept wounded and sick from the RAPs, to assess and treat these casualties and evacuate those fit to travel who did not need immediate treatment. The MDS/HQ would have four motor or horse drawn ambulances, whilst the sections would have three. The HQ and sections would be divided into stretcher bearer party (for collection/ movement of the wounded) and the tent party (for the treatment of casualties).

Next in the chain was the Casualty Clearing Station (CCS). Transport to here was done as far as practicable by motor transport, but light railways were also used. The CCS was normally allocated at one per division and usually comprised around 120 officers and men, commanded by a Lieutenant-Colonel, with three chaplains normally attached. In an ideal world a CCS would be situated just out of enemy artillery range, as close to the front line as possible and most importantly of all, enjoy good communications both forward and back.

The name Casualty Clearing Station was adopted in early 1915, up till then they had been known as Clearing Hospitals. During the early part of the Great War at Mons and Le Cateau most of the Clearing Hospitals did not even manage to unload their equipment from the trains that were carrying it. It was not until early 1915 that they became really effective units. Surgeons who had dealt with wounded from the First Battle of Ypres were convinced that facilities were required to enable surgery to take place nearer the front line and so prevent a potentially fatal delay in the treatment of infected wounds. Fortunately the onset of trench warfare meant that the railheads and their associated units, which included the CCSs became static. The CCS's now became virtual 'hospitals' in which the bulk of the surgery on the Western Front was carried out.

A more appropriate title in today's language would be field hospital. However, most CCS's were of semi permanent construction and were able to treat casualties of all types including the most dangerous of injuries such as head and abdominal wounds. In the present day RAMC, such casualties are known as 'Priority One' and the aim would be for them to be operated on within six hours of being wounded. It is worth adding that the CCS was the first place in the evacuation chain where successful surgery could realistically be carried out.

The equipment scale for a CCS amounted to 22 1/3 tons including 31 marquees and 20 bell tents. To move one would require 17 General Service (horse drawn) wagons or 8 3-ton lorries. The space required for a CCS was 205 x 190 yards. However, these figures are assuming an in-patient strength of 200. During the Great War some CCS's had accommodation for 1000 so would need an area almost 1000 x 1000 yards. From the CCS the wounded soldier would be taken (normally) by rail to one of the huge base hospitals, such as those at Etaples, Rouen and Boulogne. A typical ambulance train to hold 350 casualties would contain four or five ward carriages for stretcher cases, four or five carriages for sitting cases, together with carriages converted to sleeping and cooking accommodation for the staff. There were also carriages converted to offices and an operating theatre, stores, dispensary and so on. A typical Base Hospital on the coast would have around 35 wooden huts each able to contain 27 beds, a total of just over 1,000 patients/casualties. More seriously ill patients would be housed in the forerunners of Nissen Huts. The operating theatres and x-ray departments would also be housed in these galvanised iron huts. In times of offensive actions using tents could double the capacity of the Hospital. Around 21 officers and 300 men and women would form the staff.

Finally, should his wounds dictate a trip home to Blighty (hence the term a 'Blighty One', which would ensure a time away from the front line), the soldier would be moved by one of the hospital ships and on to full hospital, specialist care and convalescence in the UK.

This, then, is a brief outline of the casualty evacuation chain. There is just one more small important point to add - that due to the expansion of the British Army there was the obvious need for more commanders and administrative appointments. The difficulties that the infantry faced in finding senior commanders are well known and many medical units in France were forced to give up experienced officers (up the rank of Lieutenant-Colonel) for the same reasons. For the medical services it was to take up command and training of new field ambulances and CCS's, as well as for administrative medical duties and the command of hospitals allocated to the lines of communication. This may have had the effect of putting people in jobs before they were ready for them, and by this I mean having enough experience and seeing how others undertake the role before being thrown in. I suspect that many officers were literally thrown in at the deep end without sufficient training and experience. Although this is only the author's opinion the *Official History of the War: Medical Services General History* Volume II (hereafter known as the *Medical Services Official History*) also alludes to this, albeit in the spin of the times when it was written, using a very careful wording.

It is now appropriate to examine at the medical planning and preparations for the battle.

On the 9th September 1915, Haig gave his DMS Surgeon-General W. MacPherson, full details of the forthcoming operation and discussed with him the medical arrangements. MacPherson, for his part, then flowed the plans down to the top man at corps level (known as Deputy Director Medical Services- DDMS) and then to those at divisional level (known as the Assistant Director Medical Services- ADMS). It fell to these ADMS's to come up with a detailed scheme for clearing the divisional field ambulances to the CCS's, for the evacuation of these by railway, and for the resupply of units with stretchers, blankets and supplies. The plans submitted after the usual amendments were accepted and issued in the form of an operational memorandum for the battle dated 22nd September. Some of these instructions included authority for each field ambulance to hold a reserve of 50 stretchers and a special dump of additional reserve stretchers at each CCS (it is normal for a unit to be resupplied by the unit behind it in the chain so a RAP would be resupplied by a field ambulance, the field ambulance by a CCS etc). Motor ambulance convoys were instructed to carry spare stretchers and blankets on all journeys and hand these over to the field ambulances in exchange for those taken away with the wounded. Should more stretchers be required the field ambulances were told to send a message by one of the motor ambulance convoy vehicles to the CCS they were using, asking for a quantity of stretchers and then the CCS was responsible for sending this number back in the vehicle on the return journey.

At GHQ a reserve of 2,000 stretchers and 4,000 blankets had been stockpiled and were available as required. The ambulance trains were required to automatically bring up 100 stretchers on each trip from the base hospitals to top up the reserve at each CCS. It was incumbent upon the DMS of an Army to access the likely casualty figure for the forthcoming fighting and make sure he had enough resources to cope with the figure. In his planning MacPherson estimated the probable casualties as follows:

> 5,000 in the III Corps
> 7,000 in the Indian Corps
> 12,000 in the I Corps
> 15,000 in the IV Corps

This then gives a total of 39,000 in a battle, which, it was anticipated would last several days. This, of course, means that the medical services must have sufficient resources to cope with this number. The most important link in the chain is usually the CCS as it is where most of the casualties 'back' up. A field ambulance does not have the facilities to keep casualties for any great number of days and when you consider there were three field ambulances to a division but only one CCS it is fairly obvious which unit would see the most casualties. There were 12

Table 12.1
1st Army casualty clearing stations

CCS	Location	Normal Capacity	Expanded Capacity	Total
No 1	Chocques	730	900	1630
No 6	Lillers	484	540	1024
No 9	Lillers	390	570	960
1st W Riding	Lillers	300	530	830
No 7	Merville	433	720	1153
2nd London	Merville	449	547	996
No 18	Lapugnoy	320	372	692
No 23	Lozinghem	200	300	500
Meerut	St Venant	296	710	1006
Lahore	Merville	402	600	1002
No 1 Canadian	Aire	420	500	920
No 22	Aire	302	553	855
Total		4726	6842	11568

CCS's in the 1st Army as below.

This then gave the 1st Army facilities to hold over 11,500 casualties in relatively good conditions and at a place where surgery could be carried out with relative ease on those who needed it. It is reported that this expanded capacity took many shapes. Obviously tents formed a major element of this but it is reported that 23 CCS 'borrowed' two hangars from a nearby RFC airfield and a large wooden structure belonging to a travelling theatrical company and these were all erected in the grounds of the chateau at Lozinghem they were using as a location. However, it was also important for casualties, where necessary, to be moved away from the CCS's and this revolved around the ADRT located at Béthune keeping them busy with incoming trains. As well as the proper ambulance trains, there were also the temporary ambulance trains. These, as the name suggests, were trains brought specifically into service at times of stress to move large numbers (up to 1,000) of lightly wounded. These would have to be sitting cases and most likely walking wounded. The DMS advised the ADRT on 21st September that at least six trains would be required daily. At this time there were sixteen ambulance trains in France and the estimated capacity of these is set out over the page.

This then, in theory, should have given enough capacity to move the estimated number of casualties daily expected at the CCS's. Together with the equipment kept ready at Chocques, Lillers and Merville for equipping three empty supply trains at each of these railheads and by the use of the temporary ambulance trains, it was hoped any congestion in the CCS's would be rapidly eased.

Table 12.2
British ambulance trains in France, September 1915

Ambulance Train	Number With Maximum Lying Down			Number With Maximum Sitting Up		
	Lying	Sitting	Total	Lying	Sitting	Total
No 1	188	77	265	88	461	549
No 2	184	182	366	0	561	561
No 3	215	20	235	135	340	475
No 4	227	74	301	160	267	427
No 5	130	133	263	48	298	346
No 6	144	72	216	35	513	548
No 7	176	134	310	94	401	495
No 8	235	90	325	111	600	711
No 9	144	188	332	72	466	538
No 10	158	284	442	92	516	608
No 11	234	0	234	0	410	410
No 12	220	40	260	0	370	370
No 14	144	256	400	48	448	496
No 15	174	220	394	58	458	516
No 16	152	320	472	48	532	580
No 17	120	210	330	120	280	400

Another vital link in the chain of things were the motor ambulance convoys (MAC). There were 14 of these units in France in September 1915, moving casualties between the field ambulances and the CCS's. The DMS of 1st Army decided to keep these under his own control and allocated each MAC definite areas of responsibility. The CO of each MAC was made responsible for ascertaining, by use of the motorcycles within each MAC, the position and situation of every field ambulance in the area they had been allotted to, and for keeping it clear of wounded. Of the 14 MAC in France just four were in the 1st Army area, these being Nos 2, 7, 8 and 12. The stations to which the ambulance trains were running were Merville, St Venant, Aire, Chocques and Lapugnoy, these being the locations of nearly all the CCS's. One Medical Officer and ten cars from No 2, 7 and 8 MAC were based at Merville, Chocques and Lillers respectively for use at the stations to help loading. Ten cars from No 12 MAC were based at St Venant and Aire for similar duties. The odd one out, No 18 CCS based at Lapugnoy, was actually sited in a railway siding an almost perfect location! Should an ambulance train be brought up to another station than those already mentioned during the battle, the DDMS of the Corps, in whose area the station was situated, was made responsible for controlling the loading of casualties, but instructions were issued stopping loading from field ambulances direct without express permission from the DMS. It was also the theory that at places where there was more than one CCS, the CO of each unit was meant to keep the others informed of the number of lying and sitting cases awaiting evacuation so that the capacity of the incoming ambulance train was not exceeded.

Therefore we have seen that there was in place (on paper at least) a complete plan for bringing the wounded from the point of wounding rearwards and if necessary all the way back to the base hospitals. As well as all the integral resources for transport (each division had in theory 21 motor and 9 horse ambulances), the transport of the CCS's, divisional sanitary sections and the transport of the field ambulance workshop units were also converted to 'ambulances'. These were told to be ready to supplement the MAC and field ambulance transport sections. Finally, there were a few medical barges on the Aire-La Bassée Canal that were going to transport a few of the more seriously wounded.

There was a final innovation that was first used at Loos that would later became standard practice. This was the use of several Advanced Operating Centres (AOC). These were for early surgery on penetrating wounds of the abdomen. Before the outbreak of the Great War medical thinking was that it was best to leave these wounds at rest because of the unfavourable results of operating on them during Boer War. But several surgeons, notably from No 1 CCS and the 2nd London CCS, were saving many lives from early treatment and the DMS of 1st Army had issued orders that men wounded in the abdomen should be sent at once to these CCS's by field ambulance transport without waiting for them to be removed from dressing stations by the MAC. Consequently in the medical plan for Loos these two CCS's were again nominated to receive abdomen casualties but with the additional resource of two AOC, one on the banks of the La Bassée Canal at Bac St Maur and the other near Noeux les Mines. Specialist surgeons, nursing sisters and orderlies, together with specialist equipment, were sent to both these locations. The early treatment proved its worth and early operative treatment of wounds of abdomen became the rule, perhaps one of the few positives from Loos. These then were the arrangements for the rear areas, but I must admit I always find it more interesting to look at the action up at the blunt end with the field ambulances and the RAP's.

Much effort was made to put all the field medical posts in suitable places such that they were protected from German artillery fire. Some facilities were specially constructed but as usual natural features such as cellars were used. Many of the ADS's were connected with the RAP's by communication trenches and where the distance was greater use was made of light railways and trams. As with the actual fighting divisions I will look at the medical support position on the 25th September from north to south, so we start with the 2nd Division in the north around the La Bassée Canal.

2nd Division

This Division had three field ambulances attached to it and these were spread out as follows:

Advanced Dressing Stations

> Harley Street - south of the Canal
>
> Lone Farm - north of the Canal

Collecting Stations for walking wounded

Beuvry for southern area

Le Preol for northern area

Main Dressing Stations

All three field ambulances were located around Béthune

5th Field Ambulance Ecole Maternelle

6th Field Ambulance Seminary St Vaast

19th Field Ambulance Ecole des Jeunes Filles

The ADS's were near the start of the communication trenches and there was also an ADS south of the La Bassée road and Harley Street, but wounded received here were transferred to Harley Street for subsequent evacuation. An overhead mono-rail had been previously constructed to bring stores to the trenches from Harley Street and use of this was made during the fighting to bring back wounded.

9th Division

This Division was positioned facing the Hohenzollern Redoubt and Fosse 8 and it was noticed that a railway line neatly divided the areas for collecting the wounded into a north and south area. Arrangements were made to bring the wounded from the northern area back down a special trench, known as Guy's Alley, which was solely for the use of the medical services. This trench was wide enough for wheeled stretchers. An ADS in dugouts was positioned at the point where the La Bassée-Vermelles road crossed the railway. After the usual checking etc. they were taken to a factory further back where Guy's Alley began. They were then taken by trolleys, of which there were six (each able to hold six casualties) back to the Noyelles-Cambrin road and on to Cambrin. South of the railway line a similar trench, called Bart's Alley, was dug for wounded, which connected with a dressing station known as Bart's where it crossed the La Bassée-Vermelles railway line. The trench was continued from here to the La Bassée-Vermelles road where the wounded were taken by road to an ADS in cellars of the brewery at Vermelles. Additionally there were two divisional collecting stations for walking wounded, one west of Annequin on the Béthune-La Bassée road and the other at the northern end of Sailly Labourse. The remainder of the three field ambulances were positioned in and around Béthune. The 27th and 29th field ambulances were positioned respectively in the Ecole Jules Ferry and the grounds of the French Civil and Military Hospital. The 28th Field Ambulance was at Vendin, west of Béthune. Finally a tent sub-division of 29th Field Ambulance was located here and one from the 27th Field Ambulance at Annezin, ready to act as MDS's in the event of the main unit being shelled out of Béthune and also to act as a supplementary MDS.

7th Division

This formation located its ADS's in Hulluch Alley with a large divisional collecting station in the cellars of the chateau at Vermelles. A trolley line ran to Vermelles from the support trenches. Twenty three trolleys, each capable of taking two stretcher cases or four sitting cases, were used on it, supported by two relay posts for bearers. These were formed along Hulluch Alley for the wounded brought back on stretchers to the ADS at the start of the trench. The MDS's of the field ambulances were located at Gonneheim (21st Field Ambulance) and two at Fouquières (22nd and 23rd Field Ambulances).

1st Division

Perhaps the best way to describe the medical set up here is to look at the following table:

Advanced Bearer Post - Le Rutoire Farm

1st Field Ambulance - 3 officers and 27 men

2nd Field Ambulance - 3 officers and 27 men

Advanced Dressing Stations - Philosophe

1st Field Ambulance tent sub-division

1st Field Ambulance bearer division less detachment at Le Rutoire

2nd Field Ambulance bearer division less detachment at Le Rutoire

Main Dressing Stations

1st Field Ambulance Mine School Bracquemont

2nd Field Ambulance Verquin

141st Field Ambulance Les Charmeux (in reserve and for sick)

In this area the ADMS had specifically asked the CRE to make sure there were enough trench bridges to help the work of the stretcher bearers. It is also important to note that the MDS's were about four miles away from the ADS's at Philosophe, certainly not an ideal distance. The 141st Field Ambulance had only recently arrived in the Division to replace the 3rd Field Ambulance, which had gone to the Guards Division and was in theory acting as a reserve and for the sick. It did however receive a large number of wounded during the battle, owing to the congestion in the MDS's of the other two units.

15th Division

The medical facilities started at Mazingarbe, where an ADS was set up in the abattoir run by 45th Field Ambulance. Other ADS's were located at Quality Street (46th Field Ambulance) and Fosse 7 (47th Field Ambulance). These apparently were large affairs, with the ADS at Mazingarbe being capable of holding more than 200 casualties, the one at Quality Street for 500 and at Fosse 7 nearly 250. There were divisional collecting stations set up at Mazingarbe and Philosophe and the MDS's were located two at Noeux les Mines and one at Vaudricourt. The ADMS had managed to get special communication trenches set aside for the movement of wounded from the RAP's to the ADS's at Quality Street and Fosse 7, then a tramway had been constructed that would take the wounded back to Philosophe and Mazingarbe. From here the movement of casualties was by normal field transport,

Walking wounded in Vermelles returning from the attack on the Hohenzollern Redoubt on the 13th October 1915. (IWM Q 29005)

although GS wagons were available if required. The Division's medical resources were strengthened by the fact that nearly all the men from the 32nd Sanitary Section RAMC volunteered for duty with the field ambulances. This Section's lorry was fitted with seats sufficient for 24 sitting cases and carried many men from the collecting stations to the MDS's.

Advanced Dressing Stations

    45th Field Ambulance Mazingarbe

    46th Field Ambulance Quality Street

    47th Field Ambulance Fosse 7

Divisional Collecting Stations

    45th Field Ambulance Mazingarbe Chateau and Brewery

    46th Field Ambulance Philosophe Brewery

Main Dressing Stations

    45th Field Ambulance Noeux les Mines

    46th Field Ambulance Vaudricourt

    47th Field Ambulance Noeux les Mines

47th Division

The RAP's of this formation were all set up in the cellars of houses along the road and railway running from Grenay towards Loos. Each of these was again a large affair, as it is reported each RAP was able to hold 250 wounded! This Division was somewhat lucky in that the ADS had found space in a well equipped French auxiliary hospital at Les Brebis, about two miles from the RAP's. This was not a problem as there were reasonable roads between the two, and wheeled stretchers and ambulance cars were able to use it with ease. The MDS's were located at Noeux les Mines (4th London Field Ambulance), Houchin (5th London Field Ambulance) and in a school building by the railway crossing at Noeux les Mines (6th London Field Ambulance). Again there were excellent road communications between these places and the ADS, so transport was not a problem.

These then were the divisional medical arrangements, so how did they work on the actual day? Regretfully this is not an easy question to answer. The author served for a number of years in the RAMC and studied the medical services in a number of different conflicts, yet the picture at Loos is unclear. Looking at the Great War after such a time one source of information is the Medical Services Official Histories, and these are quite willing to take criticism of their performance at places such as Gallipoli and the Somme. It is the author's opinion, after research on the Western Front, that it was not until Arras in 1917 that the RAMC can really be said to have got their act together. Yet the *Medical Services Official History* on Loos gives an almost 'sterile' account of the battle as the following few paragraphs show:

As a general result it was found during the battle that the divisional arrangements were so good that the wounded came in more rapidly to the main dressing stations than the motor ambulance convoys could evacuate them to the casualty clearing stations. Consequently, the DMS arranged with the ADRT for ambulance trains and improvised ambulance trains to run to Noeux les Mines and Béthune, for direct evacuation from the field ambulances at these places. Also on the 28th September he sent the 33rd CCS to take over the Seminary St Vaast in Béthune, where 5th and 6th field ambulances had previously been instructed to act as casualty clearing stations for evacuating wounded by train. With few exceptions the scheme for collecting and evacuating the wounded worked well and smoothly.

The clearing of the casualty clearing stations by railway transport worked well, and with the aid of improvised ambulance trains for sitting up cases, more specially for those accumulating in field ambulances at Noeux les Mines and Béthune, and with the road transport to St Omer, there was steady relief of congestion in the casualty clearing stations, and the estimate made before the battle of the requirements of accommodation and means of evacuation proved sufficient.

One point, however was brought out. It was found that the system of sending the severe cases to the most advanced casualty clearing stations and the slighter cases to those further back was inconvenient. Many of the trains could not be fully loaded with lying down cases only and had either to go to other entraining stations to fill up with sitting cases, or go to the base partially filled. Also the number of severe cases in the casualty clearing station receiving them was often more than one ambulance train could take, so that there was a gradual accumulation of these cases at times. It was obvious, therefore, that the best use of casualty clearing stations was to fill them in rotation with both lying down and sitting up cases. The DMS consequently issued orders on the 1st October to the motor ambulance convoys to fill the casualty clearing stations up to 500 each in rotation; and this was the practice in subsequent operations, modified to the extent that the numbers sent in rotation became more and more limited as the surgical work in casualty clearing stations became more and more important and more extended. This method of filling casualty clearing stations also led to a redistribution of the personnel sent to reinforce temporarily the casualty clearing station establishments. Twelve or fourteen medical officers were sent to each of the casualty clearing stations to which wounded were being brought from the area of active fighting, instead of a comparatively larger number to the advanced casualty clearing stations for severe cases and a smaller number to those further back.

The RAMC did take on board these lessons and incorporated them into the medical plan for the next big attack, that on the Somme in 1916. The major problem with that plan was an estimated daily casualty figure of 6,000 - the number on the first day threw the plan out of the window. However that is not to say everything at Loos went smoothly. A major problem that is glossed over is the problems of the MAC on the 25th and 26th September in negotiating the crowded roads. I suspect that the drivers suffered the same problems as the 21st and 24th divisions on these days. There are reports of some casualties taking three days to reach a CCS after being wounded. I think it is unlikely that many were actually in the chain for so long but there are always the stories of men lying wounded in No Man's Land for some time before crawling back to the British lines and entering the chain. So the claim of taking three days may be entirely valid, but this includes time spent outside the chain. It also seems that on the ground relations were strained between the very top men. The Director General Medical Services (the top man), General Sir Arthur Sloggett, visited the battlefield on the 25th September and apparently saw large numbers of lightly wounded waiting at a field ambulance on the main road to Noeux les Mines in Béthune. He decided to do something about this himself and so on the following morning 30 London buses arrived at Noeux les Mines (without the knowledge of the DMS 1st Army), with orders to take all the sitting cases back to the 4th Stationary Hospital at Arques. These moved around 700 but were not really required, as arrangements had been made for a temporary ambulance train with capacity for 1,200 lightly wounded to come to Noeux les Mines. When the train left it was less than half full and led to a strong complaint from the ADRT. Another small but very time consuming incident occurred on the 27th September when someone not involved in the chain (but in a senior staff position with XI Corps), noticed a large number of walking wounded waiting at one of the field ambulances at Noeux les Mines. He ordered them onto an apparently empty but waiting ambulance train. Perhaps he thought the area was looking untidy with these men sitting doing nothing. This train had been specifically brought up for stretcher cases and when they started to arrive, the lightly wounded had to be got off and sent back to where they had come from. But it did cause a delay. It seems there were others who felt that things did go wrong. Here is an account from a nurse working at a base hospital:

When the convoys started to come in, they were very different from any we had seen before. The casualty clearing stations simply couldn't cope and many of the wounded arrived with their first field dressings on. Stretchers were scarce, and it was no uncommon sight to see one wounded man carrying another. There was one man who came to my tents who had a large piece of shrapnel in his side and at least one fractured rib. One of the other men told me that he'd seen that man put on a stretcher three times, and each time he had given it up to someone he thought worse than himself.

We were terribly overworked. One Sister and I had six tents to cope with alone. The orderly was fully occupied with the man's kits when he wasn't carrying the stretchers of the new arrivals. Normally, when a new patient was admitted, the orderly undressed him and took his clothes to be deloused; but in this rush I very often had to see to the undressing of the men myself. Their things, as can be imagined, were in a pretty foul condition, and as all the pockets had to be emptied before they were taken to be deloused, it was almost impossible to avoid the creatures swarming all over you.

For over a fortnight we worked unceasingly, just as hard as we could go. The Sister of my ward handed over to me three of the tents, and told me to carry on with them and appeal to her only if something unusual occurred or if I were in any difficulty. There was no off-duty time for over a fortnight and we slept with one ear open in case the 'Fall In' went, which meant the arrival of a fresh convoy of patients.

After the rush, rather belatedly, in about the middle of October, a new lot of trained nurses were sent to us straight from the Cambridge Hospital in

Dud Corner Cemetery and Memorial to the Missing. Located on the main road between Béthune and Lens, on the crest of the Grenay Ridge on the approximate site of the Lens Road Redoubt. This positioned was attacked by the 9th Black Watch on the morning of 25th September 1915. It contains around 2,000 graves and 20,700 names of those who have no known grave. (Niall Cherry)

Aldershot. They were very smart and grand and critical of our rough and ready ways. One new nurse was horrified to find she would have to keep the linen in packing cases stood on end. 'In the Cambridge,' she said, 'we had wonderful linen cupboards. I never imagined we should have to put up with this sort of thing.' I'm afraid that I was a bit irritated and couldn't resist pointing out that we were, after all, on active service.

There is much evidence to back up this claim that stretchers were in short supply, as the following excerpt from the War Diary of 21st Field Ambulance for the 25th September shows:

Daily State 0600 25th September to 0600 26th September 3,000 wounded admitted. During the night the supply of stretchers ran short - patients were lifted off stretchers, so as to enable the ambulances to run back with their proper supply of four stretchers.

But again this problem is glossed over in the Official History.

The commander of IV Corps visited several medical facilities and kept his thoughts to himself for a few months until he was commanding the 4th Army on the Somme, when he wrote a famous memorandum to the Q branch at GHQ in Montreuil. With the benefit of hindsight, it seems that the RAMC at Loos had no problems and everything went well, at least, according to the Medical Services Official History. Perhaps I am a cynical old medic, but recall the name of the DMS of 1st Army...General Sir W.G. MacPherson, and the name of the compiler of the post war Medical Services Official History? General Sir W.G. MacPherson.

Table 12.3
Casualties by Corps, 25th September to 20th October 1915

I Corps

9th Division	5480
2nd Division	4910
7th Division	2128
28th Division	1030
Total	13548

IV Corps

15th Division	4308
1st Division	3625
47th Division	2340
3rd Cavalry Division	418
Total	10691

XI Corps

Guards Division	2444
12th Division	2423
21st Division	1821

46th Division	1811
24th Division	485
Total	8984

Indian Corps

Meerut Division	1781
19th Division	525
Lahore Division	262
Total	2568

III Corps

8th Division	692
20th Division	514
23rd Division	222
Total	1428

Casualties

The total number wounded in the 1st Army between the 25th September and 20th October was 37,219, a number which was very close to the estimate of 39,000 made before the battle.

The wounded in the III and Indian Corps were suffered in actions at Piètre and Bois Grenier, part of the demonstrations intended to withdraw attention away from the main sector, but nevertheless they still needed treating.

Just to digress a little, the only RAMC Victoria Cross during the period of Loos (and indeed during 1915 on the Western Front) was won by Lieutenant G. Maling on the 25th September. He was attached to the 12th Rifle Brigade of the 60th Brigade, part of the 20th Division. This New Army Division took part in one of the diversionary attacks for Loos on the morning of the 25th September, which later became known as the action of Piètre. The Garhwal and Bareilly brigades from the Meerut Division carried out the main attack here. They were supported (in theory) with covering fire from the units on their flanks. The left hand supporting unit was the 12th Rifle Brigade. They were positioned about 20 yards north-east of Winchester Road, which ran from Fauquissart to Mauquissart. One of the units of the Bareilly Brigade, the 2nd Black Watch, managed to advance as far as the German second line, and so a company from Maling's Battalion moved into the German front line and took over the manning of trench barricades from men of the Black Watch. A German counter-attack within the next hour or so was launched which forced the men of the Rifle Brigade back from their positions. This withdrawal had a knock-on effect and soon the Bareilly Brigade were forced back to their starting point. Many casualties were incurred during this counter-attack, on top of those caused during the initial attack. As the RMO of the Battalion, Maling was busy treating the wounded from early in the morning of the 25th for the next 24 hours or so. His citation, which was gazetted on 18th November, gave some details of his actions:

> For most conspicuous bravery and devotion to duty during the heavy fighting near Fauquissart on 25th September 1915. Lieutenant Maling worked inces-

santly with untiring energy from 6.25am on the 25th until 8.00am on the 26th collecting and treating in the open, under heavy shell fire, more than 300 men. At about 11am on the 25th he was flung down and temporarily stunned by the bursting of a large high explosive shell, which wounded his only assistant and killed several of his patients. A second shell soon covered him and his assistants with debris, but his high courage and zeal never failed him, and he continued his gallant work single-handed.

Maling had been commissioned into the RAMC in January 1915 and went to France with the 12th Rifle Brigade in July of that year. Maling served in the RAMC for the rest of the war in various units ending up in the 34th Field Ambulance in 1918. After leaving the Army he worked at a variety of hospitals and in a general practice before his untimely death at the age of 40 in 1929.

The number of wounded received day by day in the field ambulances of the 1st Army between 9.00am on 25th September and 9.00am on 1st October was

Table 12.4
Admissions into field ambulances and casualty clearing stations, and evacuations, 1st Army, 25th September to 1st October

Date	Admissions into		Evacuations by		
	FA	*CCS*	*Train*	*Road*	*Barge*
25th/26th	13910	7464	1894	0	0
26th/27th	7107	5935	6200	649	0
27th/28th	5348	5389	5107	1364	24
28th/29th	2038	2220	4211	0	89
29th/30th	854	895	3803	0	0
30th/1st	463	412	2258	161	0
Total	29720	22315	23473	2174	113

29,720. Of this number 22,315 were shipped in the same period to the CCS's, and trains evacuated 23,473 to the base hospitals. The apparent discrepancy in these numbers can of course be explained by reasons such as wounded not having to go back to the base hospitals from the CCS's and a number going direct from the

Table 12.5
RAMC casualties, 25th September to 1st October

	Killed	*Wounded*	*Missing*	*Gassed*
Officers	8	18	1	1
Men	16	68	0	9
ASC attached	1	0	0	0

MDS's to the base hospitals. A breakdown of these numbers is as follows:
FA - Field Ambulance, CCS - Casualty Clearing Station

The number of casualties amongst the RAMC was, relatively speaking, not high.

I would like to end this chapter by quoting from a report written by the ADMS of the 15th Division, Colonel G. Rawnsley, which is probably typical of everyone's experiences:

On the morning of the 25th September the infantry assault was preceded at 5.50am by a gas and smoke attack; at 6.30am the infantry stormed the enemy's trenches with the bayonet and casualties very shortly began to arrive at the advanced dressing stations. The process of clearing the field worked well. As the troops advanced the regimental medical establishments followed up, forming new aid posts in more advanced positions; contact was well maintained between these regimental stretcher bearers and those of the bearer divisions of 46th and 47th field ambulances. The wounded unable to walk were conveyed by stretcher carriage to the advanced dressing stations at Fosse 7 and Quality Street. The tramway from the advanced dressing stations worked to the divisional collecting station at Philosophe and by this means the wounded were rapidly evacuated; those able to walk followed in most cases the branch of the tramway to Mazingarbe and were admitted to the rest post and advanced dressing station of 45th Field Ambulance at this place.

From Philosophe brewery evacuation was by 21 motor ambulance cars of the Divisional field ambulances, and the Sanitary Section motor lorry, to the main dressing stations of 45th and 47th field ambulances at Noeux les Mines, and of 46th Field Ambulance at Vaudricourt. The motor ambulance cars also cleared on 25th September Quality Street and Fosse 7 by day, but on the following day, owing to heavy shell fire, they were driven back and were unable to clear from there until the evening. The horse ambulance wagons and general service wagons cleared from the Divisional collecting station and advanced stations at Mazingarbe to all the main dressing stations. On the afternoon of 25th September I sent a bearer sub-division of 46th Field Ambulance under Lieutenant J. Turner to Loos to endeavour to bring in wounded from there. He went forward collecting them, but his party was subjected to shell fire and was also gassed by asphyxiating shells. This officer was subsequently wounded and admitted to a field ambulance.

On Sunday 26th September, I ordered C Section 45th Field Ambulance to proceed to Loos and there open a dressing station. The Section opened one in a house on the main Béthune-Lens road 1,000 yards south-west of Loos and collected wounded until Monday at noon 27th September, when they were shelled out of it. The officer in charge, Captain H. Friedlander, was badly gassed but had all his wounded removed by stretcher carriage to Quality Street. He remained behind and endeavoured under heavy shell fire to put his horses in the

Table 12.6
Admissions as given by Colonel G. Rawnsley (ADMS, 15th Division), 21st–28th September

21st September 1915 to 6am 25th September 1915	66
6am to noon 25th September 1915	153

Noon 25th September to noon 26th September 1915	2434
Noon 26th September to noon 27th September 1915	1662
Noon 27th September to noon 28th September 1915	448
Total	4763

vehicles and bring them away. Several horses were killed and others stampeded, and the equipment was left. He showed very great gallantry on this occasion.

The casualties in the Division during the course of the operations were enormous. I think I am correct in saying that they exceeded those on any previous occasion during the war. The figures speak for themselves. The admissions were as follows:

Some of the above casualties were amongst men of other divisions, but none the less the work entailed by the field ambulance was the same. The total number of these was 889. The total of casualties of the 15th Division reported as admitted into other Divisional field ambulances was 423. The total of the 15th Division casualties accounted for was thus the large number of 4,297 of all ranks.

With the exception of about 100 cases, all the casualties admitted to our field ambulances, which meant about 4,600 cases had been collected, their wounds dressed and all ranks fed and housed by Sunday, 26th September, at midnight. It was obviously impossible to accommodate such large numbers in the field ambulances, so the difficulty was overcome by billeting the lighter cases, which entailed much extra work for the medical establishments. Owing to the blocking of the roads by troops, the motor ambulance convoy was unable to clear sufficiently to do very much to ease the pressure on the field ambulances until the evening of the 27th September. The task, therefore, of maintaining and redressing the wounded had thus to be continued until Monday, 27th September. The work of clearing the battlefield of wounded had been done so rapidly and well that on the morning of the 27th I was able to place at the disposal of the DMS 1st Army, 14 motor ambulances to assist the motor ambulance convoys in evacuating wounded. Evacuation by the 8th MAC from the 27th was rapid, and by the 29th all cases had been sent to casualty clearing stations except 48 mild gas cases, which remained in 46th Field Ambulance on 30th September. The scheme for removing the wounded worked admirably, and it is entirely due to the zeal and devotion to duty of all ranks, both of the regimental medical and field ambulance establishments, that such splendid results were obtained, and the battlefield was cleared of 4,600 casualties by Sunday night. All ranks worked day and night for three days. In conclusion I should like to place on record the heroism displayed by the wounded which lightened the task of those who had to minister to them. No murmur or groan was heard amongst this vast assembly of stricken heroes, many with grievous wounds, joking and making light of them, and cheering up their wounded comrades. It was an honour appreciated by all ranks of the medical service to serve such men. In closing this report I wish to place on record the courageous and devoted services rendered to the British Army by Mademoiselle Emilienne Moreau, the particulars of which were furnished to me by Captain F. Bearn, officer in medical charge 9th Black Watch. This girl, who is only 17½ years old, was living with another woman in a shop at Loos in the Church Square. These premises were taken as Regimental Aid Post by Captain Bearn and these two women spent the whole day and night (25th/26th September) in helping to carry in the wounded and carry out the dead, also preparing food and coffee for all, refusing payment. This work was done continuously for twenty four hours. When the British troops were making ineffective efforts to dislodge two German snipers from the next house, who were firing on the stretcher bearers, this young girl seized a revolver from an Officer and went into the back of the house and fired two shots at the snipers. She came back saying "C'est fini," and handed the revolver back to the Officer. It is uncertain if the two shots actually killed the men but the diversion in the rear enabled our men to effect an entrance in front. Captain Bearn states: "I saw many examples of cool courage that day, but none that excelled hers."

13

The demise of Sir John French
and other repercussions

In the days and weeks after the end of the Battle of Loos there was much political wrangling and intrigue and apportionment of blame for the failure of the attack. Much of the criticism was directed at the Commander-in-Chief Sir John French, and it seems Sir Douglas Haig cleverly orchestrated a lot of this.

It is clear that Sir John French certainly stirred the pot up in his post-Loos despatch. In this he stated that he had placed the 21st and 24th divisions under Haig's command at 9.30am on 25th September. Additionally, in this despatch of 2nd November he stated that the Guards Division was placed under Haig's control on the morning of 26th September. Relations between French and Haig, already at a low point, were not helped by this and things were to get a lot worse. Haig, in fact, had already been meddling behind the scenes well before the 2nd November.

Perhaps a good place to start is the controversy over the handling of the 21st and 24th divisions. Sir John French had recognised the value of putting in freshly arrived, unbloodied troops not yet corrupted by their first experience of trench warfare but it was for exactly these reasons that he felt reluctant to commit them until a breakthrough had been achieved and success almost certain. He had advised the two divisional commanders that all that would be required of them would be to pursue a fleeing German army, and not the intention to throw them against the unbroken German second line defences. It was of course, entirely proper for Sir John French to retain a proportion of the troops as reserves, entirely under his command and to release them only when in his opinion it was the correct moment. As we have seen it had been agreed with Sir Douglas Haig that some reserves would be held a short distance behind the front. It was the classic dilemma, because if Sir John had given Haig his *only* available reserve the likelihood is they would have gone in much earlier than they did, with the same results as Haig's other six divisions. Everything depended on an initial success, which was achieved in some sectors, notably the 15th Division in the area of Loos. News did reach French that the German line had been broken, men were swarming forward and Loos had been taken, and after these reports he did release the reserves to 1st Army. It was on Haig's instructions that the 21st and 24th divisions were sent into the attack, and of course he issued his orders in good faith based on the extent of the information available to him. When he issued the orders he understood that his men were already attacking the German second line defences, but as we have seen the fog of war came down thickly and the orders were virtually out of date by the time they were issued.

There was certainly no love lost between the Commander-in-Chief and his 1st Army Commander and people were looking for reasons for the failure of the attack. It seems to me that Haig decided who should bear most of the blame. During a meeting between Sir John French and Sir Douglas Haig on the 28th September,

Sir John informed Haig that he was withdrawing the 21st and 24th divisions for more training. It was a private meeting and it seems no official record of what was said was taken or has survived but shortly afterwards Haig wrote in his diary about Sir John: "It seems impossible to discuss military problems with an unreasoning brain of this kind. At any rate, no good result is to be expected from so doing."

In any case, on the 29th September Haig wrote direct to the Secretary of State for War:

Wednesday 29th September
1st Army HQ
Hinges

My dear Lord Kitchener,
    You will doubtless recollect how earnestly I pressed you to ensure an adequate reserve being close in rear of my attacking divisions, and under my orders. It may interest you to know what happened. No reserve was placed under me. My attack, as has been reported, was a complete success. The enemy had no troops in his second line, which some of my plucky fellows reached and entered without opposition. Prisoners state the enemy was so hard put to it for troops to stem our advance that the officers' servants, fatigue-men etc, in Lens were pushed forward to hold their second line to the east of Loos and Hill 70.
    The two reserve divisions (under C-in-C's orders) were directed to join me as soon as the success of the 1st Army was known at GHQ. They came on as quick as they could, poor fellows, but only crossed our old trench line with their heads at 6pm. We had captured Loos 12 hours previously, and reserves should have been at hand then. This, you will remember, I requested should be arranged by GHQ and Robertson quite concurred in my views and wished to put the reserve divisions under me, but this was not allowed.
    The final result is that the enemy has been allowed time in which to bring up troops and to strengthen his second line, and probably to construct a third line in the direction in which we are heading viz Pont à Vendin.
    I have now been given some fresh divisions, and am busy planning an attack to break the enemy's second line. But the element of surprise has gone, and our task will be a difficult one.
    I think it right that you should know how the lessons which have been learnt in the war, at such cost, have been neglected. We were in a position to make this the turning point in the war, and I still hope we may do so, but naturally I feel annoyed at the lost opportunity. We were all very pleased to receive your kind telegram, and I am,

Yours very truly,

D Haig.

As well as this letter there was much gnashing of teeth about the training, composition and performance of the 21st and 24th divisions, but much of the washing of the dirty linen did not emerge till post-war. The British Official History went into great detail and these are a few of the points raised.
    The 21st Division, originally commanded by Lieutenant-General Sir E. Hutton, but from the 1st April 1915 by Major-General G. Forestier-Walker (who had been with the BEF from August 1914 until that date as BGGS of the II Corps

and 2nd Army), was raised from the third hundred thousand (K3) during the early part of September 1914. Its infantry consisted, except for two battalions, of Northerners from Northumberland, Durham and Yorkshire. Of its General Staff officers when it went out to France all three had passed the Staff College course, two had previous staff experience in France and one had not. Of the Admin and Quartermaster staff, none of the three had passed the Staff College course but one had had experience albeit only in the UK. Of the four Brigadiers in the Division, two were Regulars and the others retired Regulars. All the battalion commanders were ex-Regular, mostly retired from the Indian Army. But after this, in the 13 battalions in the Division, out of a total of about 400 officers only 14 were either Regular or ex-Regular. The Official History states that the remainder of the officers were newly commissioned, mostly without special training. In the ranks were a few old soldiers and some ex-NCO's attached as instructors, but of these the earlier K1 and K2 divisions had got the pick. The 21st Division was originally billeted around Aylesbury and Tring and was still not concentrated together as a unit until May 1915 when it moved initially to Halton. Shortly after this move it was transferred to the Aldershot Command at the end of July, when it moved into huts in the Godalming-Frensham area. Around this time the Divisional transport was issued to it. Owing to the shortage of weapons, clothing and equipment, and to the fact that the officers themselves required instruction before they could in turn instruct, the training of the Division did not progress well and by April 1915 was little advanced. Until the middle of June 1915 nothing could be attempted in the way of divisional or brigade training except a weekly route march combined with a tactical scheme. After this time, it is reported that a reasonable amount of brigade training was carried out with a few divisional exercises thrown in for good measure. But this training was disjointed as range work claimed priority and indeed a lot of the men did not get to fire their weapons for the first time until they were at Aldershot in August 1915. Also the divisional artillery spent most of their time on Salisbury Plain learning how to use the guns.

Meanwhile the 24th Division had a similar experience. It again was a K3 Division and consisted of battalions drawn from 13 different regiments recruited from the Midlands, Eastern and Home Counties. Its GOC, Major-General Sir J. Ramsey, was a retired Indian Army Officer. Its General Staff consisted of officers who had passed the Staff College course and had served in France but not with actual staff experience, two of them having recovered from wounds received earlier in the war. One of the Admin and Quartermaster staff was psc but was an Indian Army Officer again without staff experience. No battalion in the Division had more than one Regular or ex-Regular officer beside the commanding officer, who with the exception of one who was a retired officer, either Regular or Militia. All the Brigadiers were retired officers, two of them being from the Indian Army.

At Loos the GSO I of the 24th Division was a gunner, Lieutenant-Colonel C. Stewart, who post-war wrote a letter to the Official Historian, stating:

> In the 24th Division, there was no staff officer who had acted in that capacity with troops in the field during the war. The GSO's I and II (General Staff officers) were serving Regular officers who entered on the war as regimental officers; both had been badly wounded in the first two months in France, and had spent months in hospital or convalescing. Both had been through the Staff Col-

lege, as had also the AA & QMG who was a retired officer of the Indian Army. None of these officers had had any opportunity of approaching to what extent everything connected with staff work before and during battle had developed in France, since the commencement of the war. They had paid one visit of a few days to France in the interim but had been then more concerned with instructional duties of other officers who accompanied them. The GOC himself was a retired officer, who had commanded a District in India.

The 24th Division was originally based on the South Downs near East Shoreham and Patcham until the end of May 1915 when it was also moved to the Aldershot area. It suffered the same problems with training and equipment as the 21st Division, except that weapons were even slower in being issued. The artillery arrived in May but small arms did not appear till the Division was at Aldershot around August. It is unclear whether all the men actually fired a practice shoot in the UK but it is believed some men arrived in France never having fired a rifle. It seems most of the training consisted of digging trenches with less marching than the 21st Division. There were very few brigade and divisional exercises. These two divisions when they arrived in France only had about three weeks in the rear areas before being sent into action. Whether it was known if these divisions had only a small amount of training in the UK and needed more could not be ascertained, but given the benefit of hindsight, it is unfortunate that they were thrust into a situation they could not really deal with and paid a high price.

Another problem with the handling of these two divisions was the time taken on the 24th September to reach their pre-allocated positions. They were faced with a journey of between nine and fourteen miles. The 24th Division moved off at 6.30pm and the 21st at 7.00pm. This should have given all troops ample time to reach their destination by midnight and grab a few hours rest before coming under the command of 1st Army at 6.30am around the time of the initial attack. The march as we have seen was a disorganised fiasco. With the benefit of hindsight it is easy to lay the blame at the door of GHQ who failed to ensure that their routes to the front were properly signposted and marshalled. There is an interesting post-war letter written by Lieutenant-Colonel Maurice who in September 1915 was GSO Military Operations at GHQ and this states:

> GHQ should have made arrangements for assisting the march of newly-formed divisions. I think now this was a bad oversight on my part. The reason or excuse was that we were pressing Sir John up to the last to have these divisions handed over to Haig as soon as they came into his area and we didn't know from hour to hour what the decision would be...I went through the march orders for XI Corps with Haking and his BGGS...The only difficulty was that for the night of 24th/25th when they would be in the 1st Army area and crossing the roads and railways of that Army. I warned them that they would have to look out for that and said that probably by that time they would be under the 1st Army, which was perhaps injudicious. I still think now, that as there was so much friction and discussion about the employment of the General reserve I ought either to have insisted on the 1st Army making arrangements for clearing the roads or seen to it myself.

The following comments are taken from various officers who suffered as a result of the inactivity of GHQ to ensure adequate route-marking:

As Staff Captain of the 64th Brigade I spent the whole night trying to get battalions through a mass of traffic, which was completely uncontrolled. The chief cause of the delay lay in the constant blocking of the road at level crossings to permit trains running and shunting. It poured with rain all through that march; transport horses unused to the drivers and heavy draught, slipped, stopped and caused checks. The road from Busnes to Gonnehem is very narrow - with deep ditches full of water on either side. We were constantly meeting motor lorries and vehicles of all sorts along the road, and, to permit passage units had to get into file. At every road junction there were blocks from cross traffic.

It can be gauged from this range of comments that it was not an easy march and to make matters worse the planners billeted the 21st and 24th divisions next to artillery batteries which fired most of the night - not the most easiest noise to sleep through!

Anyway this was now history and news was reaching London by various means of the disquiet amongst the Generals on the Western Front, Haig again fuelling this. On 10th October French's Chief of staff, Lieutenant-General Sir W Robertson, travelled to London "to do a bit of lobbying for Haig and himself", as one observer has put it. Robertson attended a Cabinet Meeting and was also contacted by the King's Private Secretary who advised that King George wished to see him as a matter of urgency. What happened at this meeting is speculation but it appears that on his return to France on 17th October, Robertson asked Haig for guidance about what to report back to the King regarding a possible change of command in the BEF. Haig apparently left Robertson in no doubt as to what to say by replying:

> I told him at once that up to date I had been most loyal to French and did my best to stop all criticism of him or his methods. Now at last, in view of what had happened in the recent battle over the reserves and in view of the seriousness of the general military situation, I had come to the conclusion that it was not fair to the Empire to retain French in command on this main battlefront. Moreover, none of my officers commanding corps had a high opinion of Sir John's military ability or military views; in fact, they had no confidence in him.

It is alleged that Robertson wholeheartedly agreed with these comments and said these views would get back to the King through his Private Secretary Lord Stanfordham. Robertson also related the fact that it appeared that several Cabinet members who had previously supported French had now swung round to the other point of view. On hearing of Haig's attitude from his Private Secretary Lord Stanfordham, King George decided at pretty short notice to visit France to see for himself the lie of the land. Sir John French met him upon arrival at Boulogne, but as the King's Mess at Aire had not been completed, it was decided he would stay in the Royal Train for a few days. On hearing this, Sir John almost bizarrely decided that his interests would be best served by visiting London to consult friends and colleagues there. As usual Murphy's Law came into play and the King's Mess was finished early and Haig was invited to dine there with the King. Haig's recollection of the conversation that took place is as follows:

> I told him that I thought that the time to have French removed was after the Retreat, because he had so mismanaged matters and shown in the handling of the small Expeditionary Force in the field a great ignorance of the essential princi-

ples of war. Since then, during the trench warfare the Army had grown larger, and I thought at first there was no great scope for French to go wrong. I have therefore done my utmost to stop criticisms and make matters run smoothly. But French's handling of the reserves in the last battle, his obstinacy and conceit showed his incapacity, and that it seemed to me impossible for anyone to prevent him doing the same things again.

The King told Haig that he had seen Haking and Gough previously that afternoon and that they both had given forthright views on Sir John's capacity for command. Robertson had said: "It was impossible to deal with French, his mind was never the same for two consecutive minutes." The King's diary recorded:

After tea Generals Gough and Haking came to see me and we had a long talk; they pointed out that there was a great want of initiative and fighting spirit and no proper plans made in high quarters and that everyone had lost confidence in the C-in-C. They had seen more fighting than anyone out here, they complained that only the 1st Army did any fighting, the other two did nothing and that unless a change was made we should never win this war...They had no axe to grind, but only wanted to win the war...Douglas Haig came to dinner and I had a long talk with him afterwards. He entirely corroborated what the other two had said, but went much further and said the C-in-C was a source of great weakness to the Army, and no one had any confidence in him anymore. He also thought Robertson ought to go home to England as Chief of staff at once, but he, DH, would serve under anyone. All these things add to my worries and anxieties...

So as we can see nearly everyone was lined up against Sir John French. The words "Infamy, Infamy, they've all got it in for me" comes to mind! It was only a matter of time. But then an almost hilarious incident nearly put paid to the plans. Whilst reviewing some troops the King was thrown from his horse, which then rolled on top of him leaving him badly bruised and shaken, so he retired to his bed for a rest. The twist is that Haig had provided the horse at the King's request and he supposedly specially picked a quiet one; it is a good job he didn't pick a lively one! News of this accident obviously dominated the newspapers and therefore any speculation about a change at the top in France was either relegated to the inside pages or non-existent. On 30th October Sir John visited the King but apparently only saw him for a minute or two. After this Sir John again went to London to seek advice and support and crucially for him to arrange for the publication of his Official Despatch on the Battle of Loos in *The Times*. He also arranged for a supportive article written by *The Times* military correspondent Colonel Repington to appear in the same edition. I suppose Sir John hoped this 'good news' would strengthen his position but they actually turned into his downfall. By the time his Despatch was printed on 2nd November he was back in France. As the question of his handling of the reserves had already caused much speculation, it would make common sense to make sure that whatever you said was 'squeaky-clean' and entirely accurate. Instead Sir John made an easily refutable misstatement of fact, which simply played straight into the hands of his enemies, particularly Douglas Haig. The critical passage in the Despatch was as follows: "At 9.30am I placed the 21st and 24th divisions at the disposal of the General Officer Commanding 1st Army, who at once ordered the General Officer Commanding XI Corps to move them up in support of the attacking troops." To add additional credence to this statement Repington 'span' along the following lines in the accompanying article:

> The despatch does not enable us to ascertain why the first line of attack remained unsupported throughout the day of September 25th. Sir Douglas Haig had the 3rd Cavalry Division, less one brigade under his hand. The 21st and 24th divisions of the New Armies, posted at Beuvry and Noeux les Mines, were placed under his orders at 9.30am on September 25th and were at once ordered up by him in support, but do not figure at all in the report of the operations of this day...It is not, therefore, possible for me to say whether the current criticisms for the failure to support the two corps in the first line are justified or the reverse...We are not even made acquainted with the hour at which the 21st and 24th divisions went into battle on September 26th...If we have to regret anything it is that, as the Army grows, the very great qualities of Sir John French as a leader of troops are no longer available in the fighting line and that he is forced to delegate to others fighting duties of which no one else but he, since the death of Lord Roberts, is so great a master.

Even if it doesn't state it clearly, the implication behind these words is that the reserves were handed over to Haig at 9.30 on the morning of 25th September and are not heard of doing anything that day. Additionally if Sir John had been able to spare time away from his duties as Commander-in-Chief to oversee their action, then there might have been a different result to the Battle of Loos and the elusive breakthrough achieved. It is easy to imagine Sir Douglas spluttering over his eggs and bacon when he read this, indeed he confided to his diary:

> It is too disgraceful of a C-in-C to try to throw dust in the eyes of the British people by distorting facts in his Official Reports...On my way to Gonnehem, I met General Gough, also riding. He was perfectly furious about Sir John French's Despatch published on 2nd November. The 1st Corps is scarcely mentioned, in spite of its splendid conduct. But a similar feeling to Gough's is universal throughout the Army. Everyone knows that Sir John French is alone to blame for the want of troops at the decisive point on 25th September...I sent a letter to GHQ today calling attention to the two paragraphs in Sir John French's recent Despatch which are incorrect...I enclosed copies of three telegrams which showed that the 21st and 24th divisions were not placed under my orders at stated, nor did I issue orders to GOC XI Corps, as he was not under my command.

When this letter arrived at GHQ Sir John, clearly on the verge of a nervous breakdown to his subordinates, did the honest thing and claimed he was ill and went to bed. Haig noted in his diary on hearing that Sir John was unwell: "Sir J French has returned from England and is in bed with a heart attack. We wonder whether that is a result of my letter to GHQ." Perhaps reassessing his options after being called a liar by one of his subordinates, Sir John decided to try and tough it out and instructed his Chief of staff Robertson to reply accordingly. Two letters were sent which arrived around 8th November and Haig recorded the following in his diary:

I received two letters from GHQ. One commenting on my report on the papers which I forwarded re the 21st and 24th divisions and the actions of the reserves at Loos. This correspondence the C-in-C directed to cease. The other letter is in reply to mine of the 4th instant calling the Field Marshal's attention to certain inaccuracies in the Despatch which was published on 2nd November. The CGS is directed to state that the statements in question are substantially correct and call for no amendment.

Haig, again probably spitting feathers, wrote once more to GHQ setting out the facts as he saw them and concluded his letter stating the following regarding Sir John's view of the transfer of the reserves: "This was not the case and I beg to request that this fact may be placed on record." On the morning of 9th November Robertson visited Haig at 1st Army HQ, and said that Sir John was very upset over the controversy that had cropped up as a result of the handling of the reserves. Haig replied that his only concern was for the true facts to be placed on record and handed over the letter mentioned above. At this meeting, however Robertson did admit that Sir John had agreed to send all the relevant correspondence to the War Office in London, together with a covering letter, which Haig would be allowed to see. Haig was probably pretty happy at this, as it ought to prove that he was right and French was wrong. But historians over the years have argued long and hard about why Haig launched two divisions which he himself admitted were, amongst other things, tired, hungry, thirsty and inexperienced against strongly-held and un-damaged German positions. The answer will never be known but an insight into this episode can be judged from a post-war letter he wrote to the British Official Historian in 1927, when the 1915 volumes were being prepared. Haig wrote: "To think of the reserves at Loos is like a nightmare!...With so much anxiety before the Battle about the reserves you can understand what I felt, as the Battle progressed and all my fears became realities." Perhaps this is looking at the situation through Haig-tinted spectacles. There was nothing to stop him issuing orders cancelling the 'pursuit' of the demoralised Germans. It has been recorded that it seems Haig took the view that the 21st and 24th divisions were on some pre-destined course to di-saster, brought about by French's decision to keep them under his command until the last minute, and there was nothing that he could do to stop this disaster hap-pening, which of course he could have. But, if, on the other hand he wanted the top job it would be better to do nothing and later lay the blame (very skillfully) at Sir John's door. The two met at St Omer on the morning of 10th November and Haig noted:

> Sir John French seemed shaky and nervous at the outset of the meeting...After the conference I saw Sir John in his own room regarding the correspondence which I have had on the subject of the reserves and his recent Despatch. He was most anxious for me to know that he had nothing to do with an article by Repington on 2nd November.

I suspect Haig did not believe this as Sir John's footprints were all over the 'revelation' of the shell shortage earlier in the year as reported by Repington. He did add to his diary a cutting comment: "I gather that no one of importance takes much notice of Sir John when he goes to London and that he feels his loss of position."

Over the next couple of weeks things moved on swiftly, Lord Esher (a member of the Government) visited France and had several meaningful discussions with key players such as Haig and Robertson. Around the middle of November Robertson again visited England, but before he left he wrote to Haig:

> Stamfordham writes that the King is quite sure of the two changes he ought to make in France and at the WO but that he cannot make them...I feel sure I know exactly what ought to be done, in fact I think and feel the same way as you do, but what I can really do is doubtful. I am now off to begin to try. I see the King tonight and the PM this morning...At any rate I mean to tell them the Army in France must be given a chance. Do you know that French is in bed again - till Wednesday? I think the first thing is to get you in command.

Also, just to make doubly sure, around 20th November General Butler, Haig's Chief of staff just happened to be in London and met the Prime Minister Mr Asquith, and gave him copies of the correspondence between 1st Army and GHQ on the subject of the alleged discrepancies in Sir John's Loos Despatch.

Robertson then sent another letter to Haig, stating that it would 'help matters along' if he visited London for a few days, so on 21st November he left his HQ and travelled to England. On the afternoon of 22nd November he went to the War Office and had discussions with the Military Secretary General Robb. According to his diary, Haig learnt that the papers, which should have been sent to the War Office, had not yet come forward, but he did write that privately 'off the record' Sir John was fighting for his life. The following day he lunched at 10 Downing Street, again noting in his diary: "The matters we discussed were of such vital interest to the Empire that I never alluded to my own affairs, and the differences which I had had with Sir John French over the Despatch he published on 2nd November." That same day Lord Esher recorded the outcome of a meeting with Asquith:

> I then saw the PM at the War Office at five...the Government, he said, have come to the conclusion that a change must be made in the Supreme Command on the Western Front...he was driven to the conclusion that Sir John was physically not now equal to the work before him, his health was deteriorating, and he was constantly being laid up, which was undesirable in a commander in the field. Finally that recent events had shown that a change was desirable...he had asked me to come over in order that I might, as an old and personal friend...return and break to Sir John the conclusion at which he had arrived...he suggested that, in Sir John's own interest, he should take the initiative, and tender his resignation on the grounds of age and fatigue...I said to him that he had imposed a very disagreeable task on me, but I would think over the matter and see him again on the morrow.

Lord Esher did think about it overnight and went back to see Asquith, as Esher said he wanted to make sure that Asquith's decision to sack French was final and did not have any strings attached. Asquith after a few moments in response to this request was: "Yes, you must take it that the decision is final." Lord Esher replied that he would leave for France the following day and recorded in his diary: "It was necessary to get this answer clearly from Mr Asquith, as I had no intention of being used as an instrument of manoeuuvering Sir John out of office."

Esher's gut feeling that things were not quite right had been aroused when he had been at the War Office, before his first meeting with the Prime Minister. He wrote:

> It was difficult to avoid all suspicion, because although I believe the PM's standard of honour to be of the highest, politics is a dirty business, and because yesterday morning I had a message from Sir William Robertson that he would like to see me for a few minutes at the Defence Committee. He was evidently a good deal perturbed. His first words were, "Do you know what Mr Asquith has sent for you about?" I said "No.", and then he told me. He asked me not to mention that he had spoken to me on the subject. It was evident, therefore, that there had been something going on in a circle rather wider than that of the Cabinet. Robertson is perfectly loyal to Sir John, but his own position must be considerably affected one way or the other by a change in the Supreme Command and that he had clearly been told of the impending blow.

On that day, 24th November, Haig was going back to France but before he left Robertson visited and told him that Lord Esher was going to France tomorrow. Haig wrote in his diary: "Esher is going to break the news to Sir John that he is to be recalled...he added that the selection of a successor lay between him and me, but that there was no one in it but me." Lord Esher left on 25th November arriving at St Omer with the difficult job of handing over bad news. His diary records:

> The FM...arrived late at GHQ. Directly he came in I told him exactly what had occurred in the plainest langauage...he said at once that he could conceive of nothing that he had done to provoke Asquith to remove him from his command; the strain, no doubt, had been very great during the last fifteen months, and he had felt it at times, but on the other hand, his health was not affected, all the threads were in his hands, and he was better acquainted with the personnel of the Army than anyone else was or could be, and, after, he did not see who could do any better...After dinner the FM sent for Brinsley. I had to tell the story again. By this time the FM had reacted and his mood had changed. He was keen to show fight, to dare the Government to turn him out and do their worst. There was nothing to be done but to give him time to calm down.

The next morning Sir John French went to London to meet with Asquith for 'an interview without coffee', while Lord Esher stayed behind at GHQ and dined with Robertson. Esher stated that he felt it would be a great sorrow for Robertson to quit the Army in the field, but that his knowledge of military affairs led Esher to think he would be best suited at the War Office. Esher confided to his diary:

> It is impossible to talk to this man and not appreciate his fine, disinterested outlook. He may think of himself, as we all do, but primarily he sees the peril of his country and casts about for safeguards. That he would subordinate his desires and personal advantage for his duty. I feel confident.

Meanwhile what of the meeting between Asquith and French? French must have spoken with his friend Repington as a report appeared which stated that Asquith advised Sir John, that he had previously been the only supporter of Kitchener in the Cabinet, but had now decided he could no longer support him. Asquith therefore wanted Sir John to come back to England as Commander-in-Chief

Home Forces, so that the Cabinet could have the benefit of his military advice. Asquith added that there was no hurry to make the change. Sir John asked who was to succeed him as C-in-C BEF, and was told the decision had not yet been made. When he heard this with a touching loyalty he nominated Sir William Robertson, probably not aware that he was suggesting one of the conspirators who had lobbied against him.

A second version of this meeting can be provided from Lord Esher's diary, which reports in a verbatim style:

> PM: Yes, Lord Esher has exactly rendered my meaning. I wish you to clearly understand that, unless you yourself take the first step, I will take no action. Your case is quite different from that of some others. They were recalled and given no option. You are in no sense recalled. FM: I quite understand. I realise that under certain circumstances it might be your duty to insist upon my relinquishing my command, but you do not think that the circumstances at present require such insistence, or that the occasion for such action on your part has arisen. For my part, I must first consider my duty to the officers and men under my command...I must first consider whether, in my judgement, it is to their advantage that I should relinquish the command into other hands. Should I be satisfied that I could do so rightly, there are two conditions to which I attach such importance that their fulfillment will absolutely govern the situation at which I may arrive. The first is that I should be consulted about my successor, and the second is that you should confirm what I understand is your intention of appointing a civilian Secretary of State. You must realise it would be impossible for me to act as your military advisor, which is what you say you desire, if a Field Marshal of higher rank remains as Secretary of State. If you can satisfy me on these points, I hope to place myself, unreservedly in your hands. Asquith then spoke freely and openly to the FM about his future, and reiterated that the FM's retirement was to be his own act, and that if he decided to retain the command, the Government would make no move. It was finally agreed that the FM was to write and communicate his decision.

If this account is a true record of the discussions then no one emerges with any great credit. The Prime Minister Asquith apparently did not have the necessary resolve or will power to actually sack Sir John. On the other hand Sir John French was desperately trying to salvage 'something' for himself by attempting to get Kitchener sacked and to have a say in who should be his successor; he obviously did not want Haig. Lord Esher must also be tarred with the same brush, for he negotiated French's elevation to the peerage and also pleaded that he should be granted a large gratuity because he was a poor man; this meant he did not have a large inherited fortune but had to survive on a Field Marshal's salary. Perhaps the underlying trend in all of this was the fact that the leading figures both politically and military were out of their depth and all would go over the following months.

Lord Kitchener, who had been to see Gallipoli for himself, returned to London at the end of November and on 1st December there was a meeting in London between Haig and himself. This is what Haig recorded in his diary:

> He asked me first of all what I knew about Sir John French and his position. Kitchener then told me that Sir John was ready to resign on account of ill-health, provided that he was given a peerage etc...After lunch I returned to the

War Office. About 5pm Lord K sent for me regarding the letters I had sent to GHQ re the mis-statements in Sir J French's last Despatch and re the question of the reserves on 25th September. The copies of the correspondence had been obtained by the Prime Minister from General Butler and so could not be used officially...the issue was how to get the papers officially from Sir John. He had promised me he would send them to the WO, so I presume he will do so. I saw Brade after my interview and he wired to GHQ with reference to another paper dealing with the 21st and 24th divisions, asking for reports by Corps and Army Commanders which have not been forwarded!...I feel I have some good friends at the War Office.

This entry is interesting as it shows that Sir John French had not sent the papers as he had promised he would on the 10th November about his Despatch to the War Office. Haig obviously suspecting a double-cross, as we have seen, made sure that Asquith got the relevant papers! Two days later Haig had another meeting with Kitchener and according to Haig's diary this is what happened:

Lord K was most friendly...As regards myself nothing has been definitely settled, but today he had written to the Prime Minister recommending that I should be appointed to succeed Sir John French. If the PM did not settle the matter today, he would again press for a settlement tomorrow, but, in any case he had taken the matter in hand and I must not trouble my head over it. As soon as I was in the saddle he would see me again, meantime he said that I must not be afraid to criticise any of his actions which I found unsatisfactory; he had only one thought, viz., to do his best to end the war...He again kindly told me he would look after my interests and wished me good luck.

Around 5th December as a result of pressure from Kitchener, a junior Government Minister wrote to Sir John's Secretary, Brinsley Fitzgerald, saying that the Prime Minister really wanted Sir John back in the UK and urging him to write his letter of resignation without any further delay. It is interesting that this letter came from a junior subordinate of Asquith and Sir John now realised the game was up. He wrote his letter forthwith and decided (or forgot) not to include his two conditions on the future of Kitchener and Haig. Haig travelled back to France on the 4th December and obviously the news was out as a staff officer at GHQ, Brigadier J. Charteris, wrote in his diary: "DH is back, apparently it is all settled that he will succeed French and Robertson is to go home as CIGS. The immediate cause is the Loos trouble. But it would have happened in any case."

On the 10th December Haig received his long-awaited letter from the Prime Minister Asquith, this stated:

Sir John French has placed in my hands his resignation of the Office of Commander-in-Chief of the Force in France. Subject to the King's approval, I have the pleasure of proposing to you that you should be his successor. I am satisfied that this is the best choice that could be made in the interests of the Army and the Country.

One week later soon after approving Haig as the new chief, the King wrote a letter in his own hand to Haig expressing his view that the fighting on the Western Front would be successfully concluded under Haig's able direction. But it seems that behind the scenes the King had some reservations over 'his' choice, if Lord

Esher's private diary is to be believed: "The King sent for me this morning...he feels profoundly every pang the war can inflict, and while he approves, he frets about the change in the High Command in France and the decision to bring Robertson to London." Anyway it was realistically a bit late as on 18th December Haig went to St Omer to visit Sir John to make the formal arrangements for the change-over of command which was to occur at noon on the following day. Haig's diary entries for this and the next day contained the following:

> I saw Sir John at 3pm, he did not look very well and seemed short of breath at times. I took over the command of the Army in France and Flanders at noon. I sent a telegram to the War Office announcing the fact, and asking who was to take command of the 1st Army. I recommended Sir H. Rawlinson, up to 11pm no reply reached me. Then Sir William Robertson arrived from England and telephoned from St Omer that the Prime Minister and Lord Kitchener had gone out of London for the weekend, and nothing could be settled till Monday! And this is war time.

Sir John went back to London to become Commander of Home Forces and was granted a peerage and became the 1st Earl of Ypres.

The official hand-over was 1st January 1916 and Brigadier Charteris recorded this about the GHQ New Year's Eve party: "DH never shines at dinner, but he was obviously in very good spirits, and kept silence merrily." So Sir Douglas Haig had got what he wanted, but it would be nearly three years before he was able to bring the war to 'be successfully concluded' albeit with a casualty figure running into the millions. Whether Haig's 'interfering' behind the scenes was necessary at all is open to question. It appears that in August 1915 Haig had a meeting with the King at which it seems he was told that Sir John French's job would eventually be his. But Haig was an ambitious man in a hurry and he used all his contacts to try and hurry up the slow-moving Whitehall bureaucracy to gain his appointment quickly. In the process he made the maximum possible use of what was virtually a conflict of opinion between himself and Sir John French as to how the Battle of Loos was to be fought. Haig readily capitalised on French's bungled attempt to make the disaster of Loos more acceptable to the general public, when he made a plain mis-statement of fact in his Despatch. Haig pounced on this error and exposed it for all it was worth. The rest is now history. Haig was able to plan for his big attack in 1916, again aiming to end the war by Christmas. Whether any lessons were learnt and the knowledge retained from the 'defeat' at Loos is debatable. In all the 1915 battles no major breakthroughs were achieved and 'bite and hold' seemed to be the best option for future attacks. Yet in 1916 again it was expected that huge gaps and gains would be made and the Cavalry could exploit these. But it is not my place to talk about 1916.

The final British casualty of the Battle of Loos was the divisional system itself, not a fatal injury, but more of a corrective surgery. After the poor performance of the two K3 divisions on the 26th September it was decided to carry out a wholesale exchange of units between as many of the later New Army divisions and the Regular divisions then in France as possible. The divisions affected were the 21st, 23rd, 24th and 25th. The other two K3 formations - the 22nd and 26th divisions - left the Western Front and went to Salonika where they remained for the rest of the war. It is interesting to point out here that the 22nd Division suffered the lowest

46th Division Memorial at Vermelles. (Niall Cherry)

casualty figure of the whole war for any New Army Division of 7,728. This indicates the relative safety of the Salonika area compared to other sectors. The 26th Division has the second lowest with 8,022, while the 21st Division heads the casualty table for the New Army divisions with a total of 55,581, the 9th Division is second with 52,055. Of the four K3 divisions, three divisions exchanged complete brigades with Regular divisions and the other was sent three Regular battalions to, I suppose, 'stiffen them up.' The 21st Division was the formation to get the three Regular battalions, while in the 23rd Division the 70th Brigade was swapped with the 24th Brigade from the 8th Division. In the 24th Division the 71st Brigade was exchanged with the 17th Brigade from the 6th Division, and in the 25th Division the 76th Brigade went to the 3rd Division swapping with the 7th Brigade. This process was also extended to some K4 and K5 divisions then in France, the 30th, 32nd and 33rd divisions all swapping brigades with Regular divisions. But there were not enough Regulars to go round and the last eight New Army divisions, the 34th to 41st and the 31st (when it came back from Egypt), were without any 'stiffening' Regular presence.

It was also decided to leave the Territorial Force divisions alone, as some had done well in the fighting they had already experienced. I am thinking here of the 42nd (East Lancashire) Division at the Third Battle of Krithia in June 1915 on Gallipoli, where a General remarked they performed like Regulars, and the 47th (2nd London) Division at Loos on the 25th September and after. But one Territorial Division seemed to suffer as a result of experiences at Loos, the 46th (North Midland) Division. This Division was the first complete division to have reached a satisfactory level of training to be considered ready to go and serve on the Western Front. It crossed to France in February 1915 and held the line in the Ypres sector for the next six months or so. At the end of September, as we have seen, it was moved south to Loos, where it had the first of two misfortunes. Their problems at Loos we have looked at. Then in July 1916, on the opening day of the Somme offensive, it again suffered badly. On this second occasion they, together with the 56th (1st London) Division, had to undertake a diversionary action for the main attack at Gommecourt. The 46th Division again suffered heavy losses, the Divisional commander was sacked, and as a result of these two failures (which were not really the fault of the men involved), the 46th Division seems to have been given the reputation of only being suitable for line-holding duties. This tag stuck with them until September 1918 when the Midlanders carried out a successful attack crossing the St Quentin Canal, which formed part of the Hindenburg Line.

There is little more to say about the Battle of Loos save that it gained the British Army experience in attack, although it seems the errors of Loos were repeated for a few more battles yet. Perhaps the best way to conclude is to say that the initial assault in certain places went very well, but fresh divisions to exploit this success were not immediately available, and if they had been, it is possible a relatively major success would have been achieved. As it was, the attempt by Sir John French to influence a battle by holding back divisions in reserve was ill considered, tactically out-of-date and eventually cost him his job. In spite of the virtual stalemate and the heavy losses, Loos did not dampen the faith of the men of the BEF. They knew that the line had been broken and they had captured men and equipment. Some of the gains were at locations that the Germans had fortified strongly, but the BEF had

SECRET.

Information Regarding Asphyxiating Gas.

1.—It appears that a certain amount of doubt and misgiving exists among the troops in regard to the use of gas. The operations of the 25th September have disclosed information which should be of value in restoring confidence and which should, consequently, be made known to the troops.

2.—There is no doubt that our gas is effective against the enemy under certain conditions of weather and surprise. Evidence from responsible persons has been obtained that in the village of LOOS and in certain places in the German trenches where the wind was favourable, the gas had great physical effect on the enemy. Many were found dead in dug-outs and cellars who had received no wounds, their death being due to gas.

3.—On the other hand, there is conclusive evidence that if our troops are properly practised and trained, and **accustomed to the wearing of the tube helmet**, there is no cause for alarm at the bursting of a gas cylinder or the defective discharge of gas in our own trenches, especially if vermoral sprayers are kept handy. The fact that our helmet **is an** absolute protection if properly worn must be impressed on all ranks.

4.—It was undoubtedly the case that a certain number of our own troops were gassed owing to the bursting of cylinders and to the defective discharge of the gas. This was to a large extent due to the want of knowledge and practice in wearing the tube helmet, and is evidence of the fact that considerably more training in the use of tube helmets is required.

5.—A large number of men reported sick at the dressing stations and field ambulances purporting to be suffering from the effects of gas. Nearly all these men, however, were merely out of breath from running and were suffering from excitement and fright; they required no treatment and were discharged at once. A considerable proportion of them were recognised as habitual malingerers.

R. BUTLER, *Major-General,*
General Staff.

19th ~~September~~ October, 1915.

1st Printing Co., R.E. G.H.Q. 1922

FIRST ARMY

Leaflet written in October 1915 intending to provide the troops with information that gas worked but in the event never issued. (PRO WO 95/159)

still done a good job. All in all, in places the British troops had advanced over two miles from their front line, which was the largest advance made on the Western Front since trench warfare had begun. The expectation was that they would do better next time.

The ultimate tragedy of Loos is that it was a foreseen disaster, but political decisions ensured that the BEF rushed headlong into a 'Valley of Death'. The 'pale battalions' still hold areas of Loos around such places as Dud Corner, St Marys ADS, The Quarries and Fosse 8; the men who really did the job are dead and in their graves.

Appendices

Appendix A

1st Army Order of Battle

Army Commander General Sir D. Haig

I Corps

Corps Commander Lieutenant-General H. Gough

2nd Division
Divisional Commander Major-General H. Horne
    5th Brigade
        1st Queens
        2nd Worcestershire
        2nd Ox and Bucks Light Infantry
        7th Kings
        9th Highland Light Infantry
    6th Brigade
        1st Kings
        2nd South Staffords
        1st Royal Berkshire
        5th Kings
        1st Hertfords
    19th Brigade
        2nd Royal Welch Fusiliers
        1st Scottish Rifles
        1st Middlesex
        2nd Argyll and Sutherland Highlanders
        5th Scottish Rifles

7th Division
Divisional Commander Major-General Sir T. Capper
    20th Brigade
        2nd Border
        2nd Gordon Highlanders
        8th Devonshire
        9th Devonshire
        6th Gordon Highlanders
    21st Brigade
        2nd Bedfords
        2nd Green Howards
        2nd Royal Scots Fusiliers
        2nd Wiltshire
        4th Cameron Highlanders
    22nd Brigade
        2nd Queens

2nd Royal Warwickshires
1st Royal Welch Fusiliers
1st South Staffords

9th Division
Divisional Commander Major-General G. Thesiger
    26th Brigade
        8th Black Watch
        7th Seaforth Highlanders
        8th Gordon Highlanders
        5th Cameron Highlanders
    27th Brigade
        11th Royal Scots
        12th Royal Scots
        6th Royal Scots Fusiliers
        10th Argyll and Sutherland Highlanders
    28th Brigade
        6th KOSB
        9th Scottish Rifles
        10th Highland Light Infantry
        11th Highland Light Infantry
    Pioneers: 9th Seaforth Highlanders

28th Division
Divisional Commander Major-General E. Bulfin
    83rd Brigade
        2nd King's Own
        2nd East Yorkshire
        1st KOYLI
        1st York and Lancaster
        5th King's Own
    84th Brigade
        2nd Northumberland Fusiliers
        1st Suffolk
        2nd Cheshire
        1st Welch
        6th Welch
    85th Brigade
        2nd Buffs
        3rd Royal Fusiliers
        2nd East Surrey
        3rd Middlesex

IV Corps

Corps Commander Lieutenant-General Sir H. Rawlinson

    1st Division
    Divisional Commander Major-General A. Holland
        1st Brigade

1st Black Watch
1st Cameron Highlanders
10th Gloucestershire
8th Royal Berkshire
14th London
2nd Brigade
2nd Royal Sussex
1st Northamptonshire
1st Loyal North Lancs
2nd KRRC
9th King's
3rd Brigade
1st South Wales Borderers
1st Gloucestershire
2nd Welch
2nd Royal Munster Fusiliers

15th Division
Divisional Commander Major-General F. McCracken
44th Brigade
9th Black Watch
8th Seaforth Highlanders
10th Gordon Highlanders
7th Cameron Highlanders
45th Brigade
13th Royal Scots
7th Royal Scots Fusiliers
6th Cameron Highlanders
11th Argyll and Sutherland Highlanders
46th Brigade
7th KOSB
8th KOSB
10th Scottish Rifles
12th Highland Light Infantry
Pioneers: 9th Gordon Highlanders

47th Division
Divisional Commander Major-General C. Barter
140th Brigade
6th London
7th London
8th London
15th London
141st Brigade
17th London
18th London
19th London
20th London

142nd Brigade
  21st London
  22nd London
  23rd London
  24th London
  Pioneers: 4th Royal Welch Fusiliers

3rd Cavalry Division
Divisional Commander Major-General C. Briggs
  6th Cavalry Brigade
    3rd Dragoon Guards
    1st Royal Dragoons
    North Somerset Yeomanry
  7th Cavalry Brigade
    1st Life Guards
    2nd Life Guards
    Leicestershire Yeomanry
  8th Cavalry Brigade
    Royal Horse Guards
    10th Hussars
    Essex Yeomanry

XI Corps

Corps Commander Lieutenant-General R. Haking

Guards Division
Divisional Commander Major-General The Earl of Cavan
  1st Guards Brigade
    2nd Grenadier Guards
    2nd Coldstream Guards
    3rd Coldstream Guards
    1st Irish Guards
  2nd Guards Brigade
    3rd Grenadier Guards
    1st Coldstream Guards
    1st Scots Guards
    2nd Irish Guards
  3rd Guards Brigade
    1st Grenadier Guards
    4th Grenadier Guards
    2nd Scots Guards
    1st Welsh Guards
  Pioneers: 4th Coldstream Guards

12th Division
Divisional Commander Major-General F. Wing
  35th Brigade
    7th Norfolk
    7th Suffolk

9th Essex
5th Royal Berkshire
36th Brigade
  8th Royal Fusiliers
  9th Royal Fusiliers
  7th Royal Sussex
  11th Middlesex
37th Brigade
  6th Queens
  6th Buffs
  7th East Surrey
  6th Royal West Kent
Pioneers: 5th Northamptonshire

21st Division
Divisional Commander Major-General G. Forestier-Walker
  62nd Brigade
    12th Northumberland Fusiliers
    13th Northumberland Fusiliers
    8th East Yorkshire
    10th Green Howards
  63rd Brigade
    8th Lincolnshire
    8th Somerset LI
    12th West Yorkshire
    10th York and Lancaster
  64th Brigade
    9th KOYLI
    10th KOYLI
    14th Durham LI
    15th Durham LI
  Pioneers: 14th Northumberland Fusiliers

24th Division
Divisional Commander Major-General Sir J. Ramsay
  71st Brigade
    9th Norfolk
    9th Suffolk
    8th Bedfords
    11th Essex
  72nd Brigade
    8th Queens
    8th Buffs
    9th East Surrey
    8th Royal West Kent
  73rd Brigade
    12th Royal Fusiliers
    9th Royal Sussex

7th Northamptonshire
13th Middlesex
Pioneers: 12th Sherwood Foresters

46th Division
Divisional Commander Major-General E. Montagu-Stuart-Wortley
137th Brigade
5th South Staffords
6th South Staffords
5th North Staffords
6th North Staffords
138th Brigade
4th Lincolnshire
5th Lincolnshire
4th Leicestershire
5th Leicestershire
139th Brigade
5th Sherwood Foresters
6th Sherwood Foresters
7th Sherwood Foresters
8th Sherwood Foresters
Pioneers: 1st Monmouthshire

Note this is not a full listing of the formations in the 1st Army, but those we were concerned with in the text. Formations such as the III Corps, involved in diversionary attacks, have been ignored.

Appendix B
Lessons learned from Loos

In 1929 a small booklet written by Lieutenant-Colonel A Kearsey (who had been a staff officer in the Great War) was published, entitled *1915 Campaign in France - The Battles of Aubers Ridge, Festubert and Loos considered in relation to the Field Service Regulations.* It was primarily intended to be a study of these battles with regard to the planning, preparation and events of the fighting from a staff point of view. Reasons for the failures were also given, and the following are Kearsey's main lessons learnt from the fighting at Loos:

(a) The attack on a limited front against an enemy in very strong positions will lead to indecisive results, unless reserves are at hand to exploit success.

(b) The necessity of maintaining at every point the momentum of the attack until the objective is gained.

(c) The necessity of close liaison and co-operation to prevent salients being formed and open flanks being left after a temporary success.

(d) The necessity of a vast amount of heavy artillery and a large supply of shells of all kinds and of mortars and grenades if an attack is to be made in daylight across open ground against very strong, well-sited trenches.

(e) The standard of leadership must be very high in all ranks, and the discipline among the troops must be very firm, to deal with the many unforeseen incidents and checks in an advance across the open against entrenched positions.

(f) The training also of all ranks requires to be very high, in order to maintain direction in the advance and the assault, so that objectives are not mistaken and gaps are not formed in the assaulting lines, and so that initiative is shown in the use of local reserves to exploit success.

(g) The necessity for thorough staff work to enable troops to reach their starting lines with the minimum of hardship and discomfort, so that reserve divisions arrive in the best fighting condition.

(h) The necessity as to a clear understanding of the use of the reserves. In this battle, there was not a concentration of the general reserves at the decisive point, after the local reserves of the first-line attacking troops had been used up on the understanding that the general reserves would be available to exploit their initial success. An opportunity was thus lost of breaking through the German second line before their reserves arrived.

Field Service Regulations states: "With large forces there can be little, if any, hope of being able to strike with the general reserve at the right moment unless its place of concentration is determined with reference to the approximate place in which it is to be used, and the communications available. In such circumstances, therefore, it is essential to make this decision as early as possible, and to place the general reserve accordingly."

At 0900 hours on 25th September, when the divisions had used up their local reserves, the head of our general reserve was six miles from the area in which it was required to be used.

(i) The difficulty of pressing through a second strongly entrenched position, in which the enemy are prepared for an attack, unless there is a preponderance of ammunition. Otherwise, there will be heavy losses and little result. In this battle we lost 50,380 men.

(j) The value of consolidation after any check in an assault. This was done at Loos Crassier and at Hill 70.

(k) The difficulties incurred in trying to break through, in one battle, a whole defensive position disposed in depth, when the enemy has power to manoeuvre in rear and has time to bring up his reserves from areas where he is not engaged, will always lead to unnecessary losses.

Appendix C

Second Lieutenant K. Kershaw, G Company, 9th Gordon Highlanders

One of the many casualties at Loos was a young Second Lieutenant – K. Kershaw - who was killed in action on 25th September 1915. A few days after his death, on 2nd October, his Company commander Captain T. Taylor wrote to Kershaw's father. I am sure this letter was typical of many that were received in homes up and down the length of Britain around this time:

I had to send two platoons up with the assaulting columns and I could see it would have broken his heart if I had not sent him for one. I don't think I could do better than quote what I wrote about the work of his platoon in my despatch, as I feel sure you would like the actual words used best.

"Number 11 Platoon followed the sixth and seventh lines of the 9th Black Watch. Seeing that the left flank of the Black Watch was exposed Lieutenant Kershaw led his platoon half left and charged some German first line trenches immediately on the left of the Black Watch, who at this time had not been able to reach the German first line trenches owing to a hot fire from machine guns, rifles and bombs. These trenches he took unaided. The second line was captured almost without opposition and an advance made on Loos. Within 300

The author standing behind the headstone of 2nd Lieutenant K. Kershaw. (Niall Cherry)

351

yards of Loos where a road crosses the front a hot fire was encountered from machine guns. Lieutenant Kershaw was killed at this point after having been previously wounded. All accounts agree that this officer performed most gallantly leading that part of the line to the assault to Loos."

His men say he was perfectly splendid, always in front and leading the whole way. I called for volunteers from his platoon as soon as we were withdrawn from action and we bought him in on Monday. These are the names of the men I selected. The whole platoon volunteered.

3878 Private M. McIntyre
6836 Private T. Dempsey
9496 Private T. Kirkwood
and the Platoon Sergeant 6414 Sergeant G. Henderson.

They went out under a heavy shell fire and brought him in. I had the padre to read the service. We laid him in a little soldiers cemetery near Quality Street the village of pit or Fosse Number 7, a place which he had so often passed by on his way to work, in fact every day for the past seven weeks. His men made a cross and we wired in the grave.

Second Lieutenant K Kershaw is still in his original grave although the cemetery is now known as Fosse 7 CWGC Cemetery Mazingarbe Plot 2 Row B Grave 2.

Appendix D

Report from M Company 10th Gordon Highlanders 44th Brigade on actions 25th/26th September

A number of men were gassed right at the beginning, and in trying to avoid the gassed bays the two front platoons were separated before leaving the trenches. One party under Lieutenant Boyd joined on to some 9th Gordons and were with the Black Watch when they charged the first line trenches. The other party under Sergeant Aitken reported to L Company but later joined on to the two rear platoons of M Company under Lieutenant Robertson. This party carried right on through Loos and onto Hill 70 without much loss. When they crossed the crest of Hill 70, they found several machine guns in action and a line of KOSB on their left. They joined up and advanced down the hill. There seemed to be some doubt as to whether there was any of our own troops in front. Suddenly they found a strong line of barbed wire concealed in the grass and at the same time a heavy machine gun and rifle fire was opened on them. They lay down and tried to make some cover. Lieutenant Robertson was the only officer left. The party was about 600 strong of different regiments. Various attempts were made to communicate back. Sergeant Cavers got up under a heavy fire and signalled back for support with flags, but he was soon hit. Sergeant Aitken and Private McKeller crawled back and the former reached OC 7th Camerons who was digging in on reverse slope of Hill 70. Private Davidson also went back with a message. None of the three attempts produced any result, and the line had to retire as the enemy were getting round the right flank. They retreated to reverse slopes of Hill 70 where they held on till early next morning when they were relieved.

Sergeant Aitken's account: When we started away from the front line numbers 3 and 4 sections got through one of the bays where there was gas and some of our men got gassed there and had to turn back and come through the support trench. We went round the support trench and we came to the rear of L Company where I reported I had lost communication with Mr Boyd. Captain Angus told me just to attach ourselves to the rear of the Company, and when we got into the open to rejoin Mr Boyd. When we got into the open we were in the rear of L Company and Major Crichton instructed me to keep to the left as we had to go on to the support the Camerons. On making to the left I met Lieutenant Robertson and about two platoons of our Company and joined in with the line.

We advanced in an extended line right onto Loos village and when we were coming near the village the whole line took a left incline and passed the left hand side of the village. We advanced right over the moor on to Hill 70 and some unknown officer told us that the Camerons and Black Watch were occupying the village in front and we pushed over to support them. When we got over the crest we found a number of machine guns firing on men in front. Lieu-

Picture taken 28th September 1915 of a captured German machine gun position near Loos village. (IWM Q 28976)

tenant Christison joined our line and instructed the machine gunners to stop firing, as they were firing on the Black Watch and Camerons. We then proceeded down the hill towards the village in front when a murderous machine gun and rifle fire opened on us. Instead of it being the Black Watch and Camerons as we thought, we found it to be the retreating enemy who ran down a road through houses and manned a trench heavily barbed wired.

We advanced until we were about 150 yards from this trench and Lieutenant Robertson, who was in command of the line, gave orders for the men to make head cover. The enemy's fire was causing a great deal of casualties in the line. I was there over 2 hours when Lieutenant Robertson asked for volunteers to go back with a message to Major Crichton. McKeller and myself went back and reported to Colonel Sandilands what was happening in front. McKeller was wounded on the way up. I found Colonel Sandilands with men digging themselves in on the reverse slope of Hill 70. When we were in the advanced line I saw Sergeant Cavers signalling back for reinforcements.

Special Divisional Order, 15th Division, 28th September

September 28th 1915
15th Division HQ

Special Divisional Order

The following message has been received from Sir Henry Rawlinson:

The Corps Commander is anxious that you should communicate to all ranks of the 15th Division his high appreciation of the admirable fighting spirit which they displayed in the attack and capture of Loos village and Hill 70.

Sir Douglas Haig has also desired the Corps Commander to convey his congratulations to the Division.

The Major-General wishes to say that he is very proud of his Command.

Signed J.T. Burnett-Stuart,
Lieutenant-Colonel, General Staff.

Appendix F

The experiences of an infantry unit at Loos, a contemporary report

Acontemporary report after Loos concerning what was no doubt a typical example of the experiences of an infantry unit:

The 9th King's and the part they played in the Great Advance

The recent big advance on the Western Front had long been in the minds of those who were to take an active part in it and the chances of its immediate success and its effect on the War generally were the subjects of great deliberation. The 9th Battalion the King's Regiment (Liverpool) TF under the command of Lieutenant Colonel F Ramsay 2nd Middlesex Regiment had for three weeks immediately preceding the advance undergone a vigorous training some distance behind the line with a result that the Battalion was in a very fine condition to undertake the arduous task that would be given to them in the near future. That they would have an important part allotted to them was only to be expected, and at the same time hoped for as they had already established for themselves a very high name for general proficiency and good work in their Brigade.

On the night of the 24th September, the Battalion left its reserve billets which it had occupied during the last stages of the preparations for the attack and took up its position in the trenches allocated to it. The weather conditions were extremely bad and a continual deluge of rain quickly churned the trenches into a quagmire, but even this was not calculated to damp the spirits of the men in the trenches who had braced themselves for a mighty effort and were only conscious of the work to be done and the fact that the Germans would be in retreat on the morrow.

It was known that the 9th King's were to advance in cooperation with the London Scottish, the two Battalions constituting a force known as 'Green's Force'. This fact alone was sufficient to brace the boys of the 9th for any eventualities in view of the fact that they were to work with a Territorial Battalion that had already created for itself a name. The time for the assault was not communicated to the Battalion until one hour before it was to take place. Our artillery had for the past three days bombarded the enemy's lines continuously and the bombardment was renewed on the morning of the 25th at daybreak becoming very intense. At 8am the 9th King's moved forward towards the first line of British trenches which had just been vacated by the remaining battalions of their Brigade, who had now moved forward to the attack on the German front line. The enemy were keeping up a hot fire on our attacking force and at this stage in the advance we sustained our first casualties, Major J. Hunt, second-in-command being wounded at about 8.30am. Our communication trenches and front line were during the whole of this time being heavily shelled and all movements were carried out over the open, the ground being perfectly flat and affording no cover to the attacking force. At 9.00am the Battalion after moving over the open occupied a position immediately behind the old firing line where they remained until 10.00am, several casualties had occurred in the Battalion and companies were now reformed and the position taken up in the open, between the old firing line and new support trench, ready for the attack. At 12.15pm, the Battalion received orders to advance and attack the German front line, a distance of 600 yards from the British front line. Led by Colonel Ramsay, whose great fortitude and brilliant work had already inspired all the officers and men, the Battalion pushed on eagerly and at 12.30pm, the two leading companies had jumped the British front line and were moving in splendid order towards the German lines. During the whole time that the Battalion were advancing, the enemy maintained a heavy machine gun fire on our lines, inflicting many losses in both officers and men, amongst the number being Major Evans and Captain Howroyd, commanding C and A companies respectively, and Captain and Adjutant P. Lederer, all of whom received leg wounds. The latter officer is very well known in Liverpool banking circles as the assistant manager of the Liverpool, City and Midland Bank Ltd., and has done very fine work since his appointment as Adjutant of the 9th King's on the 10th May last. In the face of a very hot fire from the enemy the progress at this stage of the advance was not so pronounced, but at 2.00pm our machine guns were brought to play on the enemy's front and this had the effect of reducing considerably the German fire. Our losses had now become very severe but in spite of this the Battalion continued its advance in short rushes and by crawling through the grass and at 3.30pm they had succeeded in establishing themselves in one line within 100 yards of the German trenches. The London Scottish now came up to their support on the left rear. At 3.35pm the Germans surrendered to the King's who had stuck to their work with great tenacity and were rewarded by the capture of some 300 to 400 prisoners. Colonel Ramsay, who had led his men with great dash and spirit, receiving the token of submission from the now shrinking Huns who had once more shown their fear and dread of the British bayonet. The prisoners were quickly sent to the rear and the Battalion again reformed with orders to advance on the remaining lines of German trenches and at 4.30pm, the Battalion, its strength then being 5 officers and 120 men took up a position on the.... Road. This position was maintained until 4.00am on the morning of the 26th when orders were received to retire on the first line of German trenches, the Brigade having been relieved and here the Battalion remained during the whole of the day and the following night. On the morning of the 27th we were again withdrawn to the original British front line where we remained until the early morning of the 29th. The 25th September will ever be remembered in the 9th Battalion The King's as a day of achievements. On this day another testimony was given to justify the good name that the Battalion has always enjoyed under the command of Colonel Ramsay.

On the 29th September the Battalion left the trenches and moved into billets some three miles behind the line, the general opinion among the men being that they were now to receive a well earned rest. Accordingly they settled down to take things easy for a little while, but at 7.00pm the same night orders were received to proceed to hold a section of the trenches recently captured from the enemy in the south east of the village of L.... At 9.00pm the Battalion left their billets and in a deluge of rain marched back to the line in splendid spirits in spite of the fatigue resulting from the recent heavy fighting. This line was held until the night of the 1st October and during the whole of the time the enemy's artillery was very active and our line was shelled incessantly. We were relieved late on the night of 1st and marched to billets. After a week's hard fighting the Battalion were now able to obtain a well earned rest and at the same time take advantage of the few days at their disposal to reorganise and refit in readiness for the next engagement. On 4th October movement orders were again received and the same evening our former billets some three miles behind the line were again occupied by the Battalion until the evening of the 6th. On the 6th the Battalion was temporarily attached to the ...Brigade and orders were received to take over a portion of their line north of the village of L....It was found necessary to at once carry out extensive digging operations, the trenches being extremely shallow and offering no cover to the fire of the enemy's artillery which was very active. At about 10.30am on the morning of the 8th the enemy's artillery opened fire on our front line and support trenches and maintained a steady fire throughout the day with great accuracy, the fire evidently being directed by a hostile aeroplane which remained over us for some time.

Considerable damage was done to our line during the bombardment but at 2.30pm it became terrific, the enemy guns enfilading our trenches from the north and south east. At 3.30pm the enemy also concentrated machine gun and rifle fire on our front and the Battalion sustained very heavy casualties. At 3.50pm the Germans advanced to the attack in mass, marching in four ranks shoulder to shoulder. In spite of the severe losses already suffered, the remaining men in the front line trenches stuck to their posts with great tenacity, but it was found necessary to reinforce the front line from the supports. The enemy advance, which was strongly supported, having reached midway between the lines, was now met with a rapid rifle and cross machine gun fire, the Germans falling in great numbers. The enemy had been severely checked and small groups could now be seen endeavouring to regain their own line in great disorder under a hot fire from our machine guns and rifles. During the attack the enemy succeeded in establishing a very intense *tir de barrage* of shrapnel, HE and machine guns, and the casualties in our front line were by this time very heavy, further reinforcements being brought up on the flanks. At about 5.00pm our artillery obtained superiority of fire and this had the effect of reducing the enemy fire considerably. At this period of the fight, the Battalion had not more than 300 rifles holding the line but the spirit of the men was magnificent, even the wounded who were unable to leave the trench cheering their comrades with shouts of "Go to it the King's," "Stick it King's, give it them hot." Worn out but not dismayed the Battalion or what then remained, still held on and bravely carried out Colonel Ramsay's command to 'keep cheerful'. At 8.15pm a company of the London Scottish came up as reinforcements and the situation became slightly easier, the enemy making no further attempt to attack the position again the night. At 5.00am the following morning the Battalion was withdrawn into the old British support line, having finished a terrific day, and were rewarded for their fine work by congratulations from the GOC's of the Corps, Division and Brigade.

For the second time in a fortnight, the 9th King's had been called upon to play an important part in the advance on the Western front, and on each occasion they have carried out their part with great credit to their Colonel, themselves and the King's Regiment.

The following Special Order of the Day by Major General A Holland. CB, MVO, DSO, commanding 1st Division, was issued and received by Colonel Ramsay on the 10th October:

The Corps Commander has desired the General Officer Commanding to convey to the General Officer Commanding 2nd Infantry Brigade and all ranks under his command, his appreciation of the gallant defence made by the Brigade against the German attack on the 8th instant, and especially the good work done by the 1st Battalion Gloucestershire Regiment and the 9th Battalion Liverpool Regiment.

Appendix G

Notes from the History of the 10th Battalion York and Lancaster Regiment for September 1915

This unit was, at that time, part of the 63rd Brigade from the 21st Division.

September 21st. The men's first pay day - 5 Francs to all privates, the remainder divided amongst the NCOs. Billets, rifles, ammunition, iron rations, gas helmets, boots, socks and feet inspected and the daily certificate rendered to Orderly Room. The Battalion paraded about 6.30pm and marched through Aire to St Hilaire. Trouble was experienced with a farmer who refused to find straw for the men but the situation was eased by taking some from a loft.

September 22nd. Maps were issued and officers were again told that there would be no trench warfare and fighting would be entirely in the open. How many times were we to hear that before the war ended and how utterly wrong this assumption proved to be until the last month of the war, except when the Germans advanced early in 1918. Practically the whole of the training of the New Army had been based on this assumption - near guards, advance guards and attacks across the open were the favourite amusement of the old die-hards who were so slow to learn modern conditions. The Battalion marched 8 miles to Auchel where the billets were good, but ASC NCOs objected, without success, to handing them over to our officers. Instructions were given for all ranks to stay in billets during the day - all marches were to be done at night.

September 23rd. Auchel was a colliery district. D Company caught a 'spy' and imprisoned him in their guard room, but unfortunately he had to be released. The chief interest here was a large munition dump and the departure of 150 lorries, loaded with shells, for an unknown destination and their return for a second load.

September 24th. At 7.00pm the Battalion marched off again, the progress being slow and finally bivouacked near Houchin.

September 25th. The Battalion had breakfast at 7.30am and the CO left for Brigade HQ, as reserve Brigade Commander, Major Raven taking over command. The men saw their first aerial battle. At 9.45am Operational Orders were read with instructions to move off. The attack was to be on a 10 mile front, the troops in front were to carry on as far as Pont à Vendin and make good the crossing of the canal when the 63rd Brigade was to follow on to Carvin. The Battalion marched off at 11.30am in a drizzling rain, stopping every few hundred yards and progressing at a maximum rate of 1½ mile an hour. At 3.30 p.m. D Company were in a field behind some heavy guns and saw the first casualties coming back. Slow progress continued, the Battalion passing Noyelles, Mazingarbe and reaching Vermelles about 7.30pm. At 8.30pm there was a long check, stew being served from the cookers, the first meal since breakfast. Progress continued slowly until Loos was reached and skirted, the Battalion turning

Lieutenant A. Jamieson and other members of the 10th York and Lancasters at Halton Park in 1915, shortly before moving to France. (Rob Elliott)

northwards. The heavy casualties at the Loos crossroads and the burning Loos pylons and Cité St Pierre made a deep impression on all ranks. A shell whined overhead and gave the Battalion its first experience of shell fire. The smell of gas was now discernible as the Battalion passed the old front line. The roads were blocked with transport which necessitated proceeding in single file.

It is very difficult to trace the movements of the Battalion about this time owing to the various accounts but as far as can be ascertained on this night in the neighbourhood of the Lens-Hulluch road it deployed into four lines of companies in line and attacked towards Hill 70 and dug in with entrenching tools before dawn. At dawn there were no signs of the enemy in front and later during the day the Battalion was ordered to retire and moved to a sunken road. All companies were mixed up and after being spotted and shelled advanced slightly up the rise towards a wood in front. About 6.30pm they moved back near the field guns which were firing in the open without any attempt at camouflage.

Captain Mitford was wounded early in the morning of the 26th, Captain Loftus taking over command of B Company and after Second Lieutenant Robinson had reconnoitred in front of the B and C company positions, these two companies advanced by platoons in alternate rushes up the slope towards Hill 70. During this attack Captain Loftus was shot through the head and killed, Lieutenant Whitaker was shot in the leg, which was broken, and was captured next morning along with his batman, who had remained by his side all night. 2nd Lieutenant Robinson was hit in the shoulder which was patched up by Captain Loftus's batman. Between 7.30 and 8.30am on the 28th September, a

Guards Brigade relieved the Battalion. The first roll call was answered by only 3 officers and 71 men but later others joined the Battalion.

At 7.30pm the Battalion marched off and at 10.30am reached the railhead at Noeux les Mines after marching in heavy rain through the thick mud.

Captain Henry Loftus of B Company the 10th York and Lancaster Regiment was just 19 years old at the time of his death on 26th September 1915. Regretfully his body could not be later identified and he is commemorated on the Loos Memorial to the Missing at Dud Corner.

Another member of the 10th Yorks and Lancs present at Loos in September 1915 was Lieutenant A. Jamieson. Alexander Jamieson was to become famous after the War as a painter, before his untimely death in 1937. It was said at the time that his work was reminiscent of Constable. He concentrated on landscape painting, one of most famous works being 'The Mill-Pond, Weston-Turville.' This village in Buckinghamshire was close to where the 10th Battalion trained before going to France, perhaps no coincidence, as Jamieson had been born in Glasgow. He was a regular contributor to the Royal Academy Exhibition and also at the Royal Society of Oil Painters, of which he was a member. In his obituary in *The Times* it said:

Whistler said of Velazquez that he dipped his brush in light and air. No truer description of the work of Jamieson could be given. As a man and sincere friend he was beloved by every one who had the privilege of knowing him.

Appendix H

Report by the 12th Battalion Royal Scots on Operations 25th/27th September 1915

Report by the 12th Battalion Royal Scots on Operations 25th/27th September 1915 Lieutenant Colonel G. Loch in command.

The Battalion being in Divisional Reserve left the assembly trenches at 6.20am the 25th September with orders to advance on the line of Douvrin church. Crossed our firing line trench in four lines at 8.00am in support of 8th Gordons, whom we reinforced at Pekin Trench at about 8.45am. The Battalion then advanced through the 8th Gordons in one line. Advance was carried out by rushes for about 300 yards. We were then unable to advance further, being entirely unsupported and subjected to heavy enfilade fire from Haisnes and Cité St Elie on both flanks as well as from the front. The Battalion was in touch with the 7th Division on its right and the 11th Royal Scots on its left. The Battalion lay here in the open till about 4.00pm and suffered fairly heavy casualties. At that time a message was passed from the Queens on our right that the enemy was working round their right. Major Dutton, who was in command of the firing line, then withdrew the Battalion to Pekin Trench. At about 6.00pm the situation was as follows: a detachment of 11th and 12th Royal Scots with Gordon Highlanders and a few Black Watch on the left were holding the line Pekin Trench up to its junction with Cité Trench on the left to a point about 500 yards on the right. As already pointed out, our right was in the air and being enfiladed from Cité St Elie, our left was also enfiladed from Haisnes and being attacked by bombers down Pekin Trench. Darkness was setting in and the situation was critical. Our bombs, being soaked with rain, were useless and the men's rifles were clogged with mud. The flanks, particularly the left, became very unsteady and it was necessary to rally the men three times and to reoccupy Pekin Trench, which the men had been leaving in large numbers. OC 12th Royal Scots, after conferring with OC 11th Royal Scots, decided to report the situation to GOC. This was done. Reinforcements of the 6th Royal Scots Fusiliers were ordered up to the left. These reinforcements proved useless. It was now dark and the bombing very severe; it was therefore decided to withdraw to Fosse Alley. There a similar situation arose. Our right which lay about G.6.C.8.7 was completely enfiladed by rifle and machine gun fire, and to our rear a heavy bombing attack developed which is now believed to be the retaking of the Quarries by the enemy. Large casualties had occurred, no touch was obtainable on either flank, the situation was quite obscure with the exception that the enemy had worked completely round our right flank. In the absence of the Brigadier, a consultation was held among the COs present, and it was decided to withdraw to our front line trenches to get touch and to reorganise. This was eventually done. Shortly after, Lieutenant Colonel Loch was informed that the Brigadier was missing and that he was now in command of the Brigade. Major Dutton took command of the Battalion.

Appendix I

Comments from Lieutenant-General Sir H. Rawlinson on 9th October 1915 regarding the performance of the Artillery at Loos

Some lessons drawn from Operations 21st-25th September as regards artillery fire.

Deductions:

(a) The fire of 4.5", 5" and 6" howitzers is demoralising and to a limited extent destructive to the enemy's personnel, and therefore well worth employing with these objects.

(b) The destructive effect, however, of these field howitzers on deep well-constructed trenches is small.

(c) No artillery, except howitzers of the heaviest natures, are likely to cause material damage to such trenches, and even these will produce no great effect unless the bombardment is a heavy one.

(d) The dug-outs, constructed on the German plan at a great depth under the parapets, appear to be almost proof against artillery fire of any kind. If the exits of these dug outs can be blocked up, the result is good, but it is impossible to locate, even from air photos, where these exits are, and their destruction is therefore a matter of chance.

Glossary

AA and QMG
Assistant Adjutant and Quartermaster General. A staff position found at division level and above, usually this person was looked on as the senior administrative officer. At division level usually a Lieutenant-Colonel, at corps a Brigadier.

ADMS
Assistant Director Medical Services.

ASC
Army Service Corps.

BEF
The British Expeditionary Force. The name by which the British and Commonwealth Forces in France and Flanders were known.

C-in-C
Commander-in-Chief. The top man; the first person to hold this post as C-in-C BEF was Field Marshal Sir John French.

CRE
Commander Royal Engineers. The Chief Engineer of a division or corps.

CWGC
Commonwealth War Graves Commission.

FEBA/FLOT
Forward Edge of the Battle Area/Forward Line Own Troops.

GOC
General Officer Commanding. The initials by which the position of the officer commanding a brigade, division, corps or army was known.

K1, K2, K3
A useful term for dividing the Kitchener New Army Divisions. Originally intended to call for 100,000 volunteers to form six new divisions, many more than this volunteered. The first six New Army divisions (the 9th to 14th) were known as the K1, the second six (the 15th to 20th) the K2 and the third six (21st to 26th) the K3.

psc
'Passed Staff College', the initials an Officer could put after his name to signify he had successfully been to the Staff College. Usually unless you had passed the course promotion prospects to high command were limited.

RAMC
Royal Army Medical Corps

RE
　　Royal Engineers

SAA
　　Small Arms Ammunition

Bibliography and Sources

Unpublished material

Numerous War Diaries and other related files from the National Archives Kew
Documents held in the Liddle Collection, Brotherton Library, Leeds University
Recordings held in the Sound Archive, Imperial War Museum

Published works

Anon *The War History of the 6th Battalion The South Staffordshire Regiment (TF)*,
    William Heinemann 1924

Atkinson, C. *History of the Devonshire Regiment in the Great War*, Eland Brothers
    1926

Atkinson, C. *The 7th Division 1914-1918*, John Murray 1927

Batchelor, P. & C Matson *VCs of the First World War: The Western Front 1915*,
    Sutton Publishing 1997

Cherry, N. *I Shall Not Find His Equal. The Life of Brigadier-General Noel Lee*,
    Fleur de Lys Publishing 2001

Christian, N. *In The Shadow of Lone Tree: The Ordeal of Gloucestershire Men at
    the Battle of Loos 1915*, published privately 1996

Coppard , G. *With a Machine Gun to Cambrai. The Tale of a Young Tommy in
    Kitchener's Army 1914-1918*, HMSO 1969

Edmonds, J. *Military Operations France and Belgium 1915 Volumes I and II*,
    Macmillan 1927/1928

Ewing, J. *The History of the 9th (Scottish) Division*, John Murray 1921

Farndale, M. *History of the Royal Regiment of Artillery, Western Front 1914-18*,
    Royal Artillery Institution 1986

Fox, C., Chapman, J. et al. *Responding to the Call: The Kitchener Battalions of the
    Royal Berkshire Regiment at the Battle of Loos 1915*, Dept of Extended
    Education, University of Reading 1995

Headlam, C. *The Guards Division in the Great War*, John Murray 1924

Kearsey, A. *1915 Campaign in France, The Battles of Aubers Ridge, Festubert and
    Loos: Considered in Relation to the Field Service Regulations*, Gale & Polden
    1929

Macdonald, L. *1915 The Death of Innocence*, Headline 1993

MacPherson, Sir W.G. *Official History of the War. Medical Services General
    History Volume II*, HMSO 1923

Maude, A. *The 47th (London) Division 1914*-1919, Amalgamated Press 1922

Meakin, W. *The 5th North Staffords*, Hughes and Harber 1920

Middlebrook, M. *Your Country Needs You: Expansion of the British Army Infantry
    Divisions 1914-1918*, Leo Cooper 2000

Richter, D. *Chemical Soldiers: British Gas Warfare in World War I*, University
    Press of Kansas 1992

Sigmond, R. *Off At Last: The 7th Kings Own Scottish Borderers*, R Sigmond
    Publishing 1997

Stewart, J. & J. Buchan *The 15th (Scottish) Division 1914-1919*, William Black-wood 1926

Wyrall, E. *History of the 2nd Division 1914-1918*, Thomas Nelson 1921

Articles from *Stand To! The Journal of the Western Front Association*:

Bryant, P. "The recall of Sir John French" (issues 22, 23, 24)

Cherry, N. "The RAMC on the Somme" (issue 64)

Cook, D. "The agony of Loos" (issue 14)

Fellows H. "The Battle of Loos. An eyewitness account of the attack on Hill 70" (issue 5)

Holt, T. & V. "Have you news of my boy Jack?" (issue 37)

Index

Index of Places

Index of People

Index of Military Units